Praise for *Leade*

"In her second *Upheaval* book, Michele DeStefano continues to tap into key issues for any business. Collaboration, innovation, and culture change take center stage as DeStefano provides very direct and helpful tips on how to lead, manage, and inspire teams, while emphasizing the need to really understand and serve the client. The book also invites the leaders to take a more introspective approach and provokes the seasoned or an emerging leader to work, first, on self-awareness and humility in order to become an effective leader. These teachings and practical recommendations are more relevant now than ever considering the complexities of the world. This book stands as a very important resource for leaders determined to not only navigate change but to lead it and become a catalyst for positive transformation in any organization."—**Marco Araujo, Chief Legal & Compliance Officer, Nubank**

"A thought-provoking account of the unthinkable truth: All professional service providers should learn how to innovate, even if their business model isn't broken. A necessary read for anyone who wants to differentiate in the professional services marketplace."—**Augusto Aragone, EVP, Secretary, and General Counsel, Ingram Micro**

"Finally! A book by a LawLander, a member of the guild's academy no less, that directly and persuasively makes the case for culture, service, and people. In a LawLand obsessed with itself and convinced of its privilege and uniquetitude, to find our way to sustainability takes a new generation unafraid to show empathy. To learn from mistakes. To embrace servant leadership. In reality, people are our most important asset—our most critical tech. Make no mistake, Prof. DeStefano is no normal LawLander— her career outside law in, OMG, Corporate America, and in Big Law, as well as her development of and dedication to LawWithoutWalls, shines through each and every page. This is a manifesto for the bedrock necessary to build a customer-centric service credo. When you read this book—and you must read it if you care about a sustainable LawLand and your place in it, I ask only that every time you read the word "client" you replace it with "customer." In so doing you will stretch away from the narcissistic LawLand of today. Then you'll be able to take the risk to step toward that vision. Finally, you'll find the courage to make the leap to

NextLaw—where optimization of legal matters is the norm. Prevention of legal problems is the destination. And a culture creating truly marvelous customer experiences is the objective. Let Prof. DeStefano be your inspiration, your sherpa, your whisperer."—**Jeff Carr, Former SVP, General Counsel, Corporate Secretary, Univar Solutions and Former SVP, General Counsel, FMC Technologies**

"*Leader Upheaval* stands alone as the most informative, helpful, and comprehensive book available today for lawyers and other professional service providers undertaking transformative change initiatives in their organizations. The learnings presented by Professor DeStefano could not be more timely, as they coincide with the advent of democratized generative artificial intelligence and the resulting acceleration of client demands for even more client-centric, experience-based innovation and collaboration from their professional service providers. DeStefano methodically and convincingly makes the case for the digital transformation imperative for multinational companies, and then masterfully and interestingly guides the reader through the essential success factors for leading impactful organizational transformation. The clarity and depth of her writing is made highly practical and relevant to the reader through an extensive presentation of meaningful quotes from legal and other practitioners. As a general counsel continuing to pursue the digital transformation of legal services, I will no doubt consult *Leader Upheaval* on a regular basis, and it is gratifying to know that future legal leaders will have such valuable guidance and advice available to them as they lead in their own transformation journeys."—**Bill Deckelman, EVP & General Counsel, DXC Technology**

"Michele DeStefano has done it again! Thirteen years of research and leadership on the ground in innovation, collaboration, and culture creation shine through in her sparkling *Leader Upheaval*, all delivered with plain speaking and leavened with common sense."—**Adam O. Emmerich, Partner, Wachtell, Lipton, Rosen & Katz**

"Ask any lawyer and they will tell you they consider themselves an innovator in what they do because lawyering requires a large dose of adaptability and creativity. But lawyers are notoriously resistant to change when it comes to how they deliver their services. This book makes a needed and extraordinary contribution to the topic of innovation and collaboration in the delivery of professional services, starting with a review of the factors that compel change today, before delving into the leadership, cultural and procedural levers, and as well as practical tools that leaders can use to make change happen. I expect it will be required reading in many law firms and in-house legal departments around the world."—**Horacio Gutierrez, Senior Executive Vice President and Chief Legal & Compliance Officer, The Walt Disney Company**

"This book by Professor Michele DeStefano is simply a must-read for professional service providers who aspire to add real-life, long-term value to business partners, stakeholders, customers, or colleagues beyond pure and technical legal solutions. Professor DeStefano provides numerous examples, anecdotes, and case studies that make the guide a compelling and captivating read."—**Clifton Richard Harrison, Global Market Leader, EY Law**

"Michele provides many useful tools for supporting collaboration and innovation. But her most powerful idea is a simple one—focus on your client's experience—and let that drive innovation. Clients who are delighted with how you deliver the service will drive the mindset shift that will create a sustainable innovation culture within your firm."—**Michael Hertz, Chief Marketing Officer, White & Case**

"In a time of rapid change, Michele's latest work provides the practical guidance needed for leaders to rise to and meet the challenges that professions have not had to meet before. It builds on her earlier works and clearly drives home why there is a need to do things differently now in professions that have to date only known slow incremental change. A must-read for those looking to lead diverse people across generations in digital times when the only constant is change."—**Alan Keep, Managing Partner, Bowmans**

"Michele DeStefano's *Leader Upheaval* is a high-octane book of hard truths for successful organizations to thrive in the complex global economy today. Just as Michele pleads for leaders to have courage to trust in collaborative problem-solving, have courage to read this book with an "open mind" and you will be reaping rewards in both your professional and personal growth. From the pairing of humility and curiosity to create safety nets in enabling risk taking, to the consequences of disruptive technology in new workplace environments and markets, this book has been distilled from hundreds of interviews, case studies, and years of highly acclaimed training and consultancy work undertaken by Michele globally. Her incisive 3-4-5 Method™ is another invaluable tool for professional organizations attempting to drive collaborative innovation and the iterative steps within gives structure to her novel concept, helping leaders to drive toward certainty of positive outcomes for their organizations. This book is not simply another manual on what good leadership is supposed to look like to everyone else. Michele's "Three Rules of Engagement" guides leaders to be self-aware, to be focused as individual contributors and vested owners of team wins, while not being egotistical or selfish. Providing a blueprint for leadership to cultivate an environment for multidisciplinary teams to thrive, the book gives deep insights to help organizations concoct winning formulas toward self-determined success. This book is a worthy adversary to anyone serious about leading teams and driving change, as well as to hone and sharpen adaptive leadership skills. Candid, refreshing, and pragmatic, I would recommend it as essential reading for leaders in professional services firms to contemplate Michele's hard truths within."—**Jerry K. C. Koh, Managing Partner Allen & Gledhill LLP**

"Michele DeStefano has written a thorough and extremely practical book on managing collaboration, innovation, and culture change in professional services firms and corporate units. If you are a team manager or project leader in professional services, then read it before you embark on your next assignment in the area. You will profit tremendously and improve your performance in the role right away."—**Peter Kurer, Former Chairman, UBS; Chairman, Sunrise Communications; and author of** *Legal and Compliance Risk*

"Michele takes the reader from macro trends impacting professional services firms to adaptive leadership skills to redefine how we think about service delivery. She examines the important role digital mindsets and culture play in enabling real innovation to thrive. As well as bringing to life innovation tools and techniques which seek to unlock breakthrough client-centric experiences and provide a roadmap for business leaders to follow to build their adaptive leadership capabilities and drive growth."—**Michelle Mahoney, Executive Director, Innovation, King & Wood Mallesons**

"Professional service providers (including lawyers in corporations and in law firms) are, by nature, change resistant. Professor DeStefano offers a practical approach to breaking through this change-aversion by laying out a planned approach to leading organizations through the unprecedented changes the professional service providers industry will continue to see at an ever-accelerating rate."—**Joe Otterstetter, Former Associate General Counsel, 3M**

"In *Leader Upheaval*, Professor DeStefano utilizes interviews, critical analysis, and conversational writing to convince all of us that honing the mindset, skillset, and behaviors of innovators is the key to sharpening our skills, opening our minds, and changing the way we work to delight our clients."—**Yvette Ostolaza, Chair, Sidley Austin Management Committee**

"In the ever-evolving legal landscape, the traditional lawyer archetype of technical expertise and unwavering adherence to established practices is no longer sufficient for success. Tomorrow's lawyers must embrace a client-centric approach, prioritizing innovation, and service excellence to truly thrive. Michele DeStefano's *Leader Upheaval* serves as an indispensable guide for legal leaders seeking to navigate this transformation. DeStefano masterfully outlines the fundamental shift required for lawyers to excel in the 21st century. She challenges the notion that technical proficiency alone can guarantee success, emphasizing the need for a holistic approach that encompasses collaboration, creativity, and a deep understanding of client needs. With a conversational and anecdote-rich style, DeStefano provides actionable insights and practical strategies for legal leaders to cultivate a culture of innovation within their teams. *Leader Upheaval* is not merely a theoretical treatise; it is a practical handbook brimming with concrete examples and real-world applications."—**Stacey Quaye, Global Head of IP, Innovation & Design**

"*Leader Upheaval* is a must read for anyone in professional services. It captures the essence of great client service and how we need to continue to hone those skills in a fast-changing world."—**Lisa Sawicki**

"Michele is a driving force in the legal industry. She makes a compelling case in her new book that being a trusted legal advisor is not good enough in today's world. Clients want to hire lawyers who can innovate, who know how to collaborate internally and externally, and who are strategic. Most importantly, lawyers need to understand a client's wants, needs, and desires and to develop strong teams. Michele has done the research—she has interviewed well over 200 lawyers and clients for her new book. The insights from these interviews provide real-world examples of how the legal services industry needs to adapt and do better."—**Craig Seebald, Co-Chair of the Global Litigation Department, Vinson & Elkins**

"Again, Professor Michele DeStefano focuses her attention on innovation in the professional services space and provides us with a well-researched, executable method for innovation that weaves marketplace needs into the creative process."—**Paul Silverglate, Partner, Vice Chair–US Technology Sector Leader, Deloitte & Touche LLP**

"Michele DeStefano's great talent is seamlessly blending practice and theory. *Leader Upheaval* is an invaluable book in this spirit, drawing on her experience of managing a successful global change program and on her evident mastery of the academic literature on innovation and collaboration. All thoughtful leaders should buy this book and follow its guidance."—**Professor Richard Susskind OBE, co-author of *The Future of the Professions***

"This powerful and practical book provides lawyers and service professionals of all kinds with the tools they need to forge a culture of innovation, collaboration, and creativity within their teams."—**Bjarne Tellmann, Founding General Counsel and Member of Executive Committee, Haleon**

"In law firms, change is hard. Even rudimentary change can easily fail, and when it comes to driving change as profound as innovation in a law firm, something special is needed. And that's what Michele DeStefano provides in this book. It's the method, techniques, and insights she has developed leading change initiatives in law firms, and few if any have more experience of it. She acknowledges that her 3-4-5 Method™ may not work for everyone, but in grappling with difficulties that any law firm leader seeking real change must confront, she offers a useful blueprint to help them on their own journey."—**Hugh Verrier, Former Chair, White & Case**

"Michele DeStefano is the extraordinarily rare visionary who also has a great gift for making things happen and getting things done—the right way. *Leader Upheaval* brilliantly provides professional services firm leaders with years of her research-based insights and expertise and most importantly is a book—and workbook—that they can pick up and quickly apply to drive change. Whatever other changes may be coming, generative AI will supercharge competition in the markets for professional services and there will be clear winners and losers, with complacency no longer an option. My best advice: use *Leader Upheaval* across your firm as your playbook for winning."—**Scott Westfahl, Professor of Practice and Faculty Director Harvard Law School Executive Education**

"Michele DeStefano's last book, *Legal Upheaval*, established her as a master alchemist in turning theory into practice for law firm leaders trying to cope with growing disruption in the market for corporate legal services. In this book, DeStefano urges leaders to take the next step by confronting the single biggest obstacle for achieving collaboration, innovation, and culture change: themselves. In simple and direct prose backed by years of interdisciplinary research and unparalleled experience teaching and practicing innovation, DeStefano guides readers through a step-by-step process for leading and managing change. The result is an eminently readable and immediately useful guide that belongs on the shelf of every professional service provider who understands that the first step in overcoming any challenge is to acknowledge, to paraphrase the great cartoonist Walt Kelly's philosophizing opossum Pogo, that when we meet the enemy, they is us!"—**David B. Wilkins, Lester Kissel Professor of Law and Director of the Center on the Legal Profession, Harvard Law School**

"Backed by her experience leading over 230 multidisciplinary teams on a four-month journey and creating an inclusive culture, Professor DeStefano provides concrete strategies and tactics on how to enhance your leadership style and transform the culture of your team, department or firm."—**Petra Zijp, Partner, NautaDutilh N.V.**

"This book is different! As DeStefano says in her introduction, there are many books that talk about innovation, collaboration, and culture creation. What DeStefano does in this book is walk the walk. She explores the nitty gritty of leading and managing and explains how to do it. All of this is done in a very readable style with plenty of real examples. My favorite statistic in the book is that "75% of change efforts fail due to poor management or execution." Leaders need to radically improve! This book will help. The overall distinction of this book is practical advice. Every firm leader should read it!—**Stephen Revell, Consultant, Former Partner, Freshfields**

LEADER
upheaval

A Guide to Client-Centricity,
Culture Creation, and Collaboration.

MICHELE DESTEFANO

AMERICAN**BAR**ASSOCIATION
ABA Publishing

Cover design by Carolina Martinez/ABA Design

Printed in the United States of America.

28 27 26 25 24   5 4 3 2 1

Library of Congress Cataloging-in-Publication Data

Names: DeStefano, Michele, author.
Title: Leader upheaval / Michele DeStefano.
Description: Chicago : American Bar Association, 2024. | Includes
   bibliographical references and index. | Summary: "This book provides an actionable
   roadmap for leaders to enhance client-centricity, shift mindsets, and create the right
   teaming climate so that a culture of collaboration, innovation, and inclusivity can thrive.
   Derived from over 280 interviews with senior executives in professional services and their
   clients—along with hands on experience leading hundreds of multidisciplinary teams on
   innovation journeys—Professor DeStefano reveals the path to successful collaboration and
   innovation efforts in professional services, including how to avoid the pitfalls that lead to
   failure."--Provided by publisher.
Identifiers: LCCN 2023056585 (print) | LCCN 2023056586 (ebook) |
   ISBN 9781639053490 (hardcover) | ISBN 9781639053506 (epub)
Subjects: LCSH: Practice of law--Social aspects--United States. | Practice
   of law--Technological innovations--United States. | Lawyers--Effect of
   technological innovations on--United States. | Leadership--United
   States. | Success in business--United States.
Classification: LCC KF318 .D475 2024 (print) | LCC KF318 (ebook) |
   DDC 340.023/73--dc23/eng/20231214
LC record available at https://lccn.loc.gov/2023056585
LC ebook record available at https://lccn.loc.gov/2023056586

Discounts are available for books ordered in bulk. Special consideration is given to state bars, CLE programs, and other bar-related organizations. Inquire at Book Publishing, ABA Publishing, American Bar Association, 321 N. Clark Street, Chicago, Illinois 60654-7598.

www.shopABA.org

CONTENTS

PART II

PART III

Managing Collaboration, Innovation, and
Culture Change   185

Introduction

There are too many books that *talk* about innovation, collaboration, and culture creation without actually teaching—how to lead it, staff it, manage it, and inspire it. This book fills this gap. This book, and the method it is based on, is the fruit of 14 years of my experience leading more than 230 multidisciplinary, multicultural, intergenerational teams on a 4-month innovation journey—from business problem to viable solution. However, as much as my method is for leading and managing collaboration and innovation in professional services,[1] it also helps leaders drive change, client-centricity, and culture creation.

This book provides practical recommendations to enhance leadership style and develop the right climate, team structure, and processes so that a culture of creativity, collaboration, and innovation can thrive. It also unpacks why collaboration and innovation efforts in professional services so often do not succeed. Given that more than 75 percent of all change management initiatives fail in corporations,[2] understanding these failures is critical to any hope of success. In my experience leading multidisciplinary collaboration efforts and innovation journeys within professional service firms and corporate legal departments, I have repeatedly witnessed three failures, by leaders, that contribute to the efforts' demise.

The first is a failure on the part of the leader to truly understand what mindset, skills, and behaviors (beyond expertise and collegiality) are required to collaborate and innovate on multidisciplinary teams and *delight* clients and other key stakeholders. Therefore, Part I of this book begins by exploring the new priorities and demands of corporate clients and the leadership gap that exists in professional services. It then identifies the new expectations of professional service providers, explores what is (and what is not) client-centricity and highlights the importance of adaptive, inclusive leadership (which includes leading and following others). It concludes by arguing that the new value equation in professional services is learning how to collaboratively problem-solve on multidisciplinary teams the way that innovators and design thinkers (and adaptive, inclusive leaders) do.

The second common pitfall is a failure by the leader to focus on further developing their own leadership skills and undertaking the hard facets of culture creation. Therefore, Part II identifies what it takes of *you*, the leader, to inspire, lead, and create a culture that embraces collaboration, innovation, and change. It identifies the Three Rules of Engagement that can help leaders meet the changing expectations, lead collaborative initiatives, and transform relationships with internal or external clients and stakeholders. Then, it spells out the recipe (and emphasizes the tough work that is required) to create inclusive environments where diverse professionals can thrive—because there's nothing soft about culture creation.

The third failure is neglecting to actively *manage* innovation or change efforts. Collaborative initiatives (whether geared toward innovation or cross-industry practices within an organization) do not happen on their own. Without the right management, they are doomed. To this end, Part III unpacks what needs to be managed in any collaboration or innovation effort, including how to create effective multidisciplinary teams that are set up to—and actually do—collaborate in the "right way." This involves paying attention not only to behavior but also team makeup, structure, and processes. It also requires the employment of a calculated preplanned method to move a team from a broad challenge or opportunity to a discrete initiative that adds real value—along with a communication strategy. Therefore, in addition to unpacking how a marketing and measurement plan should be developed to secure buy-in internally, Part III provides an overview of The 3-4-5 Method™ I created (and refined over the past decade), demonstrating why it works and why professional service providers need a method like this one that is geared toward their ways of working. Instead of being all about embracing messiness and failure, my method focuses on step-by-step progress and ensures that the only failure that occurs is the competent (vs incompetent) kind. There are two complements to this book. First, there is a handbook that goes with it: *The Leader Upheaval Handbook: Lead Teams on an Innovation and Collaboration journey with The 3-4-5 Method(™)* that includes week-by-week instructions, exercises, checklists, and timelines that have been used successfully on hundreds of diverse teams to inspire, lead, and manage collaboration, innovation, and culture change within professional services. Second, my prior book, *Legal Upheaval*, provides some similar content in more detail and with a focus on legal professionals specifically.

This book, however, is for anyone who yearns for more successful multidisciplinary collaboration in professional services. This book is for anyone invested in transforming how professional service providers provide service to clients. This book is for anyone who is searching for concrete ways to lead and inspire change, culture creation, and client-centricity among their teams, firms, or departments. If you've gotten this far in this introduction, then this book is likely for you.

Why You Should Hone the Mindset, Skill Set, and Behaviors of Innovators

> *"Start with why."*
>
> —Simon Sinek, *Start with Why*[1]

Your business model isn't broken. The sky is not falling. So why should you learn how to innovate? Even if you agree that professional service providers could use a refresher on creativity and collaboration, you might still be skeptical or even shaking your head and asking why they (and you) should learn how to innovate. The answer to that question is explained in Part I of this book.

Part I is designed to convince you to at least *try* to hone some parts of the mindset, skill set, and behaviors of innovators. Through the voice of clients and professional colleagues, Part I demonstrates that clients' focus is changing from *what* professionals do to *how*—how professionals work. The focus is changing from individuals to diverse and inclusive teams and from providing services to delivering experiences that delight.

So Part I is dedicated in Simon Sinek fashion to "starting with why"— the reasons you should try to innovate, to collaborate, and sharpen your adaptive leadership skills—even if your business model isn't broken. The next three chapters will take you through what I believe are four whys:

Why #1: Your clients' needs and challenges are changing, and these changes are creating *leader upheaval* in the professional services marketplace, and contributing to what has been identified as a leadership gap. Chapter 1 highlights three key priorities of corporate clients that are transforming what they need from professional service providers. These priorities all require the ability to innovate and to lead innovation and change with a human-centered, client-customer-centric approach.

Why #2: Clients' focus is changing from *what* we do to *how* we do it. Clients need their service providers to help manage change, to leverage technology differently, to learn new skills, to partner on multidisciplinary teams to problem-solve collaboratively and creatively—often in sprints to find innovative solutions. Chapter 2 identifies the new expectations of professional service providers including the new mindset and skill set (above and beyond expertise) that today's professionals need to provide client-centric service and become adaptive and inclusive leaders with a digital mindset.

Why #3: The way to delight clients is with client-centricity, which requires a shift in focus from *services* to *experiences* and from a *traditional* style of leadership to an *adaptive*, inclusive one. Chapter 3 unpacks what clients mean by client-centricity and why being an adaptive and inclusive leader with a digital mindset helps you be more client-centric.

Why #4: Clients are asking for and rewarding innovation, even if in the form of simple incremental changes that add lasting value. Therefore, the New Value Equation in professional services is innovation. Chapter 4 presents the ABCs of Innovation: by individually attempting to innovate our *A*ttitude about innovation changes; it also changes how we *B*ehave because we hone the skill set and mindset of an innovator and, over time, it changes the *C*ulture that suffuses our teams, our departments, and our firms as new kinds of relationships are formed when professionals collaborate on multidisciplinary teams to create innovative solutions to complex, adaptive problems.

CHAPTER 1

The Key Priorities of Corporate Clients Require Innovation

> "Certain things they should stay the way they are. You ought to be able to stick them in one of those big glass cases and just leave them alone."
>
> —J. D. Salinger, *Catcher in the Rye*[1]

People like things to "stay the way they are." So, it is not surprising that professional service providers are often described as resistant to change. For this book, I interviewed more than 280 subjects in professional services, including senior executives in business, finance, technology, compliance, and law, from large, international corporations and firms from all over the world. Given the rapid enhancements in and adoption of technology, shifting socioeconomics and demographics, and globality (not to mention the pandemic, spiking inflation, the "Great Resignation," "quiet quitting," and "bare minimum Mondays"),[2] my interviewees consistently report how much has changed over the past 5 to 10 years, how much is continuing to change, and how hard it is to lead change efforts among professional service providers of many kinds (lawyers, compliance officers, accountants, management consultants, advertisers, marketers, insurance brokers, etc.).

One of the reasons professional services have changed and will continue to change is because the world is changing. According to the World Economic Forum's recent report on the future of jobs, the job marketplace has undergone major transformations driven by enhanced social and environmental pressures, geopolitical and economic disruptions,[3] and "the coming of age of generative artificial intelligence" (AI).[4] It makes sense, therefore, that corporate clients' needs and desires of their professional service providers have evolved along with these transformations. Although the key priorities of clients will change, new buzz word labels will be adorned, and pendulums will swing, this chapter presents a short overview of three of the priorities of corporate clients that are directly impacting the nature of professional services today: (1) enhancing diversity, equity, and inclusion (DEI); (2) creating environment, social, and governance[5] (ESG) strategies; and (3) harnessing technology (especially AI) and leading digital transformation (DT) efforts.

True, books could be written about each of these subjects. However, the point in highlighting these specific priorities is less about their substance and more about what they mean for—and what they reveal about—professional service providers today. Therefore, after providing a short overview of the priorities, this chapter explores what these three priorities have in common and what they lay bare. To help clients manage and leverage any of these three priorities, professional service providers need to proactively collaborate, innovate and create culture change (unsurprisingly, all of these things are also a big priority of CEOs).[6] This, in turn, requires today's leaders to take a human-centered (and customer-centric) approach to problem solving and transformation—like innovators do. That is what these priorities have in common. What they reveal, however, is a special kind of leadership gap in professional services. This is because professional service providers of many kinds (lawyers, accountants, consultants, financial advisors, insurance brokers, etc.) generally haven't been trained to do what innovators do. Therefore, they may not have their mindset or skill set or exhibit their behaviors.

So, if you are one of those professionals that already knows a lot about these three key priorities, I recommend you skip to the next section of this chapter to read more about this potential leadership gap because that's when things start to really get interesting in this book.

A. Diversity, Equity, and Inclusion

The first priority of corporate clients is one that has existed for decades. This is enhanced DEI. It is a top priority for them internally at the corporations and within the departments in which they work, but also for their external service providers.

The business case for DEI is well documented.[7] Research demonstrates that enhanced diversity is linked to enhanced profitability and financial health.[8] Studies show that companies that are more diverse are 25 percent to 36 percent more profitable.[9] Studies also show that companies in the top quartile in gender diversity outperform those in the bottom.[10] Similar increases in performance occur for those companies that are ethnically and culturally diverse.[11] In keeping with that, companies that are leaders in their industry for DEI perform better than their market average in decision-making because they are almost 30 percent better at spotting and reducing risks.[12]

Another reason why DEI is a priority is that it may also help companies and firms recruit and retain diverse talent[13] (a key priority for CEOs).[14] DEI at the workplace is extremely important to both millennials[15] and Generation Z (Gen Z),[16] aka "digital natives."[17] Gen Z want their employers to mirror their diversity,[18] which is a big task given that Gen Z is the most diverse generation yet[19]—and their definitions of diversity continue to change over time. Also, studies show that when their companies embrace diversity, and their leaders lead with inclusion, millennials and Gen Zers are more actively engaged at work and more productive[20] and less likely to leave.[21] In addition to retention, there are many benefits tied specifically to age and generation diversity, including increased engagement/productivity, breadth of skills, and mentorship opportunities.[22] Diversity of all kinds (economic, race, expertise, education, sexual orientation, gender, etc.) has the potential to enhance the culture of the entire organization. For example, recent research shows that companies that employ people with disabilities create an enhanced culture of collaboration and inclusion that increases productivity and a company's value proposition with—and loyalty from—employees and customers.[23]

The other major benefit of diversity (as will be discussed more in Chapter 6) is innovation. Studies report that companies that outperform in DEI have higher rates of innovation and almost 20 percent higher revenues from innovation.[24] Although diversity can create conflict,[25] when managed appropriately,[26] diverse teams are more productive and provide a competitive advantage.[27]

Given these benefits, it is unsurprising that corporate clients want their professional service providers (or professional service firms, PSFs) to enhance their own DEI efforts. When their external PSFs are diverse and inclusive, it enables them to increase the benefits of their own efforts. They can tap into a bigger talent pool, creating more opportunity for innovative thinking along with a more diverse, and healthy, environment for their professionals to work and find mentors within. Unfortunately, despite the potential benefits and the many initiatives by PSFs to enhance DEI,[28] the professional services market is not very diverse. For example, general counsels have been calling on their law firms to enhance DEI for decades, looking for proof of their commitment not only in the numbers but a range of other indicators, such as the people who are actually doing the work on their projects, meaningful promotion opportunities, and inclusive flex-time policies.[29] Some have even started asking their law firms to bill them in diversity hours. Others, like Microsoft,[30] Hewlett-Packard,[31] Shell,[32] and Novartis[33] reward and punish law firms based on their diversity achievements or lack thereof.[34] Despite this loud call to action by their clients, and millions of dollars being spent on DEI initiatives,[35] law firms have made minimal progress in the last decade, and underrepresentation at law firms (especially in positions of power)[36] persists.[37] The legal marketplace is not alone. Research shows there is a lack of DEI within other types of PSFs as well, including in insurance,[38] management consulting,[39] accounting,[40] and advertising, marketing, and public relations.[41]

And the reasons for this sad state of affairs is often the same: lack of an inclusive culture,[42] leaving diverse professionals without a sense of belonging or the ability to be themselves at work.[43] In the law marketplace, for example, the un-inclusive culture of law firms is transferred over to corporate legal departments because many in-house lawyers began their careers working at law firms, and firms are where legal departments recruit talent.[44] The same can be said of marketing and PR departments within corporations that recruit their talent after they have had some training and experience at an external agency in the industry. Recent research by Gallop surveying thousands of employees in the United States, U.K., and Ireland demonstrates that only 25 percent strongly feel included and only 30 percent strongly feel a sense of belonging within their organizations.[45]

The lack of safe, inclusive environments in which diverse professionals can thrive is extremely problematic even if you believe that the "Great Resignation" is over.[46] There remains what one Harvard Business School professor calls the "Great Rethink,"[47] wherein employees are questioning the culture, mission, and values of the organizations in which they work. Therefore, a heightened need for corporate cultures in which employees feel engaged, included, and connected persists. Corporations and firms that fail to answer this need risk not only that their employees will move to a different company (or retire),[48] but also profit loss. It is not only the entity's employees but also their customers and/or clients who care about an organization's values and how it treats its human capital—which leads us to the second priority of corporate clients: ESG.

B. Environment, Social, and Corporate Governance

The second priority of corporate clients is the need to better manage their ESG strategy. Evidently, global ESG assets could exceed $53 trillion by 2025,[49] and with that comes both risks and opportunities. Of course, like with DEI, books could be written about ESG. Therefore, I only include a snapshot of the issues that professional service providers can help their clients navigate. However, please do not equate the shortness of this section to the breadth of the need as the demand for help with ESG is literally booming.[50]

First, clients need help developing a balanced ESG strategy which historically was under the umbrella of corporate social responsibility. It was treated as part of reputation upkeep, as opposed to ESG, which is part of a corporate strategy to enhance profits while also creating long-term value for employees and customers alike.[51] As evidenced by the exit of Danone's CEO and chairman who tied Danone's success directly to its environmental performance,[52] companies need to strike the right balance between meeting ESG objectives and shareholder capitalism, that is, growth, market share, and profit goals.[53]

On the one hand, in addition to potential loss of profits, too much emphasis on ESG can weaken a company's competitive positioning—especially in countries like China that have less rigorous ESG standards. The Danone example is evidence of that. Although turning Danone into a mission company, similar to an American B-Corp, with a mission of "One Planet, One Health," pleased climate activists, sales and shares decreased dramatically.[54] On the other hand, if a company does not focus enough on ESG, it can have negative PR issues. Companies like ExxonMobil and Tyson Foods have been called out for claiming they are committed to sustainability and the environment while in other ways they continue to negatively impact the planet.[55] In addition to PR impact, there can be financial repercussions if a company does not focus enough on ESG.

Investors are now placing emphasis on ESG criteria (including climate change and diversity), and so are banks in the lending process.[56] They are offering funds made up of only environmentally friendly industries and prioritizing finance for companies in industries that are attempting to address climate change.[57] However, on the flip side, this has been met with some political backlash, with people on the right calling this practice woke capitalism.[58] On those lines, some analysts claim that "funds investing in companies that publicly embrace ESG sacrifice financial returns without gaining much, if anything, in terms of actually furthering ESG interests."[59]

That said, employees' and customers' expectations about the role businesses play in society has changed and, as mentioned above, they care greatly about how companies are performing with respect to ESG. The exodus of 30 percent of Basecamp's employees after its announcement that they weren't going to "do" ESG proves the point.[60] Today, employees and customers are tracking ESG scores and choosing employers and vendors that are aligned with their ESG thinking. Therefore, meeting certain ESG criteria may help employers of all kinds recruit, engage, and retain talent and customers. Employees and buyers of services alike care about the E in ESG, that is, climate change, carbon emissions, water and air pollution, energy efficiency, deforestation, recycling, etc. They also care greatly about the S or "social" in ESG, which involves a focus on an organization's relationship with people, including employees and customers and the community and society at large. This includes corporate responsibility related to human rights, product safety, and the labor standards of the company and its suppliers. It also includes protecting data and privacy of its customers and also ensuring the company has an inclusive culture that supports diversity and income equality and that engages their people with purpose.

Relatedly, employees and customers care about the G, the governance of the corporation which, in addition to being concerned about bribery and corruption, corporate management structure, board composition, company policies regarding executive compensation, compliance, standards, and disclosures, is also concerned about many of the factors involved in the S in ESG. For example,

> . . . *gender diversity and equity is another high-profile governance issue, with many institutional shareholders demanding better representation of women on corporate boards and in executive ranks, and equal compensation and mobility for women and people of color. More companies are emphasizing the financial*

benefit of creating inclusive workplaces in an effort to increase diversity and inclusivity.[61]

More and more companies are also elevating the role of the chief sustainability officer (CSO) to help identify the ESG issues that have a direct impact on the financial health of the company, long-term value creation, and its risk profile.[62] However, research shows that organizations are failing to identify the material ESG priorities and "distinguish between value-creating and ethical concerns, or between risk-reduction measures and strategic opportunities"[63]—which leads to the next area in which clients are in need of help from their professional service providers related to ESG.

In addition to corporate strategy, clients need help with ESG reporting and compliance. Along with the recent proposed legislation in the United States[64] and Europe[65] to require climate change and sustainability disclosures (and the already existing regulations in the U.K. requiring certain companies to adopt disclosure practices)[66]—corporate clients need help now more than ever in managing the risks of ESG noncompliance. Especially with respect to the E and G in ESG, if corporations don't meet the requisite standards, corporate clients may face litigation, as evidenced by the recent rise in litigation related to corporations' environmental footprints. Interestingly, professional service providers, themselves, are also in the hot seat when it comes to compliance and litigation. They are now being scrutinized based on their clients' ESG-related practices and some activists are targeting PSFs, specifically accounting companies, who are responsible for auditing and reporting.[67]

Clients also need help leveraging the opportunities that exist in new legislation. As an interviewee at a large U.K.-based financial services institution explained:

> *We are doing a lot on the ESG front to become a market leader. We want law firms to help us efficiently navigate and work with the changing legislative landscape. A lot of people are coining this as a legislative tsunami. But we'd like to see law firms take a more positive approach and not just avoiding the doom and gloom. We want them to help us identify what are the possibilities i.e., what can we do that we couldn't do before?*—IT and commercial lawyer, one of the UK's largest financial services organizations[68]

Unsurprisingly, the only way clients will be able to leverage the benefits of its ESG strategy and limit the risks is if it collects, processes, and analyzes the right data in the right (and compliant) ways. In addition to devising metrics to track ESG progress against the evolving regulatory standards, companies also need to create data collection, metrics, and measurement processes to compare their ESG (including their DEI) progress to that of competitors and other industries[69] and also to measure (and demonstrate) whether the corporation is striking the right balance between revenue/profit/market share growth and meeting the needs and expectations of its employees and customers. For these reasons, ESG has become an important part of digital transformation efforts at corporations and specifically within professional service providing departments, like the legal and compliance departments, as well as the marketing and PR departments. As espoused in a paper I cowrote with Dan Wu and Bjarne Tellmann, the general counsel of Haleon, general counsels are now leading DT journeys of their legal departments and part of that effort is helping companies articulate, measure, and leverage their ESG activities to create new forms of value and limit risks related to disclosure (and failures of disclosures), including liability, public criticism, and regulatory harm.[70] Further, in-house legal departments are developing tech tools to allow the department to "drive social agendas like DEI as much as the cost agenda" with outside law firms to force their professional service providers "to come to the D&I table."[71] This discussion of DT as it relates to ESG leads us to the third related priority of corporate clients.

C. Artificial Intelligence and Digital Transformation

Like with the other two client priorities, this section will be brief, although books could be written on the subjects. The point of this section is simply to highlight the importance of helping clients harness new technology (especially AI) and lead digital transformation (DT) efforts (not to mention doing the same internally within your own firm).

Beginning with technology, in the fall of 2022, the first public-facing, easily accessible generative AI[72] chatbot built on a state-of-the-art large language model (LLM)[73] was introduced to the masses.[74] In its ability to be trained to interact with humans in a conversational way and generate new content, Open AI's Chat GPT (like Google's Bard and Microsoft's Bing) greatly opened up professional service providers' eyes to the power of AI and the need not only to understand it but to harness its benefits.

Although it feels new, the reality is that the theory behind AI, generative AI, and LLMs is not. As early as 1965, theorists such as British mathematician Irving John Good hypothesized the "Intelligence Explosion"—when AI surpasses the cognitive ability of humans.[75] Also, around that time, Joseph Weizenbaum, a Massachusetts Institute of Technology (MIT) computer scientist, created the first chatbot "Eliza," named after the protagonist, Eliza Doolittle, in *My Fair Lady*, that simulated a conversation between it, as the therapist, and a patient.[76] So it is unsurprising, now in 2024, that we have entered the era of being impacted by what is coined the "law of accelerating returns." This means essentially that in terms of technology, innovation begets innovation. Disruptive technology is being discovered faster and faster because existing technologies are used to improve the latest technology inventions and to create new ones. Technological inventions are reaching the mainstream faster, and innovation in technology is not graphed as a linear movement forward, but as exponential leaps.[77]

In addition to predicting that technology will enable immortality by 2030, futurist Ray Kurzweil predicts computers will be as smart as humans by 2029 and that "singularity, which is when we will multiply our effective intelligence a billionfold by merging with the intelligence we have created," will happen by 2045.[78] Similarly, AI expert Professor Richard Susskind claims that "we are still at the foothills," with what generative AI can do, and that "the pace of change is accelerating and we can reasonably expect increasingly more capable and accurate systems. In the long run, AI systems will be unfathomably capable and outperform humans in many if not most activities."[79]

So simply put, AI is everywhere and has been for some time, and its impact on the professions is going to continue to increase—as it has for the past 10 years—only faster and bigger.

In the last decade, PSFs of all kinds have been utilizing predictive analytics (the use of existing data to provide customer insights, inform decisions, enable risk mitigation, and predict future outcomes) and classic or analytical AI (which includes machine learning wherein algorithms are fed data enabling the tech to make assumptions, test, and learn autonomously).[80] That kind of AI has been replacing tasks and augmenting the work of professional service providers of all kinds for some time, helping them spend less time on low value and more time on high value strategic work.

For example, law firms, corporate legal departments, and the Big Four legal departments use AI every day to help with compliance and due diligence and to help accelerate contracting cycles, automate contract analysis, conduct legal research, and do document review exponentially faster and more cost efficiently.[81] They also use it to identify opportunities for revenue generation. For example, they use it to cross-check specific clauses with payment or other records to efficiently identify breaches, and generate and send standard legal letters for collection. They also use AI and data analytics to identify repeated breaches in a contract structure to negotiate the restructuring of commercial arrangements and deal structures in ways that generate greater revenue or to identify secondary assets acquired through a merger and acquisition deal that can be turned into revenue-generating opportunities. They also use it for litigation analytics and outcome prediction. Companies such as Premonition Analytics sell you just that—a premonition based on that type of case, country, court, lawyer, and judge (and yes, it takes into account race, religion, and gender). Insurance providers are using AI to make underwriting more efficient, to help identify potentially fraudulent claims, to identify ways to decrease accidents, and to streamline the claims process.[82] The Big Four accounting firms are using AI to analyze voluminous amounts of financial data and streamline auditing and accounting processes.[83] Marketers and advertisers use it to enhance their marketing strategies, enabling them to identify new target audiences, measure the effectiveness of advertising campaigns, and create tailored, personalized messaging campaigns to different customer segments that are delivered at optimal times and ideal locations.[84]

And companies of all kinds are using AI to personalize the customer/client/user experience and make our lives easier (which is what client centricity is all about). Think Apple's Siri, Amazon's Alexa, or Spotify, which learn from the music we play, the alarms we set, the grocery lists we create and then generate suggestions tailored to our likes. In our homes, we are now able to connect many of our electronic devices—our lights, our doorbell cameras, our alarm systems, our cable television, and we can ask our friendly, almost human-sounding AI to manage them for us—"Alexa, turn off the lights." "Alexa, set the alarm for the house in 15 minutes." "Alexa, give me options where I can eat breakfast close by." "Alexa, play songs by Fleetwood Mac." Now with generative AI, we can ask our tech tools to do tasks that we used to have to do ourselves at work, such as "Write that client memo for me." "Write that keynote address for me." "Write that contract for me." "Create the logo and tagline for me." "Come up with a new way to productize my services for me!"

When I wrote *Legal Upheaval* in 2018, I noted that experts believed these advancements were not far off. Now, we are there. Generative AI has opened the door to what MIT's Eric von Hippel coined the "democratization of innovation." Generative AI tools like Midjourney, ChatGPT, and Stable Diffusion can be used to create new art, new products, and new services that are more novel than what humans can ideate on their own, and that overcome expertise bias.[85] They can help support problem and solution refinement and can even evaluate the viability, feasibility, and novelty of a solution.[86] And the various tools can collaborate and be used by humans to collaborate.[87] The opportunities to assist in connecting dots that are seemingly unconnected, to create beauty, to build innovative solutions to the world's important problems, to enhance productivity and efficiency are endless for corporate clients and for PSFs alike. For PSFs, both generative and analytical AI will (continue to) help them enhance knowledge management and sharing, improve resource utilization, retain top resources (by saving them from the mundane work and identifying those most likely to leave), optimize productivity and increase overall efficiency, better identify business targets, answer requests for proposals (RFPs) with more precision and persuasion, enhance invoicing and collection processes, and even avoid scope creep.[88] It will also help them develop novel innovative products and services that do not yet exist. And it may help them better brand, market, and differentiate themselves in a marketplace. Importantly, as Susskind points out, clients need their professional service providers to use AI "to deliver client outcomes in entirely new ways."[89] They also need help managing the risks that AI poses.

Putting aside the much-debated risk that AI will replace some types of professional service provider jobs altogether (because too much could be written on that and leave us very depressed),[90] there are other risks to address. Although AI can be used to eliminate bias (as some insurance companies and banks have done),[91] big data and AI can have bias baked in regardless.[92] For example, a study conducted at the University of California Berkeley found that its AI-powered algorithms worked to eliminate some face-to-face bias in the lending process. However, it still assigned extra mortgage interest to minority borrowers.[93] Also, generative AI tools can "amplify biases and perpetuate stereotypes" and it can "hallucinate."[94] It can also contain errors and misinformation. Recently, a lawyer was sanctioned for citing cases that didn't exist that were provided to him by Chat GPT. This resulted in a mandate by the judge that lawyers not use generative AI but if they do, they have to disclose it and verify that they checked the information for accuracy.[95] Further, generative AI tools may also violate existing data protection, privacy, and copyright laws and regulations. Comedian Sarah Silverman sued Meta and Open AI for copyright infringement.[96] And the Federal Trade Commission is investigating the potential risks to consumers that OpenAI's ChatGPT poses, including the reputational harm that can occur from ChatGPT providing false information.[97] It is an understatement to say that there is likely a great deal more regulation (and litigation) about generative AI and analytical AI on the horizon.[98]

This is, in part, why clients are calling not only for their professional service providers to understand and harness new technology and become more digital[99] but also help them in all of their digital transformation initiatives. As I have written about in a prior article, the scalability and interconnectedness of networks together with AI and machine learning technologies[100] are transforming how companies and firms operate and compete and define their scope and scale.[101] Critical to survival, DT has become an enterprise-wide imperative for most multinational companies (MNCs).[102] As described in a McKinsey Guide, the goal of DT is to increase competitiveness by continuous integration and deployment of tech at scale to improve the customer experience, enhance efficiency, and lower costs.[103] And unlike "regular" transformations, that conclude once new processes and behaviors are achieved, because technology is continually changing, DT is a long-term—and continual—rewiring of how an organization operates. As the McKinsey Guide aptly points out, this means most executives will be on this journey for the rest of their careers and will be continually challenged to reinvent themselves to keep up.

The name of the game is customer centricity, which is more than minimizing wait times or suggesting products and services that the client wants. It's about using individual customer data to tailor the customer journey—the experience with the product or service—at every touch point. True, AI is essential to achieving "precision and scale in personalization," however, experts aptly note that AI is only "about 10% of the secret sauce. The other 90% lies in the combination of data, experimentation, and talent that constantly activate and inform the intelligence behind the systems."[104] Moreover, DT is a multidisciplinary change management process of the most difficult kind that demands a thorough redesign and reimagination of the organization's (or department's) core purpose, operating environment, and service delivery model.[105] As my coauthors and I (and other experts) have pointed out, ["the] real challenge lies in the softer dimension . . . internally, you need to have the right culture to harness and quickly develop what works, and just as quickly stop what doesn't, and you have to have the right skill sets working in the right way, collaborating to successful outcomes."[106]

As such, it requires talent to be upskilled and reskilled across all facets of the department, along with behavior and culture change.[107]

Thus, like leveraging ESG and enhancing DEI, harnessing AI and leading DT initiatives require a human-centered, proactive collaborative approach that tailors its efforts to the end user/key stakeholder to continuously improve their experience.[108] This is something innovators and design thinkers excel at doing, but something that many professional service providers have never been trained to do, which may account for the undeniably loud and persistent call by corporate clients for innovation from its professional service providers. Another reason for this loud and persistent call for innovation is also likely due to the fear that jobs will be replaced. A recent study by Goldman Sachs predicted "roughly two-thirds of current jobs are exposed to some degree of AI automation, and that generative AI could substitute up to one-fourth of current work" *and* that 44 percent of legal tasks will be replaced.[109] However, as Thomas Malone, a professor at the MIT Sloan School of Management and founding director of the university's Center for Collective Intelligence, aptly points out: "the reason it's so easy for us to get worried about loss of jobs is because it's very easy to imagine what jobs might be lost . . . It's much harder to imagine the jobs that might be created."[110]

Since innovators excel at imagining and creating, this call for professional service providers to innovate, or to at least hone the skill set and mindset of an innovator so that they can collaborate with others to harness the risks and opportunities involved with DEI, ESG, and technology, makes sense. After all, how we do our jobs, how we work—with data and the machines and with other professionals—and how we lead in this new world, will be valued even more in the future workplace.

D. Leader Upheaval and the Leadership Gap: A Call for Innovation and a New Mindset and Skill Set

Combined with the rapid enhancements in and adoption of technology, shifting socioeconomics and demographics, and globality (not to mention the pandemic),[111] the three priorities discussed above are causing *leader upheaval* in global industries and professional services. Being a successful leader in professional services today and in the future is different than it was before and it requires one word: innovation. To keep up with clients' needs, professional service providers need to innovate and adapt not only *what* services they provide but also, as mentioned above and discussed in more detail in the next chapter, *how* they provide them. And this call for innovation is probably the largest call to action by corporate clients, which makes sense given that enhancing DEI, leveraging ESG, and leading DT efforts all require the type of human-centered approach that is the hallmark of innovators and design thinkers (that is, putting the end user front and center and focusing on experiences [versus products and services]). A recent EY CEO Imperative Study sums it up aptly:

> *The challenge of delivering value to a widening range of stakeholders requires strong, decisive, empathetic and human-centered leadership, with a focus on innovation, fostering trust and modelling desired traits. Increasing digitalization, the prominence of data and analytics in decision-making and the ongoing shift to remote work is making the human qualities of leadership rise to the forefront.[112]*

However, as discussed in a previous article of mine, the call by corporate clients for their professional service providers to innovate and take a design-thinking approach to challenges creates a chicken-egg dilemma.[113] This is because many were not trained and don't know how to innovate or lead innovation, change, and culture creation in which diverse individuals thrive.[114] Experts in innovation agree that "the innovator's method" requires a different type of leadership, a different type of thinking from traditional business thinking and that the challenges posed with leading innovation are different than leading strategic planning.[115] Moreover, they posit, too many leaders do not have the requisite mindset and skill set of an innovator—which, uncoincidentally includes that of an inclusive[116] and adaptive leader[117] (discussed in more detail in Chapter 3). Further, as

Richard and Daniel Susskind have repeatedly pointed out, professional service providers continue to "dive for cover" and "advise on transformation rather than change themselves."[118] Like the quote this chapter began with, they desire that things "should stay the way they are"[119] when what they should be doing instead is innovating, adapting, and "acquiring skills needed to build and operate the systems that will replace their old ways of working—knowledge engineering, data science, design thinking and risk management."[120]

Given this aversion to change and this desire to hide, it is unsurprising that many companies and professional services organizations are suffering from a leadership gap. A study by Deloitte found that 86 percent of businesses worldwide claim new leadership development is their number one challenge.[121] Seventy-one percent claimed that they do not believe their leaders are able to lead their companies into the future.[122] These confidence levels are lower than they were pre-pandemic.

One of the largest and longest-running global studies on the current and future state of leadership found in 2023 that only 40 percent of leaders believe their leaders were high-quality—reflecting a 17 percent decrease from 2022, the largest decline in a decade.[123] According to the data, a reason for the decline is lack of trust in existing leaders,[124] which also isn't surprising given that research indicates that current leaders do not have the requisite skill set and mindset to inspire others, manage change, and build collaborative relationships.[125] They do not have an innovation mindset and they are not supportive and consultative, inclusive and adaptive.[126] Tie that to research that shows that ineffective leadership is a top reason why talent walks out the door,[127] and it makes perfect sense that the leadership skills gap is a top strategic priority of CEOs at large, multinational corporations around the globe.[128]

The question is: What are the mindset and skill set that are required of a leader to answer clients' call for innovation and to harness the opportunities and decrease the risks that the future holds? It is to that question that the next chapter turns.

...Reflection Point Take a moment to jot down the mindset, attributes, and skill set you believe leaders need to innovate and collaborate and help clients with the three priorities outlined above (DEI, ESG, and AI/technology). Later, compare your list with those described in Chapter 2 in the Professional Skills Delta.

▄▟...Reflection Point Lead a discussion among your team to generate ideas of how clients might demand change and/or innovation in the future given their changing priorities and pressures related to DEI, ESG, and AI/technology. Discuss how and why these new demands may frustrate or energize the team.

CHAPTER 2

New Expectations Call for a Move from *What* We Do to *How* We Do It

> ## *"How We Do Anything Means Everything"*
> —Dov Seidman[1]

One of the hardest lessons I learned during my first job after college was that *how* I worked was at least as important—if not more important—than how *hard* I worked or how much I accomplished. And I learned this the hard way. As an assistant account executive at Leo Burnett, my job was to manage everything having to do with developing, creating, and placing the advertising for my assigned products (which at that time were Kellogg's Nutri-Grain Cereal Bars, Kellogg's Pop-Tarts, and Kellogg's Smacks). This meant I had to corral my immediate bosses from the Client Service account team; and people from Creative (the copy writers and artists); Media Buying (the executives that bought the TV, billboard, magazine, and radio space); Production; Research; and also, sometimes, Events—none of whom reported to me, yet all of whom I needed to make sure were on-strategy and on-time. This required a ton of proactivity on my part and an immense level of attention to detail, as well as, of course, the organizational skills to manage every phone call, email, and meeting. Still, none of this was the most demanding aspect of the job. No, that was in communicating what needed to be done without simply seeming like a demanding 23-year-old assistant account executive hammering away at people all the time. It's true, I never missed a client deadline. Our meetings and projects ran smoothly and on time and I received great client reviews, but I wasn't very well liked internally (by my colleagues and internal clients).

My flatmate, let's call him Alex, on the other hand, couldn't have been more my opposite. He wasn't proactive. He wasn't organized. I don't think he understood what the words "project management" meant or what details would make an advertising campaign successful. And he was definitely not demanding. Instead, he was mellow and nice. Like Mr. Magoo,[2] Alex bumbled forward yet things worked out for him regardless, because everyone *loved* Alex. He was their go-to guy for golf, a drink, or lunch. Unlike that other assistant account executive (i.e., me), he didn't harass folks all the time about when the work would be ready or when the strategy would be finished.

You likely won't be surprised to hear that Alex was promoted a few weeks before I was. But I was surprised by this big lesson in life: *How* we do things matters as much if not more than *what* we actually do. If this was true in professional services back then, it is truer than ever now—especially given the advancements of tech and AI. Our clients care as much about HOW we provide services, the EXPERIENCE of the interaction with us, as WHAT services we provide. Moreover, they care about our business and professional skills that are unrelated to our substantive expertise because those skills add value: they make us better able to harness the opportunities that AI, tech, and data provide; they change the way we communicate to and collaborate with others. And they impact the overall experience we provide, making it more efficient and effective, more tailored to the clients' needs and wants (i.e., client-centric), and more delightful.

Therefore, the goal of this chapter is to bring to life the mindset and skill set needed of professional service providers to meet the demands and desires of the changing marketplace and that of clients. Simply put, this chapter contends that professional service providers need to master the skill set and mindset that enable them to make three moves: (1) a move from behaving as expert advisors to innovation consiglieres, (2) a move from a focus on services to experiences, and (3) a move from the traditional notions of leadership (with a capital L) to becoming adaptive, inclusive leaders with a digital mindset. This chapter focuses on the first move, leaving the second two moves to Chapter 3.

Over the past decade, based on my research, consulting, and work in LawWithoutWalls,[3] I have created the Professional Skills Delta (Skills Delta; see Figure 2.1). The word delta signifies **change,** an area where many of us have big, gaping holes. The Skills Delta is shaped like a pyramid that contains three levels of skills (or attributes) that are needed and desired of professional service providers that go beyond the base expertise skills required of that type of professional expert. The skills ascend vertically from required skills (which are relatively easy to procure) to desired skills that may be more difficult to procure but have the potential to differentiate service providers. The skills and attributes on this Skills Delta are those that every professional should seek to hone no matter what future job they envision (whether it is a job that already exists but is aided by tech, or one of the new jobs predicted by Richard and Daniel Susskind,[4] or something not yet even imagined). This pyramid, not coincidentally, also ranges from dissatisfied, to satisfied, to ecstatic clients along the same vertical access. The purpose of the Skills Delta is for us to identify the skills, mindset, behaviors, qualities, and attributes we need to hone so that we can become inclusive, adaptive, leaders who can embrace change and innovation in our constantly evolving, unpredictable environment with multiple uncertainties that are trans-dimensional.[5] In addition to becoming adaptive leaders, as we master that on the Skills Delta, we are able to be client-centric with a focus not only on products and services

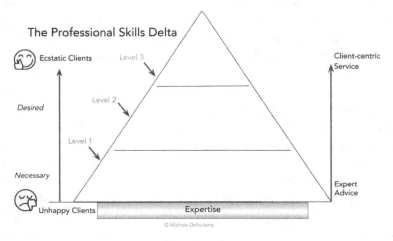

FIG. 2.1. Outline of the Professional Skills Delta.[8]

but on experiences that are meaningful and multifaceted. This is what our clients expect of us today[6] and this is how we can move our unhappy clients to the top of the Delta, where they become ecstatic clients.

You may be familiar with the Skills Delta from my book *Legal Upheaval.*[7] This version, however, applies to all professional service providers, such as accountants, consultants, insurance brokers, human resources professionals, engineers, marketing and advertising professionals, financial advisors, and IT professionals. It turns out, we *all* have clients, especially when you include the professional service providers who work *inside* our companies. That was another lesson I learned the hard way. After I had worked in advertising at Leo Burnett for a few years, I was sick of having all these clients! I wanted to be a client too. So, I got a job as a marketing executive at Levi Strauss & Co. in San Francisco, California. When I started in my new role, I realized very quickly: *Oh no, I have just as many clients now, and actually, it's even worse because I can't get away from them . . . there are all these people within my company that are now my clients!* The Skills Delta is all about working with clients, both internal and external. Note that at the base of the Skills Delta is the professionals' specific expertise (legal, insurance, banking, etc.). That is at the base because it means expertise in your specialty is a *given*. It's why you need a degree or certification in what you do. You will also note by the unhappy face at the bottom of the Skills Delta, that if all we give our clients and our teams is our substantive expertise, they will be unhappy. To delight our clients, we need to be client-centric, focused on experiences, on providing full service, which is our expertise plus the skill set and mindsets on the Skills Delta.

As noted in Chapter 1, clients' needs and desires are changing. In addition to the three priorities highlighted in Chapter 1, another big priority of clients can be summed up in three words: *cheaper, better, faster.* I don't know a professional service provider who isn't sick of hearing those three words. The reality is that they aren't going away. Clients within corporations are increasingly sophisticated, with more access to information. As a result, they are demanding more transparency from their service departments on budgeting, outside spending, and prioritization. Clients of external firms are demanding the same—more transparency and certainty on project staffing, management, and billing. Clients are demanding that their firms utilize tech (and AI) to maximize efficiency and increase effectiveness. Clients are demanding that their professional service providers are savvy with data, data metrics, and predictive analytics. More than that, clients are forcing a more efficient unbundling and repackaging of services to move toward not only value billing but also value production. Clients want value produced every step of the way as the firm journeys toward project completion—not just at the end.

A. Skills Delta Level 1: The C.O.S.T Skills (Sunk Costs)

The first level of the Skills Delta is designed to meet these needs. It contains what I call C.O.S.T skills. This acronym describes the skills in this tier, that is, those that are concrete (in that they can be taught and then sharpened with practice), related to the organization your client works in, service-oriented, and tech-enabled (as everything is these days). I also call them C.O.S.T skills because they are sunk cost skills. They take time (and money) to learn but they are the cost of doing business. For the most part, the value these skills deliver for clients (and the revenue they return for professional service providers) isn't measurable. These skills include project management, facility with technology, knowledge of our clients' industry, understanding our clients' business, knowing the difference between marketing and branding, knowing how to network, presenting, mentoring, giving and receiving feedback, and, of course, the ability to use technology and data to measure results, aid in decision making, and predict future outcomes. These skills are at the bottom third of the pyramid because they are considered necessary to compete (Figure 2.2).

The skills at this level aren't new and they can be mastered over time. But that doesn't mean many still *haven't* been mastered by professional service providers—even though they can add so much value along the way, as we work on projects for and with our clients.

Take a simple example of a client calling his lawyer because he wants help getting from A to B. The legal service provider might assure the client that they have called the right person and they can help them. Then they go off and work *really* hard to do their very best to exceed their clients' expectations (and get paid more), and eventually they do get them from A to B and in first-class style. Think Rolls Royce. But what if the client was absolutely fine with coach-class or a Honda Civic? Not only has the lawyer overdelivered, they have underdelivered because they gave no value along the way.

Figure 2.3 shows a chart of a Minimum Viable Product developed by Henrik Kniberg, a coach and consultant at Crisp, that brings this to life.[9]

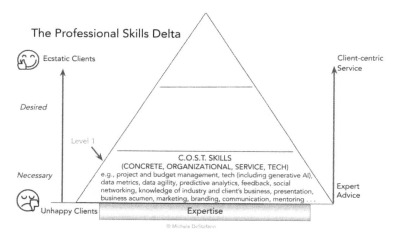

FIG. 2.2. Level 1 of the Professional Skills Delta.

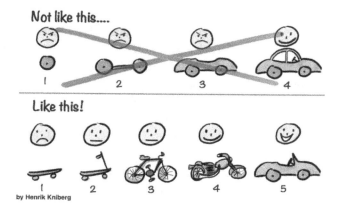

FIG. 2.3. Henrik Kniberg's Chart Depicting a Minimal Viable Product.

Instead of providing value with, for example, a skateboard, then a scooter, then a bike, then a motorcycle, etc., the lawyer provides only the car—and in this case, it is a luxury car. This often makes the end product not worth the costs because it either overreaches the goal (maybe the client only needs to go a few blocks, making a car superfluous altogether) or underreaches its value-add potential—in the top picture, the client only gets the car, whereas in the bottom picture, the client gets the car in addition to the motorcycle, bicycle, scooter, and skateboard.

Clients are frustrated with their professional service providers for not providing value along the way and for giving them the Rolls Royce job when all they needed was the scooter, the quick and simple view.[10] The professional service providers haven't exemplified business acumen or an understanding of their clients' business, and overdelivering does no one any favors. Probably one of the most common complaints I receive about lawyers from their clients is reflected in this quote by the CEO of a real estate management company in Australia: "If we ask you one question, we don't need seven answers for five times the price. And we need it packaged up and in a language so the business unit person can understand the advice and put it in practice versus needing an intermediary to translate."[11] In addition to internal business clients being frustrated with their in-house and external lawyers, in-house counsel are frustrated with their law firm lawyers:

> *Some professional service providers are incapable of having a normal basic conversation, of bringing the advice down to a level that gets rid of complex words or impressive terms and understanding how to get from A to B. Some wrap themselves around in convoluted advice. I think they are trying to cover all the bases, but they haven't understood how or why the client is trying to get from A to B.*—IT and commercial lawyer, large U.K.-based financial services institution[12]

Many professionals, especially lawyers, may be shocked to hear the suggestion that they lack business savvy. Yet, a recent study by LexisNexis in partnership with the Judge Business School at the University of Cambridge reports that although "clients repeatedly emphasized that they look to law firms for solutions to business problems, . . . 40 percent noted that senior partners of their law firms appeared to lack more than a basic knowledge of their business [. . .] and 75 percent mentioned they get little help from law firms when analyzing the complex portfolio of legal work given to them."[13] And it's not just lawyers. Other professional service providers, like HR professionals, also come up short when it comes to business acumen.[14] To provide information in business-minded language is a concrete skill that can be learned. It may take time, but that effort to learn is valued by the client.

In addition to overdelivering, lawyers can also underdeliver in the A to B scenario because they haven't served in the role as project manager or communicated with the client, nor have they tracked budgets. Instead, the lawyers racked up hours (without keeping the client in the loop) and then showed up with something off the mark.

The skills in the bottom part of the Skills Delta can change the game. They can deliver that value-add. Consider the following quote about project management from a chief financial officer of a boutique investment advisory firm who is an expert in merger and acquisition (M&A) deals:

> *It goes back to coordination. For diligence, you have your law firm review the contract and diligence and outside accountants reviewing diligence and only certain aspects of the contract. And then the non-legal insurance experts. But from the law firm side you have no one coordinating it all. The bankers and accountants in M&A do a better job because they have a person in the middle trying to pull it together who is thinking about project management, and they have reporting formats established on how they are going to review and report on diligence whereas the lawyers basically do free form diligence and a big memo without identifying what is important even when they include an executive summary.*—Chief financial officer, boutique investment advisory firm.[15]

Consider this quote by the general counsel (GC) of a large media and telecommunications company:

> *"What we have seen is more and more a need for lawyers to migrate from the classic role of just giving legal advice and yes-no answers and more and more becoming project managers. Our demands have changed for lawyers. We need them to be a part of the team . . . the world is more complex with more areas overlapping and lawyers can see these overlaps that most people in business units can't. So, the lawyer's role has naturally grown into the project management role. And we ask them to change to assume the role of speaking their mind and assuming the project management role versus only providing narrow legal advice. It's about transitioning people from legal experts to being project managers and business partners. This is the main change (beyond tech) that we are asking of lawyers."*—GC, large media and telecommunications company in Australia[16]

Budget predictions and updates, communicating in concise business style, and highlighting key areas of import are a way to add value. This is one of the reasons why I have all my teams learn how to present in Ignite style (20 self-moving slides in 5 minutes or less). It is a great way to communicate in a very short time period—much shorter than most professionals talk in a meeting—and limited to the essentials (which is what clients want). In addition, doing an Ignite with your colleagues takes trust and vulnerability (all attributes clients want their professional service providers to hone). Essentially, clients do not just want more for less, but they sometimes just want less—which sometimes means more work spent on utilizing and exemplifying the C.O.S.T. skills. You know that famous saying that has been attributed to many people, including Mark Twain and Blaise Pascal: "I didn't have time to write a short letter, so I wrote a long one instead."

> *A firm will send seven pages of advice but is it something I can act on and do something with? Because I can read the law as well. I want an executive summary and a recommendation—so my business clients only have to read the first paragraph. The issues are attached on the back. Presenting legal advice in a way that helps me and the business make a decision rather than legal advice I have to decipher and figure out what to do.*—Senior corporate counsel, multinational insurance company headquartered in Australia[17]

Clients want their professional service providers to help get them from A to Z, but to help differently (harkening back to the title of this chapter). Clients want lawyers to give executable advice. If they want the car, clients want the scooter and the bike as well. Moreover, they want to know *how* to ride the scooter and drive the car.

As indicated, clients need professional service providers that approach their problems from both industry and business focal points and provide actionable direction. Take lawyers, for example. Most of the lawyers I have come across believe they are meeting this need already—when many are not—at least not according to the clients with whom I have spoken. I hear the same complaints about law firm lawyers from all over the world—from those at the big, elite firms to those at the mid-tier and midsize firms. Clients are sick and tired of advice that does not take into account their industry and their particular business, their brand, and culture, and advice that does not provide a clear point of view. In addition to wanting concise advice that is easy to understand, they want advice that is in the same style and tone as the client. Consider the following quote by an interviewee:

> *I asked an external firm for a note that I could provide to the other side to negotiate; to just set out a few terms and what I got, I had to read three times to understand it—and I knew the partner! I wish they knew how I communicate. They see how I communicate but they just go about doing it the way they see fit whereas they should adapt their*

approach to their client in tone, length, complexity/simplicity. The law can be complicated, but you don't have to talk about it in a complicated way. That's a choice. At the bank, no one is impressed when you make something sound complicated. Law firms should be capable of writing better emails and better pieces of advice, so I don't have to re-write their emails which is not my job.—IT and commercial lawyer, one of the U.K.'s largest financial services organizations.[18]

As indicated in Chapter 1, the problems facing corporate clients are uncertain, ambiguous, volatile, and require proactive collaboration on multidisciplinary teams. This means clients are not looking just for help related to that professional's area of expertise. Consider the legal industry again, for example. It's not just help with their "legal" problems that clients are looking for. They want their experts to be business professionals who can communicate with the right positioning and branding and target audience in mind and provide advice that is not related only to their expertise.

Strategic (not just legal) advice is considered the highest value output of the legal department . . . It is this kind of advice that directly adds value to the company's projects and overall strategic goals. For this kind of highly valued work, understanding the business is a critical success factor.—Max Hübner, executive director, Legal Management & Operations (formerly director, Corporate Legal and Tax, PGGM N.V.)[19]

In-house clients also want help in managing their department better. They want their external professional service providers (including law firm lawyers) to figure out a way to utilize technology to provide solutions for their business (not just legal) problems to help manage the inefficiencies and bureaucracies that in-house counsel are experiencing. They want their external professional service providers to help them deal with the intense and immense demands of their internal business clients,[20] who prioritize everything as high and want everything right away—not to mention the endless repetitive requests and questions by the business about contracts and marketing language and nondisclosure agreements, for example. They need help suppressing demands from their business clients.

We need more self-service for non-legal users . . . The time saved can be used to deliver more value-added services in the field of ever-increasing regulatory matters.—Max Hübner, executive director, Legal Management & Operations (formerly director, Corporate Legal and Tax, PGGM N.V.)[21]

Indeed, law firms are winning awards for doing just that type of work: for providing neither *legal* advice nor *legal* services in the traditional sense, but instead law-related services to help legal departments suppress demand from their business clients and manage their departments as a business. For example, Herbert Smith Freehills won a *Financial Times* award in 2017 for helping Telstra lower internal legal department costs associated with meetings, overhead, and inefficient processes.[22] Gilbert and Tobin won a *Financial Times* award in 2017 for hosting a hackathon in conjunction with its client Westpac Banking Corporation and Legal-Vision in which teams hacked on challenges to help free up lawyers from time-consuming, inefficient tasks. One such example is an app created by Gilbert and Tobin that provides corporate legal teams with tips and draft clauses so that they can service their business clients' contracting needs faster.[23]

Clients want you to get to know them and their department and to help them run their business or their department.[24]

> *I think what works really well is when the firm takes a lot of opportunity not just to get to know maybe the GC, but to get to know multiple levels throughout the organization because that really pays dividends . . . I would love to hear from law firms, and I would love for someone from a law firm to come to me and say "We have a point of view on the kinds of technologies that are gonna make your legal services better in the next five years. Would you like to talk to us about them? Would you like for us to present to you on them and take a look at some of your internal processes and look out how you could maybe tweak those to deliver better services for your clients and help your business?" I would love to have those conversations—and I'm rarely asked that. In fact, I'm never asked that.*—VP and associate general counsel, American multinational enterprise information technology company.[25]

Clients want all of this now—all of the time, from all their professional service providers. And they want them to oversee, that is, quarterback, what Steven Walker, former vice president and associate general counsel of Hewlett-Packard Enterprises, calls "end-to-end solutions," which are solutions that provide "the optimal combinations of people, process, tools and technology, and hybrid inside/outside sourcing models, to meet their client's business and legal challenges."[26] This is the future for professional services of all kinds and clients are asking for help in envisioning and shaping it. Consider this quote by the GC of a multinational enterprise information technology company:

> *The question is: if I am going to invest in you for the next two to three years' worth of fees, how can you invest back in me? What is your tech strategy? How can you help me unbundle? What are you doing in the legal management space? . . . How can law firms help GCs manage the consumption of legal services?*—VP and associate general counsel, American multinational enterprise information technology company[27]

This requires a more consistent and intense relationship as opposed to the sporadic transaction-based relationship that often occurs between service professionals and clients (i.e., client and lawyer interact when client needs legal advice, and then when that is over, the interaction lulls; accountant and client interact when client needs tax advice, and then when that is over the interaction lulls, etc.).[28] This requires a shift from being expert advisors or even consultants to *counselors* like consiglieres (ethical ones of course).

> *There are a couple of firms that we use that kind of see the advice of the legal adviser as a little bit removed and their job is to provide the technically correct legal advice in relation to the question that is asked whether or not that is particularly helpful and whether or not that is what is wanted. And it is almost like a high moral ground. We are here to tell you what the law is and you can go away and deal with it . . . we have other firms who are much more attuned to what it is the client (not me but our business areas) wants to achieve and find a way to do that and delivering advice that while still accurate takes into account where the client wants to go—and the law is very rarely black and white. There are lots of grays and it's how you work with grays to find the way through. The firms that don't do that well, do at times very much frustrate me—because they are not really delivering the service we need.*—General counsel, government department of Australia[29]

This also requires a shift from being experts to being business leaders:

> *So, what we need to do is make sure that the lawyers are participating fully as leaders . . . getting to the space where they are business leaders who happen to be lawyers, can bring that experience and expertise, and are also participating in the business calls being made.*—Siobhán Moriarty, General counsel of Diageo[30]

But to do that? Professionals need to master those skills and attributes (and mindsets) in Level 2 of the Skills Delta.

> *I do think there are quite a number of things lawyers need to develop. Leadership starts with self—emotional intelligence and self-awareness. There is a huge difference between being a great lawyer versus a great leader. Do they actually lead people? Inspire, motivate, collaborate, and drive a team to high performance? There's a whole skill set required for lawyers around leadership and that requires a huge amount of investment.*—Senior corporate counsel, multinational insurance company headquartered in Australia[31]

B. Skills Delta Level 2: Collaboration and Creative Problem Finding + Solving Skills

In the middle tier of the Skills Delta the challenges become even more difficult. The skills and attributes presented here require not only a different mindset but also continual attention. They are the collaborative and creative, problem finding and problem-solving skills that are often also cited as key to inclusive, adaptive leadership (Figure 2.4).[32]

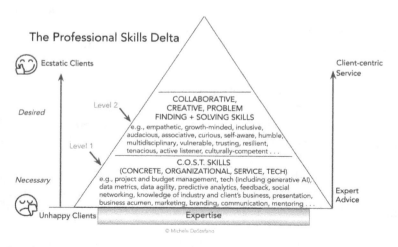

FIG. 2.4. Level 2 of the Professional Skills Delta.

Leaders who excel in this tier as well as the preceding one have growth mindsets, are curious, courageous, and flexible. These leaders associate things that might not otherwise be associated and lead with audacity when necessary—which they can do because they trust others on their team, which they have assembled to take advantage of the power of diversity. And they do that because they are not only humble and self-aware, resilient, and tenacious, but also culturally competent.

Perhaps most importantly, leaders at this tier know the difference between problem finding and problem-solving. Research has shown that the best problem solvers are the best problem finders. Both Tina Seelig and Daniel Pink have written on this subject[33] which is described well in Albert Einstein's famous quote: "If I had an hour to solve a problem and my life depended on the solution, I would spend the first 55 minutes determining the proper question to ask, for once I know the proper question, I could solve the problem in less than five minutes."[34] There are problems all around us, and they are ripe for solutions. But if we don't spend the time asking questions and listening with empathy—if, instead, we jump to solve—we can miss the mark because sometimes in our rush to "serve" our clients by fixing something, we solve for a symptom instead of the problem.

> *What is important is: how do they then add value to make strategic decisions? We need more law firms to invest in the front add and provide a value add to go through the problem at an early stage and talk to us—and not charge us—and not jump to advice.*—Senior corporate counsel, multinational insurance company headquartered in Australia[35]

However, clients need their professional service providers to be problem finders and to work in multicultural, multidisciplinary teams—to move, in other words, from the role of service provider to partner, partnering *together* with their clients (and other types of professionals including HR, marketing, data scientists, PR) to find the problems before attempting to solve them.

Clients want their service providers to partner together and with them to find the problems and create new opportunities. As one business client explained:

> *The biggest bit of contract work I did last year, when I got the legal team involved, they behaved as a real ally and their work ethic*

was phenomenal. Their creativity . . . was absolutely outstanding. But it was a problem-solving activity vs a problem finding one. I'm a really big advocate of genuine partnering. My team works close with HR, finance and supply chain partners.—Head of Colleague Platforms & Network Services, major retail and commercial bank in the United Kingdom[36]

I've shown the quote above to professional service providers and they don't get how it is negative. And I agree it is a bit obscure. It is hard to see the "problem" within and hear what the client is saying by what they are *not* saying—which is one of the reasons that listening is part of Level 2 on the Skills Delta. Instead, they glean that the work was "phenomenal" and "creative" and "outstanding." However, what this client was saying is that HR, finance, and the supply chain departments were true partners who collaborated with him in problem finding, whereas the in-house legal team were not "genuine partner[s]" in their approach and problem-solving work.

In addition to problem finding, clients also want them to harness multiple skills so that they provide nontraditional expertise and advice. Consider the following responses from a GC interviewees:

The challenges we have are multifaceted. The legal issues are a manifestation of a problem but the way you solve it is not the law. Sometimes it's the relationship, sometimes it is with lobbying or public relations and communications. It is with a variety of skills that are not inherently legal in nature. It requires sometimes acting with others in industry or coalitions. You have to understand the business and that a lot of legal issues cannot be solved by changing the law or with a legal solution but through changing the business model. You can't start with a legal discussion. You have to have a vision and a combination of skill sets that come from a number of disciplines.—General counsel, global music streaming service[37]

I ask them to be innovative . . . but they are going on an old model. I find this with my team as well—they are getting frustrated with law firms. As time goes on, it's becoming less and less connected with what you need . . . Figure out what do I need? You could be providing training that I can't do because I'm too busy. You are selling me templates, but I want to buy your judgment.—General counsel, Australian division of a worldwide healthcare group based in the United Kingdom[38]

These are the value adds. The things that they can provide us that are not the traditional model of advice or documentation . . . a transition to thinking away from tech to the softer side, to developing that broader set of soft skills . . . Some law firms are running [training] programs . . . and offer some spots for us to come along. That's been interesting, inviting us to piggyback on their efforts. But what we keep saying to our panel firms is let's do something together—let's develop together—bring in an external provider and work with them to together develop a training program and give us an opportunity to work together on learning opportunities.—Head of Knowledge and Development, Compliance and Secretariat, a Big 4 Australian bank, and financial service provider[39]

The operative words in the quote immediately above are "that's been interesting." Although many Americans might not interpret those words the way they are intended, I learned the hard way that when a person from Britain or Australia says that something is "interesting," it means "there is no bleeping way *that* is interesting." Here, the point is, GCs want to collaborate with their professional service providers—as in together—not just have them bring them a solution, or even more often, a new problem.

This may seem obvious, yet it is exactly the opposite of how legal professionals are trained to work with clients. They are not taught to collaborate like this. They are taught to problem-solve for sure. But collaboration for a lawyer often means that I deliver my part and you deliver yours . . . and then we'll put them together. And it is not just lawyers who struggle with the idea of collaborative value creation! Researchers have demonstrated that other professional service providers often "offer value propositions that prioritize their own products and services over collaboration with [customers and clients], taking a one-sided perspective that lacks critical customer [and client] input."[40]

Clients want professional service providers who are creative problem solvers, problem finders, and opportunity finders who seek to understand their clients' needs and collaborate with them with empathy and ingenuity to create value. They want professionals who are cross-competent leaders with wide networks and can team across countries, cultures, and disciplines. They want professionals who have a growth mindset and will put their egos aside and work with people of different levels of experience and expertise. And they want professionals who not only have passion and perseverance but also take risks and embrace failure. They want professionals who have accepted the idea that they don't know everything and will ask for help from a wide and diverse set of inputs—in other words, those with self-awareness and a dash of humility who do not always think they are the smartest and best in the room.

> *A level of professional creativity in terms of helping you devise innovative approaches to deal with legal problems has always been seen as a part of the legal profession. That's not a new trend. Lawyers are creative in finding the right answers to the right problems. Competence in this type of creativity in advice is a commodity. It is a prerequisite. But most successful lawyers are not necessarily the ones with the right IQ and substantive expertise. They are the ones that combine those skills with soft skills . . . It takes a lot of dedication and commitment and empathy and ability to listen.*—General counsel, global music streaming service[41]

An exercise we have all LawWithoutWalls teams do multiple times, to help teams learn how to listen and empathize and thereby separate the sources of a problem, its root causes, from its symptoms is *The 5 Whys & Root Cause Analysis Exercise*, based on a concept created in the early 1930s by Sakichi Toyoda, the founder of Toyota Industries.[42] This exercise is designed to help teams better understand the problem and empathize with the target consumer audience. If conducted properly, by the end, teams should be able to tell a *real* story from beginning, middle, to end that highlights the various aspects of the problem that exist and brings the target audience to life.

The 5 Whys Exercise is best conducted if the person being questioned is someone who has truly experienced, witnessed, or researched the problem and understands the frustration. That said, the people that ask the 5 Whys have the hardest job. They must really listen to the answer to each "why" and they must respond to the answer provided. When asking the 5 Whys, we are trying to connect the dots—we are not asking a bunch of unanswerable "why" questions that are unrelated. Also, there should be no judgment during this exercise, no right or wrong answers. The goal is to empathize and better understand the pain points of the person experiencing the problem. After all, the person experiencing the problem likely doesn't know the answers either. They may not know the root cause but only feel the symptoms. This is why, during the exercise, this person might get emotional, frustrated, or even angry. "Why are you asking me why? If I knew the answer, I wouldn't be hiring you!" they might say. Or "Why are you asking me why? The why doesn't matter. Just fix it." To risk irritating people in pain even further, sometimes you must ask more than 5 Whys to get to the root cause. Sometimes the person being asked can be a bit recalcitrant, that is, they don't answer our "why" questions. When that happens the person that can get frustrated is the questioner and it can take more like 15 Whys.

Regardless of how many questions it takes, you know the team has asked "why" enough times when they get to the "aha" moment: that moment when the person experiencing the problem understands better why they were so frustrated. Simultaneously, the people asking the question now have a better idea of what they should focus on fixing because they have a greater sense of "why" the problem is happening. They also have participated in an important type of client-centric listening, with empathy and that, in and of itself, adds value (after the client gets past the frustration of course).

It sounds easy. Yet, it is really hard for people who are in professional services who are good at problem-solving.[43] We like pleasing our clients; we are trained that the client is queen or king, and we should drop everything (even vacation) to help them. We are also taught that the order of events is that, first, clients tell us their problems. We listen. Second, we go off and collaborate internally to solve the client's problems. The irony is that in trying to treat clients like royalty and do all the work for them, we do them a disservice. We give them what they say they want (or what we think they want) instead of what they need.

I use the following example with my teams, so they realize that asking 5 Whys and resisting the urge to jump and fix things does not come easy. Instead, it takes work every day to overcome our nature and our training and our desire to please. If *I'm* still making this mistake after leading 230 plus teams for over a decade, then it must be really hard to avoid. My example happened when I was working with Microsoft. I led an experiential learning program on collaboration and innovation for five years with their internal corporate external and legal affairs department.

The program was similar to LawWithoutWalls in that teams of business and legal professionals were assigned a real challenge facing Microsoft and they had to create a viable solution to the problem along with a prototype and business plan, and then present it to the most senior people in the department. The program was almost 4 months long and the format was blended (part in-person and part virtual). In the fifth year of the program, my lead client at Microsoft and I decided to test a new form: five days in person at Microsoft's headquarters in Redmond, Washington (outside of Seattle), beginning on a Monday. On the Friday morning before the program's scheduled launch, I received an email from my client, Mark, that bore the dreaded red exclamation mark. Who wants that on a Friday? In the email, Mark explained that he was really worried about our program because a huge, historic snowstorm was expected to hit the greater Seattle area on Sunday and Monday. *"Do you have time to jump on a call immediately?"* he asked.

Well, of course, I did. I'm a client service provider and I aim to please. But like a good service provider, I didn't want to show up unprepared or empty-handed. I called my team to brainstorm solutions. We had Microsoft professionals traveling from all over the world to the Seattle area to attend this in-person program. What would we do if they couldn't get there, if they were stuck at home or in an airport somewhere? We brainstormed lots of options so that those who couldn't make it physically could attend virtually (which was OLD HAT For LawWithoutWalls but foreign to most professionals at the time, believe it or not—remember this was 2019 and well before COVID-19 forced the world to go virtual).

Thirty minutes later, we were on a call with Mark. My first question was, of course, *"I know this is hard; how are you?"* (That was the empathy—check!) For my next point, after listening to his general concerns that the program might fail due to the storm, I jumped in with: *"My team and I met briefly to discuss some options that we thought we could present to you to get your feedback so we can tweak and improve them."* (You know, collaborate—check!). Then I began listing a few of the ideas we had for the travelers from outside the country. But Mark, who never interrupts me, broke right into my speech: *"Wait a minute,"* he said. *"Wait . . . a . . . minute. I don't care about the people flying into Seattle. I care about the people already here. The roads will be closed. And even if they can drive, the schools will be closed. And even if that wasn't the case, Microsoft headquarters might be closed entirely.*" His words jarred me like the sound of a record needle being dragged across my favorite album. I had committed the ultimate problem-solver sin. In my rush to solve, to please the client, I missed the mark. What I should have done is started the call by asking 5 Whys: *Why are you worried about the snow impacting our program? Why is that your biggest worry?* I would have learned with the first "why" question what was troubling him and that we had assumed wrongly. My heart was in the right place. I wanted my client to know how dedicated we were to him, and I wanted to help ease his worries by finding a solution that could save the program. But we failed to empathize with the client. Even if we are trained to conduct the type of open-ended pain point discovery interviews that are needed to really understand the problem, the genuine observing and questioning that is part of the innovator's DNA is only done with empathy and listening.[44] Only when we empathize with and listen to the target audience experiencing the problem can we reach the root cause. And only then can we create a solution that resonates. This is why empathy and listening along with humility, curiosity, cultural competency, and tenaciousness are essential skills in the Level 2 of the Skills Delta.

These skills in the second level are also at the heart of effective collaboration. There has been a lot of research about why collaboration is important: how it increases revenue, but also about how it is more than just cross-selling.[45] However, the research that I've done over the last couple years with hundreds of general councils and law firm partners from around the world points to a new type of collaboration that is desired. This enhanced kind of collaboration is not just about collaboration between service providers of different kinds who are hired to work on different pieces of a problem by the client, or between teams within firms or within companies, or even between professionals from lots of different areas of expertise. Rather this is about a new type of togetherness which is a proactive co-collaboration. Our clients want us in the boat with them. Our clients need their professional service providers to counsel them on everything related to the service provided. There is no problem that is just about one discipline or that only needs one expert's advice. Clients need counsel on the unintended (and intended) consequences of their choices. They want help with digital transformation, and they need their service providers to be looking around the corner for what's next. Consider the company Philips. It started selling light bulbs and lamps, then electric shavers, then radios and television sets, then records and cassette tapes, then VCRs, and eventually became one of the largest electronics companies in the world.[46] Now it's a health technology company![47]

Based on data about nutrition and the concerns of its customers, Nestlé began developing nutritional supplements now found in pharmacies and hospitals (and paid for by insurers).[48] The company's most profitable and fastest growing division is nutrition and health science—not candy.[49] Take that KitKat! This type of industry blurring is happening at an even faster pace given technology and data collection. Imagine if you work for a rental car company. Whether you are a lawyer, or a data scientist, or a compliance professional, or marketer, or in HR, your job is to predict where that rental car company will be making most of its revenue in 10 years because it may not be from renting cars. Maybe it will be from the data it collects, for example, selling maps of its drivers. Who knows? But if this is so, it impacts what professional advice you give, how you set up data lakes, who you hire and retain, how and to whom you market your services because as the company's business model changes, so too does its needs. Therefore, clients need internal and external professional service providers to be their eyes and ears looking out for them in the back alleys and helping them see the future and lead them to it so that they can protect the client's future, prepare for it, and help generate revenue.

Firms can come with a POV for GCs and say look, we are here to look around the corner for you. We know you can't always look around the corner for yourselves, but we can help you on that journey. Here is our POV on the technology you need and the type of investments you might like to consider making and here are the independent experts we can bring to you . . . To me, that is the opportunity for law firms. To come with that point of view and that expertise makes them stickier, stickier, and stickier rather than less relevant.—VP and associate general counsel, American multinational enterprise information technology company[50]

So professional service providers do not just need to move from advisors or counselors to consiglieres but also to *innovation* consiglieres. This leads us to Level 3 on the Skills Delta, which is all about innovation.

C. Skills Delta Level 3: Innovation (Client-Centric, Adaptive, Inclusive Leaders with a Digital Mindset)

As mentioned in Chapter 1, one of the loudest calls by corporate clients is for innovation (which is at the top level of the Skills Delta as indicated by Figure 2.5). And I'm sure you are likely sick of hearing it. In fact, one of my interviewees called the word innovation "the newest four-letter swear word."[33] I pointed out that the word has more than four letters and they responded, "OK, but it has four syllables—so there!"

Even if you feel as that interviewee does, there is a silver lining. In fact, there are three of them.

First, my work and research indicate that when clients ask for innovation from their professional service providers what they are really asking for is service transformation in disguise. They may want new, innovative services and products but what is also driving this request is a desire to have those services delivered *differently*—which goes back to the subtitle of this chapter and its focus on the "*how*" versus the "*what*."

> *I think innovation in how we deliver our legal services, it's not even just an option, it is a necessity for us now in my view . . . Unless we innovate how we do things, we will not keep up in my organization with the pace at which my organization wants to transform, and that is the thing I'm really trying to solve.*—Head of Legal, a large international airline[51]

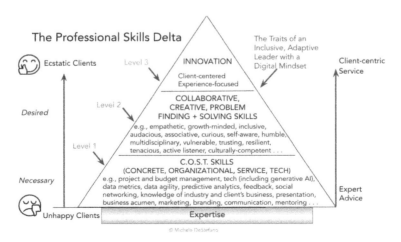

FIG. 2.5. Level 3 of the Professional Skills Delta.

To reach the top of the pyramid, to scale to the top of the Skills Delta, we need to create a culture of innovation with our clients to transform how we work together. This is what clients are asking: to create a new mindset and culture. They want the mindset, skill set, and behaviors of innovators, who have what is called "digital mindsets," which according to experts is "attitudes and behaviors that enable people and organizations to see how data, algorithms, and AI open up new possibilities and to chart a path for success in a business landscape increasingly dominated by data-intensive and intelligent technologies."[52] Having this new mindset and culture results in innovation and increased revenue opportunity but also, in what one interviewee aptly coined: "service delivery transformation"[53] that enhances the professional's ability to be "client-centered" and "experience focused"—words also included in the Level 3 of the Skills Delta.

> *How do we create a mindset and culture of innovation? How can we be relentlessly curious in terms of understanding the new and what is happening and challenge the status quo? . . . I want to light a fire under my lawyers so that they see an urgent need to change the way we do things and to innovate. And it is not about tech or a particular innovation. It is really a mindset.*—Senior corporate counsel, multinational insurance company headquartered in Australia[54]

So clients are fired up about their service providers having an innovation mindset and skill set and the transformation of services.

The second silver lining is that the innovation that is desired does not have to be some bewildering magic trick. In fact, the key ingredients to innovating are right there in the middle part of the Skills Delta. The word *innovation* may conjure up images of the scientist alone in their lab when along comes a "Eureka!" moment. But these "ahas" are rare; instead, innovation is far more likely to come from collaborative, creative problem-solving on diverse teams where one person's ideas impact another person's ideas that then impact another person's ideas. Slowly, over time, the ideas change and migrate. As Steven Johnson points out, it is that migration that delivers the "pearl of the oyster."[55]

As a great *Harvard Business Review* article points out, depending on capital costs, people either concentrate on finding new opportunities for growth or on improving upon that which is already profit-generating.[56] The C.O.S.T. skills help with the latter. Collaboration, creative problem-solving, and innovation skills help with the former. And the former does not have to be "disruptive" in the Clayton Christensen sense like what Netflix did to Blockbuster. As another great *Harvard Business Review* article points out that there is great good to be created from nondisruptive innovation, that is, innovation that generates a new market without destroying the old one.[57] "Nondisruptive creation occurs outside the boundaries of existing industries, giving rise to markets where none existed before. Thus, it fosters economic growth without incurring social costs, enabling business and society to thrive together."[58] Some examples include the dishwasher, female sanitary napkins, luxury cruises, Square (now Block), e-Sports, GoPro, and microfinancing.[59] Additionally, as described in more detail in Chapter 4, the type of innovation that many clients are looking for is not like TNT—explosive and disruptive—but instead it can be TNT as in T for Tiny, N for Noticeable, and T for Things that add lasting value. That's what James Batham, head of Innovation and Partner at Dentons calls it and appropriately so. I'm not saying clients don't ever want big changes. I am saying that they can be delighted with small, incremental changes that add lasting value. For some examples of TNTs at each level of the Skills Delta, go to Chapter 4.

The third silver lining is that firms that innovate *together*, with their clients, are considered special. I heard this time and time again from the client interviewees. When a firm innovates with a client, that firm is considered special.

> *To me, it is essential that my law firm is helping me innovate because if they are not, there are other law firms I can go to. . . . When a firm innovates with me, this is something really special and makes me think very highly of what a great business partner the firm is.*—General counsel, large media and telecommunications company in Australia[60]

When I asked this GC what it means to be *special*—does this mean you will hire this firm more? He replied, "It's actually the other way around. If you don't want to be an innovation partner with me, then I'm going to be inclined *not* to give you business."[61]

> *If the law firms don't do it, then new entrants will. And then the law firms will become less significant and less relevant. And the conversation will be less about demanding law firms to innovate and more about the opportunity that law firms continue to miss out on and their ever-decreasing pie because they are not being proactive*

in helping us in areas that they had not traditionally helped us in the past.—General counsel, large media and telecommunications company in Australia[62]

Similarly, when I asked this GC, whose firm innovated with him and whose company was a recipient of an innovation award, whether he gave more business to the firm, he replied, "My gut feel is that it stayed the same, but I would also say that it could have gone down but for it."[63]

Putting the two together? With innovation, a professional service firm is considered special. Without it, a firm in this market is at risk of losing business. If a firm doesn't innovate, the client will seek a firm that does. After all, clients themselves are being pushed by their clients and customers to innovate as well.

I think innovation in how we deliver our legal services it's not even just an option, it is a necessity for us now in my view . . . Unless we innovate how we do things, we will not keep up in my organization with the pace at which my organization wants to transform, and that is the thing I'm really trying to solve.—Head of Legal, a large international airline.[64]

You might ask: *"Is that my job to do all this and to innovate?"* I say, Yes. As I describe in more detail in Chapter 4, I see mastering the Skills Delta and attempting to innovate with clients as the New Value Equation in professional services. It makes cents and sense. At the top of the Skills Delta, yes, there is innovation, which might make financial cents. But the true heart of the Skills Delta is not the innovation—it's the change in mindset and skill set that come from going on an innovation journey. It's that move from what Carlos Valdes-Dapena calls parallel play and/or reactive collaboration to proactive collaboration—to what I call proactive co-collaboration.[65] And that requires a shift in focus and attitude. It is not a mere coincidence that as you move up in the Skills Delta, the focus shifts from expert advice (from an almost-paternalistic "experts know best" attitude—I exist separate from you) to a focus on client-centricity, which is all about experiences and embeddedness—I am in the same boat with you. The focus also moves from traditional leadership skills to that of an adaptive, inclusive leader with a digital mindset. Let me unpack why honing the skill set and mindset on the Delta helps us accomplish both of those moves in the next chapter.

■...Reflection Point Consider the Skills Delta above. How are profes-sional service providers currently upskilled and reskilled? Do those training programs hone the skills on the Skills Delta? If so, which skills/attributes/qualities are being honed effectively and how? If not, which skills are *not* being honed effectively and why not? What type of training might work to hone those skills/attributes/qualities at your firm or in your department?

■...Reflection Point What are some of the best training experiences you had before you started your career (i.e., in high school, undergraduate college, extracurricular activities [e.g., sports, music, and hobbies])? What stands out about those experiences? What made them so effective and/or enjoyable? Make a list of what made them so. How might you exapt some of the techniques and experiences you enjoyed in your external non-career training into how we train our future and current professional service provid-ers so that they can be adaptive inclusive leaders with a digital mindset that delights their clients?

CHAPTER 3

Client-Centricity: A Move from Services to Experiences and from Traditional to Adaptive Leadership

> *"What got you here, won't get you there."*
>
> —Marshall Goldsmith[1]

The reason why learning how to innovate and take a design thinking approach to problem solving enables professional service providers to be client-centric is because innovators are trained to focus on and empathize with the end-user. In fact, as discussed in Chapter 6, empathy is a key ingredient to innovation. Consider the movie *Joy*. As it makes clear, it is only by empathizing with the people who had to wring out the heavy dirty mop heads that innovators developed mops with detachable heads that could be put in the washing machine. Innovators always put the end-user front and center. They create user-journey maps and consumer-user stories so that they can see and experience and feel what they feel so that their solutions do not just eliminate the pain points but also delight. Like innovators, this is what great businesses do as well. For example, when I worked at Levi Strauss & Company in the mid-1990s, the research, marketing, and merchandising team collaborated to determine the next coolest type of jeans Levi Strauss should develop. To do that we elicited help from urban male teens. We visited them in their homes and had them show us their closet and how they selected their outfits. We gave them video cameras so they could share their daily lives with us, what and where they ate, what they and their friends were wearing, and why and what they were listening to and what they were doing in their free time. Although this was way before the world of social media and the ability to text, we were essentially part of these youths' daily lives and when we worked, it was as if they were always in the office with us. As a result of this customer-centricity, we were able to create the very first pair of wide-leg jeans sold to the masses and we were able to create commercials that really talked to and resonated with trend-setting male teens—both urban and suburban because the suburban teens aspired to be more like the urban teens.[2] This is why Amazon's founder Jeff Bezos places one empty chair in each meeting. He does this to represent the customer/user so that they are always there with his team for the decisions they make so they can ensure that the experience they provide is personalized and delights. Every product and service needs to be created with a human-centered approach. A recent EY CEO imperative study aptly sums it up:

> *"As leaders advance their strategies, they must view every decision, every technology implementation, every product, or service innovation through the human lens. Companies need to focus on how they make or deliver the products and services to delight customers and offer them compelling value propositions. Inherent in this is the understanding that personalized experiences have now become far bigger drivers of consumption, requiring a different approach to innovation and customer engagement."[3]*

Client-centricity is, as this chapter's title indicates, a move from services to experiences, ensuring every touchpoint with the client (or customer or key stakeholder) is delightful to them (based on their wants and desires). However, many professional service providers fail to see that there is a difference between focusing on providing great client service and being client-centric. When I explain this to senior partners attending Harvard Law School's Executive Education Leadership Program, I often receive head nods, but upon further probing, I realize that they aren't *really* with me in the nuance. They think high quality service delivery that meets or exceeds client expectations is client-centricity. Here is a typical definition of client/stakeholder-centricity by a law firm partner who believes they get it and who is very well-intentioned and a fantastic lawyer:

It's doing our best to meet client's expectations workwise. It's working really hard to meet clients' tough timelines and to keep clients happy and to deliver good quality. Also, it's doing some good marketing efforts like conducting client seminars. Some of our clients in Malaysia were interested in investing in Vietnam and we have an office there and some expert lawyers in that area, so we had those partners come and give clients a talk on that. We also had a seminar on Malaysian foreign exchange relationships.—Partner, one of the largest corporate law firms in Malaysia[4]

It's not that this partner is wrong. It's that client-centricity is so much more than being responsive, friendly, approachable, reliable, prompt, thorough, and exhibiting a high knowledge and level of expertise. It is so much more than offering seminars for free that are of interest to the client. Also, calling the seminars "marketing efforts" is the first clue that this partner may be talking the talk but not walking the walk. But it's hard to teach this nuance. Yes, client-centricity can involve big steps, yet it also requires small tweaks in what we say and do and how we say and do it and most importantly, our internal attitude about all of that. In other words, it must be done with authenticity—and without an expectation (or even a hope) of quid pro quo. More than that, it must be approached *without* what one of my interviewees called the cult of "professional service provider exceptionalism."[5] For that reason, he suggested I change the title of this chapter to "Customer-Centricity" and drop the word *client* altogether. While I use the two terms interchangeably in this book, I agree with him that the client-centric label might be one reason why some professional service providers (especially lawyers) are just a little bit *off* on what client-centricity means:

The term client *suggests a more formal, long-term relationship . . . where the service provider offers specialized expertise and advice . . . [and] can . . . . lead to a subtle . . . yet significant barrier between the provider and those they serve. This barrier often manifests in a somewhat inflated and superior self-view among providers, distancing them from the very people they are meant to assist. In legal services, this issue is compounded by the lawyer/nonlawyer distinction . . . . This hierarchy not only undermines the provider-client relationship but can also hinder the provider's ability to fully empathize with and understand the client's situation.*— Senior vice president & general counsel, global chemical distribution company[6]

So how do we teach these nuanced differences?

What I have found as a professor is that sometimes it is easier to teach what something *is*, by first defining what it is *not*. For example, throughout my years of guiding teams on innovation efforts, I'm often asked to give examples of successful collaborations or innovations. However, time and time again, I can offer examples of what is NOT successful collaboration or innovation. Therefore, in the first section of this chapter, based generally on all my interviews and more specifically on the 40 short interviews that focused on unpacking what service providers think is client-centricity, I begin by providing examples of what is NOT client-centricity before demonstrating what IS client-centricity. And I conclude the chapter with an overview of what is adaptive, inclusive leadership—which given today's unpredictable, complex challenges is the only client-centric way to lead.

A. Client-Centricity: What It Is—And What It Is Not

"Nothing ever becomes real 'Til it is experienced."

—John Keats[7]

To bring to life what is client-centric service, let's start with a few examples of what is not.

Consider law firms for a moment. Many of them are organized by practice area (as opposed to industry). That is actually not client-centric, given most clients are a part of a discrete industry or group of industries and most want solutions that span multiple practice areas. However, law firms, in this regard, put themselves first. Often their processes and services are designed largely to serve the firm's own wants and needs (to be efficient and to make it easier for internal professionals) rather than those of clients. Why is this so? My interviewees think it is due in part to a lack of trust and in other part to how partners are compensated and how origination credit is given. As one interviewee aptly pointed out:

> *Law firm partners know that clients want them to know their sector/industry, and their business but individual lawyers and law firms have pushed back on an industry and sector approach because that approach doesn't work in law firms because in some practice areas, it is logical but in some it is less logical. If I am a corporate lawyer and I say I do M&A across all industries to my clients, I'm nervous because I likely do not trust all my partners e.g., like those in banking and finance. I would rather keep a wider broader practice and I might be tempted to do a bigger piece of work and not specialize in sectors. There is low*

level of trust among the partners which leads to suspicion and back biting around clients and if you have origination credit. This is why we continually have partners going to see the client and not telling their colleagues. From the clients' point of view this is not client-centric, especially when they have had two or three partners from the same firm meet with them this week. The client thinks: "Holy shit, they don't know anything about each other, and they aren't putting me first, and when it came to the Christmas party, I received 7 separate invitations. Man, you can't even coordinate your relationship with me, who cares if you are a good lawyer?"—Cofounder, professional services consulting company[8]

In addition to law firms, consider the large well-known consulting firms (like McKinsey, BCG, Bain, and the Big 4 accounting firms). Like law firms, they are organized as partnerships, which are networks of independent entities. They are often pyramid-shaped in terms of structure, with many junior consultants or associates at the bottom and fewer in the middle and even fewer at the top (partners/senior managers). Further, compensation is often based on the rates that the professional service provider can charge for their own time and, as noted in the quote above, at some firms, origination credit is given (into eternity). All of this works to create a culture that is unsupportive of the type of collaboration and innovation clients need and want, which means it goes against client-centricity:

The problem with firms as a source of innovation is that most are not really a cohesive whole. They are a group of small business owners that share an office and do some profit sharing. Each partner has their own business and their own clients. Firms don't have a lot of central strategic control over what their people are doing, especially their most successful people . . . Some firms are talking about innovation and putting people in charge of it. But does the head of innovation at a firm have the ability to influence and convince the individual partners and senior associates to do anything differently?—General counsel, American nonprofit that designs public competitions for technological development[9]

And the sad truth is, professional service providers know it:

A [significant] element in our firm is that revenue and revenue production on an individual basis still runs how people are remunerated, so there is a great deal of self-interest and fear, and fear breaks down collaboration. In its dumbest form, I'll collaborate with you if I can get something from you. It is not collaboration for collaboration's sake. I want a dollar number to come out of it . . . Our firm talks about it a lot. Nice words in a well-put together policy that doesn't translate into hard and fast rules on how to weigh behaviors vs how much revenue you made.—Chief executive partner, top-tier Australian law firm[10]

I think it has to do with a culture and a fear. The firm values the "friendly be nice" culture above all else. That word "culture" comes out all the time. We say we have this innovation focus. But when they say culture, they mean something totally different. It harkens back to a thick wet blanket over the whole place. It's a culture of non-confrontation because you have to be nice. Nice is everything. If you draw criticism from anyone, then people want to put you through a fire squad. You cannot perform or you can have paper files and commit all these sins that are against "our culture," but if you are nice? All of that is absolutely fine. And that really frustrates me, and it is holding the firm back, the fear of conflict.—Partner, leading independent Australian law firm[11]

So, what we end up with instead of a culture of collaboration is, at best, a culture dedicated to being nice, to being collegial. I often ask partners and other leaders of professional service firms to describe the culture of their firm in only three words. Besides proving to be a difficult request time and time again, one of the three words they often choose is "collegial."

I chose the word collegial because people like working together and there is a good vibe and feel around the firm, but they don't necessarily work through how they can use that vibe to sort of make it truly collaborative. I'd say we are friendly without being engaged for a purpose.—Chief financial officer, one of Australia's "Big Six" law firms[12]

But collegiality is not collaboration. Although this interviewee doesn't say this specifically, it is clear that collegiality is not what management consultant Subir Chowdhury would consider "good enough."[13] If the partners dominate the firm and its culture and they don't want to change, to move from collegiality to collaboration, the structure and incentives of the firm need to change.[14]

And this is the point clients make. Clients don't want "good enough"; they want what Chowdhury calls "the difference."[15] What they care about is whether innovation and collaborative problem-solving has infiltrated the culture of the firm in a way that is intrinsic and not just external, not just a few well-chosen words on the innovation page of a firm's website. Without this shift from collegiality to collaboration, professional service firms and service providers within them cannot collaborate internally, and as a by-product, they also cannot collaborate externally with clients in the way clients want them to and that adds the value that clients desire.

Now consider in-house legal departments. Just the title itself suggests something separate from the other departments. True, the name "in-house" supports the idea that the department is internal versus an external law firm. However, by calling it in-house, it sets it apart from other departments that are simply part of the business. The marketing department inside a large corporation is not called an "in-house" marketing department. The same is true for finance or IT, etc. That the legal department is called in-house suggests that it is a department that is separate as opposed to embedded, which further implies that it is reactive instead of proactive, that it is there to defend as opposed to strategically align itself with the business. In a podcast I hosted in my role as chief faculty advisor to the Digital Legal Exchange, Spyros Mello, director of strategy and transformation at Coca Cola HBC, put it this way:

> *The legal department cannot be merely a cost center defending the company from risk. Its strategy must be tied to the business and not lost into functional dreams or as a controlling function. And the lawyers cannot be thinking, with arrogance, how important we are and what terrible things will happen if we are not there.*—Spyros Mello, director of strategy and transformation, Coca-Cola HBC[16]

Instead, the lawyers in the legal department need to be what Mello refers to as "frontline growth leaders" who own the success of the company as much as others with whom they work,[17] who are grounded and engaged with the real-world activity of the company. Importantly the professionals who are frontline growth leaders have the mindset reflected in Level 2 of the Skills Delta. They don't wait to get a seat at the table. They win that seat and their relevance by proactively engaging with the client. A lot of in-house professional service providers are the opposite. They assume that the client is happy and will come to them when they need their expert advice; and therefore, they don't believe they need to conduct a client listening interview nor do they need to propose any additional services. Yet, the reality is likely that they are scared to poke the bear. They are afraid of what they could hear or find out, which might mean they have to change how they work, how they are structured or organized, or do something more—in addition to something *different*. But this is a mistake. It is a post-hoc approach that leaves client-centricity to last and that adds unnecessary duplicative costs in the long run and threatens the credibility of the relationship with the client.

This is also a mistake as it relates to any digital transformation (DT) initiative because it threatens its viability. As mentioned in Chapter 1, in the past few years, in part due to the COVID-19 pandemic, DT has become an enterprise-wide imperative for most multinational corporations.[18] As a result, every service department inside the corporation needs to accelerate its own digital transformation. However, as they do so, they need to collaborate with their internal clients to make sure the changes they are making are not creating new problems or inconveniences for their clients and that future interactions with their department are the way the client wants them.

There is a great scene in the movie *The Founder* that brings to life what proactive co-collaboration and client-centricity is all about. To better and faster serve its customers, that is, clients, the burger company looks internally at the processes in the kitchen of its fast-food restaurant.[19] The owners map out the kitchen from the lettuce station to the drink station on a big basketball court. As they work on it and overhaul the organization and processes, they practice the new procedures with the staff (and they time how long the processes take).[20] At first, the staff is bumping into each other, so they overhaul the organization of the kitchen again, then again and again.[21] They start from scratch three times.[22] Eventually, they decrease the time it takes from receiving an order to serving the burger to 30 seconds and the staff are literally dancing.[23] The viewer hears the exalting music like a symphony and feels the triumph of the team. They were improving customer service, right? And they didn't stop at minor improvement. They went for the full-on fluid dance overhaul. But then . . . we hear the record needle scratch, and halt the music. Their customers hated the changes and were extremely annoyed.[24] You see, they used to get their food delivered to their cars. Now they had to get out and get it from the window. They also didn't like the new paper wrapping. The point of this is that the burger company owners and staff had good intentions and were thinking about the client (and their own increases in efficiency and profits), but they didn't co-collaborate with the client to find out what their pain points and bright spots were. Even if they were right, that is, that every customer would want their burger faster, they didn't account for the other unintended consequences and how that would impact customers. They started with an inward focus and made assumptions about what the customer would want. Sure, they had good intentions. They were thinking of the customer: Who doesn't want a burger 30 seconds faster? But they weren't really empathizing with the client. They were seeing it from their own point of view.

I call this the Kellogg's Apple Jacks problem, which my coworkers and I learned the hard way at Leo Burnett (explained in detail in Chapter 8). Failing to do the work it takes to understand the customers' wishes jeopardizes the relationship with the customer, not to mention adds costs and inefficiencies in having to reorganize and redo the processes inside the kitchen again. Instead, they should have started with the 5 Whys in customer interviews and proceeded in collaboration with the customer. That's customer/client-centricity—focusing on the customer/client experience: How the customer wants it, not how the provider wants to provide it. It is likely why Burger King's slogan is "Have it your way." (Yes, I also worked at Burger King in my past!).

I have the great fortune of being a co-creator of the Digital Legal Exchange, which is designed to help general counsels accelerate digital transformation of the legal function to drive commercial value. And, unfortunately, I have witnessed in-house legal departments doing exactly what the burger company in *The Founder* movie did—focusing inward, revising the department's processes and procedures to be more efficient and effective, with very good intentions, that is, with the client in mind. Like in the movie, the clients were not delighted, and, unlike the movie, the legal department is forced to redo what they already redid. (Note: as discussed in Chapter 10, in *The Founder*, the burger company sidestepped the disaster by creating a huge advertising campaign explaining "why" they made the changes to convince their target audience that the inconvenience was worth it and evidently this worked!). I'm sure you might be wondering why legal professionals would not naturally include their clients when reorganizing and changing processes and procedures with their clients in mind. You might also be wondering why law firms spend hours and hours putting together hand-crafted responses to request for proposals (RFPs), fail to ask the current or potential client any questions during the process (prior to the RFP meeting), and show up and give a dog and pony show in the RFP meeting and fail to ask ANY questions about what the client wants or needs or desires during the meeting as well! (This happens ALL THE TIME and there is research to prove it beyond my own anecdotal and interview evidence.)[25] Yes, I have asked why this is so in my interviews many times. It is not that they are "stupid," because as you will learn I'm a big believer that we should erase that word from our vocabulary and especially our minds as we listen to others. It is not that they are not trying to be client-centric. Instead, what I have learned is that their failure to involve the client (conduct the 5 Whys, ask questions, learn what motivates the client) stems from a combination of two things.

First, fear: fear of poking the bear as I mentioned earlier, but it is also a fear related to how the professional service provider will be perceived. It's more (but less) than a fear of actual failing. It's a fear of not looking put together, or perfect, in front of the client, which may be a lesser but more debilitating type of failure than complete failure itself.[26] One of my interviewees aptly summed it up as follows:

> *Clients say the partners are arrogant, but the perceived external arrogance is the internal imposter syndrome. They are not trained how to ask questions and get close to the clients. The stupidity is that they will spend the 10 minutes talking about their firm instead of trying to find out more about the client. They are not comfortable asking clients about their problems because they assume that the client knows what their problems are, and that the client thinks the firms know what their problems are. So, the firms pretend they do, even when they don't.*—Cofounder, U.K.-based professional services firm[27]

The professionals of those firms that regularly do investigative research as part of their business are ahead in this area because they have expertise and knowledge about the sectors and are prepared to discuss what they know and, therefore, are comfortable asking open ended questions about what the problems are.

The second reason for not probing into clients' wants/needs/desires? It's an authentic well-intentioned desire to "wow" the client. Though in this effort, the opposite of the intended effect happens. Ross Shafer's research on customer-centricity hammers home that wowing customers (or clients) does not build loyalty.[28] Instead, what does enhance loyalty is client/stakeholder/customer empathy and the elimination of what he calls "POW moments": "the gut punches" when "we disappoint them" and "don't do what we said we would do." In *The Founder*, they didn't wow their customers and, in fact, opening day was what Shafer would call a "complete POW moment." The same is true of a redesigned legal department that didn't elicit input from the internal business client before creating a "front door portal to legal," or an accounting firm that didn't ask what the client meant by "innovative" before delivering a PowerPoint presentation that was off the mark, or a consulting firm that held a hack-athon to solve problems the client was facing (without including the client or even telling the client beforehand). In the latter situation, when the senior partners of the firm presented the "innovations" from the hack-athon to the client, they thought they were in for a WOW, but oh boy, did they receive a POW. The client was flabbergasted at their gall. Even if this firm had had a WOW moment in the past with this client, as Shafer makes clear, the WOW moments don't offset the POW moments. "Determine what customers want and deliver that. . . . The bigger risk to loyalty is when you fail or disappoint them." And I agree with Shafer, it is about client/customer/stakeholder empathy—not service. Service happens as a response. It's delivered with the product or advice. It's reactive. Client-centricity is a proactive, ongoing mode of communicating and behaving with forethought and a real understanding of and empathy *with* the client—which necessarily means communicating with them regularly and asking questions (not assuming answers).

True, some professional service providers just don't "get" client-centricity *at all*. For example, I had one partner explain that client-centricity is "training clients to be better clients instead of complaining about them."[29] I kid you not. In their view, this training will enable clients to provide better direction to their professional service providers. Only after that could the partner provide better, "more client-centric" service. However, most of my interviewees were not this clueless. Nevertheless, despite understanding the gist of it and having great intentions, many have done things that are not client-centric and that are definite POWs, to use Shafer's term. The following are some examples.

Client-Centricity POW #1: Providing services that feel transactional and like the basic services of a mid-scale hotel as opposed to the concierge service of an upscale, luxury hotel, like the Ritz:

The relationship has historically felt quite transactional, and it definitely does not feel like the Ritz experience. When I joined as a tech leader there was no intro to the legal team or terms of reference for how and when to engage them. It came as a secondary ancillary service to the supply chain team. So, the value proposition for the legal team has emerged through a transactional business. Instead [of the Ritz], it feels like I'm walking into a Holiday Express. There is no understanding of why legal is here. They don't tell us: "Here are our core services and we have a concierge for additional services."—Head of colleague platforms and network services, major retail and commercial bank in the United Kingdom[30]

Client-Centricity POW #2: Failing to research the client and its industry prior to meeting with the client and attempting to learn about the client and industry on the client's dime:

So, when you start a conversation with the lawyers, you realize that behind their eyes they haven't thought about YOU really. Not really. They have not really thought about you. They ask questions and say they want to learn about your company and your pressures, but most of the answers, they could get from Board reporting materials or websites or various trade bodies. But, you know, they actually don't do that. Instead, they learn on your dime. And I'm not paying you to learn about our company. And that creates another conversation about the fees. . . .—General counsel, a startup and former general counsel, large U.K. mutual life, pensions, and investment company

They said they want to have a one-hour kickoff call, but really, they just want to suck off information from you; and they are sort of listening to you but also selling themselves. And it's an hour and then they bill you for it and you could have found it on my website. Then they asked five minutes of targeted questions at the end. And they assume this meeting showed their value.—General counsel, U.S.-based global cybersecurity company[31]

Client-Centricity POW #3: Failing to cultivate the relationship over time, focusing on how they can make money and grow their business and only seeking contact with the client for that reason or during transactions:

> *They are only interested in the next pitch, not interested in you. They do not cultivate the relationship. They are not feeding me info other than generic info on the sector.*—General counsel, a startup and former general counsel, one of the largest mutual insurers in the U.K.[32]

> *It's a transactional basis, not a relationship basis. The market is so good right now, the work has come to them. But they are not thinking about what the work is that the clients require and how do they develop stronger relationships to do that work. They never invest in finding out what the client requirements are and aligning their business to deliver that.*—Cofounder, U.K.-based professional services firm[33]

> *Law firms call themselves "relationship firms." That's a nice line created by marketing folks. But they are just a transaction firm. Our mission statement and vision are hanging on every wall and door. You cannot come in here and not see it. Yet, they don't know it. They don't think they need to know it. They think we will give them work deal to deal. They don't get that they can't advise the bank if they are so uninvested in us that they can't even tell me what the bank's purpose or vision statement is. . . . They are not that interested in the relationship because they can't really charge for it. They just want to go from transaction to transaction. It leaves you feeling a bit used.*—Head of outsource, tech, and IP legal team at a major retail and commercial bank in the U.K.[34]

Client-Centricity POW #4: Sending untailored emails informing the client of a rate increase without explaining why or calling to talk with them about it.

Client-Centricity POW #5: Failing to empower junior advisors at pitches and in the relationship management and work of the client and failing to let the client have influence over who work is assigned to:

> *When they come to pitch, they only let the partners talk and not the people who will do the work and they don't allow associates to have relationships with people in the company to build networks.*—General counsel, a startup and former general counsel, one of the largest mutual insurers in the U.K.[35]

I wish they would let me work with who I want to work with. They assign the work. There are times all I need is a senior associate and I can oversee the work. I don't want to pay a partner to do that work. I have to read it anyway. I want them to forget about their process of who does what and let me be the client. And when I ask this, they respond that there is liability if the quality of the work is not up to snuff. Blah blah blah, so I don't ask anymore.—Associate general counsel, an American multinational technology corporation[36]

Client-Centricity POW #6: Being over budget and tardy in letting the client know, and not checking in with the client and not providing the right amount of detail when overbilling the client:

We get these reports when we are overspending on the initial estimate. The firm sent us a bill and I asked: Can you tell us what is billed to that number? And they reply: Yeah, we don't have that data. We are paying them a number denominated in the millions and they can't tell me what they are doing. . . . That's a problem and not client-centric and a big miss. We want to know who is working on my business and what they are doing. And if they are working on a matter 500% longer than we had estimated it would take, that is a clear indication they are not doing what we asked. And they never came back and asked. Either they didn't understand the ask or they assigned the wrong person, or they are overworking. All are not client-centric.—Associate general counsel, an American multinational technology corporation[37]

The good news is that, in addition to witnessing the opposite, I have also seen first-hand GCs who have mastered the middle section of the Skills Delta. Those GCs "get" that digital transformation is all about how to deliver superior client service, not only to enhance efficiency but also the experience so that it delights the client, is fit for its purpose, and is in line with the business's strategy. These GCs are not afraid to reach out proactively to the business to ask questions the way innovators do, to conduct listening tours, and to collaborate before they transform their departments. Although it's riskier to show a business how inefficient the department may now be, in the end, they save time and frustration, and transform their relationship with their internal clients—and operationalize their legal department at the same time (without having to redo).

Professional service providers who "get" client-centricity understand that. They understand it is so much more than high quality service delivery. It is a business strategy and practice that prioritizes the client and seeks to foster a positive experience at every stage of the client's journey with your firm or department and in every moment that it connects with your firm or department. It's putting the client at the forefront of every single decision you make while developing and/or providing a service or a product. It involves tailoring solutions to each client's unique circumstances and idiosyncrasies. It's not just anticipating a client's wants, needs, and communication preferences, it's finding out what their wants, needs, and communication preferences are and getting it right (and, obviously, avoiding POW moments).

To do this, however, you need a deep understanding of the clients' goals and challenges. This requires empathy, active listening and continuous needs assessments and continuous learning and improving based on client feedback about what they care about. Evidence suggests, however, that there is a gap between what professional service providers *think* clients want and what the clients *actually* want.

Reena SenGupta and I co-developed a digital alignment survey during our collaboration at the Digital Legal Exchange.[38] In one survey involving 115 in-house lawyers and their internal business clients across 35 indicators, 97 percent of business respondents ranked value creation (including co-creating revenue streams) as an important metric, with more than half ranking it as extremely important; yet only 25 percent of legal department respondents ranked it as important.[39] Not only is there a lack of alignment in priority of metrics, often the right criteria are not being measured. For example, although GCs state that client experience is a key digital transformation objective and client satisfaction an important KPI (key performance indicator), much of the granular information that would be helpful in understanding client needs and wants (such as response time or time-to-conclusion) are typically not tracked.[40] To be truly client-centric, professional service providers should be measuring the metrics that their clients care about, "CPIs" (client or customer performance indicators) versus the KPIs they created for their own firms or departments. They should be asking their clients to rank the importance of each metric and compare it to the firm's or department's ranking to ensure alignment.

Gene Cornfield, global lead for the high-tech industry at Accenture Interactive, makes this point. For a CPI to be a real CPI, "it must be an outcome customers [or clients] say is important to them" and "it must be measurable in increments that [they] actually value."[41] Cornfield gives the example of a CPI of "nothing broke" for a grocery delivery service.[42] The key is determining the CPIs associated with the specific outcomes clients want when requesting or requiring service. As Peter Drucker points out "[t]he most serious mistakes are not being made because of wrong answers. The truly dangerous thing is asking the wrong questions."[43] When feedback surveys measure metrics that clients do not think are important, then you are asking the wrong question. Therefore, understanding your clients' wishes and priorities means asking the right questions (measuring the right metrics) in client surveys.

This may mean you should conduct client-listening interviews to find out what is important, that is, what is your client's "nothing broke" (e.g., it could be "turnaround speed" or "only necessary revisions were suggested" or "advice included a short summary that could easily be absorbed and passed on to colleagues").

It may also mean you should step into your clients' shoes to create client "consumer stories" that bring to life the clients' attitudes, wishes, and frustrations in story format so that the professionals who provide service to them can empathize with them and see the world through their eyes. It may also mean attending the clients' staff meetings (without charging for the time). It most definitely means mapping the relationship trajectory and every touch point the client has with the firm or department and keeping track of client preferences and professional and personal information (like how many kids they have, what they do in their spare time, their birthdays, etc.). It involves building and continually nurturing long-term relationships and not taking them for granted and not acting like they cannot take their business elsewhere (because they can!). And, of course, it necessarily requires what the second level of the Skills Delta is all about: proactive co-collaboration with clients in product and service development (and all the attributes needed to do this well!), including what former basketball player John Amaechi calls "a perpetual state of selflessness."[44] But don't take it from me. Let me first provide some examples of client-centricity from clients and then some of their definitions.

Client-Centricity Example #1: Keeping track of the idiosyncrasies, likes and dislikes of your client (and some personal information like birthdays, kids' names and ages) and confidentially sharing that with other professionals who work with the client, so the client is treated the way they like and in the same way by all professionals at the firm.

Client-Centricity Example #2: Providing frequent, authentic, proactive communication and seeking facetime without an agenda:

> *They reach out. They are proactive and interested in having more relationship meetings, always working to have face time with us as a firm or in house counsel . . . whereas others reach out and there is a phoniness to it. I haven't heard from them in 6 months . . . versus staying in constant contact and will ask if I'm in town if around want to grab dinner and coffee. It's more genuine.*—Global head of outside counsel management, multinational investment bank and financial services company[45]

Client-Centricity Example #3: Providing industry updates that also highlight how they might impact the company and that is in a format that can be sent to others in the company, and that is not redundant to the other updates provided by competitor service firms:

> *We have an obsession with horizon scanning, meaning figuring out what is riding toward you over the horizon like a regulatory change or a new case. Can we plan and not be caught? And can we do so in a way that we are not getting 11 PDFs in our inbox each month from each of our panel firms. We are drowning under the volume of email.*—Lead counsel, large global bank headquartered in the United Kingdom[46]

Client-Centricity Example #4: Listening to clients' needs and instead of pitching, connecting the client to others who are experiencing the same pain points:

> *We have a law firm on our panel that we haven't spent a penny with lately. And one of the partners knew I was interested in how to leverage social ambassadors and that I was struggling with motivating change and innovation. This partner listened to my needs and understood what I was trying to do. And he didn't try to pitch that he could solve all my problems for me. Instead, he connected me to another in-house counsel, about the same level as me, in an entirely different industry who had experience with what I was struggling with. And that relationship with that GC has been very helpful. . . . And because of that and a few other things this partner and that firm does right, I'll likely give them some business this year.*—Head of outsourcing, tech, and IP legal team at a major retail and commercial bank in the U.K.

Client-Centricity Example #5: Seeking continuous feedback and being willing to collaborate with the client to work through that feedback to fill the gaps:

I had a situation where I was very frustrated with one of the lawyers (who was young and just had been made partner) and not getting the quality of service expected. So, I called the Relationship Partner and said "I'm done. I can't do it anymore. They are not giving quality advice." The RP talked me off the ledge and I suggested that the entire team do DiSC to figure out work style to see if it would bridge the relationship issues we were having. I thought it was the right way to handle this and an opportunity for people to grow on both sides. . . . They were client-centric because they were open to the idea whereas another firm might not have been as open. Also, they had someone on their staff that is DiSC certified ready and able. And they didn't bill us for the time. Additionally, they suggested that this lawyer start to attend my weekly staff calls with senior leadership—Associate general counsel, American multinational technology corporation[47]

Client-Centricity Example #6: Applying (and teaching) design thinking principles and brainstorming together how might we provide services like the Ritz (vs Holiday Express):

A lot of legal teams are complacent because internal stakeholders have to use the internal legal department. They say, "no outside lawyers know the business like we do." I don't buy it. I don't think in-house are as proactive as they need to be. And I think we have been a bit hypocritical. If we expect ABCD from our outside firm, we should ask: are we really giving our internal stakeholders ABC and D? or just A and B? So, the client-centric approach we are trying to take is: if our internal stakeholders had a blank check and could use any lawyers, would they come to us? This is why we had an external consultant interview our internal stakeholders to find out how we could make our service more like the Ritz. Oh, it hurt hard to hear that we were more like the Holiday Express to them, but it started the conversation which will involve a lot more conversations. And I want my team to be on a pedestal to be the Ritz. But no firm would ever ask me how they can become the Ritz in service. They don't even ask me for feedback.—Head of outsource, tech, and IP legal team at a major retail and commercial bank in the U.K.[48]

Client-Centricity Example #7: Seconding a professional to the client to ensure engagement with the department happens earlier and learning their ways of working to co-develop a protocol so that the client doesn't reach out to you when it is too late, or the plan is fully cooked.

Client-Centricity Example #8: Taking responsibility for staffing and communication 24/7, even when the initiative involves professionals from all around the world in different time zones:

We were working on a big deal around the holidays with a Japanese company and I created a model where we had people within the legal department staff it 24 hours a day. Some people work in Japan and some on the west coast of the U.S., but decisions had to be made and couldn't wait for people to wake up. So, I created a process for every morning and every evening, we would do a "live" handover so that while others were sleeping, when they woke, they would know what happened—what parts of the documents got drafted and didn't. And all the documents were on Teams (shared) so that if a portion was not drafted, we could drop a comment "Hey this is x and here is an idea of how to draft." With the synchronous communications twice a day and the asynchronous review, we likely saved a couple weeks of time.—Associate general counsel, an American multinational technology corporation[49]

Client-Centricity Example #9: Collaborating with the other professional service firms to provide integrated solutions, for example, serving as the client's mega professional services firm as opposed to trying to highlight how great your firm is (compared to others) in order to be awarded more business (contrast this with a real POW I heard about from one of my interviewees: Client asks its panel law firms to collaborate on industry updates so only one industry update goes out per month, but the firms fight for whose letterhead is on the update and whose email the update comes from).

Client-Centricity Example #10: Navigating the internal governance and understanding your clients' business better than they do:

Some of our firms, some specific professionals, amaze me because they really understand my business better than I do. We are an incredibly complicated organization. There are so many people and approval points. The best law firms know all that and can guide me through my own processes. They know that because they worked for us the whole time and have taken the effort to do it and not see it as a cost thing, navigating our internal governance which they can't bill for. Whereas client-centric firms see it as an opportunity to get to know us better and others see it as a cost issue.—IT and commercial lawyer, one of the U.K.'s largest financial services organizations[50]

Client-Centricity Example #11: Figuring out what the client really needs as opposed to just saying yes to whatever the client requests. Asking why the client is requesting something to figure out what is motivating them and what they are really worried about and conducting 5 Whys interviews and question bursts:

We had a transactional client that requested a flat fee, and the senior partner wanted me to just do it. When I asked the partner who is requesting the flat fee his words were "These are finance guys. They know what they want." However, I followed up with the senior VP of finance to find out what was motivating their request for a flat fee. The biggest concern and value for them was wanting assurance that they were not going to get dinged if this deal went nowhere. But they were not actually concerned about cost containment if the transaction went well. What they were truly scared about was the closing part. So, I gave them a broken deal discount which is nothing out of the blue, not innovative but exactly what they needed rather than what they said they wanted. Clients say, "I need this" but sometimes if you ask them "Why do you think that?" you can figure out what they really value. For example, they could have a goal of reduction of overall costs, but they truly value extensive communication with the firm. . . . The majority of the time, it is generally better when you get with the client and ask question outside of legal ones.—Director, pricing and legal project management, an AmLaw 200 law firm[51]

Client-Centricity Example #12: Helping create and facilitate and speaking at client events, such as retreats, and offering, without a pitch, free tailored training on substantive issues of interesting new technology, design thinking, diversity, ESG, or process and operations optimization to help clients with shrinking budgets.

So, those are some specific examples of client-centricity. Here are some quotes from clients about what they think client-centricity is:

To me, it means that the client is at the center of everything you do. You don't have your own agenda. You have a focus on the client. You build

processes, structure, and systems (pretty much everything you do) with the client at the forefront to satisfy their wants and desires. How do you find out what those are? Communication. Talk to them. No. Actually listen to them. Listening is all about hearing and understanding.
—Global head of outside counsel management, multinational investment bank and financial services company[52]

It's being interested in us, caring, giving a shit; understanding us and being engaged in what we are doing and being interested. I don't find firms are particularly interested in us at all. We have a huge external budget and very few know the bank's mission and purpose statement.
—Head of colleague platforms and network services, major retail and commercial bank in the United Kingdom[53]

They come to you and ask: How can I build a relationship with you and express a vision of how my company and their firm are going to react and interact with them? They invest in the relations which means spending time with us, understanding our business, and understanding what our needs will be. It is helping us identify what our needs will be whether they will get a piece of that pie or not. It's an appreciation of the ability to get to know me and to know what the company is going to achieve and how can they help me work out what is the problem and what does it really look like and, only after analyzing the problem deeper, we move to asking: what is a solution and how are we going to deliver it? Like we do in LawWithoutWalls.—General counsel of a startup and former general counsel, one of the largest mutual insurers in the U.K.[54]

The client is at center and clients' interest drive the work and, in many ways, drive processes. And it starts from there. I have seen our organization evolve over time and develop this idea of client-centricity. It runs across a gambit of things. The way we have organized ourselves, how we organize our teams, and the way we draft our work and advice. It has changed a lot. We are creating timelines and measuring output and being driven by a desire that the work is not just high quality but also timely. Drafting is not just form. It's useful, practical, pragmatic. The latest change is not just about written work but also other kinds of support that you can lend the client. You don't have to draw those lines so clear between a lawyer and a government policy driver. It's fluid. And this is very recent. We want our image of our department to be like that of a Singapore law firm for the government. This has very much defined the interaction and approach in which we are all asked to come to things. It is very useful to have a single elevator pitch image that everyone can rally around and fill in the gaps.—Government Legal Counsel, Government Agency in S.E. Asia[55]

And if those definitions don't convince you, consider how Chat GPT3 defines client-centricity:

Client-centricity in professional services refers to a business approach or philosophy that places the client's needs, preferences, and satisfaction at the center of all operations and decision-making processes. It involves understanding and anticipating client expectations, delivering exceptional service, and consistently striving to exceed client needs.
—Open AI, Chat GPT 3, https://chat.openai.com/, July 10, 2023.

At this point, you may be thinking, this is too much. I am not Burger King. I cannot give *all* my clients *everything* they want in *every way* they want. And you would be right, and you don't have to. Think of client-centricity, instead, as a new way of doing the things you already do or are willing to do but with a new attitude and slightly different goal. In other words, of the things you *can* and *will* do for them, do them the way they want them done—and in a way that *delights* them. As one interviewee aptly put it: "it's striv[ing] for excellence in every interaction, ensuring that [the client's] or customer's journey from discovery to post-purchase is seamless, enjoyable, and fulfilling."[56] This is perhaps the most missed part of client-centricity in the definitions above (and the examples below), and it is also the most important part. Our ability to create an experience that evokes feelings of delight, of belonging, of understanding and fulfillment, of "they've got my back," is how we will be able to set ourselves apart from the machines that are coming. Yet so many (including Chat GPT 3) leave this *feeling* part out. I find this time and time again when I run workshops with in-house service departments or PSFs.

Thus, to enhance understanding of this essential nuance, I created and incorporated an exaptation exercise called *What I Love Most* into my *What Is Client-Centricity? Exercise.* After asking for participants to jot down real examples of what is *not* client-centricity that they do or their team does and examples of what *is* client-centricity that they do or their team does, I have them write down their individual definitions of client-centricity.

Then I ask the group to write a collaborative definition of client-centricity. We share the definitions out loud, and they are generally good (much like the definitions above). But they still miss the feeling part, how behaving in a more client-centric way makes the client *feel*. So, I tell everyone to pivot for a moment and to think of the service experience they love the most (e.g., at their favorite restaurant or hotel, from their favorite app like Uber or Uber Eats, or it could be at a spa or a local boutique or grocery store, etc.). Then I ask them to write down why they love this service experience the most and specifically, how it makes them *feel*. Does it make them feel special, listened to, safe, pampered, known? Then I ask them to do the same for their favorite *product* (e.g., personal-care product like face cream, cologne, shampoo, or personal-use product like their phone, car, gaming platform, etc.). And then I ask them to do this for their favorite brand, each time stressing the incorporation of adjectives that describe how they *feel*. I also give them a few examples. I start with a simple example that my son (then 13 years old) provided when I tested this exercise on him. I use this example because it identifies a fast-food restaurant that is considered by many to be low quality to be a place that provides a client-centric service (albeit to its target audience, which here is a teenager):

- The people at Subway always remember my name. That makes me feel special, known, and like I belong.
- I can pick every part of my sandwich and I can have my sandwich any way I want it. That makes me feel like I have control each and every time.
- The people at Subway always smile, even when I frustrate them. For example, I often just want ham in my Subway sandwich, which confuses them because there are so many options (lettuce, pickles, tomatoes, peppers, mustard, mayo, vinaigrette, turkey, beef, etc.). And I want bread and ham and that's it. But no matter how many times, they are required to ask me if I want any of the other things added to my sandwich, and even though they think I'm a bit crazy for just wanting plain ham and bread, they always smile. This makes me feel important, listened to, that my preferences matter.

I then provide some examples from senior in-house counsel related to the service experiences they loved the most. For example, I like to include the following examples gleaned from running a workshop on client-centricity with the in-house legal department at ENI, an Italian multinational energy company:

- My favorite hotel, which I like a lot, makes me feel surrounded by beauty, comfortable, and safe.
- My perfume makes me feel attractive, self-assured, and unique.
- My spa makes me feel catered to and relaxed . . . like a glass of champagne, bubbly, like I'm always on vacation.

After the participants in my workshops come up with their own *What I Love Most* examples, I have them revise their definitions of client-centricity to include some those feelings, those reasons why. As a result, their definitions come alive:

- BEFORE: Proactive and inclusive, tailor-made services and communications based on my clients' needs, wants, and desires that keep my client informed, and updated every step of the way in the proceeding and negotiation.
- AFTER: Proactive and inclusive, tailor-made services and communications that anticipate my clients' needs, wants, and desires that keep my client informed, and updated every step of the way in the proceeding and negotiation *and that makes them feel understood, safe, related to me, and, hopefully, just a little bit spoiled.*

To move them even further, I then introduce the idea of branding—which is what the forward-thinking service departments within big companies are doing: They are first determining the department's unique selling proposition by asking: If the department were a stand-alone business, who would be the primary target audience, what would its main offering and point of difference be? What well-known company would it emulate and why (based on the jobs to be done and client and stakeholder desires)? Then they are creating branding statements and taglines to message their purpose and their value and to justify their existence to the business, and to demonstrate that they are being more client-centric. Consider the following tagline and explanation created by the legal department of an American multinational Fortune 500 corporation operating in many fields, including healthcare and consumer goods:

On your side, by your side. *"On your side" communicates the partner and guardian point and the relationship point is "by your side." It is not enough to be on your side. We want to be by your side, which requires a combination of skills and service we provide with a human element and the EQ over the IQ.*—Senior vice president, legal affairs, & general counsel, an American multinational Fortune 500 corporation[57]

This may not seem important, but it is. Consider how different that tagline resonates (evokes feeling) as opposed to a snoring, boring mission statement by a department like this one: "developing and deploying the best legal talent to provide the highest quality and efficient legal services." First, this mission statement isn't communicating client-centricity like the tagline above. Second, there is a big difference between having a brand and a tagline versus a mission statement, as discussed in more detail in Part III. Branding, marketing, and messaging are essential to changing people's perceptions of us and our initiatives and for incentivizing and motivating our teams to meet expectations and behave within the culture and brand we aspire to emulate. As one professional service provider interviewee aptly explained, "it is very useful to have a single elevator pitch image that everyone can rally around and fill in the gaps."[58] Branding can help internal professional service departments at companies, firms, practice groups, and teams message with influence, inspire culture change, prioritize initiatives, "resonate" with clients, and add value that justifies the costs/price/resources. So, in addition to creating experiences that delight, we emulate our brand, which is a way of doing things and being that is individual to us but also synergistic with the type of services we provide and the way we provide them. And this match between who we are, what we stand for, and how we demonstrate that and message that to and with our clients is critical if it is true that "we become the stories we tell about ourselves."[59]

B. Adaptive, Inclusive Leadership: A Move from the Possible to the "Adjacent Possible"[60]

The mindset, and all the skills and attributes on the Professional Skills Delta, when mastered, enable professionals not only to be innovators but to be collaborative and ADAPTIVE, inclusive leaders (with digital mindsets) as well. Entrepreneurship expert and Stanford professor Tina Seelig explains it this way:

> *"T-shaped people," those with a depth of knowledge in at least one discipline and a breadth of knowledge about innovation and entrepreneurship allows them to work*

effectively with professionals from other disciplines to bring their ideas to life. No matter what their role, having an entrepreneurial mind-set is the key to solving problems, from small challenges that face each of us every day to looming world crises that require the attention and efforts of the entire planet. In fact, entrepreneurship cultivates a range of important life skills, from leadership and team building to negotiation, innovation, and decision-making.[61]

Thus, the skills, attributes, and mindset of an innovator help us collaborate and problem find better. They help us to recognize the adaptive challenges that stem from the complex, ever-changing, and volatile environment in which our clients work today. Pink calls this problem finding; Seelig calls it "need finding." They enable us to "see how data, algorithms, and AI open up new possibilities and to chart a path for success in a business landscape increasingly dominated by data-intensive and intelligent technologies."[62] In other words, they enable us to see what Stephen Johnson calls the "adjacent possible."[63] Think about that term—it's not about reaching the possible, but what is adjacent to the possible. According to Johnson, the adjacent possible is "a kind of shadow future, hovering on the edges of the present state of things, a map of all the ways in which the present can reinvent itself."[64] This is a very apt description of how living with a growth (and digital) mindset can help create the possibility for change and see the benefits (as opposed to the negatives) of change.

You might now be wondering how adaptive leadership differs from traditional leadership. According to experts, adaptive leaders do not rely on established methods and procedures to solve problems. Instead, they seek novel ways to handle challenges. This makes sense given that adaptive challenges cannot be solved from precedent, nor does the requisite expertise exist to solve the problem.[65] Technical challenges, on the other hand, can be handled with existing expertise and procedures.[66] As Ron Heifetz, the original guru on adaptive leadership explains:

The staff of an emergency room face a kind of problem similar to many everyday situations. These problems are technical in the sense that we know already how to respond to them. . . . They are not easy, nor are they unimportant. Their solutions frequently save lives and require great organizational effort. These problems are technical because the necessary knowledge about them already has been digested and put in the form of a legitimized set of known organizational procedures guiding what to do and role authorizations guiding who should do it. For these situations, we turn to authority with reasonable expectations.[67]

But *adaptive* challenges? They escape clear problem definition, clear solutions, and easy implementation[68] and the solution doesn't easily come from the person with the most authority.[69]

Adaptive challenges are the type of challenges our clients face. They are VUCA, as in *v*olatile, *u*ncertain, *c*omplex, and *a*mbiguous,[70] issues faced by our clients (related to cross-border compliance, the vast reach of internal investigations, the threat of bribery and corruption, cybersecurity and data privacy, and catastrophic, systemic risk)—all of which have been made more complex by boundary blurring.

Thus, successfully tackling adaptive challenges requires innovation and learning and change-management leadership skills. They also often require an intersection of varying expertise including law, marketing, PR, communication, and company governance. This means they need leaders with multiple types of skills (like those in Level 1 of the Delta) and leaders who can proactively co-collaborate on diverse teams with a focus on problem finding—given that the problems are new and need to be better understood and refined.[71] It also means they need leaders with the ability to take a human-centered approach to problem-solving and leading change initiatives. The new solutions created to solve adaptive challenges also require stakeholder buy-in and convincing the hearts and minds of many to change. It is unsurprising that in a recent Annual Leadership Development Survey of more than 2,200 professional service providers, the leadership skills that had the largest increase in priority was "change leadership." It is also unsurprising that "adaptive thinking and problem solving, interpersonal relationships, emotional intelligence, team leadership, and communication" were all in the top 10.[72] And it isn't an accident that the skill sets and mindset on the Professional Skills Delta (especially those Level 2 skills like humility, empathy, curiosity, flexibility, communication, collaboration, having an open and growth mindset, and the ability to take risks) mirror those required of an adaptive leader.

Thus, adaptive leaders are different from the more traditional, heroic types of leaders who, like Pied Pipers, often work alone or in silos, value hierarchy (a clear chain of command), are a bit more resistant to change, and prefer maintaining stability. Moreover, traditional leaders rely on expert-based authority to lead and influence a group to follow their vision. This is why we often refer to people who have top management positions as Leaders with a capital L.[73] In fact, as experts have pointed out, "in our everyday language, we often equate leadership with authority. We routinely call leaders those who achieve high positions of authority."[74] We turn to formal authority to lead and expect these leaders to do so as a fair exchange for their powers.[75] Traditional leaders can be very capable, effective, and valuable, especially in situations in which problems occur in a stable environment and precedent exists that can be employed to solve the problem. However, as mentioned, given the complex, ever-changing, and volatile environment in which leaders work today, many (if not most) of the challenges our clients face are adaptive ones and it is important that adaptive challenges are identified as such, otherwise the wrong strategy and tactics will be applied.

This leads to some more good news about the Professional Skills Delta. It serves as a 2-for-1. It includes the skillsets and attributes of both adaptive leaders *and* innovators with a digital mindset. While adaptive leaders and innovators share some of the same traits like those in Level 2 of the Skills Delta, innovators have a higher risk tolerance and are considered highly creative and driven by creating groundbreaking, novel, revolutionary solutions and disruptive change.[76] Adaptive leaders are also creative; however, "their primary focus is on applying existing knowledge and adapting it to changing circumstances."[77] Last, in terms of execution and management, adaptive leaders are great at implementation, management, and driving execution (which involve a lot of the skills in Level 1 of the Skills Delta), whereas innovators are not considered as strong in execution but instead in idea creation and refinement.[78] Thus, mastering the skills, attributes, and mindsets on the Skills Delta is a win-win for professional service providers. The combination of skills, attributes, and mindsets on the Skills Delta enables leaders to identify, face, and collaborate with others to navigate evolving situations (like adaptive leaders with a digital mindset do), but also, to come up with entirely new, novel solutions, processes, and products like innovators do.

As Chapter 1 made clear, the adaptive challenges facing (and the priorities of) clients today means a new mindset and skill set are needed. Learning how to be both an innovator and an adaptive, inclusive leader with a digital mindset who can lead change initiatives is likely the most client-centric thing a professional service provider can do. However, the reality is the quote from the beginning of this chapter: "What got [us] here, won't get [us] there." Therefore, the question is: what will? What will help us sharpen the skills and grow the mindsets on the Skills Delta? How can we increase our adaptiveness and behave more inclusively? It is to this that the next part of this book turns.

📣...Reflection Point It is important in a team or department and at a firm or organization, that there is a common understanding of what is meant by client-centricity. Just like teams need to get on the same *problem plane* before trying to come up with a solution (discussed in Chapter 8), teams need to get on the same Purpose Plane when it comes to client-centricity. Therefore, a shared vision and description can be useful here.

To develop that together, first, take a moment to have each person on your team think of an example of something that is NOT client-centric that they or someone they know at the organization does, for example, a process, a way of working, a pitch/RFP, a way of managing a relationship, a business development tactic, a type of communication, a response or completion time. Have each person write down an example and share it among the team.

Next, have each person think of an example of something that IS client-centric that they or your team or organization does and have them write it down. Then share the examples.

Now, based on the examples, ask each person to write out their definition of client-centricity. Share the examples among the team and take note of and discuss the differences. Last, try to collaboratively write out one shared definition of client-centricity and some examples of it (or dos and don'ts) that can serve as a North Star for the team.

Before settling on this shared definition, check to make sure that it has some adjectives describing the way the client will or should feel. Consider conducting *The What I Love Most Exercise* described above if your definition does not convey the feeling that clients should feel when experiencing your service.

📣...Reflection Point Consider the tagline of the legal department noted above "on your side by your side." What is your tagline or mission statement of your team, department, or firm? How might you revise it to be more client- and stakeholder-centric?

●... Reflection Point Conduct a *KPI-CPI Alignment Exercise* as outlined below:

- **Step 1:** Make a list of what KPIs your department currently tracks and measures.
- **Step 2:** Identify which KPIs are for the legal department's internal use (i.e., to enhance efficiency, understand work allocation, leverage external law firm resources better, understand churn and department or firm engagement) versus external use (to demonstrate the value of the department or firm to its clients or key stakeholders).
- **Step 3:** Add any KPIs you think are missing and that should be measured (column 1) and mark whether they are for external or internal use.
- **Step 4:** Brainstorm together to create a list of CPIs that you think your internal business colleagues might care about, that is, their "nothing broke."
- **Step 5:** On a scale from 1 to 5, put the priority of the KPI/CPI for the legal department. Then, guestimate the level of priority of your clients-stakeholders.
- **Step 6:** Now, interview some of your clients to find out (1) if your firm or department has enough (and the right) KPIs that are externally focused on demonstrating the value of the department or firm; (2) if the priority of your KPIs matches the priority for your clients; and (3) if the CPIs you created resonate or if there are others that should be incorporated.

CHAPTER 4

The New Value Equation in Professional Services: Honing the Mindset and Skill Set of an Innovator

> *"Price is what you pay. Value is what you get."*
>
> —Warren Buffett

Clients want their professional service providers to collaborate with them, and to innovate with them. However, there is a reluctance on their part to attempt innovation with clients for fear of failure of two kinds: failure to actually succeed in innovating and failure to get any real value out of attempting to innovate. Although it is true that many professional service providers may not need to innovate now to continue to make money (or even increase revenue), this is far from a static equation. Regardless, all professional service providers should learn how to innovate (go on an innovation journey) because of what I call the New Value Equation in Professional Services.

Before explaining what I mean by the New Value Equation, let's start by discussing how clients value innovation. Value generally equals benefit minus costs. Thus, one way to increase value is to provide the same benefit (same goods or services) at a reduced cost. Walmart is masterful at this; it buys in volume and pressures its suppliers to reduce costs. The other way to increase value is to give more benefit at a cost that doesn't increase at the same rate—something that more securely applies to the PSFs. But this is tricky. When lawyers innovate with their clients, how do we measure the benefit? Perhaps in some situations, for example, with e-discovery or automated contracts, we can measure the benefit in terms of the number of hours saved and then equate those hours to dollars.

But even in that situation, there is not a true one-to-one calculation. Consider digital billboards that have been proven to be more effective than static billboards. Digital billboards can track who drives by and who goes to the client's store or restaurant advertised on the sign. That's a measurable benefit, but it isn't proof that someone saw the billboard or that the billboard was the reason the person drove to the store or restaurant. Technology might improve this by tracking whether our eyes actually scanned the billboard, but even then, there are many soft factors that can't be measured. Perhaps the child in the car had to go to the bathroom, and the billboard had nothing to do with the stop at the restaurant. Perhaps the teenager in the car wanted to be able to boast to his friends that he ate at the great British wings disaster at the King's Head and had never even looked up from his phone as the car passed the billboard.

With innovation, can we really "subtract" cost from benefit to arrive at value? Value is what you get in exchange for what you give, but the value of a service provided is often *perceived* value where the values assigned are subjective. Why does a consumer spend more money on, for example, 501 button fly jeans than another style when no one else can tell whether the person is wearing button fly (or zipper) jeans? How do you determine the return on investment from a commercial? The same questions are arising in the professional services marketplace right now about innovation. Clients are saying that they value innovation, but that valuation is not linear. It affects who they are likely to hire, but in a roundabout way. As the GC of a large media and telecommunications company in Australia explained, "it won't be 'if you do this, you get that,' but you might be surprised by the benefit . . . [T]he financial benefit is likely to be further down the track."[1]

As mentioned in Chapter 2, what I have heard from clients in my interviews (and in LawWithoutWalls) is that a willingness to innovate *with* the client puts you in the "special" category. It distinguishes you and your firm as being a better business partner, and it will help you get included in the panel or the RFP (i.e., meaning the gateway to the potential for more business). Going on an innovation journey with a client translates to more because it transforms the relationship between service provider and client. They are in it together. Together they are feeling vulnerable and are taking risks, and they must trust each other. Essentially, innovating with a client is a new form of business development (that has a great deal of added value as discussed in the following).

Innovation is part of the mix. If firms are demonstrating innovation in the way of supporting us in legal content or the way they are delivering legal services, we will recognize it and it will differentiate them and get them included in the mix.—Head of knowledge and development, compliance and secretariat, a Big 4 Australian bank and financial service provider[2]

Furthermore, in the actual act of innovating, the law firm learns the company's DNA, internal processes, and communication preferences.

I think it is inevitable. I think if someone is prepared to partner in that way you will be inside in the DNA of that company and you will know how we go about our internal processes and I also foresee a building block thing. Once you build the knowledge portal, at the end of the day, you can bolt on other modules . . . so you basically have the one-stop shop.—Head of legal, large international airline[3]

If that's not enough "value" for a firm to justify investing in innovating, there are also dollars and sense behind collaborating in a way that is client-centric and yields creative problem-solving or an innovation. For example, research suggests that the highest-performing financial investment advisors are client-centric, collaborative relationship builders who have interpersonal understanding, and are "innovative and creative in the way in which they bring about results for their clients."[4] Relatedly, Heidi Gardner's research demonstrates that when lawyers collaborate, versus simply cross-sell (i.e., when two practice groups collaborate), annual revenue per client triples. A similar increase in profits accrues to individual lawyers who collaborate as well. These rainmakers? They don't just make it rain; they make it pour.

Gardner compares two nearly identical lawyers: Lawyer 1 and Lawyer 2. Lawyers 1 and 2 graduated from law school in the same year, have been with the same firm for the same amount of time, and are in the same practice area. In one year, both of them billed almost the same number of hours. Lawyer 2's total revenue, however, was more than four times larger than revenue from Lawyer 1. The difference? Lawyer 2 had collaborated with a much broader network of partners. Lawyer 1 collaborated with six other partners (only three of whom were outside his practice).[5] Lawyer 2 collaborated with more than 30 other partners (20 of whom were from outside his practice). Gardner's research demonstrates that the more a partner shares the work they originate with other partners and other practices, the larger the partner's book of business grows over time.[6]

Why is that? It is partly because, as discussed, multidisciplinary collaboration yields better, more creative problem-solving. Collaboration is a key ingredient to innovation. It is also partly because, as many client interviewees claim, the kind of collaboration that results in innovation changes focus and mindset.

> *How do you measure innovation? You could force a quantitative analysis e.g., how many new ideas have translated into something or some system. But I don't know that we need to bid ourselves up that much. Just change in the service delivered or how delivered and the how will become apparent and become part of the experience and people will accept that the difference is driven by a change in focus and mindset. They will recognize that the change has happened and there is a driver of that change and the driver is thinking in a new way.*—Head of knowledge and development, compliance and secretariat, a Big 4 Australian bank and financial service provider[7]

And this is the real value equation in innovation—the new way of thinking, leading, team building, negotiating, decision-making, and collaborating.[8] Some innovation may fail. And I could tell you that many successful entrepreneurs have failed and that failure is lauded in the start-up world. There is even a conference called FailCon that touts itself as a "one-day conference for technology entrepreneurs, investors, developers and designers to study their own and others' failures and prepare for success."[9] However, there is a difference between competent and incompetent failure. As discussed later, incompetent failure should not be allowed. But competent failure? We can learn from that as much as successes. Moreover, failure isn't a necessity. Research reported in the *Harvard Business Review* found that successful entrepreneurs were just as likely not to have failed the first time as to have failed the first time. In other words, failure didn't make it more likely that the entrepreneur would succeed in their next venture.[10] Failure for failure's sake, especially for professional service providers, is overrated. In truth, what matters are three things I call the ABCs of Innovation: *a*ttitude, *b*ehavior, and *c*ulture. They provide a primer for anyone ready to apply themself to innovation: win, lose, or draw. And the best thing about this game is regardless of win, lose, or draw, you don't fail. Let me explain how that can be so.

A. A Is for Attitude

> ### *"If you cannot do great things, do small things in a great way."*
> —Napoleon Hill

Many people have bad attitudes about innovation in professional services like insurance or law or accounting. Some don't think it's worth it; I can't tell you how many venture capitalists have said as much to me. Others don't think it's possible—at least not by these traditional types of service providers. They make comments such as "Lawyers aren't going to change and neither are law firms, especially big law."[11] Others think it's not necessary. They prescribe to that horrible model that if it *ain't broke, don't fix it.* For many professional service providers, their business model isn't broken and if the pie is getting bigger—even if their piece isn't growing at the same rate as the rest of the pie—it's still growing. So why bother?

And still others think innovation is just too scary and too big to take on. They think innovation is about doing "great things"—great, big things that are like TNT—explosive and immediately disruptive as in *boom, pow, bang*! They are wrong, and they are right. Innovation is like TNT, but it is not always explosive and disruptive. Instead, it can be TNT as in *T* for tiny, *N* for noticeable, and *T* for things that add lasting value. That's what James Batham, head of innovation and partner at Dentons calls it, and appropriately so. Clients want small, incremental changes that add lasting value. Although clients may not always know exactly what they are looking for when they call on their professional service providers to innovate, and they might not know exactly how to measure innovation or being innovative, many agree that the type of innovation they are looking for is this kind of TNT.

Innovation can simply be questioning why we are doing things the way we always have done them.

Innovation is questioning the status quo and trying to improve upon the quality of the product you provide to your client.—General counsel, iconic software and technology company from the United States[12]

Don't beat yourself up over it. It doesn't need to be world class or patentable. If it is improving and sustaining? Fantastic. Give yourself a tick.—Head of knowledge and development, compliance and secretariat, a Big 4 Australian bank and financial service provider[13]

Innovation doesn't have to be new or original; it just has to be practicable.

It's not innovation unless it has a practical impact. It has to have something unique to it. It could be taking something that exists and applying it differently. I don't think it is innovation unless it is something people want. Creativity in action.—General counsel, Australian division of a worldwide healthcare group based in the United Kingdom[14]

So, what are some good examples of innovation—of a TNT? Examples include:

- Providing one of your clients an opportunity for training they might not have had otherwise
- Creating a budget tracking tool that pushes info to professional service providers and the client
- Creating a work allocation tool that aligns with clients' diversity, equity, and inclusion initiatives and eliminates cognitive bias on the part of partners
- Developing and sharing a database of experts that tracks and ranks all the experts a firm uses in litigation and shares that with their clients
- A template database for clients of the firm (DIY via website)
- Creating an app for clients that instantly provides an overview of the professional service providers working with the company, their country, what they are working on, the budget, and also an overview of the projects currently handled by the firm for the client
- Developing a digital dashboard to track and report all deals and disputes so that legal and business have real time data on all deals and disputes in the region
- The harmonization of seven contract templates for seven business units into a single template in simple modular plain-English format

and a playbook to enable the off-shore team to handle variations from the customer (plus the use of AI tools to find the similarities/differences among the seven contracts).

• Creating a new recruitment program that helps train future lawyers and provides free legal services to corporate client legal departments, and doing something that makes GCs lives easier when they are working with you

But don't just believe me. Believe the clients:

The law firm created a collaborative recruitment strategy for trainees that included a corporate legal intern arrangement in a rotation with the firm. It really boosted our standing among trainees and provided some service to us.—General counsel, large financial services group based in Norway[15]

We have an arrangement with one of our four firms that provides us with a $10,000 scholarship for one team member to go and do an amazing leadership course. It's almost like a gift. That's one of the value-adds.—Head of knowledge and development, compliance and secretariat, a Big 4 Australian bank and financial service provider[16]

I think the sweet spot for law firms is things that make in-house counsel's life easier—the website that has any kind of piece of information you would want about insurance or securities that you can log into or shared sites where we can keep every piece of case material (all referring to things the same way). That is pretty attractive: the ability to log into a place to see the status without having to pay for 15 minutes of the attorney's time.—Deputy general counsel, global insurance company based in the United States[17]

It's that easy. Send your client to one of Harvard Law School's Executive Education Programs, or bring them to LawWithoutWalls like Pinsent Masons, EY, KPMG, Linklaters, DLA Piper, Microsoft, DXC, The LEGO Group, HSBC, and White & Case have done—get a check plus for the value-add (or a tick as they say in Australia).

Innovation, TNT, can also be the story as opposed to a product or program. The tick can be the way in which you position/frame/market. Tim Brown provides the example of the microchip Intel created that sits inside the computer.[18] The innovation was tiny in physical size but TNT in the true sense of the word for impact because the computer would be useless without it. The tick, however, was the sticker on the outside that said "Intel inside." That is how Intel built its brand. Today Intel is not just what's inside the computer, and it's not exemplified just with a sticker. Today Intel is a serious competitor in the driverless car market, having purchased Mobileye, a device that helps the driverless cars "see" without a driver, for $15.3 billion dollars.[19] But the tick with kick? It came from a Tiny Noticeable Thing, a small sticker.

Innovation does not even have to be three dimensional to provide value. It can be a new service or a new user experience, as discussed in great detail in Chapter 3 on client-centricity and adaptive leadership. As discussed in Part III, an integral component of human-centered design is understanding the user's experience with the product. You might ask how the user's experience with a *product* relates to the innovation in the professional services market. What's a consultant's or lawyer's or insurance broker's product? In most cases, the user is the client and the *product* is the service provider. If that is the case, value can be provided by simply changing the client's experience with the firm. Think billing. One of the chief complaints about external professional service firms is the billing process—that it is not streamlined, easy, transparent, predictable, or on time. Just imagine the value-add if that were changed.

As exemplified, offering to have an off-the-clock meeting focused on problem- or opportunity-finding—offering to go on an innovation journey—with a client is a tick. Another tick is demonstrating a new attitude about creativity, collaboration, and innovation. The point is that there are different types of innovations and different types of innovators. The type of innovation that gets a tick does not have to be that of an extrapreneur or entrepreneur but instead an intrapreneur—and an intrapreneur can be anyone who hones the skills of creative, collaborative problem-solving and follows the Three Rules of Engagement described in Part II of this book. In *The Man Without Qualities*, Robert Musil writes that it is easy "to think in miles when you've no idea what riches can be hidden in an inch."[20] Although this new attitude may be a movement in inches, it delivers riches. Furthermore, these riches lend a new attitude about leadership and what you value in leaders. The type of leader you aspire to be will shift just an inch from the traditional leadership traits you have been attempting to hone to that of an inclusive, adaptive leader with a digital mindset. That shift in attitude about creativity, collaboration, innovation, and leadership style? That's the *A for Attitude* in the A, B, Cs of innovation.

And this new attitude enables us to do "small things in a great way." As Winston Churchill is sometimes credited with saying, "Attitude is a little thing that makes a big difference."[21] The big difference? That's in new behaviors. That's the *B*, in the A, B, Cs, to which the next section turns.

B. B Is for Behavior

"But of course we can't take any credit for our talents. It's how we use them that counts."

—Madeleine L'Engle, *A Wrinkle in Time*[22]

As mentioned (and is worth repeating), we are moving into an era where the focus is on how professional service providers work versus what they do. The paradox, however, is that service providers still get paid for what they do and often for how long it takes. We have all heard the expression about professional service providers—that they "eat what they kill." Ironically, this premise holds true in innovation as well—even if not in quite the same way. In innovation, the main thing you eat is time and that's one of the reasons professional service providers don't like or want to innovate. It takes time. And that time may feel wasted if not undervalued, because, as stated above, it is hard to measure. A. W. Tozer said that "When you kill time . . . it has no resurrection." In innovation, the opposite is true. In an innovation cycle, the time you kill is resurrected in new behaviors (brought on by new attitudes and new skills) that help bridge the gaps that currently exist.

A key learning from my years of leading more than 230 multidisciplinary, global legal teams through 4-month innovation cycles is that in the process of learning how to innovate and actually attempting to do so, the skills and behaviors that are honed are those that clients demand, value, and want. Essentially, going on an innovation journey with a multidisciplinary team is a way to fill the very skills and training gaps we have been discussing. It's also a great form of business development, although many professionals fail to see it that way.

First, those skills at the bottom of the pyramid that were identified as C.O.S.T skills are honed. Project management, technology, business acumen, social networking, communication, presentation, mentoring, feedback, and industry knowledge—all these skills that cannot be taught in a typical classroom become second nature over the course of a 4-month innovation journey like that offered in the past by LawWithoutWalls (called LWOW and pronounced L-WOW):

> *Through LWOW, I experienced first-hand the new and evolving technologies on the market and more effective ways to communicate with my team and clients, gained a better understanding of the current challenges facing the legal market and generated ideas to help resolve some of the problems we face day to day in legal practice.*—Mentor, senior associate, Eversheds

> *I loved being involved in LWOW and felt privileged to be there. It gave me an opportunity to learn skills for the future. Dealing with the different nationalities, personalities and cultures in my team was a challenge and certainly developed my communication and interpersonal skills as well as mentoring skills. I will carry these back into my professional life.*—Mentor, VP, and legal counsel, Barclays

An innovation cycle also hones the skills in the middle of the pyramid, those skills that clients desire that are essential to collaboration and creative problem finding and solving, including a growth mindset, empathy, cultural competency, self-awareness, humility, and risk taking. As mentioned, these are the same qualities of successful and inclusive adaptive leaders: empathy, emotional intelligence, industry knowledge, open-mindedness, growth mindedness, communication skills, cultural competency, high risk tolerance, and humility, for example.[23] These skills are developed in the process of problem finding, problem-refining, problem-solving, identifying target audiences, problem analysis, business case development, prototyping, testing, solution-refining, and retesting with people from different backgrounds and cultures in different locations. In the process of co-creating a real innovation—a practicable solution (including a prototype with branding and a commercial) that solves a real problem faced by clients—professional service providers uncover hidden talents and learn to better leverage the talents they've had (but perhaps forgotten that they have) all along.

There is one central problem that remains of course: authenticity. I recently took a course with IDEO called Leading for Creativity, and it struck me that the course should have been called Leading *with* Creativity. For it is only when we walk the walk and do as we do (not only what we say) that has an effect on others. Many of my firm partner interviewees complained of a lack of authenticity, an innovation officer without any power, a management philosophy that is hammered at off-site meetings but has no follow-through or compensation/incentive structure. And they complain of too much tolerance, turning a blind eye to the proliferation of bad habits. It's criticizable but also understandable, especially when the culprits are revenue generators for the firm.

> *We talk about innovation, we talk the talk, but we don't walk the walk. So many people in the firm are very passive aggressive in their approach. They nod and say they prescribe to this vision, but they print out their emails in hard copy and hide them in file cabinets in their office because they really don't want to change. And, as a firm, we are really tolerant of it. What we need to do is shake those people up and get them on board. And too many of our partners are not on board and it depresses our younger staff. They think, this is a waste of my time and why are my leaders telling me something that is inconsistent with the message that we need to be innovative?*—Partner, a leading independent Australian law firm[24]

Individuals at firms are resisting learning the new skills that will lead to a new *a*ttitude and new *b*ehaviors. These new skills change how we utilize our talents to contribute. They enable professional service providers to leverage their talents to better practice and service clients with an Open Mind, Open Heart, and Open Door (The Three Rules of Engagement described in Part II); they enable them to behave differently. They change how we interact with others, how we provide service, how we treat clients, how we practice, and most importantly, how we build relationships. How professional service providers leverage the skills from an innovation journey to build relationships internally and externally with clients and to become more client-centric, more creative, more collaborative, and more adaptive, is what counts—even if they don't want to innovate or quit (let alone change) their day jobs. This new "how" is an innovation itself, an innovation of the self.

C. C Is for a Culture of Collaboration

"A bonfire in a strong wind is not blown out, but blazes even brighter."

—Dilgo Khyentse Rinpoche

As I have written about in prior articles, one of which was published in Harvard Law School's *The Practice*, every corporate client is seeking a culture of compliance.[25] That's a given. Yet clients are also seeking a culture of collaboration: internally across the organization, within the service departments, and with their service providers. And firms of all kinds are beginning to recognize that for this challenge—to create a culture of collaboration—innovation is the solution.

> *One of the biggest challenges any law firm has is to establish how culturally we are different from other firms. Innovation is a strategy to tie us together.*—Deputy chief executive partner, One of Australia's "Big Six" law firms[26]

But how? How can innovation help in reaching that goal? It used to be that the way companies approached culture change, whether a culture of compliance or collaboration—or perhaps both—was to do it from the top down. The operation involved infiltrating the souls and minds of leadership down to the trenches. In some ways, companies used to look at culture change the same way they did hiring a new CEO. Turn in the old one and get a new one and voila! Culture change. That protocol has begun to shift to a culture change that takes place directionally from the bottom up—or even, as I suggested in my previous articles, from the middle out.[27]

Recent research, however, has suggested an alternative approach, one that is in sync with the mission of this book, which is for professional service providers to attempt an innovation cycle within a multidisciplinary global team. In a recent *Harvard Business Review* article, Jon R. Katzenbach, Ilona Steffen, and Caroline Kronley argue that the way to make "cultural change that sticks" is to work "with" and "within" the culture, focusing on small interventions designed to change a small set of behaviors.[28] They argue that this is how companies such as Apple, Four Seasons, Microsoft, and Southwest Airlines succeeded in changing their culture to attain a competitive edge. They claim that these "targeted and integrated cultural interventions designed around changing a few critical behaviors at a time" change culture. They "energize and engage your most talented people and enable them to collaborate more effectively and efficiently." And they spread the word.

A former head of innovation at Clyde & Co, Chris White, described that his strategy to get people to innovate at his firm was to light some bonfires. That analogy lit a bonfire in me. That's what this approach is about—starting bonfires with small groups of people to attract the attention of others. That's exactly what I have been doing for the past 13 years, lighting bonfires. Whether it is through my consultancy or LawWithout-Walls, when the innovation journey ends, each person goes back and starts a new bonfire in their organization, department or team to spread and burn. Think about it. When you see a bonfire from far away, you are lured by the light, the laughter, and the embers floating in the sky. And that's the goal of a small intervention, of creating a multidisciplinary team and having them go through an innovation cycle. The goal is to lure the others to join over time to slowly create "cultural change that sticks." As the authors of *Rework* point out, culture cannot be installed in an instant big bang push; it takes time—like the aging of scotch, the good kind.[29] Culture is oxidized. Small teams working on vetted projects designed to deliver TNT to the firm and/or clients raise awareness. Over time, buy-in and momentum build like a slow-burning flame. It may be true that there is a "strong wind" going against professional service providers' attempts to create culture change within firms. However, the bonfires that are lit by the small teams (that include staff and managers from different areas in the organization) charged with creating a TNT will stay lit and "blaze even brighter" because of it.

To be clear, I am not suggesting that innovation should be a strategy in and of itself. It should not. Here, I am suggesting using innovation as a tactic to learn a new way to approach problem-solving and to create a culture of collaboration because it is by attempting to innovate—going through a 4-month innovation cycle, for example—that we learn how to collaborate the way clients desire. Also note that the goal is collaboration and not collegiality, as discussed earlier. Being collegial is not the same as being collaborative, at least not in the sense clients want. They want a culture of co-creation, energy, and change. This type of culture, a culture that embraces change, is infused with energy and, importantly, meets clients' needs at the same time it motivates the future generations of professional service providers—the digital natives, who want it too—and enables them to find satisfaction in their careers.

Thus, creating a culture of collaboration lends both tangible and intangible value to an organization. As the managing partner of Vieira de Almeida (VDA) explained after his firm won the *Financial Times* award for continental Europe in part because they created an

Innovation Forum designed to create not only innovations but also culture change:[30]

> *One is the value of innovation as far as business is concerned . . . it helps us keep clients, develop clients, find new clients. It has a business value. Then there's an intangible value . . . people sit together and talk innovation—and the simple thought that they are sitting and talking together, there's value just in that alone.*[31]

My point here is like that of Mary Doria Russell in *Children of God* who wrote, "The sign of a good decision is the multiplicity of reasons for it."[32] This rings true here as well. As described in more detail in Chapter 11, there is a "multiplicity of reasons" for investing in an innovation cycle, the most important of which is that even if you fail, you don't fail. Even if at the end of an innovation journey your team has not created a project that is viable or feasible, it is still what we call in LawWithoutWalls a Project of Worth. The innovation cycle, regardless, results in the ABCs: *A* for a new attitude and understanding of what innovation is in the law market and that it is achievable, *B* for new behaviors that come from a combination of new skills and inherent talents, and *C* for a culture of collaboration that builds a sustained platform for co-creation with clients and others in your firm or department regardless of generation. The end result is a client leadership edge opportunity. Those that follow the ABCs will have stronger and more durable relationships with their clients and a competitive advantage.

...Reflection Point Consider the following question: What do calculus, steamboats, oxygen, and the evolution of man have in common?

Answer: For the correct answer, turn to the notes at the end of this book.[33]

- After reviewing the answer, ask yourself: Why does that matter? How does knowing that impact how you feel about innovation in professional services?
- Now consider Renren.com, originally called Xiaonei.com. It was a copycat version of Facebook designed to look exactly like Facebook in terms of color scheme and layout.[34] Renren (which means "everyone") was an all-out imitation, but it was wildly successful for over a decade. Is it a tick? Why or why not?

...Reflection Point We have talked about innovation as TNT, *tiny noticeable things*. Some innovations can be big and hairy and disruptive. These are the projects that do not just add incremental value; instead,

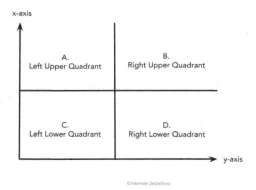

FIG. 4.1. A Basic Four-Quadrant Map to Help Diagram Innovation Goals and Value Add.

they create new offerings. Many experts have diagrammed innovation on a quadrant to identify goals and value. The goal according to design thinkers is to invest in all four quadrants. A basic four-quadrant map is shown in Figure 4.1.

For the professional services market, however, investing in just one of the quadrants may make a difference in a low-risk way. Map out the four examples described below based on the quadrants and axes information provided. Then compare them. Which one best represents how your firm or department thinks of innovation? Which one best represents how your biggest business client thinks of innovation?

- **Example 1:** A quadrant designed by Diego Rodriguez and Ryan Jacob[35] featured in Tim Brown's book.
  - Y-axis: From "Existing Offerings" at the bottom to "New Offerings" at the top
  - X-axis: From "Existing Users" on the left to "New Users" on the right
  - A. Left Upper Quadrant: "Extend Evolution"
  - B. Right Upper Quadrant: "Create Revolution"
  - C. Left Lower Quadrant: "Manage Incremental"
  - D. Right Lower Quadrant: "Adapt Evolution"
- **Example 2:** An innovation quadrant developed by Shirley Gregor, a professor of information systems (business informatics) at Australian National University, and Alan R. Hevner, a professor in information systems and decision sciences at the University of South Florida, called this the Knowledge Innovation Matrix (KIM). (Note: I especially like this

because it is the first time I have seen anyone other than me use the word *exaptation* with regard to innovation in a business context.)[36]

- Y-axis: From low to high on "an Application Domain (Problem) Maturity Scale"
- Y-axis: From low on the left to high to the right
- A. Left Upper Quadrant: "Improvement: Develop new solutions for known problems"
- B. Right Upper Quadrant: "Exploitation: Apply known solution to known problems"
- C. Left Lower Quadrant: "Invention: Invent new solutions to new problems"
- D. Right Lower Quadrant: "Exaptation: Extend known solutions to new or different problems (Or adopt solutions from other fields)"
- **Example 3:** An "innovation management matrix" by Greg Satell, an author, speaker, and innovation adviser who frequently writes for the *Harvard Business Review.*[37]
  - Y-axis: Problem Definition: From "Not Well Defined" at the bottom to "Well Defined" at the top
  - X-axis: Domain Definition (as in "who has the talent/capability/capacity"): From "Not Well Defined" on the left to "Well Defined" on the right.
  - A. Left Upper Quadrant: "Breakthrough Innovation"
  - B. Right Upper Quadrant: "Sustaining Innovation"
  - C. Left Lower Quadrant: "Basic Research"
  - D. Right Lower Quadrant: "Disruptive Innovation"
- **Example 4:** "The Four Quadrants of Innovation" developed by Hutch Carpenter, chief scientist at Revolution Credit, called Incremental Disruptive Innovations: Picking Your Spot.[38]
  - Y-axis: From "Manage Existing Market" on the low end to "Create New Market" on the high end
  - X-axis: From "Minimal Technology Change" on the left to "Radical Technology Change" to the right
  - A. Left Upper Quadrant: "Low risk, many competitors"
  - B. Right Upper Quadrant: "High risk, high reward"
  - C. Left Lower Quadrant: "Customer experience; cost savings"
  - D. Right Lower Quadrant: "High risk, defensive strategy"

PART II

Leading Collaboration, Innovation, and Culture Change

> *"First Things First."*
> —Stephen R. Covey[1]

As I mentioned in the Introduction to this book, research indicates that 75 percent of change efforts fail, often due to poor management or execution.[2] However, related research on 62 corporate transformations suggests that change efforts also fail because the leaders don't do the right thing, first.[3] The authors of the research point to JCPenney as an example. When Ron Johnson took over as CEO of JCPenney, the first thing he changed was the store design and pricing of new merchandise in an effort to lure younger, trendier customers. However, when the new target audience went to the stores, they didn't actually have the trendier (newly priced) merchandise that was showcased online. The two channels (in-store and online) were run separately, each with its own merchandise and supply chain. In failing to do the right first thing first, that is, integrate the merchandise and supply chains for online and in-store, he failed as a leader. He didn't select the correct action to take first as a CEO (whose goal was to revitalize JCPenney's appeal and attract a new target audience). As a result, the sales and stock fell drastically. Johnson's first priority should have been a better integration of JCP's in-store and online operations.

My point in relaying this story is twofold. First, it is to emphasize the importance of selecting the correct first step in transformation, which, of course, varies based on your goal. Second, it is to suggest that if your goal is to lead a change effort, then the *right* first action you should take is to focus on your own mindset, skill set, and behavior. If they aren't in line with the culture you are trying to create, your change effort will fail. So, starting with YOU is the right priority. The first thing you need to do is focus on yourself and your individual responsibility to hone and exhibit the right mindset and skill set. In fact, this is true for everyone on the team, not just the leader. The title of Chris Avery's book makes this clear: *Teamwork Is an Individual Skill.*[4] Avery posits that if every person on the team entered each teaming experience believing that it was their individual responsibility to hold up the effort—that it rested on their shoulders alone, teams would collaborate a whole lot better. I like to compare a team to a house where shelter is dependent on each individual putting up his or her arms to hold the roof up. If one person lets go, the protection comes crashing down. It is ironic that people love the saying "There is no 'I' in Team" when what they mean by that is that we should not think about ourselves individually when tending to the collective. I often disagree with this contention and point out that there is an "i" in teaming and there *are* two "i's" in innovation. The only way to innovate (which requires multidisciplinary collaboration) is if each individual keeps their eyes not only on the group goal but also on their own individual contribution to the collaboration itself.

By focusing on our own contributions, we hold ourselves accountable for the group's success at collaborating. Thus, we need YOU: your mindset, your skill set, and your behavior to enhance the collaborative nature of the effort, to hold it up—in fact, we can't do it without you focusing on you in this way.

And this is especially true for the leader. The old saying: *Do as I say not as I do,* doesn't cut it in today's leadership effort, and it definitely doesn't cut it in culture creation. Rather, the first thing you need to do is focus on yourself: identifying and shoring up your weaknesses—exactly what this part of the book is designed to help you do. Chapter 5 focuses on the importance of self-awareness and humility and recommends that you take a good look in the mirror to determine your gaps on the Skills Delta. Chapter 6 provides the Three Rules of Engagement any leader can follow to help shore up their weaknesses on the Skills Delta and improve their client-centricity, collaboration, and culture creation skills. Only after that can you focus successfully on the culture of your department, firm, or team[5]—which is what Chapters 7 and 8 are dedicated to. They are designed to provide professional service providers specific approaches to face the current leader upheaval in the marketplace. Chapter 7 provides a recipe for creating a safe, inclusive, collaborative culture that engages the multigeneration universe we all work in these days. Chapter 8 identifies the situations in which the leader needs to step in to ensure the right culture is created and to prevent incompetent failure.

CHAPTER 5

First Things First: The Art of Collaboration and Change Starts with You

> *"I'm starting with the man in the mirror. I'm asking him to change his ways. And no message could have been any clearer. If you wanna make the world a better place. Take a look at yourself, and then make a change."*
>
> —Michael Jackson, "Man in the Mirror"[1]

Your ability to lead teams and to collaborate depends on your knowing your strengths and your weaknesses. Understanding this root cause requires some self-analysis and reflection. As Michael Jackson once sang, "I'm starting with the man in the mirror. I'm asking him to change his ways." Well, Michael Jackson had it right. The only way to make a change is to look in the mirror. Before you, as a leader, can inspire change, create new culture, and lead collaborative efforts, you need to figure out if your "HOW"—that is, how you provide professional services—delights your clients and if your HOW models the mindset, skill set, and behavior you desire in your team. This absolutely needs to happen first, before you do anything else. And to honestly figure out your HOW, you need self-awareness and humility.[2] Only with those two attributes will you be able to lead—and follow—the way innovators and adaptive, inclusive leaders with a digital mindset do.

A. Lead with Self-Awareness and Humility Because There Is a Lower-Case "i" in Teaming

"Leaders are made, not born."

—Vince Lombardi[3]

Although we may have all been born creative, the reality is, we aren't all born leaders. Moreover, that saying that leaders are born, not made, is not necessarily true. Maybe some people are natural born leaders, but I know for certain leaders can be "made." The mindset, skill set, and attributes on the Skills Delta can be honed over time. There is proof that leadership training works via The 3-4-5 Method™ (and that it doesn't suffer from the typical skills transfer gap often complained about when training is provided in a classroom format).[4] By following the Three Rules of Engagement (described in the next chapter) *and* joining a collaborative, innovation journey with The 3-4-5 Method™, you can get most of the way there.[5] And there are a ton of resources to help close the last mile—over 30,000 books on Amazon alone that are about leadership[6] plus a slew of high quality executive education programs on leadership offered by some of the best schools on the globe, including Harvard, Stanford, IE, and Oxford, to name a few. In addition, there *is* scientific research supporting the notion that leaders can be trained and that companies should invest resources to promote leadership development.[7] So saying that leaders are born (not made) is just an excuse for not exemplifying the traits of a leader or not focusing on upping your leadership game. Why wouldn't you want to learn to be the best leader, influencer, and motivator? Filling the gaps in your leadership style will only help differentiate you within your organization. However, the only way to fill in those gaps is to know what the gaps are.

Some of you, like me, may have been leaders for a while and you may have become a little rusty. When you first become a leader, with a new team, you were focused on being great at it, reading the latest *Harvard Business Review* articles on leadership and taking executive education classes. Over time, however, you lost some of that zest and focus—not because you don't care but because you are busier. You have more and more responsibilities and more and more clients. Yet this is the time when it is even more important for you to keep an eye on the "i" in teaming, which means keep an eye on *you*, as an individual, and *your* individual skills that you used to cultivate and need to hone anew or that you need to develop.

There are numerous articles and books on the importance of self-awareness, self-reflection, and self-examination as a key—even the key—to changing ourselves and, by extension, our industries.[8] These writings are directed not only at our personal lives but also our professional ones and, specifically, our ability to grow as business professionals and as managers and leaders. Research and articles on the topic date back to 1964.[9] For decades, companies and executive training programs have been giving personality tests to professionals for this reason: research shows that a top criterion for successful leaders is high self-awareness.[10] This means understanding both our strengths and our weaknesses will help us lead better and team better.[11]

When we are aware of our strengths and our talents, and are cognizant that they add value, we can identify opportunities to bring them better—not to mention also attain a higher level of well-being.[12] When we are aware of our deficiencies, we are more open to ideas and help from others because we understand that others might be better at some things than we are. This is why, in LawWithoutWalls, we have everyone conduct a *Delta-Skills Vision Exercise* to identify (and write down on Post-it® notes) the two attributes, qualities, or skills they are great at and will commit to bringing and bringing even better. We then have them identify (and write down on Post-it® notes) the two attributes or qualities or skills that they need to work on. Finally, we have them reflect and write down WHY they want to achieve or hone these new skills or attributes or qualities, that is, what difference will it make and for whom? The reason we have them write all this down is because research shows that the act of writing our goals (combined with writing the WHY) has what neuroscientists call a "generation effect," which helps us remember them[13] and can double our likelihood of achieving them.[14] Moreover, having to learn new skills to reach our goals also increases our odds of reaching them.[15] The final action is to have everyone place their notes on a blank Skills Delta on an easel (in the corresponding level) and share this among their teams.

The visual aspect of this also increases the odds that we will set concrete goals,[16] while the sharing aspect increases our commitment.[17]

After the *Delta-Skills Vision Exercise*, we have teams do a *Talent & Topic Expertise Exploration Exercise* (discussed at greater length in Chapters 6 and 7), which is designed to open participants' minds to the idea that each individual can contribute something meaningful to the team, regardless of their age or level of expertise. Importantly, the combination of these exercises takes individuals out of what might be their natural, innate competitive mode, forcing them to be vulnerable, and moves them into the mindset that they can achieve more together than alone. Amy Edmondson ends her TED Talk, "How to Turn a Group of Strangers into a Team," by turning a famous quote from the movie *The Paper Chase* on its head to illustrate her point. In the movie, the professor says to the new class of 1Ls: "Look to your left. Look to your right. One of you won't be here next year." She says, "There's no better advice than this: 'Look to your left, look to your right' but not because one of us won't be 'here' in a year." Instead she urges us to look to see "[h]ow quickly can you find the unique talents, skills and hopes of your neighbor, and how quickly, in turn, can you convey what you bring? Because for us to team up to build the future we know we can create that none of us can do alone, that's the mindset we need."[18]

Following this train of thought, we eventually seek people who are different from us to fill in what would be (without self-awareness) our blind spots. To help see our blind spots, we have the participants in Law-WithoutWalls take personality tests (such as DiSC, Meyers-Briggs, and/or CliftonStrengths) and then map them out as a team to identify gaps to gain these benefits.

Self-awareness, however, isn't easy to acquire. Studies show that generally, leaders' self-perception of their abilities is not accurate; people generally fail to recognize their weaknesses and tend to overrate their abilities.[19] This is sometimes referred to as the Dunning-Kruger effect.[20] Worse yet, those who overrate their substantive abilities are also more likely to overrate their emotional intelligence (EQ) and be reluctant to attempt to improve their EQ.[21] The title of a study demonstrating this says it all: "Emotionally Unskilled, Unaware, and Uninterested in Learning More: Reactions to Feedback about Deficits in Emotional Intelligence."[22] Self-awareness is essential to great leadership. Yet, as Benjamin Franklin pointed out in 1750, like "steel" and "a diamond," "to know one's self," is "extremely hard."[23] And if you don't know yourself accurately, it is hard to change.

Despite this, according to leadership experts like Deborah Rhode, James Kouzes, and Barry Posner, "although it seems self-evident that leaders' first priority should be to know themselves, many appear surprisingly uninterested in doing so."[24] Moreover, "most leaders don't want honest feedback, don't ask for honest feedback, and don't get much of it unless it's forced on them."[25] Contributing to the problem is that many believe that they need less development at senior levels in their careers than they did earlier in their careers.[26]

Perhaps counterintuitively, research also shows that the most *successful* leaders, however, actually underrate themselves, due in part to, you guessed it, humility.[27] If self-awareness was the first "i" in the word Innovation in the title of this chapter, then humility is the second "i" and appropriately it's in lowercase and not uppercase. Moreover, the more realistic leaders are about their abilities and skills, the more effective they are as leaders.[28] So the answer is to be self-aware and humble at the same time, as the two go hand in hand. According to experts, people who are humble are "open to new ideas and to engagement in an accurate self-appraisal (of both strengths and weaknesses) . . . and are willing to accept the idea of something greater than the self,"[29] and they have a collective identity orientation and define themselves in relation to others.[30] But being humble and self-aware isn't easy, as there are more impediments to doing so that tie directly to our role as professional service providers.

B. Lead by Following Because Only Those Who Are Inspired Can Inspire

Another impediment to self-awareness and humility (in addition to and related to our faulty self-perception) is our self-concept—especially our self-concept as a "leader" versus a follower. Paul J. Brouwer explained this in a *Harvard Business Review* article published in the 1960s:

> *Each of us, whether we realize it or not, has a self-image. We see our-selves in some way—smart, slow, kindly, well-intentioned, lazy, misunderstood, meticulous, or shrewd; we all can pick adjectives that describe ourselves. This is the "I" behind the face in the mirror; the "I" that thinks, dreams, talks, feels, and believes, the "I" that no one knows fully.[31]*

It would be difficult enough to attain self-awareness if we only had one self-concept. But we don't; we have multiple self-concepts that change based on the role we are playing. Brouwer gives the following example: You may be someone who personally loves to travel. So, when on a personal vacation, you attempt to learn about the history, culture, and customs of a location. Yet, when you are on a business trip, you might not ever leave the hotel that hosts the conference—even if you have time to do so. Brouwer explains that this is because your self-concept during that trip was as a businessperson versus a vacationing explorer. This self-concept works like a filter on what we see (or do not see), what we hear (or do not hear), and how we behave (or do not behave). Sometimes our different self-concepts are in conflict with each other internally, and sometimes they are in conflict externally, with how others see us.[32] According to Brouwer, the more integrated our self-concepts are and the more realistic they are, the more effective we are in both our professional and personal lives.[33] Essentially, we wear our self-concepts like a *suit*, and they impact how we behave.[34]

Therefore, it is important for us to understand which self-concept that we rely on when we are acting as professional service providers because this professional self-concept can lock us into preferences, tendencies, and practices that impact our behavior positively, and at the same time, actually *contribute* to a skills and behavior gap even without our knowing it.

Understanding this can make all the difference. To help raise self-awareness so that you can make the first step toward change—it is important to identify the crutches that you rely on that may make you great at your job but that might prevent you from evolving higher up on the Professional Skills Delta.

Successful professional service providers are known for being strategic and great at complex problem-solving.[35] That's part of our professional identity to be this way and we live up to it. However, what part of our professional identity is holding us back? Research shows that professional service providers prefer autonomy and do not like to be told how to behave or operate.[36] Moreover, they are risk averse and reluctant to try new approaches and feel a duty to maintain traditions and ways of working. How is that impacting our ability to hone the skills, mindset, and attributes on the Skills Delta? What about arrogance? Arrogance seems to come with professional services jobs given that our roles are often as the experts, advisors, or fixers of other people's messes. In fact, according to a recent *Harvard Business Review* article about professional service firms, most PSF leaders presume their practices are more premium and valuable to clients than clients think they are and this misalignment stems from "pride that sometimes borders on arrogance."[37] In keeping with that, evidently the legal profession has been voted the most arrogant discipline for 78 years in a row.[38] And just a quick Google search makes clear that people feel other professional service providers, like accountants,[39] and financial advisors,[40] exude arrogance as well. In fact, experts contend that arrogance was one of the key contributors to the fall of Enron.[41] I was recently chatting with a senior officer who oversees strategy and market development for one of the Big 4 accounting companies and what she said sums it up:

> *There's something really weird about professional services. I do a lot of work with foreign affairs and trade, and I work with professional services folks of all kinds, including architects, and there is a scary similarity across professional services. People with a high degree of training and professional accreditation have a scary similar mindset and it is not a growth mindset. Although they do things really well, they don't know how to talk to clients, give eye contact, or talk about the business, but they sure think they do.*—Head of strategy and market development, One of the Big 4 Professional Services Firms[42]

Unfortunately, arrogance leads to closed-mindedness, a "false sense of invincibility to criticisms," a failure to listen to others' advice,[43] and blaming others for problems (vs taking personal responsibility).[44] It is also the death knell of collaboration[45] and innovation—and that client-centricity we talked about in Chapter 3—because you aren't stepping back and asking questions to find out what the client really wants. You are assuming that the client wants what you have provided in the past. As Leslie Wexner, the CEO of The Limited, aptly put it: the "more that you know a thing works, the less likely you are to think that it won't work. When you've had a long string of victories, it's harder to foresee your own vulnerabilities."[46] Arrogance, therefore, is the opposite of humility[47] and contributes to leadership failure due to biased self-perceptions and self-enhancement tendencies.[48]

Time and time again I have heard professional service providers talk about how they want to *lead*, not follow, how they want to *inspire* versus be inspired. This is driven internally by their self-concepts. In fact, according to research, "If one asks: 'Would you rather be known as a leader or a manager? A follower or a leader?' the response is usually 'a leader.' The term 'leadership' involves our self-images and moral codes."[49] And it is hierarchical in nature.

Recently, a friend introduced me to a very successful accountant who was fed up with how uncollaborative and closed minded he found fellow accountants. He had heard about what I do as a consultant and wanted to meet me because he wanted to help accountants adopt the mindset, skill set, and behaviors on the Skills Delta, to inspire them to be client-centric and focused on client experience.

When I met with this accountant for the first time, I asked him if he had read any great books that had inspired him in the way that he wanted to inspire others. He replied point-blank, "*No, I hate those leadership business books that try to teach you how to be a better leader. I don't need them.*" So, I said, "*Would you consider reading my book?*" Again, he said, "*No.*" *Wow*, I thought to myself, *Okay, at least he's honest*. Then I asked, "*Well, have you ever even tried to lead a team to change their mindset, skill set, and behaviors?*" He said, "*No, but it is so needed in the accounting profession because accountants suck at communication, marketing, empathy, and self-awareness. They suck at all the things that our mutual friend says you train professionals to do so well.*" Finally, I said, "*So you haven't read anything about how to do this and you have never done it yourself. And you are saying that you refuse to learn from others and that you don't have your own method. And you won't even read my book, but you think you can start a movement to motivate accountants to adopt a new attitude, a new mindset, learn new skills and new behaviors?*" To which he responded, "*Yep.*"

This accountant's self-concept is so tied up with being a leader and not a follower it's holding him back. Not only does he lack self-awareness, but he also lacks humility. People who are humble do not consider themselves superior or to be in "hierarchical relationships with others" but instead "are oriented toward reciprocity in relationships."[50] Additionally, this accountant lacks curiosity (another key attribute on the Skills Delta). In Amy Edmondson's TED Talk mentioned previously, she points out that humility combined with curiosity is essential to creating the type of psychological safety individuals need to take risks and have the courage to trust others in collaborative problem-solving.[51] However, "we're hardwired to think we know[,]" and "it's hard to learn [from others] if you already know."[52] This accountant's lack of humility and curiosity prevents him from seeing (and valuing) what others can bring, and failing to account for that limits his ability to lead. He is not credible. He is not followable. Until this guy is inspired, he can't inspire others.

The sign of a true, adaptive, inclusive leader is the ability to follow, to stand up and risk following someone else as opposed to having to be the one who everyone else follows first. True leaders show their teams that they understand that leaders can't lead without followers and they orient themselves toward their followers.[53] As Derek Sivers's TED Talk "How to Start a Movement" makes clear, without the first follower, the original leader may be viewed as just a "lone nut."[54] Therefore, the first follower is actually *more* important than the leader because without the first follower, there is no movement—there is no cultural change.[55] A leader of none is not a leader. The first follower transforms the person (who starts a movement) into a leader and lowers the risk for the third, fourth, and fifth persons who follow, thereby increasing the number of people who join. Sivers makes his point by showing a video of a man at an outdoor concert who stands up on the lawn and begins to do a weird dance as everyone else remains seated, looking at him as if he is foolish.[56] Eventually, the first follower stands up and begins to join him, which piques interest and eventually turns the dance from foolishness to interesting. The second follower joins in and so on until the foolish folks are those few who refuse to get up and dance. The moral of the story is that to create "cultural change that sticks"[57] (as discussed in Chapter 4), leaders can sometimes lead as (if not more) effectively by following. As in a partner dance, the leader initiates the movement, but it is the follower who actively harnesses the energy and creates the momentum. But only a humble leader can be a follower. And it is also true that humbler leaders garner followers in spades. Research demonstrates that employees are more receptive to a humble leader's ideas and more committed to their visions (which are by nature more inclusive and reflective of the opinions of others).[58] Consistent with this, research also shows that teams are more effective when the leader is humble.[59] And if you are still struggling with this, consider the following.

Margaret Heffernan has this great TED Talk entitled "Forget the Pecking Order at Work."[60] She talks about a study on productivity conducted by evolutionary biologists, William M. Muir and Heng Wei Cheng.[61] Muir and Cheng, professors at Purdue University, study productivity by studying chickens, in part because productivity in chickens is easy to assess: you simply count the eggs. (Ironically, they are based at Purdue

University not Perdue Farms, the famous chicken processing company. And yes, that is a funny coincidence!) Muir and Cheng started with one flock of average productive chickens. They selected the most productive chickens (those that laid the most eggs) and put them in what they called the "super-flock" of chickens. They did this over six generations. They then compared the average flock to the super-flock. And guess what? The average flock was healthier than they were before (i.e., they were healthier without the super chickens), and they were *more productive* than the super-flock. Indeed, the super-flock had only three surviving chickens. The rest of the super chickens had been pecked to death. This study is one of many demonstrating that energy is wasted when there is a pecking order. When there is a star who is aggressively "eating" the largest share, it has a negative impact on all.[62] This is an especially tough lesson for many professional service providers to learn given that we are often rewarded for being super chickens. We profit from the business we bring in, and the hours that we bill are counted just like eggs.

For decades, corporate America has been following the super chicken model of recruiting top performers from competitors to help boost company revenues. Like a partner dance, however, this model fails without the follower. Boris Groysberg, Ashish Nanda, and Nitin Nohria's research proves just that.[63] They tracked stars across all types of professional services (e.g., law, management consulting, public relations, advertising, and investment banking) for 6 years. They found that the top performers were more likely to burn out when they moved from one company to another. Although they shine at first, they quickly fade. To determine why stars fade, why they were unable to maintain their success level, the trio of researchers completed another study of more than 1,000 top performers working at approximately 80 investment banks across the United States over an 8-year period.[64] This research confirmed the earlier findings: stars do not stay in their new organizations for long despite the large salaries and incentives that enticed them to move in the first place.[65] Even more surprising than their lack of longevity was the fact that the superstars' performance drops on average about 20 percent and does not rise back to prior levels even 5 years after their move.[66] Furthermore, the performance of the group to which the star joined dips significantly and the company's valuation decreases.[67]

The interesting part about this research, though, is the reason this occurs. And the reason is that success doesn't come to us alone. Accomplished professionals tend to believe that they (individually) are the main contributors to their company's or team's success and that they may be indispensable. Neither is true, of course, and research shows it. For example, one study of the performance of more than 2,000 mutual fund managers over a 6-year period found that 70 percent of the fund's performance was attributable to the manager's company and only 30 percent to the individual manager.[68] It was the institution's resources, processes, leadership, internal networks, training, size, and culture that were predominant factors in success—and in failure, such as when a star moved from one institution to another—that varied in these dimensions.[69] In addition to the institution, the team is key to a star's success. Groysberg et al.'s research shows that stars moving from one service firm to another are more successful when they move with their teams.[70] Research on chief legal officers at corporations listed on the S&P stock market index (that I co-conducted with Harvard Professors John Coates, Ashish Nanda, and David Wilkins) supports the theory that clients are moving away from hiring individual lawyers or law firms. Instead, the relevant unit of choice is teams and departments.[71] Perhaps this is why we are now seeing more and more teams of lawyers moving laterally from firm to firm. The following is a commonplace headline: "Breaking: Freshfields loses entire Paris real estate team to Jones Day."[72]

This appears to be true for individuals in varied lines of work, from lawyers to creative artists. Musicians who perform in bands, for example, tend to outlive those who are predominantly solo acts.[73] Think Bruce Springsteen and the E Street Band or Keith Richards and the Rolling Stones versus Michael Jackson, Elvis Presley, or Amy Winehouse. Although a lifestyle rife with drug and alcohol abuse plays a role, research by a team at Liverpool John Moores University in the United Kingdom studied 1,500 rock stars from North America and Europe over a 50-year period and found that solo stars were twice as likely to die young than those who were a part of a band.[74] Why? Musicians in bands have greater peer support, which can help stars better manage the rough, lonely, and temptation-filled lifestyle options that come with fame.[75]

Importantly, when leaders can step away from being super chickens and play the role of first follower, they have the power to transform those whom they follow into leaders. And frankly that's what great leaders do. They mentor, support, outwardly praise and recognize, and help develop their followers.[76] They work *with* as opposed to *above* followers, understanding that they can learn and grow from interacting with followers; and they act self-sacrificially.[77] They get inspired by inspiration and they follow it and others, and in turn, they inspire others to do the same. Consider this example: Researchers followed 218 marine recruits during a 32-week training program to determine if individuals who identify as followers may, perhaps counterintuitively, emerge as leaders. In their study, recruits were asked to rate whether they identified as leaders or followers five times over the training period. The recruits' commanders and peers also evaluated each recruit's leadership and followership tendencies. Perhaps unsurprisingly, those recruits who saw themselves as leaders were also more likely to be rated as leaders by their commanders. However, perhaps more surprisingly, it was the recruits who self-identified as followers and also were perceived as followers by their commanders who emerged as leaders among their peers in the peer evaluation. This study suggests, therefore, that there are different aspects of leadership, and these different aspects are recognized differently by others—depending on who they are and the role they play on the team. So, to be successful leaders, we may need to be seen as part of the team as opposed to set apart.[78] Leaders who are good at leading *and* following understand that they don't have all the answers and are flexible and good at adapting[79]—traits that, of course, are integral to the second tier on the Skills Delta. In fact, most leaders are followers by design and often report to another leader (e.g., we aren't all Bill Gates or Elon Musk or Steve Jobs). So, just as they need to know how to set goals and provide direction to others, leaders need to know how to take directions and pursue goals set by others.[80]

Moreover, the type of adaptive challenges facing our clients today require us to be both leaders and followers, that is, to lead when we don't have the formal authority and to follow others who may not have the formal authority. Research on adaptive leadership demonstrates that there is value in leading without authority. As Ron Heifetz, the expert on adaptive leadership, points out "the absence of authority enables one to deviate from the norms of authoritative decision making. Instead of providing answers that soothe, one can more readily raise questions that disturb. . . . *One has more latitude for creative deviance.*[81] Also, "operating with little or no authority places one closer to the detailed experiences of some of the stakeholders in the situation. One may lose the larger perspective but gain the fine grain of people's hopes, pains, values, habits, and history. One has frontline information."[82]

It is this very type of frontline information that makes innovators and adaptive leaders successful and that hammers home the point that if we hone the mindset, skill set, and attitudes on the Skills Delta, especially empathy, resilience, self-awareness, and humility, we can become the type of leaders that can identify and face the adaptive challenges of today and tomorrow, that can be both *"in* and *above* the fray" seeing the details but also the big picture.[83] As research indicates, with self-awareness we can get out of the way of ourselves; and with humility we can "refine, sharpen, and broaden [our] thinking, keep [our] mind[s] clear and open to the unlimited possibilities . . . contain selfishness, and prepare one for ethical decision making in real-world situations."[84] More than that, we can embrace the loss that comes with tough decisions that necessitate change[85] and help our teams do so as well and, as Heifetz recommends, at a rate they can bear.[86]

So, to repeat the answer: we need to be self-aware and humble at the same time. To return to where we started, the answer is to focus on ourselves as individual contributors, owners of the success of the teaming. We need to do so in a way that is not egotistical or selfish but instead (as the next chapter makes clear), with an Open Mind, Open Heart, and Open Door: The Three Rules of Engagement. But this can be very hard. Just as it is easier to learn a new language when we are younger, it is easier to learn these skills while we are in college. Plus, this type of training cannot be accomplished in a classroom or a concentrated 5-day course where participants are often like-minded and similarly situated, having little diversity in age, education, experience, or discipline, which is the exact opposite of what is needed for creative problem-solving. It takes time and multicultural, multidisciplinary teaming, hands-on doing, and practice. As Aristotle said, "For the things we have to learn before we can do them, we learn by doing them."[87] Moreover, learning by doing them is made even harder because it is a matter of retraining rather than just training. To adopt the mindset, skill set, and behaviors of an innovator and adaptive leader requires professional service providers to unlearn some of their own—especially those attitudes that prevent them from honing what are sometimes referred to as "soft skills" but are so hard to master. As Gloria Steinem aptly stated, "The first problem for all of us, men and women, is not to learn, but to unlearn."[88]

How should *you* start the unlearning? Well, first of all, you already started by being open enough to read this book. So, what's next? Ideally, you would go on a 4-month innovation journey with a multidisciplinary team in LawWithoutWalls or through your own organization or firm. But even before you do that, there are simple actions you should take first.

Start by following others. Follow their writing, their podcasts, their talks. Follow other leaders in your organization. Follow people who might not as quickly be followed, or recognized as leaders, either because they are moving against the current, or because they are more junior or less experienced. Second, follow the Three Rules of Engagement (described in the next chapter) to enhance and finesse your adaptive, inclusive leadership style.

💬...Reflection Point As discussed, self-awareness is an essential ingredient to great leadership and teaming. To aid in this, conduct a *Delta-Skills Vision Exercise* among your team as follows:

Take a moment to consider the Skills Delta in Figure 2.5. Which two qualities or attributes or skills are in your sweet spot and that you can commit to bringing better next time you collaborate with your team? Write these down on a sheet of paper. Which two can you commit to honing over the next 4 months? Write these down on a sheet of paper. Next, reflect and write down WHY you want to hone these new skills or attributes or qualities, that is, what difference will it make and for whom? Ask everyone on your team to do the same. Then schedule a virtual team meeting to review together. In preparation, open up some type of virtual whiteboard (e.g., Google Jamboard, Miro, or Mural) and, as shown below, draw two triangles with three levels each (corresponding to the Skills Delta). Label the one on the left "What We Got" and the one on the right "What We Will Hone," as shown in Figure 5.1 below. Then, during the meeting have everyone fill out four virtual Post-it® notes with their initials with each of the four qualities or skills or attributes they selected and have them

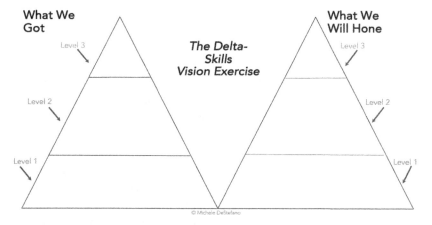

FIG. 5.1. *Delta-Skills Vision Exercise* Image.

place the notes in the correct triangle on the correct level on the virtual white-board. Then, have each individual share in one minute or less. (As discussed, in Chapter 9, we won't take the time to work on our team if teaming takes too much time!). Then, take a moment of silence for everyone to reflect on the team's strengths and weaknesses. Now discuss how you will fill in the gaps and how this information might help the team better leverage some of the team members' strengths. Perhaps, you might even consider moving some tasks and roles around based on this new information.

CHAPTER 6

The Three Rules of Engagement: Transforming Leadership Style and Enhancing Collaboration

> "*What you do speaks so loud that I cannot hear what you say.*"
> —Ralph Waldo Emerson[1]

As you will learn when you reach my bio at the end of this book, my very first paying job was as a mini-magician. I learned three important lessons from that job. First, making magic is, at best, tricky. Second, lots of people are born skeptical (and remain skeptical—especially professional service providers like lawyers).[2] Third, I love motivating people to change the way they see the world, think about the world, and the way they behave. Convincing people to suspend disbelief is really, really hard (i.e., tricky), but that's what this chapter is designed to do. My number one goal is to change your minds and open your hearts so that you see, think, and feel differently about collaboration and innovation, and most importantly, so that you can begin to hone skills and attributes in Level 2 of the Skills Delta—which will in turn change how you approach (and attempt to lead) collaboration and innovation efforts at your firm or company.

This is not to say that honing the skills and attributes in the second level of the Skills Delta won't be difficult. Just the opposite. It will be as hard as making magic. This is due, in part, to existing gaps in certain skills and attributes that all senior leaders have and may be unaware of having. Indeed, "the further up the organizational ladder people progress, the less feedback they are apt to receive. But senior leaders need coaching too, particularly around team behaviors."[3] This is because many professional service providers were not trained in adaptive leadership or change management, that is, they were not trained on the skills and attributes in the second level of the Skills Delta.[4] In keeping with that, a recent global study by McKinsey of 1,500 companies across a representative sample of industries found that few business leaders demonstrate the positive behaviors (found in the second level of the Skills Delta) that can instill the environment essential to an innovative and collaborative climate.[5] Uncoincidentally, the most important leadership qualities involve emotional intelligence and interpersonal skills, such as integrity, empathy, compassion, humility, communication, and the ability to listen, inspire, influence, and take risks.[6]

The difficulty in honing those Level 2 skills is also due, in part, to simple human nature.

First, humans are prone to believe that after they have done something a certain way for a long period of time, it must be good.[7] And the longer we do things a certain way the more we believe that it must be a good way to do things. So, changing the way we do things means stopping what you believe is working and has passed the test of time. Attempting to change our behaviors might seem illogical especially when we are successful professionally. If we are doing things the same way and continue to make more and more money, why change?

Second, successful senior professionals like to know *how* to do things and do them competently. If they are asked to change how they do things, to lead, team, and collaborate differently, this means they will be in a state of ambiguity, having to exhibit new behaviors that they are unfamiliar with (which can create a lack of confidence and fear of failure).[8]

Third, research shows that we are born selfish. It's true! And this means collaboration and inclusive leadership skills are not part of our nature. Have you ever heard of that saying: *strategy eats culture for breakfast*? Well, Carlos Valdes-Dapena says our individual achievement motivation eats the vague goal of collaborating for breakfast.[9] He writes that professionals often think they are collaborating when what they are really doing is coordinating or, worse yet, they are in a state of parallel play, like young children.[10] This is a problem given that what we want to achieve in the second level of the Skills Delta is proactive co-collaboration. However, collaboration requires self-less-ness, and it is exhausting. John Amaechi describes collaboration as

> . . . *incredibly energy expensive because it is a commitment to a perpetual state of calculated self-less-ness . . . [and] allowing yourself to have a percentage of your energy that is always going to be available to support someone else . . . to augment somebody else's position even if it means personally inconveniencing yourself. . . . It's constant vigilance . . . proactive connectedness, this idea that you've got a constant sonar that sweeps through your team so that you know ahead of time when and what kind of support a teammate might need.*[11]

So I get that asking professional service providers to follow the Three Rules of Engagement to change how they work, to collaborate on multidisciplinary teams, is a HUGE ask. When the problem requires collaboration and adopting an innovator's mindset, tons of professional service providers would prefer to work around the problem than face it— much like ants do. If you take a rock and plop it in the middle of an ant pile, they just go right around it, marching around the problem. A great scene from the movie *A Bug's Life* brings to life this preference for doing things the same way. The ants are marching in single file carrying bits of food toward their home when a huge leaf falls in front of them. The leading ant stops abruptly and screams *"I'm lost!!! Where's the line?"* This creates panic for all the following ants who begin to scream: *"Where do we go? Help!!"* The conductor ant, Mr. Soil, hurries down the hill toward them saying *"Do not panic. Do not panic! We are trained professionals. Now, stay calm. We are going around the leaf."* The original leading ant questions with fear in his voice: *"A-a- a-around the leaf? Uh, I don't think we can do that."* The conductor says *"Nonsense, this is nothing compared to the twig of '93!"* and prods them along saying, *"That's it, that's it, good! You are doing great! There you go. There you go. Watch my eyes. Don't look away."* Finally, when all the ants are around the leaf and back in single file, the ants are beyond grateful and relieved to be back to the way things were and doing things the way they always did.

I have just listed three reasons why following the Three Rules of Engagement will be hard. However, note that missing from those reasons is the contention that people are *innately* resistant to change. Indeed, research on change management efforts suggests that believing in an "inherent resistance to change" may be a "fundamental flaw" to change efforts of any kind.[12] One group of researchers felt so strongly about this that they suggested that all bodies of work that include the words "Overcoming Resistance to Change" in the title should be titled: "Overcoming Perfectly Natural Reactions to Poor Management."[13] It is essential that you *believe* that you can change (and that *people* can and will change). So, check your attitude to avoid this self-fulling prophecy.[14]

Habits are really hard to break, and new habits are really hard to create (especially those that require us to be self-less!).[15] The good news is that this chapter is designed to make both of those actions easier. It provides the Three Rules of Engagement any leader can follow to help shore up their weaknesses on the Skills Delta and improve their client-centricity, collaboration, and culture-creation skills. These rules are having an Open Mind, an Open Heart, and an Open Door. Before you yield to the proverbial eye roll you feel coming on, give me a chance to explain—and I promise these rules have NOTHING to do with religion.

I call these the "Rules" of Engagement because I'm a lawyer by training and lawyers are taught to think like lawyers, that is, with rules and strategy. In law school, we are taught to construct syllogisms or legal rubrics by connecting different rulings from different cases and putting them together under one analytical framework. I developed these rules the same way. I collected different theories from different types of research and put them together in one framework: Open Mind, Open Heart, and Open Door.[16] These rules are important to learn even if—or especially if—you are a leader and you *yourself* do not want to innovate. There are two reasons for this.

First, you can't lead your team, department, or firm to collaborate or innovate if you don't know what you are asking of them and are not exemplifying the mindset and behavior you want them to emulate. As Ralph Waldo Emerson stated, "What you do speaks so loudly" that others "cannot hear what you say." This may seem obvious, but I think it is worth repeating. I have led multidisciplinary teams of professional service providers of all kinds in creative problem-solving and developing innovations for 14 years. What I have learned is that it cannot just be about inspiring others to be creative—it cannot just be about leading *for* creativity. Instead, it must be about leading *with* creativity. Some may believe it is sufficient to promote and support and even incentivize collaboration, creativity, and innovation in their firm. But as the director of knowledge and innovation delivery at an international law firm (who is not a lawyer) remarked, "It is not just being on a soapbox making the case for change [it is] working together . . . to implement change."[17] Research demonstrates this is true. Leaders who exemplify the desired behavior and promote the positive parts of change are more likely to positively affect their team members' motivation to, adoption of, and readiness for change.[18] In fact, according to sociologist Dr. Jennifer Cross, the number one predictor that influences behaviors is seeing others exemplifying the behavior.[19]

At this point, I likely still have skeptical readers questioning why in the world they should be reading these silly Rules of Engagement let alone following them. My response? Suspend your disbelief. Even if you don't want to innovate or you will never attempt to innovate or you don't want to hear about innovation, you should follow these Three Rules. Why? Because (as repeated multiple times) the focus is changing from *what* professional service providers do to *how* they do it. If you follow these Three Rules (professionally and/or personally), you will be better at listening, teaming, and creative problem-solving. And you will be a more inclusive, adaptive leader.

The best news about the Three Rules of Engagement is that in the mere act of following them, we adopt the feelings and behaviors that go with them and, in doing so, we may end up liking the rules, even if we didn't at first. Dr. Wiseman calls this the "As if Principle."[20] Common sense suggests that when we feel happy, we smile. There are myriads of examples and research that the opposite is true as well. If we smile as if we are happy, we eventually feel happy. So, if we behave as if we want to follow the rules and as if we already have an Open Mind, Open Heart, and Open Door, eventually we feel as though we do; and we will enjoy it even if we set out with the opposite view. In fact, our views change in the process. When we are persuaded to do something, we are convinced we don't or won't enjoy, psychology research shows that we often end up justifying our actions and convincing ourselves that what we are doing is not that bad—and eventually, it is even okay. So even if you are skeptical at this moment, try out these Three Rules. You may end up convinced that following them isn't so bad after all. And as you get inspired, you will, in turn, inspire others to follow them as well.

However, given that we are born selfish, it is really hard *not* to revert to our more primitive, innate selfish ways.[21] So think of these Three Rules

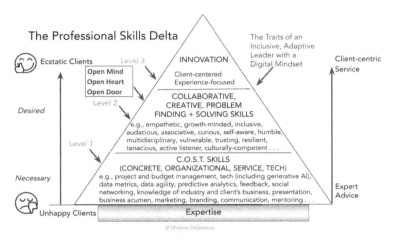

FIG. 6.1. The Three Rules of Engagement and the Professional Skills Delta.

as a diet, a "collaboration diet," if you will, and the Three Rules are (and will feel) like eating vegetables when you really want the fries. I promise if you follow these Three Rules of Engagement, you will master the second level of the Skills Delta (Figure 6.1) and see a difference in how your friends, family, colleagues, and clients respond to you. By following these rules you will instill trust, and trust is the most essential ingredient to good teaming. In fact, you can't lead to results without it.[22] However, you must trust not only others, but also yourself—which requires you to be vulnerable[23] (another key attribute on the Skills Delta), which these Three Rules of Engagement will also lead you to be.

Please suspend your disbelief as we run through the Three Rules. If this is new for you, you can read a longer version of The Three Rules of Engagement in Part II of *Legal Upheaval*. The Three Rules of Engagement overview will be briefer here—just enough to remind us what we as individuals can do to up our game in the second level of the Skills Delta, to be proactive co-collaborators, team players, and leaders.

A. Rule #1: Open Mind

> *"A mind is like a parachute. It doesn't work*
> *if it is not open."*
>
> —Frank Zappa

Let's start with Open Mind. There are 3 key aspects to this rule.

1. Say "Yes, and . . ."

Most successful professional service providers learned how to say *no* a long time ago. There are times we have to say no to our clients to protect them. Our bandwidth is also limited, so to get things done, we must be selective about how we use our time. Learning to say no (the right way) is a necessary skill.[24] The problem with being good at saying no, however, is that we lose the benefits of saying yes.

The first element or foundational principle of Open Mind is the power of "Yes, and . . . ." As part of our training at Leo Burnett Company, we took improv classes at Second City in Chicago. Yes, that is where Jerry Seinfeld was trained, and no, we weren't in his classes! Leo Burnett paid for its employees to attend improv classes because its leaders believed that learning how to improvise on stage would make us better listeners and communicators with our clients. It did. The backbone of improv, the one rule that everyone must follow to create a scene, is listening to a conversation or suggestion and saying, "Yes, and . . . ." If you don't say or use these words, you can actually literally stop the scene on stage. Now, of course, some professional service providers are excellent at stopping the scene (the conversation) in real life, because other than "it depends," their favorite words seem to be "no" and "but"—which I will tell you to erase from your vocabulary going forward.

Here's how "Yes, and . . ." works. Let's say we are videoconferencing and I say: "*I have this apple and this glass of water. Do you want to go on a virtual picnic with me where we can eat the apple and drink the water?*" And you say, "*No. I hate apples. And I'm so sick of Zooming.*" You essentially stop the scene and all collaboration. If you had instead practiced "Yes, and . . ." you might have said something like, "*Yes, and I'm going to bring my vodka and tonic. And while you eat your apple, I will drink my vodka and tonic and it's gonna be a fantastic, albeit virtual, picnic.*" That way, you built on my idea. You added to it. Now you might think, this "Yes and . . ." thing is just a trick. You just use it instead of "no" and put what you want to say after the words "Yes, and . . . ." But that's where you are wrong. When you say the words "Yes, and . . ." to something (especially when you *really* want to say no), it makes you stop and think, "*Oh no! What did I just say yes to?*" And when we stop like that, we replay what the person actually said, and then we *really* hear them. We attempt to really listen to figure out what they want or need that is behind the words that they said. This is so very important because evidently we only hear about 25 percent of what people say.[25] In fact, as we have all experienced, most of the time when people are talking, we are just thinking about what we want to say,[26] waiting for our turn to talk.[27] "Yes, and . . ." actually makes us listen (or re-hear in our minds), absorb what other people say, and respond in a way that lets them know we actually heard them—even if you disagree with them. As Daniel H. Pink explains in his book *To Sell Is Human*, we spend too much time listening for something and not enough time just listening and letting the scenario unfold, like the actors do in improvisation.[28] Pink explains that doctors tend to interrupt their patients in the first 18 seconds. Just as a doctor can't diagnose an illness in a patient if they don't listen to the patient, a professional service provider can't solve the problem (or even understand what the problem is) if they don't listen to the client. This is why I tell all the professionals that I teach in executive education programs and everyone who participates in LawWithoutWalls to erase the words *no* and *but* from their vocabulary and to start every sentence with "Yes, and . . . ." I tell them—and I tell you now—that doing this one thing, saying "Yes, and . . ." will change the relationships in your life because you listen differently.

According to Otto Scharmer, there are four levels of listening.[29] The first level he calls "downloading." At this level we are simply confirming what we already believe. Someone is talking and you simply respond, "uh huh . . . uh huh" as if to signal "yes, I'm listening." But at best, we are just agreeing with what we already believe is true. We know this is true because the moment we hear something in conflict, we pop our heads up out of our nodding reverie and say *"Wait, what?!!! Your car was STOLEN?"*

This leads us to the second level, which is called "factual listening." In this mode, we focus on what is different than expected, that is, we debate (out loud or in our heads) what someone is saying because it conflicts with what we believed, assumed, or expected. You can imagine that legal professionals are really good at this level. What's interesting about this level is that evidently our minds get rid of things that don't confirm what we believe. It is for this reason that Darwin would write down the observations that contradicted his theories. He didn't trust his mind not to purposefully forget them![30] What's also really interesting about this level is that although we "hear" the conflicting information, we don't "feel" it. This is evidenced by our response to the stolen car, which was not *"Oh no! that must have been terrifying to have your car stolen,"* or

"Are you ok? Was anyone hurt?" This is what the third level of listening is all about: empathy.

At the "empathic listening" level, we are listening with an Open Heart, the next Rule of Engagement. As for the last and fourth level of listening, I tell the law firm partners in Harvard Law School's Executive Education program on Leadership, *"We don't need to even go there because it is way out of our league right now. Let's focus on mastering the third level first."* That usually gets a laugh, but, inevitably, someone will ask, *"So what was that fourth level of listening?"* Scharmer calls it "generative listening." He explains that at this level we are connecting to the possibility of the moment. It is more than just being in *flow* (discussed later in the chapter).[31] It is as if we are in "flow" *with* the other person and this is when true collaboration and co-creation can abound.

It is in the third and fourth levels of listening that "Yes, and . . ." really helps us build on each other's ideas, a skill intrinsic to creative ideation and one that some people are naturally better at—women, for example, excel here. When IDEO, a design and consulting firm, was helping Nike create a new shoe, it brought some children together to help brainstorm, but it separated the boys and the girls. The girls came up with four times as many ideas as the boys. This is because the girls built on each other's ideas. *"How about if we made the shoes pink?" "Yes, and . . . how about if we made the pink part butterflies?" "Yes, and . . . maybe the butterflies could flutter as the shoe moves." "Yes, and . . . they could flutter and light up at the same time."* The boys, on the other hand, cared more about talking about their ideas than about listening to the ideas of others. Our job as leaders of teams is to help people let go of the idea that ideas can or should be owned and instead to teach our teams how to build on each other's ideas with "Yes, and . . ." so we can find *the* idea, not *my* or *your* idea. This is why my closest friend from college, founder of a successful venture capital firm, won't sign NDAs. If an entrepreneur asks for an NDA before pitching an idea, it is an immediate red flag. Clearly, this entrepreneur hasn't bounced his idea off enough people to get to "the" idea.

2. Think Silly Not Stupid (and Let Go of Preconceptions)

The second aspect of the Open Mind rule is: Think Silly not Stupid (and Let Go of Preconceptions). In my family, because my sister has Down's syndrome, we weren't allowed to use the word "stupid." My mom would always correct us: *"Say silly not stupid, Michele."* Of course, I would roll my eyes and say through clenched teeth, *"That is such a stupid rule"*—and be sent to my room. But now I think my family's rule was brilliant. Here's why. I'm pretty sure most senior professional service providers think other people's ideas (including or especially mine) are stupid. When I teach team building exercises or ideation techniques to professional service providers, I can see it on their faces. Although many have perfected the under the eyelid eyeroll, most of them do not have great poker faces. This is something I point out because the *"that's so stupid"* face is a collaboration killer. I point out that if they just replaced the word "stupid" with the word "silly," their facial expressions would change dramatically—along with how they categorize the idea. You might ask: How does that help? If you search the internet right now for the silliest ideas ever, you will find that many have turned into great inventions (some of which were unintentional). The list is incredibly long and includes products and services like silly putty, chia pets, the slinky, pet rocks, and Twitter (now X).[32] This is true in part because silliness is tied to creativity. Research shows that if a group is shown a funny video right before an ideation session, they are more creative.[33] Swapping stupid for silly helps us have an open mind and wash away our preconceptions.

Having a think silly, not stupid mindset might also help us to let go of other preconceptions about hierarchy and who can and should add value and when. The professional services marketplace is filled with hierarchies. There is a pecking order (especially at law firms). These hierarchies, for whatever good they may do in terms of preserving the traditions of an organization, stop the flow of communication. They create preconceptions about who should speak and when—protocols that subconsciously dictate the value of any person's contributions. When we have the mindset that even the silliest, craziest ideas lead to better ideas, we are more open to hearing what others say no matter their level of expertise (no matter if the client is in the room). Yet, in most professional settings, the most senior people often speak the most and speak first.[34] When they do this, they skew the rest of the meeting and prevent creative thinking. According to research by Cass R. Sunstein and Reid Hastie, people generally follow the statements and actions of the person who speaks first in a meeting, and if that first speaker has power, people are more likely to silence themselves.[35] This is due to "cascade effects" and "reputational pressures," which can lead to groupthink—the opposite of the kind of thinking and collaboration we want for creative ideas to thrive.

In two different studies, joint researchers at Carnegie Mellon and MIT studied what makes teams smarter or more successful.[36] One of the three characteristics identified was that team members contributed equally to discussions over the course of the meeting day or project.[37] In other words, team discussions were not dominated by only a few[38] and, just as importantly, not by the most senior few. This same elimination of hierarchy has been identified as one of the four principles that is key to the Toyota Production System, an immersion program that trains managers.[39] New managers work on the manufacturing line with production workers, breaking down the walls between manager and employee and between client and staff. In the PSF context, given the hierarchies and incentive structures, partners might have to be explicit about their intentions of equal airtime and require it. I interviewed a partner who admitted, "Most of my best ideas are not my ideas. They come from the associates. But I have to force them to put their ideas on the table and make them speak at meetings . . . to ensure that others do not crowd out their voices."[40] I'm not suggesting that a leader *always* needs to speak last, or the least, or that a leader should *never* speak first. To the contrary, if a leader speaks first in a way that shows humility and vulnerability,[41] they may be able to make space for others to do the same. Instead, let go of the preconception that talking time should relate to hierarchy and embrace "Yes, and . . ." and the silly, not stupid mindset.

3. Make Yourself Lucky (and Have a Growth Mindset)

The third aspect of Open Mind is: Make Yourself Lucky. Research on lucky people demonstrates they are not lucky by accident. They have different, more positive attitudes about life events and slim chances. Lucky people follow their gut, expect positive outcomes, look at the bright side of failure, and maintain a good attitude when things go wrong. Compared to unlucky people, lucky people are more likely to see and take advantage of slim chances because unlucky people are too focused on looking for something specific.

Daniel Simons, coauthor of *The Invisible Gorilla*,[42] is famous for his *Monkey Business Illusion* video on YouTube. He asks people to watch a video of a basketball game and count the number of times the ball is passed by one team. During the video, a gorilla walks into the middle of the game. Evidently, only about 50 percent of people see the gorilla. This can be attributed to what is called inattention blindness, an inability to notice something when you are not looking for it.[43]

This is where some readers might be putting on the brakes because it sounds as though we can't be focused (or goal oriented) and open-minded (or lucky) at the same time. How do we square this with our need to focus to be successful?[44] The good news is that, as mentioned above, we can train our brains. We can train them to turn off. For example, we have trained our brains to unsee banner ads, one of the most popular advertising tools. Banner blindness, according to advertising research, occurs when a person is surfing the net for a specific purpose—to find something.[45] But we can also train our brains to turn on. According to psychologists Chabris and Simons, we can do this simply by accepting (and remembering) that we all suffer from what they call the "illusion of attention"[46] (i.e., we believe we are seeing what is before us because we aren't aware of what we don't see).[47] That is, we can miss important details even when they are right in front of us. Staying conscious of this makes us less apt to presume that we are seeing all things or even things as they are. According to Dr. Wiseman's studies, by practicing certain habits of lucky people (in mindset and behavior), we can overcome the *Monkey Business Illusion*—and make ourselves lucky (or luckier).[48]

Another key attribute of lucky people is that they actually approach and experience things differently.[49] They have what Carol Dweck calls a growth mindset as opposed to a fixed mindset.[50] People with fixed mindsets can be successful as well, of course. They might figure out early on what they are good at and do it over and over again, keep getting better at it, and keep making more money doing it—does that sound like anyone you know? Any law firm partners, or accountants, or even any famous people? As we do the same thing over and over and get better at it and become more prosperous doing it, however, we become less open to doing anything new or different—let alone taking any risk. Why would we do something different when we know we're good at what we're doing and no one wants to look incompetent? Additionally, we become less open to feedback because we *know* we are good at this. It must have been *that* associate we brought along that caused the issue. People with a growth mindset, on the other hand, don't believe they are just born good at certain things or that our IQ limits us in any way. Instead, they believe talents, abilities, and intelligence can be developed.[51] People with a growth mindset are not, therefore, scared to take on challenges; they are better at thinking "maybe" and less defensive when receiving feedback and they "feel empowered to learn, innovate, and create."[52] The good news is, a growth mindset can be honed,[53] and lucky people "get" that!

The other thing that lucky people "get" is the ability to connect dots that might not otherwise be connected. As Louis Pasteur famously said, "chance favors the prepared mind." Lucky people prepare their minds for chance, increasing the likelihood of connecting the dots when it matters most. Consider Alexander Fleming, who is credited with discovering penicillin by "lucky accident."[54] But Fleming wasn't "lucky" to discover penicillin. He had spent his life studying cures for diseases and while studying influenza, went away on vacation for two weeks. Upon his return, Fleming saw that a mold had formed on a staphylococcus culture plate. He realized that the mold that had formed prevented the growth of staphylococcus. After that, he did many more tests to finally develop penicillin. In other words, by searching into the accident and connecting what went wrong to his existing knowledge from investigating antibacterial substances to cure diseases, he was able to get to what we talked about before in Chapter 3, "the adjacent possible."[55]

The "adjacent possible" certainly does not equate to saying that *anything* is possible. In fact, only certain things are possible based on what has happened in the past, what is happening in the present, and what choices are made—what is adjacent, in other words. Johnson describes the process as a magically expanding house: "You begin in a room with four doors, each leading to a new room that you haven't visited yet. Those four rooms are the adjacent possible" opening up yet new rooms to explore.[56] My teenage son would describe it like Minecraft, a computer game in which you make interconnected rooms, cities, or galaxies out of virtual blocks and doorways and paths. But how do you get to the adjacent possible? Ironically, it's not that different from mastering Minecraft.[57] The answer is courage, curiosity, teamwork, and associating. According to research by Jeff Dyer, Hal Gregersen, and Clayton M. Christensen, associating is one of the five essential skills of disruptive innovators (the other four are questioning, observing, networking, and experimenting.)[58] Association is the act of connecting things that might otherwise not be connected—even crazy things. Steve Jobs said famously, "Creativity is just connecting things."

Here's an example of associative thinking (and keeping an Open Mind): In the early 2000s, the city of Glasgow hung blue lights on the streets to make them prettier. After the lights had been hung, crime decreased by approximately 9 percent. Although a causal connection couldn't be proven, Nara, Japan, decided to try it in its town—not to beautify the streets, but to see if crime would decrease. It did. Continuing to move along an associative track, the city of Yokohama thought that if blue lights could help reduce crime, it might help reduce that city's problem with track-jumping suicides, a real problem in modern-day Japan.[59] So the Keihin Electric Express Railway Co. changed the color of eight lights on the ends of platforms at Gumyo-ji Station (which had multiple suicides per year). The result? Suicide attempts went down to zero.

Even though the value of such associative thinking can be demonstrated in myriad ways, research shows that senior executives—especially at large companies—don't connect different things. According to Dyer et al., executives are great at analyzing, executing, implementing, and delivering results against defined goals.[60] They claim, in contrast to innovators, however, that senior execs don't know how to associate, which, as mentioned above, is one of the core attributes of innovators: how to connect the unexpected, such as a cancer tracker to a puffer fish (discussed below). As mentioned above, you can move from a fixed to a growth mindset, and you can learn to associate and think differently with practice.

B. Rule #2: Open Heart

"Now here is my secret. A very simple secret:
it is only with the heart that one can see rightly;
what is essential is invisible to the eye."

—*Antoine de Saint-Exupéry*, The Little Prince[61]

The second Rule of Engagement is Open Heart. It's the hardest one for me and I struggle in each of its three main aspects.

1. Empathy

The first facet is all Empathy. Empathy is what promotes bonding among team members and creates psychological safety, which is more important to a team's success in collaborative problem-solving than the team's expertise, ability, efficiency, or IQ.[62]

This won't surprise many readers but research on lawyers shows that compared to other professionals, we don't just test low on empathy—we test REALLY low on empathy, period. But lawyers are not alone. Other professional service providers, such as accountants and engineers, also notoriously test low on empathy[63] and are viewed as lacking empathy and warmth.[64] Evidently, there is good *reason* for that. Accountants and engineers, like lawyers, rely on analytical *reasoning* to make decisions. This is critical because research conducted by Case Western University shows that when we engage the network of neurons used for analysis, our brains actually suppress our ability to empathize.[65] It's one or the other. Since we can't be empathetic and analytic at the same time, it is no wonder that professional service providers who rely on analytics to do their jobs engage the analytic network over the empathetic when presented with a critical task.

This is a bit disheartening because empathy is the key to innovation. Being able to empathize with the target audience, the person whose problem you are solving, is essential to solving the problem and seeing the perspective of the audience experiencing the problem. It is the core tenet of human-centered design. Think for a moment about the movie *Joy*. *Joy* is a story about a working-class, divorced mother with two children who developed the first self-wringing mop (with a removable head). It is only because Joy truly understood and empathized with women having to wring dirty mops by hand that she was able to create a mop as it should be. In *Joy*, the person who created the solution was the person who experienced the problem. The goal in innovation is to be able to experience the problem of the user or consumer to the same degree that they experience it. Successful innovators, design thinkers, and creative problem-solvers are empathetic. They put themselves in the shoes of the consumer.

Empathy is essential not only to solving problems but also to preventing them, especially when collaborating on multidisciplinary teams. Various studies, including those undertaken by MIT and Carnegie Mellon identify empathy as one of the top characteristics of smart, successful teams.[66] Teams are more effective when they are more socially sensitive to each other (that is, when they can sense how others feel by reading verbal and nonverbal cues and relate to each other's differing vantage points and perspectives). The research shows that this ability to infer about other people's mental states, often called "theory of mind" (ToM) is also important for teams working virtually.[67] Those team members often need to be able to sense how others feel from nonvisual communications such as texts and email. There's also research conducted by Cass Sunstein that demonstrates teams fail when members misread or receive incorrect informational signals from each other. Therefore, we have our work cut out for us given that professional service providers often work on global teams.[68] This means that we must be good at both receiving and sending nonverbal messages (in person and virtually); otherwise, the team will not feel safe, and that can overshadow everything the team is trying to accomplish.

The good news is that with a growth mindset and the right kind of effort, we can improve our empathy, albeit slowly.[69]

The ability to be able to improve empathy is key to relationships of all kinds (including those with clients). Empathy (and projecting empathetic concern) is critical to communicating warmth and building rapport and trust. Stephen Covey, author of *The Speed of Trust*, argues that trust impacts speed and cost. With trust we enhance the speed of business and lower the costs.[70] Without it, the opposite is true. Trust also enhances the likelihood that a client will follow a professional service provider's advice. However, research suggests that accountants, engineers, and lawyers, instead of being viewed as warm and competent, are viewed as cold, calculating. and untrustworthy.[71] This is tough because research by Professor Amy Cuddy reveals that people make judgments and decisions about people they meet within seconds based first on a person's warmth.[72] Warmth was found to be more important than competence or imagined status. When someone is perceived as warm, they are also perceived as trustworthy. It is only when people trust us that they will share their true problems. This, of course, ties back to listening (which we talked about in Open Mind). If, as Simon Sinek states, "Listening is not the act of hearing the words spoken but the art of understanding the meaning behind those words . . . and creating an environment where the other feels heard,"[73] empathy and warmth become even more important. Brené Brown, an expert on leading with empathy, vulnerability, and courage, has a fantastic video that brings to life how sympathy is very different from empathy.[74] She explains that "[e]mpathy fuels connection. Sympathy drives disconnection." When we are empathetic, we listen without judgment, we try to relate to what the other person is feeling. And it requires courage and vulnerability because we have to connect with the other person. To do that, we have to reach inside ourselves to feel what the other person is feeling.[75] When we are sympathetic (vs empathetic), however, we seek to make the person feel better. We start sentences with "at least."[76] In Brené Brown's video one of the characters says, "I had a miscarriage" and the sympathetic friend says, "*at least* you know you can get pregnant." Then the character says, "I think my marriage is falling apart." And the friend responds, "*at least* you have a marriage." Sympathy, essentially, is a cop out, a way for us to avoid the messy, tough moments that empathy requires. Empathy is "tell me more" as William Ury is famous for recommending.[77] Sympathy is what Brene Brown calls "silver lining it"[78] or trying to fix things, which leads to the second facet of Open Heart.

2. Helping Not Fixing

The second aspect of the Open Heart rule is Helping not Fixing. Research shows that one of the best ways to contribute to a team as an individual is to be helpful.[79] It may be obvious, but it's not as easy as it seems, and it requires yet another kind of empathy and group awareness. Shel Silverstein knew this well. He writes in a poem:

> *Some kind of help is the kind of help*
> *that helping's all about.*
> *And some kind of help is the kind of help*
> *We all can do without.*[80]

I'm sure many readers have had experiences wherein someone (likely someone more senior or experienced than you) tried to help you and their "help" was anything but helpful. This is a common trap for professional service providers because our job is often to fix things, but fixing something is very different from helping someone fix something. When we help someone, we listen with empathy (that third level of listening we talked about earlier) and we offer open-ended help—not help tied to our area of expertise. As leaders, we need to remember that sometimes coaching may be more helpful than fixing and that it can lead to higher satisfaction among our teams. Indeed, the idea that leaders should coach as opposed to fix is one of the four lessons identified as integral to Toyota's production system noted above—and is also one of the key lessons often missed by corporations trying to mimic its success.[81] So keep an Open Heart to helping because sometimes buying a pizza for a group that is grappling with a work conundrum is more helpful to the team than the leader coming in and giving (or pushing or requiring) a certain solution or way forward. But holding back from trying to fix things or force your way forward takes some of the other skills on the Skills Delta (as we mentioned earlier in discussing the 5 Whys), such as courage, humility, and vulnerability. The courage to take a risk on others solving the problem takes humility in that you are not assuming you, yourself, have (or own) all the right answers. This makes you vulnerable, but according to research by Brené Brown, leaders are absolutely off the mark in thinking that vulnerability is a sign of weakness.[82] Instead, it shows a willingness to remain curious,[83] to focus on asking the right questions.

It also shows an understanding of this famous quote by Peter Drucker: "The important and difficult job is never to find the right answers. It is to find the right question."[84] This is because when we jump to fix, we are not listening (and not empathizing), and we risk solving for symptoms instead of root causes.

There is this great video called "It's Not About the Nail" by Jason Headly. It opens with a woman sitting on a couch complaining to her boyfriend about the pounding pain in her forehead. At first, the viewer can't see all of the woman. We hear her speak but only see a part of her face However, we see her boyfriend's face as he is trying desperately to hold his tongue while the woman describes the pain in her forehead in great detail. Then the woman turns, and we see that she has a nail in her forehead. As soon as she is done explaining how she is feeling, the boyfriend points out that she has a nail in her head and suggests getting it out. Of course, she explodes and tells him that he always does that. He always rushes to fix things instead of really, really listening to her and trying to help her. "*Can you just listen?*" she begs. That is what she needs, she pleads. He says, "*I'm just trying to point out that maybe the nail is causing this . . .*" Then she gets even angrier. Finally, he acquiesces, and we watch him struggle (big time) to simply listen and to resist the urge to pull the nail out of her head as she continues to talk about her pain. It isn't until he stops trying to fix the problem and instead listens and says compassionately, "*That sounds really hard,*" that she eventually thanks him for helping.

This video is a lesson about empathy and the importance of listening, as we discussed earlier. It is also a lesson about helping and how, sometimes, fixing is not helping. This may seem foreign to many who watch this video. Of course, it is the nail in her head that is causing her "sweaters to snag" as she complains about. But until we understand "why" there is a nail in her head, we won't solve the problem. If she puts the nail in every morning on her own, pulling it out isn't going to fix the problem. Further, in rushing to solve, we might cause another problem or unintended consequence. In the nail scenario, if the man pulls the nail out of her head, at worst she might bleed to death. At best, they might just get blood on the couch. This is yet another reason why asking the 5 Whys is essential to problem finding, empathy, and listening (as discussed in Chapters 2 and 3). By being humble, curious, and empathetic, we can provide "the kind of help that helping's all about."

3. Cultural Competency

The third key aspect of having an Open Heart is Cultural Competency. I tell all my students from around the world that I become a little *less* culturally *incompetent* every year. Research shows that we suffer from a slew of deficiencies when it comes to cultural competency.[85] As Nancy Adler points out, we wear subconscious cultural blinders that filter our interpretation of other people's behaviors based on how we behave in our own culture.[86] Further, we assume other people are more like us than they might be and that other people feel similarly to how we do. This is called projected similarity.[87] To illustrate this point during a workshop, I like to ask participants to raise their hands if they prefer aisle seats over window seats when flying. You will likely not be surprised to find out that people have strong preferences. You may, however, be surprised that many people prefer a type of seat different from what you prefer, and that research shows that the split between window and aisle seat lovers generally is about 50/50.[88] This is a classic case of "projected similarity."

Now consider that research also indicates that window and aisle seat lovers are different from each other. Those who prefer window seats like to be in control, prefer to "exist in their own bubble," and are more selfish and irritable.[89] If you are a window-seat-lover and this is disheartening (or funny), there is a positive. Those who prefer window seats like to "nest."[90] Those who prefer aisle seats are more reserved, sociable, considerate, and amenable—yet they are also less likely to rest and sleep on planes.[91] When I share this information some laugh and others disagree, and it doesn't matter. The point is not whether these are our true attributes, rather it is that we send messages by simple actions such as sitting in an aisle or window seat, and we make assumptions about others' preferences especially when they are different from our own. Imagine all the other kinds of choices we are making that are sending messages and the assumptions we are making as a result.

When we assume other people behave the way we do, and do things the way we do them, we wear subconscious cultural blinders.[92] To illustrate this point during a workshop, I love playing this video where a team is at an offsite doing the trust fall—a trust exercise where you fall, and your teammates catch you. Except in this video, the first person to do the exercise falls forwards instead of backwards. It is hilarious! Laughs aside, clearly the team was doing some things right—they were focusing on teaming and building trust. Where they went wrong is in their assumption that everyone knows that you fall backwards instead of forwards in the trust fall. How many other things are we assuming about our teams and in our meetings? How many things are we doing or not doing that are having a negative impact on people on the team?

When we try to improve our cultural competency, unfortunately, we often don't focus on the right thing. For example, before we visit another country, we might read about the culture to try to be more culturally competent when we are there. *"Ah yes,"* we say to ourselves sagely, *"in Australia when ordering a scone, say SCAHN instead of SCONE, and eat it with jelly and cream (and never with butter)."* We think: this is being culturally competent. But that's actually not accurate. To be culturally competent we need to focus on ourselves—what is it about *us* that will make people in Australia uncomfortable. For those of you that have ever been to Miami, you will know that, as part of our culture, we air-kiss cheek to cheek as a way of greeting. We do this even with people that we have never met before. That's how we say hello. Well, when I moved from Miami to the northeast to attend Dartmouth college, my leaning in for an air-kiss was a nonstarter. People were like *"Whoa, there! Back up, Michele!"* In the United States, we are often taught to clear our plates, that is, finish everything on our dishes in front of us. What visitors to China may not know is that doing that can send the wrong message to our hosts. In China, generosity in entertaining guests is essential and gives "face" to the hosts. For this reason, hosts typically go all out with thoughtful gifts and elaborate multi-course meals for important guests. When you clear your plate, it signifies to the host that they were not generous enough with their provisions. If you leave a little food behind after each meal, it signifies you are full and that they were indeed generous with their provision.

Cultural competency is about being aware of your own cultural differences, which includes self-awareness of your behaviors and mindset. It's also about being open to cultural and behavioral differences, which leads us to the Third Rule of Engagement.

C. Rule #3: Open Door

"If the doors of perception were [open], everything would appear to man as it is, infinite."

—William Blake, "The Marriage of Heaven and Hell"

The last rule, Open Door, is my favorite because it's named after the Doors, who named themselves after an Aldous Huxley book, *The Doors of Perception and Heaven and Hell.* Huxley's book, in turn, was named after a William Blake poem, "The Marriage of Heaven and Hell" which had the following quote in it: "If the doors of perception were cleansed, everything would appear to man as it is, infinite."[93] Blake uses the word cleansed, I like to substitute the word "open." "If the doors of perception were [open], everything would appear to man as it is, infinite."

There are three key aspects to this Third Rule of Engagement.

1. The Story of Stone Soup

"Bring what you've got. Put it in the pot."

—Heather Forest, *Stone Soup*[94]

The idea of the *infinite* possible (suggested above in the quote) may seem a bit lofty and far-fetched. But it isn't; it is as simple as the story of *Stone Soup.* There are several different versions of this tale. In the one I present, two hungry soldiers visit a village to beg for food. At first the townspeople try to shut out the soldiers: they are poor and don't have anything themselves—how can they give to strangers? The soldiers then gather in the center of the town and announce that they are going to make soup with a stone. The townspeople greet this proclamation with disbelief, but eventually they bring what little they have (half of an apple, the root ends from some onions, a tomato) and throw it in the pot. Although their individual contributions were not enough to make a meal on their own, together the soldiers and the villagers make the richest and most flavorful soup they ever tasted.

Stone Soup is a story not only about the whole being greater than the sum of its parts but also about keeping an open door to people of different cultures, experiences, ages, IQs, and expertise. It is a story about diversity, in other words. Here, the townspeople (eventually) opened their doors to strangers and reaped the rewards. Just like really, really good soup, really, really good ideas come when people from different disciplines, with different expertise, and with different perspectives "bring what [they]'ve got and put it in the pot." The lore wants to tell us the opposite. The lore is that really good ideas, discoveries, and inventions occur by scientists alone in a lab in a Eureka! Aha! moment.[95] Neither of these assertions is true. Innovation is rarely accomplished solo, and it rarely happens as a Eureka! Aha!

Instead, innovation occurs through what Steven Johnson calls "a slow hunch theory": one person's ideas impact another person's idea and so on until the final "aha" moment which is really a migration and merging of the diversity of thought.[96] Jonah Lehrer in his article "How to Be Creative" explains that "We tend to assume that experts are the creative geniuses in their own fields. But big breakthroughs often depend on the naive daring of outsiders. For prompting creativity, few things are as important as time devoted to cross-pollination with fields outside our areas of expertise."[97] Notwithstanding the conflict that can develop with diversity,[98] tons of studies confirm that diverse teams, when managed appropriately,[99] are more creative, better at problem-solving, better at innovation, more productive, and can provide a competitive advantage in the global marketplace.[100] And in fact, the opposite also holds true. Although homogeneous teams are better at being "homogeneous" than diverse teams, they do not perform better despite having less conflict,[101] and homogeneity has not been shown to enhance individual or group learning.[102] Further, diversity has also proven to enhance profitability of companies by 25 percent to 36 percent.[103] Evidently, this is also true when the executive leadership is more diverse.[104] Diversity of *all* kinds has been proven to enhance the success of teams, including diversity of age, religion, race, IQ, expertise, discipline, gender, culture, value systems, socioeconomics, and even ambition.[105] A great example is how having a woman on the team enhances a team's success[106]—not to mention a company's profitability when a woman is in a leadership role.[107] Another great example is how having people with disabilities on a team can enhance the team's effectiveness. Research shows that people with disabilities have unique talents that make them better at certain tasks than others and they also have high levels of empathy[108]—an essential ingredient to innovation and problem-solving of any kind. Further, having people with disabilities on a team enhances the feelings of psychological safety of the team—an essential ingredient to culture creation, discussed in the next chapter). The idea that creativity and innovation are enhanced with diversity, that is, when talented people from different fields and with different backgrounds or levels of expertise collaborate, is called the Medici effect.[109] Its name comes from a book written by Frans Johansson, who was inspired by the prominent Medici family, who is credited with being the impetus behind innovation in Florence during the Italian renaissance in the 15th century. Evidently, the Medici family used their wealth to bring together brilliant creatives from different cultures, enterprises, and disciplines, including from the fields of art, architecture, and philosophy. So, what does this have to do with Open Door? Well, first and foremost, we need to *really* open our doors, that is, not just embrace the diversity that is around us but find ways to invite it to enter our worlds and actively seek more of it!

2. The Importance of Diverse Networks

As made clear by *The Medici Effect*, when it comes to diversity, more yields more. Diversity of all kinds, across all facets of our lives helps us—professionally and personally. This is also true of our social networks. Studies show that a key ingredient to being successful overall and having sense of well-being, in addition to being a more successful innovator, is having diverse social networks,[110] and an added benefit is that "social portfolio diversity is a high and reliable predictor of subjective well-being."[111]

But opening our doors to more diversity in social networks can prove difficult for two reasons.

First, no matter what type of professional service provider you are—if you are an accountant, or an engineer, or a legal services provider—you have been trained in the same way as other professional service providers in your industry. As such, you likely think and act like those other professional service providers (accountants, engineers, lawyers, whatever). Therefore, it feels natural to work with and interact with the other professional service providers who have been trained to (and do) think and behave like you. This is not something special about professional service providers. It's true for all people. Research shows that we like people who are more similar to us (and we believe those who are more similar to us will like us back) whether that is based on real similarity or perceived similarity.[112] Moreover, one of the top five reasons we like people who are similar to us is that we actually believe that we are more likely to expand personally and/or professionally when we are spending time with them.[113] This is called the self-expansion theory—thinking that a benefit of relationships with other people is for personal or professional growth, that is, to gain new experiences and insights.[114] Personal and professional growth is also the purpose of networks. However, given the power of diverse networks, the reality is that a person who is dissimilar to us would be more likely to help us expand as individuals than someone who is similar to us. Yet the power of attraction to those like us is sticky and hard to overcome.

The second reason opening our door to (and achieving) diverse networks is difficult—and this one is especially true for professional service providers—is because the type of diversity we should be open to in our networks is not merely related to the diversity of the "people" in the network but also the type of relationships we have with those people (strength of links). Research shows that the best networks have a combination of both strong and weak ties within.[115] Having strong ties in our networks is easy for professional service providers. Most of us were trained to be trusted advisors and to develop close, intimate, strong relationships with our clients. We are good at that. The idea of cultivating weak ties to people in our network is antithetical to us and, in some ways, tied to our empathy discussion earlier. When I said before that professional service providers test low on empathy, that doesn't mean we aren't able to establish strong emotional ties with others—we can, and we do, and especially with our clients. Empathy is the ability to sense and relate to other peoples' feelings, including those people with whom we do *not* have strong ties and with whom we may differ on a deeper level, that is, as it relates to our values and personal attitudes. So, this makes establishing looser ties even tougher and this door even harder to fully open.

One way to make it easier to open is finding a place or space that attracts people from different disciplines and walks of life—and that is not the home or the office. Ray Oldenburg calls this a "third place."[116]

These third place wonderlands flourish because they create open and eclectic environments where people from diverse backgrounds and cultures, of different ages, and with different experiences and talents can interact. Steven Johnson points out that Vienna, created in large part by Sigmund Freud, was a third place for physicians, philosophers, and scientists to share thoughts on psychoanalysis; similarly, in Paris during the 1920s, scientists, engineers, writers, artists, and workers interacted and cross-pollinated ideas.[117]

Companies have purposefully created third places for their employees for this reason. For example, Mattel's Project Platypus, a development process created by Ivy Ross, a senior VP, resulted in the successful Ello, an interactive toy for 5- to 10-year-old girls that enables them to create and build. Project Platypus consists of 12 members who work (or more aptly, play) for 3 months in a studio outside headquarters. Time is unstructured at the studio, and the members participate in exercises designed to inspire creative thinking and new collaborative behaviors not unlike the exercises we do at our LawWithoutWalls KickOff.

It is about not only the place but also the "space." This is why each LawWithoutWalls KickOff attempts to transport participants to another world with wall art, music, themes, and space in which to move and co-create. Stanford Professor Tina Seelig emphasizes the importance of space in her book *inGenius: A Crash Course on Creativity.* The way the room is set up, the color of the walls, the view outside the windows, the music that is played—all of these things can impact creativity and collaboration among people who are very diverse.[118]

As proven by LawWithoutWalls and LWOW X (and now the pandemic!), today's third place can even be virtual. LawWithoutWalls is our community's third place. For 10 years before the pandemic, the cross-pollination that gave rise to Projects of Worth occurred across geography, generation, expertise, and discipline, and it did so online in our weekly LWOW Live webinars and in the teams' virtual rooms, called "Quan" rooms.

The point is that third places can be created almost anywhere. As long as the place is off site and the space enables and promotes interaction with people from diverse backgrounds—and as Dr. Seuss reminds us, if you "dare to stay out," ask yourself "how much can you lose?" and if you "you dare to go in" ask yourself "how much can you win?"—Dr. Seuss, *Oh, the Places You'll Go!*[119]

So, you might still be a bit skeptical about opening your doors to multidimensional diversity in your networks and to weak ties (in addition to strong). You know deep down, diversity can be a double-edged sword. Although it has benefits, it can also create conflict,[120] especially when it comes to deep-level diversity (differences related to value systems and goals). One of the obvious reasons we have not developed stronger ties with our weak ties may be exactly because we have different value systems and goals. This may be true for you. However, still I persist in asking you to open your door to these weak ties, at least in part, for two reasons. First, remember that this part of Open Door is about our *networks*, upon which we rely to grow and learn new things (not with teammates with whom we collaborate and seek to build strong relationships). Second, the more diverse our networks, the better we can connect dots between ideas and concepts that might not otherwise be connected. This is what successful entrepreneurs are good at doing with their diverse networks. They leverage their weak ties when teaming with those with whom they have strong ties to get to that "adjacent possible"[121]—which isn't about reaching only what is possible but what is *adjacent* to the possible.

One example of leveraging weak ties and connecting dots comes from a story about Steve Jobs. After the success of Apple 2 in 1979, Jobs was invited to tour Xerox's Palo Alto Research Center (PARC).[122] Xerox was an indirect competitor, a weak tie, that clearly had a different value system and mission, than Apple. According to Jobs, the PARC team willingly showed him three new technological innovations when he visited but the one he was wowed by was Xerox's Graphical User Interface (GUI, the use of graphic icons on a computer screen with an easy-to-use pointing device, such as a mouse).[123] Jobs describes the product that Xerox had as "incomplete" and "very flawed" but the "germ of the idea was there and they had done it very well" and "within 10 minutes it was obvious to [him] that all computers would work like this one day."[124] It was obvious to Jobs but it was not obvious to Xerox. Indeed, they willingly gave him a full demo after his visit. These visits gave him the inspiration for how to improve the next version of the Apple (which his "strong ties" were already working on and which we now think of as a MAC) to make it more graphical and easier to use and more accessible to individuals. Jobs's goal was different from Xerox's at the time. Apple's business model was different from Xerox's. While Xerox was focused on business-oriented systems and its core business, which was making copies, Jobs was focused on developing personal computing for individual consumers.[125] Thus, his weak ties helped him connect the dots in a different arena for a slightly different purpose, which shows how important weak ties can be.

Some people have called this type of connecting the dots "stealing,"[126] but the reality is that tons of people who are famous for inventing something new didn't invent the idea itself, but instead used it in a different field or improved upon it by borrowing other people's ideas and inventions. These kinds of connecting and associating have been happening since the beginning of time. Consider that Beethoven borrowed portions of music from Wolfgang Amadeus Mozart to write "Ode to Joy" and Beethoven's First Symphony.[127] Similarly, Johannes Brahms borrowed from Beethoven to create his First Symphony. And evidently, Mozart himself borrowed from Johann Christian Bach to create his great aria, "Martern aller Arten."[128] As T. S. Eliot is known for saying "Immature poets imitate; mature poets steal; bad poets deface what they take, and good poets make it into something better, or at least something different."[129] And as Mark Twain is famous for saying, "There is no such thing as a new idea. It is impossible. We simply take a lot of old ideas and put them into a sort of mental kaleidoscope. We give them a turn and they make new and curious combinations."[130]

3. Keep the Past in the Present

Just as diversity in our networks helps us "make new and curious combinations," diversity in our individual pasts (prior fields of study, prior jobs, prior hobbies) does too. It enables us to borrow something from one field and use it to solve a problem in another field. This leads to a type of exaptation that is a result of the cross-fertilization of different disciplines and is key to innovation and idea generation.[131] It is why I created an exaptation exercise for idea generation in The 3-4-5 Method™.[132] Exaptation exercises force us to associate—connect two or more things together that might otherwise not be connected.[133]

A good example of this type of exaptation is Gutenberg's printing press. All the technologies to make the printing press were already in existence, for example, moveable type, ink, paper, and the press itself (which was first developed as a wine press for wineries). Gutenberg put them all together in a new way for a new purpose, that is, to mass produce and sell the Gutenberg Bible. Another example is how scientists recently were inspired to exapt attributes of the puffer fish to help monitor tumors and ulcers in patients.[134] As many divers have seen, puffer fishes "puff up" two to three times their size when they are scared as a defense mechanism and deflate when they no longer fear danger. Scientists, inspired by puffer fish, developed a jelly-like pill that inflates to the size of a ping pong ball. After the pill is swallowed, the consistency of the jelly enables it to expand quickly in the stomach of the patient (to 100 times its original size) so it can monitor tumors and ulcers. Then it can shrink back to its original size at any time and safely pass out of the body when the patient drinks a solution of calcium. That's an example of taking the properties of something from one field and moving it to another to problem-solve creatively. This type of cross-fertilization doesn't just happen on its own. Instead, it is driven by individuals[135] and, therefore, it comes from within and from the collective wisdom of our past experiences.

As Steve Jobs is famous for saying: "You can't connect the dots looking forward; you can only connect them looking backwards." Indeed, that is what Gutenberg did. He was only able to connect the dots and modify the existing technologies by looking backward and leveraging his prior interests in selling to religious pilgrims *and* prior training as a goldsmith and gem cutter to modify the existing movable type system.

In keeping with that, research shows that teams are more innovative when their leader has some multidisciplinary expertise. These leaders are better at selecting and leveraging cross-cutting subject matters, stimulating information sharing across different areas of expertise and drawing attention to others' knowledge and varying valuable approaches.[136] This may also be true of leaders who speak more than one language. Some research suggests that people who know multiple languages develop critical thinking skills earlier, perform better on executive functioning tasks, are more inventive, and are better able to associate things that might not otherwise be associated.[137]

So, this doorway to the past leads us to look backward to a prior hobby or job that may help us to be better in our current roles. For example, many of us have been a part of a competitive team or activity (playing an instrument, participating in a band, a sports team, a dance troupe, theater, debate, math club, etc.). We've also all had different types of jobs, including those from when we were young, such as lifeguarding, camp counseling, deliveries, waiting tables, etc. The question to ask yourself is: How might your past experiences and past learnings from those activities help you add more value today in your current leadership role? How might you associate the past jobs, roles, or hobbies to your current role within an organization in a way that you didn't think of before? I always tell people that I believe marketing and law are very similar. As a marketer, your job is to do a lot of research about people (consumers), about how they behave, why they behave the way they do, what they believe about your products or services, and then develop strategies to try to convince them to think and behave differently. For lawyers and especially law professors, this is our job as well—except it's about ethics, principles, and the rule of law instead of cereal or jeans. Making that connection helps me remember to apply my marketing expertise to my current job. For example, when I worked at Levi Strauss Company, we were trained to take an unorthodox approach to market research. We gave video camcorders to the young teenagers in our target audience so that they could record their lives and we could see firsthand what clothes they wore (and how they wore them) during which kinds of activities. We then visited their homes and asked them to describe their outfits and how they felt wearing them. I train all teams that I work with on innovation journeys to consider how they might "exapt" the Levi Strauss market research approach and take a more unorthodox approach to understanding their target audience.

So what about your past can you bring through the door into your future role? After you have answered that question for yourself, ask your team the same question. In LawWithoutWalls, we search for the hidden talents and hobbies of our participants. To that end (as described more fully in Chapter 7) we do a *Talent & Topic Expertise Exploration Exercise* to ensure that everyone's experience, smarts, and talents can be uncovered and put to good use, connected somehow to the topic challenge at hand. Indeed, when Margaret Hagan, the director of the Design Lab at Stanford, was one of my students in LawWithoutWalls, we uncovered that she had a talent as a graphic novel artist and urged her to use that talent to help her team's project, which she did (and which won by the way). Importantly, it helped open her eyes to the possibility of combining her creative artistic passions with her design thinking training in LWOW and her substantive passion for the law; check out how she brings the law and legal design to life with her artistry.[138]

Making such connections, associating things that might not normally be associated is one of the five key attributes of disruptive innovators, according to research by Jeff Dyer, Hal Gregersen, and Clayton M. Christensen.[139] And here, it may sound easy to do because all we are asking is to connect two things about which you are familiar. But it is not as easy as it seems—especially for senior leaders. Research shows that senior executives—especially at large companies—are great at analyzing, executing, implementing, and delivering results against defined goals. However, as mentioned above, senior execs don't know how to associate or how to connect the unexpected,[140] that is, the weak to the strong, wine to paper, marketing to law. Therefore, this door, although worth the effort, can be very heavy. However, the next door might help lighten its load.

In addition to applying our own diverse experiences to our current roles, there is another door to open and it is the door to our past. This is the door to our younger, innately creative selves. According to the World Economic Forum, creativity is a top (if not THE top) important skill for future success[141] and it matters more than IQ.[142] The good news for us is that this door isn't quite as hard to open as the prior one and this is because we were all born creative. But, as Hugh Macleod, a well-known cartoonist, is famous for pointing out—somewhere along the way we forgot where we put our crayons. Therefore, all we have to do is open the door and look backward to our younger selves to find where we put them. All we have to do is channel our seven-year-old self so we can find that joy, a moment of pure flow, whether playing with LEGOs or Barbies, or painting, where creativity was not just within reach, it was a given part of our kid existence. Therefore, one of the exercises I have developed to open the door to more creative ideation is to get participants to do just that. I ask people to close their eyes and attempt to open that door to the past—to channel their seven-year-old selves. I tell them to picture the apartment or house they grew up in, to picture the front door and imagine they are standing outside of it. Now, reach over and open the door. What do you see when you step in? Is your mom putting a patch on the knee of your jeans? Is your sister on the orange corduroy couch eating granola bars and watching *The Gong Show*? Now turn to go to your bedroom and open the door. What is on the walls? Is there a poster of David Cassidy or Duran Duran shining down on you? What record is next to the record player (or eight track or cassette or CD)? What color is your bedspread? Now think about the activity you loved doing most when you were seven years old. Pick up that thing and start doing it! Run outside and kick the ball. Pick up the instrument or start building. When you are truly channeling that person, open your eyes. Now you are ready to innovate. Moreover, now you are ready to connect your innate creativity to the future, and although we have to look backward to connect the dots, as Jobs explains, we also "have to trust that the dots will somehow connect in our future"— and they will if we put our minds to it.

The point is to remember we were all born creative *and* to trust that we can tap back into our creativity no matter how far away we have placed our crayons—because there is no escaping that creativity will be applicable in our future as leaders in professional services of all different kinds. We need to improve our ability to tap into our creativity. Consider that strategy is all about creating new value in new ways and that can only happen if we have the mindset to identify and recognize creative value. If you are still resisting this, read up on the literature about the role of creativity in the strategy development process and consider how, in the world of management consulting, strategy and innovation are tied together.[143]

The added benefit of having an open door to our seven-year-old selves is that it ties back to our first rule of Engagement, Open Mind. Keeping an open door to our past is representative of letting go of our inhibitions, tearing down the walls we put up and getting rid of the zippers we put on our lips (not to mention the behind-the-eyes eyeroll we have perfected so it doesn't show outwardly). Similarly, having a glass of wine can help creativity along with other relaxing activities such as taking a shower or going for a jog.[144] Essentially, keeping the door open to your past is one way to skip the glass of wine (but not the jog, of course). It is also a way for us to find our "flow," a concept first introduced by Mihaly Csikszent-mihalyi.[145] Flow is that synergistic moment when we match our talents to the challenge at hand, so much so that we forget time and place. At that moment, as Mister Rogers once said, we "aren't just the age we are. We are all the ages [we] have ever been"[146] and all the ages we will one day be—and it is at that moment that we can use the past to connect the dots into the future.

As mentioned in the Chapter 5, leaders are made not born. Because it takes effort to apply our creativity and connect the dots in the future, the whole point of this chapter is to help you start to fill those gaps on your own—to become a better leader, a leader who inspires and influences by embodying the behaviors that cultivate an environment in which others feel psychologically safe, sharing and challenging ideas without fear of negative social consequences. It is in this type of climate, led by these types of leaders, that multidisciplinary teams thrive.[147] And the recipe for creating this type of climate is what the next chapter reveals.

...Reflection Point Ask each person on your team to take this quick test to assess what type of mindset they have: https://blog.mindsetworks .com/what-s-my-mindset. Discuss your results together.

⬤...Reflection Point Consider the following Taoist short story, "The Farmer's Luck," which has been told multiple times by multiple authors. This rendition, my favorite, is by Jon J. Muth, author of Zen Shorts:[148]

> There was once an old farmer who had worked his crops for many years. One day, his horse ran away. Upon hearing the news, his neighbors came to visit. "Such bad luck," they said sympathetically. "Maybe," the farmer replied. The next morning the horse returned, bringing with it two other wild horses. "Such good luck!" the neighbors exclaimed. "Maybe," replied the farmer. The following day, his son tried to ride one of the untamed horses, was thrown off, and broke his leg. Again, the neighbors came to offer their sympathy on his misfortune. "Such bad luck," they said. "Maybe," answered the farmer. The day after that, military officials came to the village to draft young men into the army to fight in a war. Seeing that the son's leg was broken, they passed him by. "Such good luck!" cried the neighbors. "Maybe," said the farmer.

What is the main message about luck and mindset? Try to think of an example in your own life when you felt unlucky but, after a period of time, you realized that you were lucky that things unfolded as they did. How does having an Open Mind, Open Heart, and Open Door change how you view what happens in your life? Is there such a thing as luck?

⬤...Reflection Point Look at Figure 6.2 and quickly count the number of Fs in the sentence.[149]

How many Fs did you count? Compared to native English speakers, nonnative English speakers are more likely to spot all the Fs. See the footnote for the correct answer.[150]

FINISHED FILES ARE THE RESULT OF YEARS
OF SCIENTIFIC STUDY COMBINED WITH THE
EXPERIENCE OF YEARS

By Nancy J. Adler

©Michela DeStefano

FIG. 6.2. Nancy J. Adler's Cultural Competency Test.

Nancy Adler uses this example to demonstrate our cultural conditioning. She explains that the reason native English speakers miss some of the words is because they don't count words that are not essential to understanding a sentence (e.g., words such as *of*).[151]

> We selectively see those words that are important according to our cultural conditioning (in this case, our linguistic conditioning). Once we see a phenomenon in a particular way, we usually continue to see it in that way. Once we stop seeing of's, we do not see them again (even when we look for them); we do not see things that do exist.[152]

This is akin to Daniel Simon's *Monkey Business* and inattention blindness discussed above, and it is especially critical for professional service providers and especially lawyers. We learn to gloss over things that don't matter (e.g., evidence that is not *material*). Similarly, native English speakers gloss over *of's* because *of's* don't matter. How many other things are we simply discounting as inconsequential because they don't matter to us?

CHAPTER 7

S.A.F.E.T.Y.: A Recipe for Culture Creation

> *"Culture eats strategy for breakfast[1] and transformation for lunch."*[2]
> —Peter Drucker

In the previous chapter, we focused on you as an individual. We addressed the question: How can individuals bring authenticity, inspire loyalty, and influence their organizations? To that end, we talked about the importance of self-awareness, humility, and accountability for leading collaborative efforts. Leaders who inspire collaboration, innovation, and inclusivity embody the behaviors that create that kind of climate. This is critical because research shows that psychologically safe organizations are able to innovate faster, better leverage the benefits of diversity, and adapt better to change.[3] Research also suggests that it is the attitude and behavior of the senior leaders that have the most impact in strengthening creative, collaborative climates.[4] This is why the Three Rules of Engagement introduced in the last chapter are so important. If followed by the leader, they help create a positive teaming climate, as has been proven in Law-WithoutWalls, by other studies, and in the PSFs and corporate legal departments with which I have consulted.[5]

Although it starts with a focus on you and following the Three Rules of Engagement, it doesn't stop with you there. There are additional specific actions you can take to create an inclusive, collaborative, and innovative climate that will evolve over time into a culture. Not only does culture creation *start* with you, in other words, it *continues* with you, creating the right processes and practices and granting the right permissions and powers to others to develop the right climate. A recent study by Gartner defines a climate as "a group's shared perceptions of the nature of its work" which is "easier to access, influence and control than culture."[6] Climate creation is slow percolation over a long period of time. Only after the climate is created is there the ability to build the right culture—which Gartner defines as "deeply held assumptions and beliefs of a company and its employees."[7]

As discussed in Chapter 4, research on culture creation demonstrates that long-lasting change does not start with strategy. Without the climate and the culture, strategy is pretty much useless—as indicated by the opening quote of this chapter. Climate (and ultimately culture) creation begins by starting bonfires in small teams with targeted actions,[8] that is, by "starting at the periphery" with a "grass roots" approach—as opposed to mandating big "programmatic change" from the top.[9] However, just because you are a great leader doesn't mean you will automatically create the right climate that yields a great team, that is, one that is inclusive, collaborative, and committed.[10]

So *how* do you do this? This is a typical quandary:[11] teams, departments, organizations of all kinds are struggling to figure out what are the tactical steps to create, first, the climate, and then, the culture. Unfortunately, one of the answers I often hear to that question is the dreaded, "It depends" or "There is no one-size-fits-all answer to leading culture change." While those answers are true to a degree, they leave aspiring leaders a bit bereft of a "there there," with little idea as to how to improve their own organization.[12] My feeling is that if leaders truly are made and not born, we should be able to provide them a roadmap. That's exactly what this chapter is designed to do, provide specific, practical (not strategic and visionary), targeted actions you can take to create a culture of collaboration, innovation, and inclusivity that helps instill the right mindsets and behaviors to support the culture you are trying to create. Only then will true transformation happen.[13]

As I mentioned above, inclusive, collaborative, innovative cultures need a team climate that is psychologically safe, and there is nothing *soft* about creating that. In fact, there's nothing soft about creating any type of culture. Quite the opposite, you have to be hard-nosed about climate creation to build (and support) a team wherein conflict is not avoided, a mission is shared, hierarchy does not get in the way, team members are committed and engaged and hold each other accountable and of course, celebrate each other's and the team's success. That's what makes a great team.[14] In this section, I have pre-defined the desired culture (inclusive, collaborative, and innovative) and pre-proscribed the principles as the Three Rules of Engagement. However, cultures and principles can vary, of course, and it is important to know (and communicate) the culture you are trying to create. However, no matter what culture and principles your department or firm or individual team want to establish, a great team can only thrive when there is psychological safety. In that spirit, this section uses the word SAFETY as an acronym for the essential ingredients for culture creation.

> *S* is for *Surveying* the team's strengths, weaknesses, and talents and *Setting* goals
> *A* is for setting expectations to ensure *Accountability*
> *F* is for *Flattening* the team
> *E* is for *Empowering* and *Engaging* the individuals on the team
> *T* is for *Thinking Tiny* as in small versus big, short versus long, and inches versus miles
> *Y* is for saying "*Yes, and*" to those who will help you create your climate and intended culture

One word of caution as you use this acronym. Although this whole section is about creating culture change and a safe environment, this doesn't mean that there shouldn't be pressure for excellence or a sense of urgency. Nor does it mean that you are striving for total equilibrium. My experience has taught me (and experts in leading teams agree) that, what leaders should strive for is a "productive zone of *disequilibrium*," that is, one that has some degree of discomfort and pull.[15] If things are too nice and the pressure is too low, then nothing gets accomplished; but when things are too hot, the pressure is debilitating and people cannot be productive because they are in over-distress.

A. Culture Creation Ingredient #1: S is for Survey and Set

Creating a new culture generally means you are breaking the patterns of the old culture. And before you can do that, you need to know—really know—what the old culture was. You need to assess the internal culture, the team's strengths, weaknesses, makeup, and talent and expertise.

You need to know it to value (or devalue) it. Or as experts on adaptive leadership put it, you need to "distinguish . . . the DNA that is essential to conserve from the DNA that must be discarded"[16] before you can create "the new cultural DNA that will enable people to thrive anew."[17] Just as self-awareness was critical to being a leader, awareness of the team's strengths, weaknesses, and readiness for culture change and for honing an innovative and collaborative culture is essential to success in creating it.

What do you survey and how do you measure what you see? There are many tools and pedagogical frameworks to assess engagement and psychological safety levels,[18] and collaboration and innovation readiness.[19] One example is the Gartner "innovation climate index." After interviewing more than 100 leaders in research and development (R&D), surveying more than 450 R&D staff members from 91 companies in a range of industry types and revenue sizes, and testing 80 variables, this index assesses a company, department, or team based on six drivers: surfacing high-quality ideas, delivering innovative products and services, retaining the best people, continuously innovating, believing to deliver, and having a strong innovation culture. Similar to Gartner, IDEO developed the Creative Difference tool that assesses an organization across what they identify as the six drivers of innovation. These they name as: empowerment, purpose, looking out, collaboration, experimentation, and refinement.[20] Ferrazzi Greenlight identifies eight critical categories that predict high team performance: candor, relationships, collaboration, energy, accountability, teaming out, development, and outcomes.[21] More could be said about these drivers, their upsides and drawbacks in content and assessment practicability, and we can debate their fine points. However, the point is simply to convince you to survey your current culture—now: observe it, assess it, and measure it from without and within. Also, do so continuously. Many collaboration and innovation readiness frameworks focus on retrospective analysis and consist of checklists of factors for group self-analysis.[22] However, it is also important to survey as the team collaborates on a go-forward, that is, during the stages of development to assess whether momentum and climate are sustained.[23] The question should not be: how did the team perform compared to its goals but instead, given the lessons learned, should a new approach be taken?[24] To answer that question, it is important to understand WHY things are positive or negative.

You might be wondering what tools can help (other than those listed above). In addition to diagnostics, there are also the traditional psychometric questionnaires available online and *paper* surveys which, although they may be on the decline,[25] are still useful in measuring perceptions and climate.[26] You may want to consider a combination of client satisfaction, employee net promoter score, and self-reflection surveys to measure engagement and commitment. And then combine these more traditional survey instruments with other types of analysis, such as email behavior analysis[27] or social network analysis[28] (which maps the informal structure of a team so that you can understand—and visualize—which relationships facilitate and which impede collaboration, knowledge creation, and knowledge transfer). Those analysis tools, admittedly, are more time consuming. However, they can be complemented with more frequent (shorter) self-created pulse surveys to provide additional, real-time insights into team member's perceptions and beliefs about the climate and the culture.[29]

It is also important to survey subgroups (individual teams) among the larger cohort or department to assess the effectiveness of their attributes and processes. There are many analytical tools, especially in the health and science fields, publicly available to do so.[30] Although third parties can help objectivity, also ask your teams to assess themselves. What are their strengths and weaknesses? What are the challenges preventing advancement in the areas of time pressures, trust, skills, mindsets, incentives, or awareness of each other's expertise? Ask them: How can they build in these areas? How do they describe their culture now versus the desired culture of the future? How do they describe themselves versus other teams within and outside the department or organization? Self-assessments such as these are valuable. Research suggests those teams that describe their culture as "visionary, inspiring, and creative" as opposed to "behind-the-times or short-sighted" are more successful and more likely to achieve their objectives.[31] In addition to knowing and being aware of the culture that exists within the teams and the culture you want to create overall, these surveys help you protect your teams from hostile climates that can simmer and create obstacles and stymie climate change, collaboration, and innovation.[32]

Then of course, it is important to survey individuals: their attitudes, their beliefs, and especially their work style preferences. I emphasize the latter because it is important to do so to raise awareness of the differences and the gaps so that people can learn to flex and bend. I'm a fan of DiSC but there are many others to consider, such as CliftonStrengths,

Myers Briggs, Hogan Personality Inventory, Golden Personality Type Profiler, or Pioneers, Driver, Integrators, and Guardians.[33] Remember however, surveying what's there is necessary but not sufficient. In fact, if all you do is have people take a work style survey, it might give license to people on the team to use their results as an excuse for their ways of working. I have unfortunately (more than once) witnessed team members saying things like "I'm a D in DiSC, which means I am controlling and domineering by nature" to justify a controlling and domineering act . . . This is exactly the opposite goal of the S in S.A.F.E.T.Y. The point is not only to know our own preferred work styles but also those of others and to use this information to inspire our adaptation.

In addition to personalities and expertise and culture, surveying who is doing what—and why—is essential to make sure that roles match tasks, tasks are assigned to the right people, and that the team is made up of the right composition. Team science literature supports this idea: Applying task analytic methods (activity mapping, task analysis, cognitive modeling, and cognitive work analysis) help identify who is doing what tasks, what knowledge skills and attitudes are needed for tasks, and any overlap, inefficiencies, or gaps.[34] This seems like a no-brainer given that the whole point of digital transformation and operations management is to increase efficiency so that people can turn to more strategic and high value work. This can only happen if tasks are understood and properly aligned and assigned. But this step is often missed, and it is important to do it at the beginning so that old habits don't create the same old problems on a new team. It is also important to do in the middle as well for the reasons stated before in support of continuous surveying to keep your pulse on the culture.

Survey externally as well—outside the team. IDEO calls this "looking out."[35] First, look external to the company or firm entirely: How is your department or firm different or the same as competitors? What are competitors doing that is enhancing their success that you are not doing? What are other industries doing? Looking externally is a great way to source (exapt) ideas for improvement. Interestingly, a study of 21,000 employees to measure leadership development found that a leader's openness to using ideas from outside their organization was a key driver not only for innovation but also of employees' inspiration and effort.[36] (Note: it also found that most of the employees felt their leaders were not open to using ideas from outside their organization).[37]

Looking out is also essential because we often have external stakeholders (external to the department or team but internal within the company or firm) to whom we are beholden. Therefore, a key stakeholder analysis that asks who the key stakeholders are with whom this team will interact, impact in some way, or need approval from, is always a great exercise whenever you start a new teaming project. It is also important to do along the way as the timing of change changes, that is, what may be urgent for one group might not be for another. Further, for professional service providers, external key stakeholders (like clients!) often exist outside the company or firm entirely. Of course, once this analysis has been done, it is important to incorporate the stakeholder's performance indicators. Like we talked about in the chapter on client-centricity, we need to incorporate not just our own KPIs (key performance indicators for our team, department, firm, etc.) but also CPIs (customer/client performance indicators) and, then of course, also SPIs (stakeholder performance indicators).

Second, how is your team different from others inside the organization or firm? Third, what barriers exist to prevent collaboration? A great exercise to conduct with your team is to ask them to select the top two among a common list of internal and external barriers to collaboration and innovation, for example, time, resources, compensation (incentives), mindset (what mindsets are preventing, such as fixed mindsets or competitiveness or risk aversion), skill set, timing, stress, culture, power/authority, organizational structure, trust, lack of understanding of others' talent and expertise, lack of purpose (or understanding of purpose), vague values, etc.[38] Armed with this information, you can attempt to adjust the environment as needed. As Simon Sinek says "leaders are responsible for creating an environment where people are at their best"; however, we also need to keep the "productive zone of disequilibrium" principle in mind.[39]

Last, after you have surveyed, it is important to set metrics for measurement of progress and the timing, that is, *what* metric you will use to measure and *when* you will measure. There is that old saying, "if you can't measure it, it doesn't exist." However, numbers are not the only metric of measurement. For example, during your surveying stage, you could create a playbook of how a process works today and identify what needs to be improved and how. After a set amount of time, you can then compare the first playbook to the improved/enhanced process at the end. Another way to conduct your surveying is to set goals of enhancing the results/responses in certain ways. Then, measure again later with the same survey tools and compare the results side by side against the goals that you set.

B. Culture Creation Ingredient #2: A is for Setting Expectations for Accountability

In LawWithoutWalls, we always say: *The expectations that aren't set, aren't met.* And what we mean by that is, teams must set expectations early on to ensure that the right tenor for a culture is developed. This is true for both what we might consider the big things (ethics, morals, behaviors) and what we might consider the little things (like dress code and who speaks first in a meeting).

Think about the last fight you had with someone where you were disappointed in them or they were disappointed in you. Likely, part of the problem was a miscommunication based on a misunderstanding about expectations. What is true in our personal lives, how we create family dynamics, is also true in our professional lives. This is not to say we should be the same in both places, but we should set clear expectations, because that's how we increase the chance that people will behave accordingly. People often think that to change behavior, we have to first change people's attitudes. But we don't. In a recent TED talk, sociologist Dr. Professor Jennifer Cross explained that expectations work to change behaviors because they help create social norms.[40] And social norms are catchy! As mentioned in Chapter 6, research demonstrates that seeing others exemplifying the behavior influences our behavior, which is yet another plug to you, the leader, to exemplify the behaviors you want followed and, in addition, to set them as expectations with clarity and transparency. Without both, you can't hold people accountable for their behavior. It follows then that in LawWithoutWalls, one of our tenets is setting expectations. The other tenets are *forgive fast and often*, and *feedback is a gift*. We set the expectation that LawWithoutWalls is an open, nonhierarchical, friendly, inclusive community that works on a first name basis only, where suits and ties are not allowed, and jeans are highly encouraged. Last, we infuse fun into everything we do, including webinars, exercises, and tasks. This last part is especially important to make clear. In fact, having fun is one of the key attributes researchers analyze when determining the "health" and effectiveness of a team. There are strong correlations between having fun and people's happiness (and commitment).[41] Also having fun breeds positive emotions, which increase creativity and positive collaborative behaviors.[42] Although it may not sound very "fun," if you want teams to have fun, you need to set it as an expectation, put it in the community pact. More on pacts soon!

In addition, when teams set their own expectations, they are more likely to commit because they were involved in the making of the "why and what." This is supported by research: when team members feel psychological ownership of the change effort (and the reasons for it), they are more likely to embrace the change and commit to it. For change efforts to work, high levels of commitment are needed.[43]

Therefore, in LawWithoutWalls, each team makes a team P.A.C.T. which identifies the team's purpose (P), that is, the overarching goal and mission; what they are accountable (A) for, that is, the expected contribution of each participant, roles of participants,[44] how decisions will be made, the process that should be followed to resolve possible areas of disagreement, confidentiality of data and information, and in some cases, ownership (intellectual property) and authorship credit; creative cadence (C), that is, mechanisms and tools for routine communication, how often they meet, how long, what tech they will use and response times; and timing (T), that is, when they will complete certain steps, when they will measure and replan.

Sometimes it is hard to convince teams to take the time to do this. For years, I had teams commit to protocols at the KickOff and, eventually, I formally created this exercise in 2018 with Erika Pagano (the director of LawWithoutWalls then)—without knowing there was existing research in support of doing so. I was happily surprised, in writing the first draft of this book, to discover that other teaming aficionados had made similar recommendations[45] and that the P.A.C.T.s we create in LawWithoutWalls are not dissimilar to what scientific research teams do at the beginning of a project to preempt conflict and discord. For example, because it was found that problems in scientific collaborations arise from a failure to define expectations, the National Institutes of Health's ombudsman recommended research teams create a "scientific prenuptial," that is, a partnering agreement at the outset of the project that addresses many of the same things we do in our P.A.C.T.s.[46]

During the P.A.C.T. process, we also write down and share what attributes on the Skills Delta we are good at and committed to bringing and those that we struggle with and commit to improving (as discussed in Chapter 5). This last aspect is personal and requires sharing for the same reason that people who make New Year's resolutions are more likely to follow them when they share them with others. Research shows we are more likely to stick with a commitment once we make a verbal or written declaration committing to that goal with a witness present.[47]

Research also shows that we are more likely to be held accountable if we know how what we are doing fits in with the larger mission or North Star of the department and company. This is important to ensure that the project adheres to the company's core values but also to motivate individuals. There is research and data supporting that having a shared mission, purpose, or vision can add a lot of value and increase investment and knowledge sharing.[48] Rallying teams around a higher purpose or aspirational mission helps teams see how they can contribute and make a difference. It is important for the entire community, organization, or firm, to have one agreed mission or North Star. This is also true for departments within organizations (like the legal department within a company) and practice groups within a firm—which is why we are seeing this happening in the professional services marketplace.[49] Unsurprisingly, it is also important for each individual team on an innovation journey. Hence the (P) in P.A.C.T. The teams need to have a sense of ownership as to their own unique selling proposition, why they exist, and what is their purpose—which, of course, should tie into the mission or North Star for the larger community, organization, department or firm. It is also important for each individual also. In fact, when individual goals align with the goals of the team, motivation is increased even further.[50]

I would be remiss if I didn't reiterate the essential element to building accountability on a team—which I described in detail earlier—which is trust. Following the S.A.F.E.T.Y. recipe is the first step in building the trust that is essential for the kind of personal accountability that leads to real results.

C. Culture Creation Ingredients #3 and #4: Flatten, Empower, and Engage

The "F" in S.A.F.E.T.Y stands for flattening out whatever you have "hierarchized," so that you can get to the "E," empowering instead of delegating. Let's take this from the back forward: Why empower versus delegate? We may find the answer in some of the best kitchens. One of the secrets of great chefs is to inspire others to be their most creative selves, to leverage their talents to create menu items. Although the chef still has purview over every dish—to make sure that the quality standards are met, and the style of a venue is upheld—they do so without sticking their finger into everything.

Well-known chef Naomi Pomeroy, who won the James Beard Foundation Award for the Best Chef Northwest in 2014, puts it this way:

> *I don't write every menu anymore. I found that the key to my success has always been empowering the people around me. I know what I'm good at, and I know what I'm not good at. I also realize that if I'm going to be stepping away from the restaurant to come to New York or go to Minneapolis or LA, I have to have a team in place that feels 100 percent behind whatever it is that they're doing. I think that the most successful chefs are the ones that can relinquish certain controls, and give their team some creative input, and empower them to have ownership over it. I think any successful business is like that. Who needs their boss coming back in and sticking their finger in everything and being like, "Well my idea is this and my idea is that" and then walking away? Because we're not experts anymore, you know what I'm saying?*[51]

Bosses that stick their fingers in everything do not have teams that are flat, and therefore, they do not have teams that are empowered. The two go hand in hand; and when both are met, individuals and teams thrive. The authors of *Unleashed: The Unapologetic Leader's Guide to Empowering Everyone Around You* sum up this balance between presence and absence and empowerment as follows: "Leadership is about empowering other people as a result of your presence—and making sure that impact continues into your absence."[52]

A recent study by Deloitte of 3,630 executives supports chef Pomeroy's position, that organizations that thrive (versus survive) empower their professionals with "agency and choice over what work they do, unleashing their potential by allowing them to apply their interests and passions to organizational needs."[53] As mentioned in Chapter 6, to help team members figure out what their interests and passions are and how they relate to the tasks and challenges of the team, in LawWithoutWalls, we have all teams conduct a *Talent & Topic Expertise Exploration Exercise*. The point of this exercise, therefore, is not only to share the specific expertise each team member has with the topic or task but also to uncover the hidden talents and hobbies of your teammates and to ensure that everyone's experience, smarts, and talents are put to good use, connected somehow to the challenge at hand.

There is another great exercise called Alphabet Work (that I found online) that can help with this past-to-present association.[54] It is designed to identify what people excel at among their tasks. It has people grade themselves from A to F on the types of work they have to do in their job. Note: in the United States, students are graded from A to F. A is the highest (93 percent to 100 percent). B is (83 percent to 92 percent); C is (73 percent to 82 percent); D is (65 percent to 72 percent); and F is (failing, i.e., below 65 percent). So, A work, just like in school, is work that is your favorite type of work and you excel at it. "B" work is pretty good work, but you have to work a bit harder to do it and your end product is really productive but, perhaps, not best-in-class. C work is what you do at an average level. You do not excel at it, but you can handle it. D work is the work that people dread, and that people put off. It's the work that keeps going on the to-do list each week. F work is the work you should avoid entirely because it is outside your competency. When we think about productivity, we think about time for the task instead of skills. The Alphabet exercise helps team members figure out what is their "A" work, and then tasks can be divided based on skills. Doing this type of exercise, and changing how tasks are divided, helps flatten the team because tasks aren't assigned based on seniority (or availability) but on talent and expertise and desire. In fact, tasks aren't assigned at all, they are opted for based on self-grading. Combine this with some type of rotating schedule of tasks, and watch engagement grow exponentially. Consider Trader Joe's. One of their secrets to success is that in one shift, you change your tasks multiple times (from cashier to shelf stocker to cleaner or collector of carts, to helping customers find what they need, and so on).[55]

Perhaps you still believe you can empower people without flattening your organization. Even if that is true, as pointed out by Harvard Business Professor, Gary P. Pisano, there are other benefits of culturally flat organizations, including that (1) people are rewarded and provided deference based on competence not title, (2) people can respond more quickly to changing circumstances, and (3) they draw on a "broader community of contributors" and therefore "generate a richer diversity of ideas."[56] By contrast, there are multiple negative consequences tied to organizations that are not flat or at least flatter by comparison. I'm not suggesting that you do not need a strong leader. Rather, the type of flattening I'm talking about is of the layers, the pyramid shape that drags organizations down. This is like the structure of many law schools that have so many associate deans that any tenured faculty without the title feels on the out. The type of flattening I'm talking about is not just about titles, but also in the hierarchical behaviors, for example, when law school faculty insist that "staff" call them "Professor" instead of by their first name or when professors are allowed to enlist the help of an assistant who services the program while others who direct and manage the program cannot, simply because they are not professors. I am suggesting, therefore, that you consider changing or eliminating titles that exist for no other reason than to delineate the status of an all-kings lineup; this includes the hierarchy of professionals within the same professional services department who offer the same type of services (for example, partner versus associate), or who offer different services (for example, partner versus marketing director). In fact, one small boutique law firm in Florida just announced its plans to eliminate the partner and associate titles entirely, for these very reasons.[57] If that's too big of a step, consider adding extra titles to the traditional ones that communicate something important and empowering, such as associate, lead team manager.

The other type of flattening that can empower is flattening protocols and providing more permissions to take more risks and experiment, that is, one of the tenet's of LawWithoutWalls: "Ask forgiveness later." Give teams the permission (and resources) to try things fast and skip red tape.[58] Also, consider providing more direct lines of communication in all directions, and more platforms for communication. Younger generations generally don't like working in hierarchical structures. They've grown up being able to interact on social media with their sporting heroes or celebrity influencers in informal and spontaneous ways. So, they expect to be able to have direct dialogue with the boss and pitch their ideas on different platforms in forms that are not formal and that do not require scheduling and calendar invitations. In keeping with that, another way to flatten (and delevel) is to create subgroups—the importance of which is expounded upon in Chapter 9. Tied to that is the other tenet in LawWithoutWalls mentioned earlier: "Feedback is a gift." Research shows that when team members coach and develop one another with transparency and candor (regardless of hierarchy), it creates a flattening and empowering effect that enables higher performance.[59]

There are other ways to empower (and engage) in addition to flattening and one of those ways relates to accountability and purpose, which we spoke of earlier in our discussion of P.A.C.T.s. In addition to getting the team to see and align with the larger North Stars of the department or firm, consider encouraging the teams not only to create their own mission, but to create the larger mission for the community of teams on the innovation journey, and even the department itself.[60] After all, looking to the future, millennials, coined "The Purpose Generation" and Gen Z (aka, the digital natives) are aligned on this![61] So it's imperative that leaders ensure their teams are energized by purpose. Sharing the development of that purpose and giving transparency into your values and challenges—which of course, requires the vulnerability we discussed earlier in Open Heart—can motivate engagement and commitment. In a leadership development survey of more than 21,000 employees, 21 percent of employees say that their leader rarely or never openly shares the challenges they are facing and only 20 percent said the leader regularly does.[62] This is critical because this same study showed that the more a leader openly shares their challenges, the more inspired employees are to try their best at work. According to research by Professor Brené Brown, by vulnerably sharing their challenges and fears, the leader admits that they don't have all the answers and demonstrates to their team that "they don't see power as finite and hoard it; we know that power becomes infinite when we share it with others."[63]

There is yet another way to empower and engage the new pipeline of professional service providers and it relates back to that creativity and those crayons we talked about in the Open Door Rule of Engagement. Gen Z (people born after 1996) is a creative generation that self-identifies as such. In a recent poll of 5,000 participants across five countries, 56 percent of Gen Z considered themselves creative compared to only 44 percent of those born before 1996.[64] In fact, Gen Z has even been dubbed the nickname "Generation Create." This generation has not forgotten where they put their crayons, so capitalize on that by engaging your less experienced team members with creative projects that help you market your small wins and successes and at the same time empowers them to take the lead on a project. Have them create a video or a webpage. In addition to desiring creative expression, Gen Z really wants to feel part of a movement of change and that they add value. There has been a marked trend in recent years of young people quitting jobs in which they felt undervalued and underpaid. Listen to what they want and try to understand their point of view. Consider giving them important and creative roles in projects. Especially on innovation journeys that are generally not client-critical, give your teams and especially your younger colleagues more access and maybe, *just maybe*, more responsibility, perhaps even more than you think they can handle—and I'll bet you might be pleasantly surprised. If you remain worried that your team is a bit green for the enhanced responsibility, create a sponsorship/mentorship program or hire external coaches or provide external executive education and training opportunities to them. The beauty of this "double-do" is it upskills team members and also serves as another form of empowerment.

Remember, empowerment and engagement do not always come from big things. For example, it is a small thing to give someone else credit by putting the name of a contributor more junior than you on a document (in lieu of your own). It is a small thing to develop an open forum for idea submission that anonymizes the entries so that title or rank doesn't shade perceptions. It is a small thing to include *all* professionals (of all types) in your firm's online directory, as opposed to only the "practicing" service providers. Sometimes the tiniest of gestures have the biggest impact, which leads us right to the T in S.A.F.E.T.Y.

D. Culture Creation Ingredient #5: Think T as in Tiny

As mentioned earlier, of my favorite quotes is from Robert Musil's book: *A Man Without Qualities*. It says that it's easy to "to think in miles when you've no idea what riches can be hidden in an inch."[65] I am a big believer that when we begin culture creation, we need to think tiny. There is power in small wins, in moving inches. As mentioned, my dear friend and colleague calls it T.N.T., as in Tiny Noticeable Things that add value.[66] And this is the type of innovation that is earmarked in the Level 3 of the Skills Delta—which is really focused on T.N.T.—as opposed to the disruptive type of innovation discussed by experts like Clayton Christensen. Witness Amabile and Kramer's article on this topic which talks about the progress principle: "Of all the things that can boost emotions, motivation, and perceptions during a workday, the single most important is making progress in meaningful work."[67] Just progress—not winning, not completing a big project—just moving forward. In fact, the failure to preplan for short-term wins can tank a project or a team.[68] So, although big wins are a moment for celebration, the small ones happen far more frequently, and keep us engaged at work and happy.[69] This may be why our positive interactions and bonds with others at work matter more than our compensation or status and why bonding is more important to a team's success than expertise, ability, efficiency, or IQ.[70] So, recognizing those tiny but noticeable things creates the right climate, and celebrating them with recognition and praise, nourishes the team. It also comprises a kind of feedback that actually works. Recent research suggests that negative or critical feedback often fails because our brains respond to criticism like we would a threat.[71] In other words, either a fight or flight response![72] The feedback that works, however, is feedback that points out what we are doing well and asks us to build on that and to wonder how it could be different or better.[73] Celebrating small wins helps keep the feedback loop looping and can add up to a big win over time.

In addition to celebrating small wins, we should focus on starting with small groups of people as opposed to starting big. Ignite excitement with a small group of people; get them to hone new attitudes and behaviors and, over time, they will attract the attention of others, like a bonfire that slowly spreads (as we talked about earlier). The attitude of course is the new attitude that comes from the new mindset, skill set, and behaviors and helps spread the climate from one to another. The way it spreads reminds me of a Fabergé Shampoo commercial from the 1980s, starring Heather Locklear, who says when she first tried the shampoo, she told two friends and then they told two friends and so on and so on and so on. Each time she says, "and so on" more and more women's faces appear on the screen (much like a Zoom screen today, who knew?). That's how it works with culture change. As mentioned, literature on culture creation (as it relates to a culture of compliance) used to emphasize the importance of a top-down approach. Then, about a decade ago, the literature (including my own scholarship) emphasized the importance of culture creation from the middle—with an emphasis on the middle managers.[74] More recently the literature has focused on creating these small pockets of people with whom you can effect change[75] and then like a bonfire (or like Fabergé shampoo), its benefits become so irresistible that people share it and convince others to follow.

There is one caveat to this, however. Although the next paragraph will recommend going short versus long, don't go short-sighted. As others have pointed out, the mere act of breaking up a large group into smaller, autonomous, empowered subgroups to create an innovative, collaborative culture does not magically provide them the right type of spirit and attitude or values and norms.[76] The bonfire approach I'm suggesting only works with what Pisano calls "strong management efforts."[77] We will explore further what we mean by "strong management efforts" in the next chapter. Suffice it to say right now, however, that without purposeful care and oomph, these subgroups will simply "inherit the culture of the parent organization that spawned them."[78]

In addition to thinking small, you need to think short instead of long. Consider that we have four seasons that are each approximately 3 months long. Consider also that schools around the globe often offer classes in quarters or semesters that are approximately 3 to 4 months long. Coincidence or clue? I believe the latter and that a project or initiative that is longer than 3 to 4 months is too long. If a project does take longer than that, it needs to be cut into chunks of no longer than 4 months each. Spoiler alert: that's what the 4 stands for in The 3-4-5 Method™. It's the maximum, not the minimum amount of time. Indeed, when working within the now-popular "Agile method," teams often work in a "Scrum" framework in 4-week Sprints.[79] Therefore, it is not surprising that my method has been used successfully in just 4 weeks and even over a shorter period of time, in fact, less than 4 days. You might still be wondering, however, why is a time period that is longer than 4 months too long? In my experience, it's due to fatigue and loss of focus and changing objectives and, importantly, waiting too long to measure and revisit original estimations so as to replan and reestimate soon enough.

Consider the following case study:[80] In the 1990s, Denver embarked on building a new airport due to the increasing number of people using the existing airport. Part of the plan was to build an automated baggage handling system to reduce flight turnaround time. The problem was, the original estimates about the complexity and length of time involved in creating that system were wrong. However, instead of stopping and reestimating, the project just kept going, eventually delaying the opening of the airport by 16 months (which was estimated to have cost the city $1.1 million per day of the delay). When the airport finally opened, the baggage system didn't work as intended and eventually had to be completely overhauled in 2005.

So, if you have a project you *know* can't be done in 4 months or less, then set a mid-point at 4 months or shorter, a point where you stop and assess (and celebrate any success of course). This way you can make sure you don't just keep going and fall prey to what the British historian Cyril

Northcote Parkinson called Parkinson's law: that a project will always last the amount of time allotted.[81] Another good reason to minimize the time is to prevent changing variables[82] or changing objectives or priorities from sinking the project. If your project iteration is set to end at 4 weeks or 4 months, it is at that point that the team can not only reassess the estimates but also change the plan, to avoid failure.

Another practical way of thinking tiny is related to the time it takes to team. Collaborating (especially online) always takes longer than anticipated. Things go wrong. People show up late. People talk too much. So, when doing teaming exercises, use a timer to keep the talking tiny. Think tinier: If you have five things planned for a breakout session or online group collaboration jam, prepare to cut it back to three on the spot. Last, let's circle back to the quote that started this section, about thinking in inches instead of miles. One of the biggest challenges teams face is problems that are too big or solutions with extraneous bells and whistles. In innovation, a team's charge is to narrow that challenge down to a discrete problem for one or two discrete target audiences, with the goal of creating an MVP—a minimum viable product—or perhaps more aptly put in our context, given that we are not all trying to develop new products, an MVS—a minimum viable solution. The more detailed understanding we have of the problem and its discrete parts, the easier it is to pinpoint what is absolutely necessary for an MVS and, therefore, to come up with a solution that will have a snug fit. To do so I like to use an exercise I created called *The Problem Trip Mapping Exercise* which plots consumer stories and user journeys together on a trajectory map so that teams can identify who is experiencing or being impacted by the problem and when, along with all the various problems within the problem. Problem chunking helps craft a solution that fits like a glove. A glove fits because it has five spaces for five fingers—and so should a solution fit. So, if a team identifies three parts to the problem (i.e., that the syndicated loan process wasn't efficient, wasn't transparent, and it didn't provide authenticity) then the solution should solve for each of these problems, not more, not less. (Note: I have yet another exercise, which I call the *MVS Steeple People Exercise*, to ensure the solution fits like a glove without unnecessary add-ons.) The point being to think tiny when it comes to the problems, to chunk the problems into discrete problems, and to think of essentials—and in inches instead of miles—when it comes to the solutions. That way the solutions will be a perfect fit.

One small caveat to my belief in chunking things. When we are thinking "tiny," we shouldn't be thinking of only parts of a project. Giving a junior team one small piece of a bigger whole can backfire. Instead, chunk up projects into mini, holistic projects that have a beginning, middle, and end and that are true "pilots" as discussed in Chapter 10. Holistic pilots are important because they are challenging but manageable and they provide meaningfulness to the teamwork that is rewarding. They are also the "spoonful of sugar that helps the medicine [of change] go down"[83] because we know there is an end in sight and that it is not longer than 4 months!

E. Culture Creation Ingredient #6: Say "Yes, And"

The Y is for "Yes and"—as we saw in the Open Mind Rule of Engagement. We want to approach leading and collaborating with a *"yes, and . . ."* attitude that keeps our minds and hearts and doors open to questions that challenge our current ways of working, that ask *why* we do things the way we do. We need to say *"Yes, and . . ."* to those eager beavers who say *yes* to you and to the culture you are trying to create. Just as leaders need to learn how to follow, as discussed in Chapter 5, leaders need followers, but not just any kind of followers. Be selective. I'm not the only person to believe that *who* we choose to be on our teams to follow the leader (and *why* they follow) really matters.[84] As my best friend from college who is a venture capitalist always tells me: invest in people not ideas. I have learned that the people to invest in are those people who have something to bring to the project *and* really want to do so. It is why I'm a big believer in asking potential participants a double-sided question: What can they bring to the endeavor as well as what will the endeavor bring to them? The converse corollary of going after the eager beaver is to drop the negative naysayers, the Debbie Downers (who only see the negative side of things).[85] You may feel an urge to use your talents as a leader, your charisma and ability to influence, to turn these dissenters around. Save that energy for later because in the beginning of culture creation, all you will be doing is carrying their weight, and it will bring you and others down, and your efforts at culture creation to a halt. In fact, this is an important lesson to hold onto if somehow a naysayer gets on the team. Holding onto this lesson and letting the naysayers go (*mentally* and *figuratively*) isn't easy but it is especially important. I have learned this the hard way, and yet it was a lesson I already knew from a favorite book of mine, called *Zen Shorts* by Jon J. Muth.[86] In that book, Muth tells a story of two traveling monks who reach a deep stream where a woman stands unable to cross without ruining her outfit. She is scolding her attendants to help her cross. But her attendants simply can't carry her packages and her at the same time. The younger monk, disgusted by the way she is treating the attendants, walks on by her and crosses the stream. The older monk stops, picks her up and carries her across the water. When he puts her down on the other side, she doesn't just fail to thank the older monk. She actually pushes him out of her way with a huff and departs. As the two monks continue their journey, the younger monk broods . . . and broods. He just can't stop thinking about how selfish and rude *that* woman was and how she didn't even thank the older monk. He can't believe the older monk is so calm about it all. Finally, he tells the older monk how he feels. The older monk replies to the younger monk, "I set that woman down hours ago. Why are *you* still carrying her?"[87] For some, this story is a religious and moral one about whether contact with a woman is a sin for a Buddhist monk.[88] For others, this story is about letting past hurts and old resentments go.[89] For me, and for culture creation, this story means this: Carry the naysayers when they absolutely require you to—when they stand at the collaboration river, determined to cross, but cannot cross without sitting on your back—but set them down the minute you can because there is not only ONE collaboration river to cross but many and, over time, they will become an unbearably heavy load that will cause a whole team to brood . . . and brood—and *that* can take a whole team down. So you might ask: should we get rid of the naysayer *physically?* Because that doesn't sound very *inclusive.* The answer is yes, *sometimes,* for the sake of the team. As described in Chapter 8 in more detail, sometimes the leader has to remove someone from the team. That doesn't mean they have to be dismissed from the project entirely. The leader should try to find another way to include this person, to leverage their expertise or talent. But even if it is not necessary (or possible) to remove the person physically, it is imperative to remove them *mentally,* as the older monk did. And in keeping with that teaching, let's move on from the naysayers and back to the people who matter, the eager beavers.

We want to focus on the eager beavers because they become eager followers, those who can be relied on to initiate the change-oriented behavior a leader desires.[90] They are more likely to be intrinsically motivated (committed internally) to learning the requisite new mindset, skill set, and behaviors[91] and to help create a new culture and to collaborate with others towards innovation. Research shows that, to change behavior, intrinsic motivation is key.[92] Those who are motivated by a creative, intellectual challenge (versus motivated by that which is extrinsic like compensation) are more productive and creative.[93] College Professor Beth Hennessey has a great TED talk about this.[94] She explains that "motivation and creativity go hand in hand . . . that we need to approach a thorny problem, a creativity type task for the sheer pleasure, enjoyment, satisfaction, and challenge of that task itself rather than for some extrinsic goal like getting a reward someone has offered us."[95] So feed your eager beavers by ensuring that they have: (1) autonomy and control; (2) the skills and experience to make the changes and do the work, that is, they are competent; and (3) a community with whom they feel connected and are working toward a common and important purpose.[96] And appoint your eager beavers as brand ambassadors to persuade others. After all, that's how a movement begins!

So, what about extrinsic motivation? Some research indicates that extrinsic motivators (even when mixed with intrinsic motivation) can actually kill creativity.[97] For this reason, some researchers recommend saving extrinsic motivators for uninteresting tasks and warn that offering extrinsic rewards for an activity that someone already feels passionately about can devalue the task and be seen as interfering with autonomy.[98] My experience leads me to believe that as long as the intrinsic motivators are attended to, overlaying some extrinsic motivators can help—especially when other extrinsic motivators exist that work against collaboration. As Steven Kerr points out in his much-cited paper about change management, rewarding A while hoping for B is pure folly.[99] Yet that is exactly what many professional service firms do today with respect to collaboration and innovation. They reward A (individual, measurable work, e.g., billable hours or origination credit)[100] but hope for B (collaboration and innovation, which are rarely directly measured and listed as a compensation measure).

Although I believe that professionals should be compensated for collaborative work and for spending time innovating (in addition to billing hours), the good news is that compensation is not the only extrinsic motivator that works. Other extrinsic motivators that can be baked in are indirect financial benefits, for example, in LawWithoutWalls, the fact that the company is paying for the person's participation, that innovation is being made a compensated part of one's job (even if they have to do it in addition to their work) serves as extrinsic motivation even though the person doesn't get that money in their own pocket. Their travel is covered, and they know sponsorship dollars are being given to support a nonprofit and their participation in it.

Another external reward is recognition: being selected to be a part of a team going on an innovation journey to solve a problem identified by a senior leader at one's organization or by a client (within a client's organization) is an honor. The same is true of being selected to be on the strategic planning committee (especially if you are more junior). Further, there is extrinsic motivation in the opportunity to shine in a presentation in front of key stakeholders and peers, not to mention the recognition for helping create the strategy or an innovation that may save thousands of dollars or generate revenue for their company. You might be shaking your head at this, perhaps thinking that's not a real extrinsic motivator—not for accountants or lawyers or HR professionals, but oh it is. Scott Westfahl, the director of executive education at Harvard Law School shared a story with me that opened my eyes to how much of a motivator recognition can be for senior professional service providers. Scott asked associates in their own reviews to name any law firm partners who mentored them over the course of the year and to describe what these partners did for the associate to help them in their development. He then gave out plaques to the partners who were named the most. Eventually, partners who were not named (who did not receive a plaque) noticed and one by one, reached out to Scott: *"Why wasn't I given a plaque?"* They asked longingly. Scott explained the criteria, and wouldn't you know, the next year (and the year after that and the year after that) more and more partners were named by associates for good mentoring. Why? Well in part, because the partners wanted a plaque (to be recognized) for being a good mentor and this opportunity for recognition extrinsically motivated them to be better mentors to their associates.

The third extrinsic motivator that can be baked in is competition. An innovation journey is not only an opportunity to shine but also to compete to win. Although of course we want to embrace competent failure, which means we should all be able to be winners, competition is a motivator. I've seen it work with senior business professionals at law firms and in corporate legal departments. This is true for internal collaboration committees as well, not just innovation journeys. When they realize it is a competition for who will be presenting to the CEO or to the board, wow! Do they step up their game! But don't take it from me. Other experts have touted the benefits of—and other organizations have had success in—using extrinsic rewards to inspire collaboration and innovation among its professionals. For example, in a recent *Harvard Business Review* article, Scott D. Anthony, Paul Cobban, Rahul Nair, and Natalie Painchaud support the use of a combination of extrinsic and intrinsic motivators to break down barriers to innovation and build a collaborative innovative culture—although they don't use those terms. They call them BEANs (behavior enablers, artifacts, and nudges) or "interventions" that work together to motivate people to behave differently.[101] They cite as an example of a "well-crafted BEAN," a scholarship program created by DBS Bank that provides approximately $750 USD to any employee to spend on a project of their choice that supports DBS's goal of becoming a learning organization that continually questions the status quo. This of course is a type of extrinsic motivation, and they combine it with a requirement that winners of the scholarship have to teach what they discovered, learned, or created to other professionals at DBS. In less than a year, DBS provided 100 scholarships for endeavors ranging from developing artificial intelligence to attending story-telling training. If that isn't a mix of extrinsic and intrinsic motivation techniques to spur engagement in an interesting, creative endeavor, I don't know what is. If you are still not convinced, consider that the scholarship is named the Gandalf Scholarship (after the wizard in J. R. R. Tolkein's *Lord of the Rings* series). Or consider Google's 20 percent time policy, which encourages employees to spend 20 percent of their time (approximately one day per week) on creative and innovation endeavors that relate to the employee's individual interests and desires.[102] Or consider that the NASA@Work program rewards winners of innovation with nonmonetary incentives like personalized astronaut autographs, a visit to the employee's department by top officials at NASA, or a mention on the NASA X (formerly Twitter) account.[103]

So go after those eager beavers and feed them the way they want to be fed. Leverage their intrinsic motivation by baking in a bit of extrinsic motivation as frosting (e.g., with extra time, new roles, new tasks, more recognition, more power, more permissions). Appoint them as your brand ambassadors to convince others to join in. Eager beavers are the early adopters.[104] Early adopters of new systems and technology are essential, and they will help teach and encourage others in the company who are perhaps less enthusiastic or more resistant to change. People often want to see proof that a new system works before going to the trouble of learning it for themselves. So encourage younger, keener team members to take new systems, new processes, and new ways of working on board. Once they're proficient and demonstrating its value, they become a guiding coalition. As such, they can help convince other members of the organization. Indeed, they help with one of the problems innovation journeys face, identified in Part III, and that is a lack of internal marketing about the purpose and importance of the initiative.

So those are the essential ingredients for creating the right climate for culture change. However, just as a chef must at times swoop in and take things over to ensure the souffle doesn't flop, so, too, does a leader. It is to this that the next section turns.

●...Reflection Point Consider for a moment: do you really know all the talents and areas of expertise of your team? If you haven't conducted an exercise like the *Talent & Topic Expertise Exercise* described earlier, you likely don't. And if this is the case, consider doing a mini version during your next team meeting as follows:

- **Step 1:** One person on the team should state out loud to the group the team's purpose or main charge.
- **Step 2:** Each team member should then share the following:
  - **Expertise and Interest:** What ties, interest, expertise, or special knowledge do they have related to the team's purpose or main charge?
  - **Talent:** What past roles, talents, hobbies do they have that might be leveraged to help the team related to the team's purpose or main charge?
- **Note:** if you are having trouble making a connection, ask the team to brainstorm ways that your past or current hobbies, jobs, roles, talents or experiences might help the team's future success.

CHAPTER 8

There's Nothing Soft About Culture Creation: Sometimes to Be *for* the Birds, You Need to Be a *Big* Bird

> *"I learned there are troubles of more than one kind.*
> *Some come from ahead; others come from behind.*
> *But I've bought a big bat. I'm all ready, you see.*
> *Now my troubles are going to have trouble with me."*
>
> —Dr. Seuss

Now you know the mindset, skill set, and behaviors you should emulate as a leader to create the right climate and now you have a recipe for creating a culture of creativity, inclusivity, and collaboration, that is, the practical processes, procedures, and permissions you can develop. But your job (still) isn't over. Although different leadership styles can be equally effective, I have found that when it comes to building a culture of creativity, inclusivity, and collaboration and leading teams to innovate, sometimes we need to be not only support-ive and consultative leaders but also, at times, Big Birds: leaders who chal-lenge and question and push (and bring a big theoretical bat when needed).

A good analogy of what I mean by being a Big Bird can be found in the animated short film by Pixar called *For the Birds* that won an Academy Award in 2000.[1] At the beginning of the movie, we see a bunch of little birds sitting apart from each other along a telephone wire chirping in a way that might be described as "complaining." We don't know why they are not sit-ting together, but we know from the visual that they are not "together," and they aren't touching. Then the camera focuses in on a very large, gangly, awkward-looking bird, who waves their hand and says "hey!" to the birdies on the wire. The birds look at the Big Bird as if they think the Big Bird is ridiculous—they laugh and chirp, ignoring the Big Bird. Then the Big Bird calls out *"Ayy??"* almost like a scolding question and they look over at the Big Bird a bit scared and start to move, together, and away from them down the telephone wire. Now their chirping is clearly nervous as opposed to griping and they are united in their fear of what the Big Bird will do next.

Then the Big Bird flies over and lands in the middle of all of them on the wire. The Big Bird's weight causes the wire to sag and all the little birdies on either side of the Big Bird slide down and in toward the Big Bird. Finally, they appear as a cohesive group, and visually they appear as if they are one really *really* Big Bird—the little birdies on each side look like the formation of wings of the Big Bird in the middle. Eventually, however, the little bird-ies start to squawk, clearly not liking that the Big Bird has pulled them all together toward the Big Bird like this. Then one of the little birdies pecks the Big Bird in the stomach as if to say: *"Who invited you to our team?"* As a result, the Big Bird falls forward and is now hanging upside down clutching the wire by the claws to hold on. Eventually, the two little birdies nearest to the center start pecking at the Big Bird's toes, egged on by the rest of the crowd, until the Big Bird loses grip on the wire and falls to the ground (headfirst).

Commentators have stated that this animation is about being different and being seen as a threat; the little birds are rejecting, even bullying the Big Bird. I get that interpretation. However, I also see it as an example of the type of leadership that is necessary at times. As I have learned the hard way leading hundreds of teams on an innovation journey—and as Harvard professor Gary P. Pisano points out: "innovative cultures are paradoxical" and often "the easy-to-like behaviors that get so much attention are only one side of the coin. They must be counterbalanced by some thoughtful and frankly less fun behaviors,"[2] and audacity, like *landing in the middle* of a group that clearly doesn't want you around.

I play this video for all my team leaders and tell them that if one of their teams isn't coming together the way it needs to, if it is having typical teaming issues (hoarding, shirking, lack of communication and cohesiveness, or downright disruptive politics), if it is not "together" on its mission or vision or problem statement or understanding of the consumer audience, it is the leader's job to *land in the middle* and rein them all in. It is their job to ask the hard questions, challenge their assumptions, uncover and make transparent the team's weaknesses and inconsistencies in its thinking—even if this means that all the team members gang up on the leader (just like the little birdies did to the Big Bird in the Pixar animation described above). In fact, I tell all the teams I work with that if they get to a point wherein the team is dysfunctional or worse yet, acrimonious (i.e., not together on the telephone wire), I'm okay with being the reason the team members cohere and finally agree to solve the same challenge, or finally empathize and really understand the consumer audiences, or finally agree on the right solution. If ganging up on me is how they come together for a common purpose and finally start rowing in the same direction together, it's my job to be the Big Bird. And you should be okay with this too. If despite the inclusive, supportive leadership style that is the M.O. of the leader, the team isn't congealing or moving forward as needed, it is the leader's job as a Big Bird to interject with strong management efforts, to force teams to question things that might not have been questioned before, to challenge teams to rethink assumptions and think newly about old problems and also to play the heavy. Research supports this type of "transformative" or "challenging" leadership style,[3] which utilizes intellectual stimulation to encourage the team to think and behave differently and to challenge its beliefs.[4] This style has been linked to enhanced creativity, enhanced feelings of empowerment by employees,[5] and enhanced take-charge behaviors on the part of individuals.[6] There is only one caveat: this should be done *only after* the right climate is developed.[7] So don't try this at home unless you have mastered the Three Rules of Engagement (described in Chapter 6) and created a psychologically safe environment (as prescribed in Chapter 7). Only then will being a Big Bird approach be effective (as opposed to destructive). So, just as culture comes after climate creation,[8] so, too, do Big Birds.

There are countless situations that require a leader to be the Big Bird. In this chapter, I outline just a few of the most common situations I have come across.

A. When the Teaming Is Sour (Internal Dysfunction)

The first and most important situation wherein the leader needs to be the Big Bird is when the teaming itself is going sour. In other words, when the team culture is not in line with the culture of collaboration and innovation which can happen even if you have followed the Three Rules of Engagement and S.A.F.E.T.Y. recipe. Sometimes the teaming is sour because the team is being overly congenial or collegial, valuing collaboration over results or refusing to admit there is a teaming issue.[9] Sometimes folks are cooperating or coordinating instead of proactively collaborating. Other times, it can be because there is what Carlos Valdes-Dapena calls "benign neglect" of the project (which can be a result of missing incentives).[10] Worse yet, it can be because the team is working in disharmony or destructively due to personal issues within the team. I have found that, generally, the most common reasons for teams falling apart because of personal issues include personal behavioral dynamics (someone is being a jerk), someone is shirking (someone isn't pulling their weight), or there is a split in the team with two people vying for power.

Initially, I thought these problems were occurring because the Law-WithoutWalls' teams had students on them. Having taught thousands of students, I have found that students (regardless of their age or pursued degree, i.e., master's, JD, undergraduate, etc.), can behave differently at school than when they are in a business setting. For example, they don't always do their work. I guess it makes sense as they are paying to be in school (not being paid) and the immediate negative repercussions of not doing work is just a bad grade. So, originally I chalked up team dysfunction due to personal dynamics or unequal work ethic to students being students. I was wrong. As I mentioned earlier, I ran a program like LawWithoutWalls for Microsoft's internal Corporate External and Legal Affairs (CELA) department for 5 years and I am currently running a similar program for the legal department at DXC Technology. When I started the program at Microsoft, I had assumed, in error, that I wouldn't have teaming issues related to personal behavioral dynamics or work ethic. This assumption was based on the fact that the teams were made up of business professionals with 10 or more years' work experience and that they were teaming in a business set-ting and doing so voluntarily as part of their continuing education. Plus, there was an application process to be selected to participate. Despite this, every year at least one team was dysfunctional, and generally it was due to one bad apple. I learned that any team can fall apart due to an individual behavioral problem, and team science and research on team effectiveness shore this up.[11] A negative team member spoils the psychologically safe environment,[12] which, in turn, negatively impacts the team's ability to learn how to collaborate and come up with new ideas—which also negatively impacts the team's outcomes.[13] So one bad apple doesn't just prevent good teaming, it prevents the team from learning how to collaborate and also it stymies creativity and innovation.[14] When this happens, when a bad apple spoils the lot (as it invariably does), and team members cannot turn them around or remove the person on their own, I have to be the Big Bird[15] and fast![16] If I do not, then the failing of the team is my own.

Here's why. In my experience, generally when a team is falling apart, it is usually driven by one person (sometimes two)—but it is *always* the fault of *one* person if it continues and that person is the leader who does not step in and fix the problem.[17] It is the leader's job to identify any person that is the problem and address it. This could mean a tough-love discussion, rear-ranging workloads, or moving the problem-person(s) to a different team or out of the initiative altogether. The situations vary, as do the solutions (and our power to enact all the various solutions). In some situations, it is critical to remove someone entirely from an organization and replace them with someone who shares the culture. That's not always possible, however. The managing partner of a law firm cannot remove another partner from the firm (or perhaps even the project). And the solutions are made especially difficult to render when the bad apple partner is one who makes it rain for the firm. However, in that situation, something still has to be done to sequester the sourpuss from the lot—even if it means enabling that part-ner's pet project (that you believe will go nowhere) but in doing so will move their focus away from the current team's initiative. Further, if you find you have a lot of bad apples as opposed to a just a few random (or senior ones), be sure the ask the 5 Whys to get to the root cause, which entails taking a hard look at the recruitment and retention practices of the organization or firm at large or specific to your department or practice group.

Even though taking drastic measures may seem antithetical or paradox-ical to the *inclusive* culture we are trying to create, it is, as Ronald Heifetz aptly says, "one of the trials of leadership is that . . . one performs multiple little assassinations."[18] It is also unfair to the other participants and other teams to let one person or two spoil things. And yes, one person *can* create a whole lot of spoil and demotivation. True, teams sometimes are able to employ successful strategies to change the behaviors of the negative person, for example, through peer coaching (which is NOT a gang-up feedback session but instead peers within the group individually find ways to communicate when behaviors and reactions are not fitting the norm).[19] However, if that doesn't work and they do not have the power to remove them on their own, they need the leader to do it for them.[20] If the leader does not, the credibility of the change effort is threatened[21] or the team will work to isolate that person on its own. So, regardless, you will need to step in as the Big Bird.

Some people call this "draconian."[22] I think it is herculean, but I say this with three huge caveats. First, sometimes getting rid of the bad apple has the perverse effect of debilitating the substantive advantage of the team when, for example, that person is the savant of the group. However, there is still a need for a Big Bird move, that is, the leader needs to meet separately with this person to capture their expertise or set it up so that this person only attends the team meetings for such purposes and only periodically.[23] This enables the person to remain included. Second, sometimes the one person that seems to be the bad apple is serving an altogether different and important role. For example they may be playing the role of "deviant" and provide fresh thinking that is overlooked by the group; or they may represent a group of people whose opinions and voices have not been heard.[24] Third, the group may be falling under the phenomenon known as *splitting* whereby all the good in the team is accredited to one hero and all the badness in the team is accredited to one who seems to be causing the ruckus but who is actually just a scapegoat for the team.[25] The good news is that bad apple-ism of all sorts can be avoided by many of the recommended organizational, procedural, and structural recommendations in the previous chapter and that recommended in Chapter 9 in Part III. Other experts in teaming have found the same: there are fewer interpersonal issues when the team composition, roles, norms, and tasks are well-structured at the outset.[26] However, if they occur midstream, the leader must expertly diagnose the situation (this is where the "S" as in surmise from the S.A.F.E.T.Y. recipe resurfaces). Then the leader must carefully choose their interventions, whether that is repurposing a person or changing the structure and timing of the participation of the team members or removing them as noted above.[27]

All of this may seem paradoxical but so is collaboration and innovative cultures. As others have remarked, if collaboration is taken too far, decision making is stymied. If it is not emphasized enough and there is too much emphasis on individual input, people will focus on their own interests and hoard.[28] As professor Pisano points out, "Unless the tensions created by this paradox are carefully managed, attempts to create an innovative culture will fail."[29] So although we practice having an Open Mind, Open Heart, and Open Door, we need to have strong, adaptive leaders who can play the Big Bird—who are willing to bring the big bat and "break glass" as needed,[30] otherwise nothing gets done.

B. When the Team Is Not on the Same Problem Plane (Vertical Separation)

David Burkus, a leading business thinker and author, wrote a *Harvard Business Review* article titled "Innovation Isn't an Idea Problem."[31] I agree with that statement wholeheartedly—but for a different reason than him. Burkus believes, like me, that ideas are a dime a dozen. However, Burkus believes the real problem with innovation is a "recognition problem," that is, that people fail to recognize the good ideas that already exist, like Kodak failed to recognize the value of digital film. While that might be one of the problems with innovation, I believe the biggest problem is a "problem problem." Teams don't spend enough time analyzing the problem and empathizing with the people experiencing or causing the problem. They don't spend enough time in the problem finding discovery referenced in Level 2 of the Skills Delta. As a result, when they start ideating, they either can't agree on a solution, or they don't come up with viable practicable solutions.

In Chapter 7, we discussed one type of "problem with the problem" that often derails teams: when the problem is too big, and the team has failed to "think small," to narrow the problem enough. Another type of "problem with the problem" is one of misdiagnosis. In their rush to solve, teams focus on symptoms of the problem instead of the root causes and, therefore, miss the mark, as I did with my Microsoft client when I failed to ask why he was worried about our program and the snowstorm. This type of error is avoided with exercises like *The 5 Whys* and creating consumer stories (also sometimes referred to as persona journeys).

A variation on this "problem with the problem" is when, despite narrowing down the problem, the team is not in agreement on the problem they are solving (but they think they are). I call this not being on the same *problem plane*. This happens time and time again and not just on innovation journeys. It also happens on strategic planning committees, likely even holiday party planning committees. Unless everyone agrees on the exact narrow problem they are trying to solve and for whom they are trying to solve it, the team will not come up with a coherent solution. Of course, you can call any problem an "opportunity" instead, but the same narrowing issues occur and the same differences in understanding about the opportunity as well.

We might consider a plane analogy here. For example, we may all be on a plane flying toward Miami, and we may all be in the same *location* and *vicinity*, but we are actually on different "planes"—at different altitudes or flight levels. Pilots call this vertical separation. And although the pilot may see this clearly on some type of navigation device, the people on the plane don't realize there are people on a different plane at an altitude above or below them. Team members can, similarly, have no idea that this is the case, that is, that some of them are on a different *problem plane* than the others. If you ask them: are you all in agreement about what is the problem and who is the target audience? They will all say "yes" and believe it's true. Then, if you ask each person to state in their own words what the problem is, as the leader (the pilot) you can see the vertical separation between the descriptions while the team members cannot. It's almost as if the team leader has an invisible innovation navigation device.

Let me give you an example: A team I sponsored in LawWithout-Walls via my consultancy MOVELΔW was assigned the following topic challenge: *Mental floss: How can we destigmatize mental health issues in the legal profession?*

I asked one of the team members to explain the problem they were solving, and they said, "*Lawyers have disproportionately high rates of anxiety and depression. Because they are worried that they will be perceived as weak and incompetent, they do not seek help for their mental health issues which causes them to withdraw from work and leads to a decrease in productivity which is costly for law firms.*" I said: "*Okay, great. Does everyone agree with this statement?*" And everyone on the team said yes. So then I asked: "*So you are trying to help the lawyers who are suffering from mental health issues?*" Again, they all said yes. Then I probed further. I said, "*I'm confused because doesn't the topic, as it is written, challenge you to address the stigmatization— not the mental health issues themselves?*" No real response at that point.

Then, I asked another team member, "*How would you frame the problem?*" They replied:

> *Because lawyers are worried that they will be perceived as weak and incompetent, they do not seek help for their mental health issues even though many firms offer support programs like on-site psychologists, self-help seminars, and well-being apps. Colleagues that are not suffering from mental health issues are not trained for mental health awareness in the workplace and don't understand the severity of mental illness. And even if they do, they either don't recognize the mental health issues of others or they don't know how to handle it, or they ignore it.*

Ding ding ding, we are getting somewhere with this problem statement, or at least we are getting closer now to the assigned challenge. However, if you compare this student's definition to that of the prior student, it is clear that we had some vertical separation.

When this team could be operating at the second level of listening (debate), they clearly were stuck at the first level, only hearing what comported with what they believed. And believe me, they really want to be on the same plane at this point because they are itching to either ideate or share the solution they have come up with. I won't let them do either of these things, however, if they aren't on the same *problem plane*. Teams hate that I keep calling them back to the problem statement and consumer stories. The desire and urgent rush to solve is powerful. And I get it—there is beauty and peace and celebration in ideation and in problem-solving. Problem finding, however, is thorny and negative and anything but peaceful.

To hasten the problem finding phase, but in a substantive way, I have come up with an exercise (called *The Problem Plane Exercise*) to get team members on the same *problem plane*. Part 1 is silent and done by individuals. Each team member writes down the answer to three critical questions: (1) What is the problem or opportunity? (2) Who are we solving the problem (or leveraging the opportunity) for (which should include both primary and secondary audiences) and who else is impacted or contributing to the problem? and (3) Why—why do we care? Why are we solving this problem as opposed to others? Why does it matter? That is, what's the purpose?[32] I then ask them to cut and paste their answers into the group chat on whatever virtual platform we are using so they can see the separations. In Part 2, the team has to collaboratively draft an answer to the three questions, understanding that every word matters to get them on the same *problem plane*.[33]

When I conducted Part 1 of the exercise with the MOVELΔW team above, it became clear that the team disagreed about the answers to all three of the questions. They didn't agree on the problem they were solving, that is, was it to *prevent* mental health issues among lawyers, was it to *treat* mental health issues among lawyers, was it to *reduce* the stigma related to mental health issues, was it to *help* the lawyers with mental health issues feel that they were not alone? They also didn't agree on the target audience: were they targeting the lawyers at the law firms experiencing mental health issues or the firms in which the lawyers work? Or were they targeting the other people at the law firm who might be contributing to the stigma? It appeared that each of the team members had picked a different target audience.

A similar problem happened with another team. The topic challenge the team was assigned was: *A multidisciplinary approach that matters: How can law firms capture and share information about law firm matters with their internal multidisciplinary professional service providers so that they can add value that matters?* Here is what four team members wrote down during Part 1 (the silent individual part) of the *Problem Plane Exercise*:

- The problem is changing lawyers' mindsets and the culture of the law firms so that lawyers are willing to be more collaborative.
- There is no process to collect and preserve information about a lawyer's work product so that the next time lawyers work on a similar case, they have a template.
- There are insufficient technology resources at the law firm that could easily compile this data.
- We need to incentivize lawyers to be less competitive.

In other words, all four of the team members had a different idea of the problem they were trying to solve, and there was little overlap. Moreover, none of the problem statements were detailed enough and some went too far because they included hints at solutions in their problem statements, which is absolutely not okay during the problem finding stage. For example, one of the team member's problems suggested the solution is a process to collect and preserve information. Another suggested that the solution was more technological resources. Not being on the same *problem plane* AND having individual solutions in mind when entering the ideation stage is a sure-fire way to lead to incompetent failure.

This is why being the Big Bird at such points is so critical. If either of the teams had moved forward to the ideation stage, each of their solutions would have been a discombobulated mess. Solutions that try to account for varying problem statements generally do not survive a *MVS Steeple People Exercise* wherein only the minimum number of processes/parts/ benefits—and target audiences—that are necessary for the solution to be viable in Year 1 are included in the solution. When team members start ideation with a predetermined solution in mind, the group can get stuck and fail to build on each other's ideas to get to the "adjacent possible" we spoke about in Chapters 3 and 6.

C. When the Team's Tunnel Vision Is Heading Toward Failure

The third situation when the leader needs to be the Big Bird is when the team is hurtling toward failure that is avoidable. One of the reasons why I think design thinkers fail to resonate with professional service providers (especially lawyers) is because they often tout the importance of failure as part of any innovation journey. Axioms like *"celebrate failure"* or *"embrace failure"* make professionals cringe—especially those who get paid by the hour for actually not failing. What I present instead is that there is more than one type (and more than one stage) of failure. Competent failure, the kind of failure from which you can learn and move forward, the kind from which there are the seeds of a successful idea, or the learnings can be applied to a future prototype, is okay. These are what professor Pisano calls "productive failures" that "yield valuable information relative to their costs."[34] But incompetent failure—like the Denver airport's badly engi- neered baggage system that cost half a billion in delays—is just an "expen- sive flop," a waste of time and something we should have taken action on much, much earlier.

Incompetent failure can come in many flavors. It can be tactical, that is, failure to execute properly, failure to test and measure. These are called "how" failures.[35] Or they can be strategic, for example, the strat- egy doesn't deliver the intended results. These are the "what" failures. They can be the result of a team not setting a clear vision or having the right vision, or "why" failures. Many of these types of failures stem from tunnel vision. The team can't see more than one side of the same story.

Marketers understand this really well. They realize that multiple audiences are impacted by a product or solution and that it is important to understand who the product or service or tool is for but also who else may be impacted or involved. In other words, the buyers might not be the consumers.

Take for example, Kellogg's Apple Jacks, a breakfast cereal. They were given their original name Apple O's in 1965 and were advertised as having the taste of apple and cinnamon. Eventually, the name was changed to Apple Jacks. Some of you might recall the catchy jingle used in all the commercials until 1992: "A is for Apple, J is for Jacks, Cinnamon-Toasty Apple Jacks." Near the time I started working on the brand, we changed that. Why did we axe this well-established jingle? Sales were not as robust when compared to Kellogg's other sugar cereals and we didn't know why. It was a bit of a conundrum. We did some research, which confirmed what we knew—the name of the cereal "talked" to the buyer—which at that time was moms.[36] They liked that the cereal had "apple" in it because it seemed healthier than other sugar cereals. (Shh don't tell anyone. They really weren't healthier! They were basically Froot Loops with added cinnamon.) So why weren't they buying it?

We conducted more research to find out. We started with the main buyer: moms of tweens aged 9 to 11 years. The moms told us that their kids weren't asking them to buy Apple Jacks. The interesting part of this (which was new to us) was that kids had influence over what moms bought and moms wanted to buy their kids what they wanted. Next, we checked in with the real consumer, the eater and influencer, that is, 9- to 11-year-old tweens. We discovered that they were put off by the name. They didn't want their sugary cereal to be healthy and actually didn't like the taste of apples, at least not in their breakfast cereal. One option at this point would have been to simply change the name. But that would have risked incompetent failure because moms liked the name. Yet staying the course was also not an option. So we dug deeper into the minds and hearts of tweens. We learned that kids at this age, right before becoming full-fledged teenagers, liked to have control over what they did and what they ate and when they ate it. And any small chance to be a bit irreverent resonated with them. So we changed our tune entirely and started creating commercials beginning in 1992 that touted that Apple Jacks don't taste like apples and that's exactly why tweens like them because they "eat what they like"— even if the name is a misnomer.[37] We also displayed the tweens eating the cereal in the afternoons. When questioned by parents or older siblings why they would eat a cereal called *Apple* Jacks (yuk) and as a snack (in the afternoon) as opposed to a meal at breakfast, the tweens rolled their eyes and continued doing what they wanted despite the norm (indeed to break the norm). The commercials were a success and we saw an increase in sales that we were able to demonstrate was, in part, due to the new advertising strategy.

In this example, the only way we avoided incompetent failure was to check our assumptions—all of them, not just one of them. We knew moms liked the name and that the push on the "apple" made them feel less guilty. What we didn't realize was that buying habits had changed. Moms were increasingly taking into account what their tweens wanted them to buy, and tweens weren't asking for Apple Jacks. They wanted Froot Loops or Frosted Flakes. Until we really researched and developed an understanding of this new dynamic between moms and tweens and really listened to why tweens didn't like the name but realized they could get over the name, we were doomed. Without seeing both sides (mom and the tween's sides), any advertising strategy wouldn't work, and this would be incompetent failure. Moms would buy the cereal, but kids wouldn't eat it, so eventually moms would stop buying the cereal.

Creating a solution and assuming it will be bought or used by the target audience (due to lack of understanding of the full dynamics of all stakeholders) is common among teams on innovation journeys. I call this a *Field of Dreams* failure. *Field of Dreams* was a 1989 movie starring Kevin Costner that was nominated for an Academy Award. Costner plays the role of a small-town rural farmer who is inspired by a voice in his head to build a baseball field in the middle of his farming lands. The voice repeats to him "If you build it, they will come." Costner believes the voice, plows his crops, and builds a field. Now this is a movie, so of course people actually came to this hard-to-find, middle-of-nowhere baseball field, but in real life? Just because you build something doesn't mean people (your target audience) will come to it (will purchase, use, download or follow it). In fact, one of the number one reasons startups fail according to the founders themselves is a lack of market need for the product they offer![38] So when teams have tunnel vision and only see one side of the story, or fail to recognize new or other dynamics at play, or the lack of demand, they face incompetent failure, that is, a baseball field in the middle of nowhere with no attendees.

Let's go back to the MOVELΛW team mentioned earlier that was charged with solving the stigma related to lawyers having mental health issues. Given how much variance there was in their answers to the *Problem Plane Exercise*, I was worried about a tunnel vision type of incompetent failure as well. So, my next question for the team was of course: *Have you completed consumer stories for each of the audiences that are relevant to your challenge?* (Note: in conjunction with the former director of Law-WithoutWalls, I created a very easy-to-use exercise for consumer story writing that utilizes a fill-in-the-blank format akin to the old game, Mad Libs). They said yes, they had written their consumer stories but upon probing it was clear that they had only done so from the viewpoint of a lawyer who was suffering from mental health issues who feared being stigmatized if they sought help from one of the firm's offered resources. They had not considered other audiences that were impacting or being impacted by the problem. So I asked the team to create some consumer stories for the people who might be *contributing* to the problem because until they understood how other people at the firm felt and reacted to lawyers who admitted they had mental health issues—until they understood the source of the stigma—they wouldn't be able to get on the same *problem plane* and solve the problem in a viable way. Instead, they might have created a solution that didn't work, or that no one used: a classic *Field of Dreams* problem. Contributing to the vertical separation is exactly this: a failure on the part of the team to see both sides of the "story." They may have completed consumer stories for one side of the story, but they may have missed a secondary or tertiary audience like, in this example, the firm's point of view and/or the other lawyers' points of view at the firm. And without that understanding, they were at a risk of misdiagnosis and they may have developed a solution that the law firm wouldn't implement, or the lawyers contributing to the stigmatization wouldn't use. Net, a new tool or procedure or product is built, but no one uses it.

In any circumstance, when a team is hurtling toward incompetent failure (e.g., a solution without a problem or a problem that is too large for the budget or time allotted or outside the scope, or a target audience that can't be reached or doesn't care about the solution), it is the leader's job to be the Big Birds and step in and set the team back on track. It may mean chunking the problem that they are focusing on into smaller pieces for them, that is, having them start a *Problem Trip Mapping Exercise*. It may mean doing a *Problem Plane Exercise* to ensure the team agrees on the problem they are solving, for whom, and why. It may mean *telling* them what the vision should be or who their new target audience *must* be and introducing them to some people to interview to better empathize with that target audience. It also may be that the project needs to be killed entirely. Perhaps due to commitment bias, a team might continue to persist in the course of action because they are in love with the idea of their project, or they have sunk too much into it already to kill it. This is called "the double down effect."[39] Even when the team's commitment is not going well, they will be more likely to dig their heels in and increase their commitment, that is, double down on it, because they want to look like they are staying on task, on goal, even if the end result is looking like failure.[40]

One way to get teams to come to this conclusion on their own is with a *Pre-Mortem Exercise* wherein you ask the team to think of all the reasons they should kill their project or their solution[41] but if this isn't done early enough, it can be really hard to convince them to kill it themselves. When that happens, it's the leader's job to be the Big Bird and kill it for them. You might be surprised how many participants thank you afterward. In addition to commitment bias, there are other reasons teams persist in a course of action despite knowing deep down they should stop or wanting it to stop including politics, power, recognition, fear, and inertia, to name a few.[42] Knowing something should be killed, however, is quite different than putting the kibosh on a project. But either way, as a leader, it's our job to prevent incompetent failure. As a leader, it is also our job to pick our battles and to try to do what professor Pisano recommends, which is: "strike the right balance between a culture of unbridled tolerance for failure and one that is completely intolerant of any incompetence."[43]

D. And the List Goes on . . .

I have listed three of the most common conditions that require you to be a Big Bird, but there are many more. For example, sometimes the problems I identified in the previous sections happened due to another problem: the leader didn't actually establish the climate as intended or, if they did, they didn't ensure that it stuck. As discussed in greater detail in the next chapter, the most important thing to get right, right away, is teaming to build trust. It is essential that teams take the time to team almost every time—not just at the kickoff or initial meeting—because things are always fun at the beginning, but they then can become not-so-fun once the team really has to collaborate. Many professional service providers who often charge by the hour may feel they don't have time for this. After all, you can't bill a client for a teaming exercise. So you have to be an even Bigger Bird here and make sure the team knows this is part of culture creation and is essential to building trust.

Another example: research shows that there is a "negative bias against creativity in times of uncertainty."[44] In other words, when people are facing uncertainty, like that from a pandemic, they are more likely to reject innovation and to kill other people's ideas—that is another job for the Big Bird, preventing this in times of uncertainty.

Being a Big Bird is a big job, and there is no one right way to do it, and how you do it varies depending on time, place, and space, your own leadership style, and your own personal brand . In LawWithoutWalls, I put on costumes to deliver my messages and play the part in a way that lightens the heaviness of what I might be doing. I ask people to put their thick-skin suits on as a warning before delivering harsh feedback (as nicely as possible). I share my own personal mistakes with real stories (which makes me vulnerable and scares me to death every time even though I know the importance of vulnerability as it is one of the core skills on the Delta). These are some of the ways I play a Big Bird with the hopes of not over-powering. Of course, when I play the role with law firm partners at a law firm that has a different culture than LawWithoutWalls, believe me, I definitely don't wear costumes, but I still stay in keeping with my personal brand and my personal truths. To be good at being a Big Bird, you need to be authentic and good at storytelling from the heart. As an authority on courage, vulnerability, and empathy, professor Brené Brown, says "stories are just data with soul."[45] But it takes courage and vulnerability to tell your own and to play the Big Bird role. Recall the description of the Big Bird in the animated video: the Big Bird was awkward looking, and the birds were making fun of the Big Bird and avoiding the Big Bird but the Big Bird went forth anyway, firmly not meanly. Though eventually, the Big Bird was cut out of the group—the birdies stayed together—which is your intention when you are the Big Bird. Remember: sometimes being a Big Bird is an essential part of being a leader and creating the collaborative, inclusive, innovative climate and culture you desire—despite it feeling paradoxical or awkward. So embrace this otherness with vulnerability; embrace what Brené Brown would call "the suck" of being a Big Bird—and do so the way she recommends: "keeping it awkward, brave, and kind."[46]

PART III

Managing Collaboration, Innovation, and Culture Change

> *"Leadership is doing the right things.*
> *Management is doing things right."*
> —Peter Drucker[1]

There are tons of articles that tout the difference between management and leadership. They generally say that leaders inspire while managers manage.[2] In a *Harvard Business Review* article, professor Abraham Zaleznik contends that the difference is related to a person's perceptions of chaos and order. He explains that "[m]anagers embrace process, seek stability and control, and instinctively try to resolve problems quickly—sometimes before they fully understand a problem's significance. Leaders, in contrast, tolerate chaos and lack of structure and are willing to delay closure in order to understand the issues more fully."[3] In this way, Zaleznik argues, leaders are more like artists and other creative professionals than they are like managers. Best-selling author John O'Leary describes the difference between leaders and managers through their relative focus.[4] "Focus more on people and you'll demonstrate leadership, more on results and you'll perform management."[5]

Both agree that we need both leaders and managers. However, I disagree with both in two ways. First, I don't believe that we can segment leaders and managers as easily as that and second, even if we could, I don't believe we should. I believe that when it comes to collaboration efforts of any kind, whether the goal is to create a 5-year strategy or to innovate, we, the leaders, need to be managers as well. In other words, we need to be both a leader and a manager in one. We need to focus simultaneously on both people *and* results. In Chapter 5, we discussed the importance of doing the right first thing first. We also need to make sure we do the right things right, that is, correctly (as the quote above indicates). It is not sufficient to leave the management to a manager. Otherwise, like Little Bo Peep, we will lose our sheep. If we only "lead," we may inspire hearts and minds but never get the results. If we only manage, we may keep the sheep, but they will be dragging their tails behind them.

Given the kinds of challenges that professional service providers help their clients solve, it is especially important to ensure leadership is part and parcel of management. I'm not alone in making this call. Rosabeth Moss Kanter, a Harvard Business School professor, argues that managerial experience "would be a good prerequisite for leadership" and to "bring management skills back into leadership."[6] One of my interviewees put it this way:

> *"There are two types of leadership. The leaders who 'lead' the company and the leaders who also are managers. We expect everyone to be a leader but the leaders who are also managers drive clarity and energy. And that takes a lot of work."*[7]—Associate General Counsel, American multi-national technology corporation

However, in the professional services world, although *leadership* in innovation and collaboration is now being emphasized, the management aspect of *leading* innovation doesn't seem to be garnering adequate emphasis. On the one hand, it might be that professional service providers do not realize that innovation or collaboration efforts need to be project managed at all. For example, one study showed that professional service providers believe that short projects (3 months or under) don't require any project management—despite the fact that short projects are often as important to professional services firms' profitability as larger, longer ones.[8] On the other hand, even if that guess is wrong and they do realize the importance of managing projects, professional service providers are notorious for *not* managing initiatives of any kind very well. For example, they are known for failing to effectively communicate with teammates and clients, create budgets (or track them),[9] and manage scope and scope creep.[10]

In keeping with that, studies show that professional service providers, more often than not, fail to use project planning tools[11] and lack structured processes to manage collaborative change.[12] Studies of professional service providers of all kinds (lawyers, accountants, auditors, etc.) repeatedly report low scores in change management and management skills[13] And the oddest thing about all of this is, they *know* it. They *know* they are bad at managing: they self-rate *themselves* poorly on their management and change management skills.[14] So in addition to facing an incognito *"problem* problem" wherein leaders do not realize that the team is not on the same *problem plane*, collaboration and innovation efforts often face an incognito management problem, wherein the leaders don't realize they aren't actually managing and don't believe they really need to be managing the efforts.

That professional service providers may not realize the importance of management and, regardless, aren't very good at it is disconcerting on many levels. First, we have moved to a "project economy," with shorter product (and project) life cycles.[15] The value from project-oriented activity is tremendous. Although only about 35 percent of projects undertaken worldwide are successful, the economic value from project-oriented value is estimated to practically double from $12 trillion in 2017 to $20 trillion.[16] And the impact and importance of the noneconomic value is immeasurable. Social science and behavioral research demonstrate that projects can provide meaning, motivation, and inspiration for team members[17]—and that poor management is a top "destroyer of meaningfulness".[18] This makes sense given what we know about the progress principle[19] (discussed in Chapter 7).

Second, innovation is not just *a* type of change management initiative, it is a change management effort of the *toughest* kind.

Third (along with failing to do the right first thing first), a contributing culprit of the 75 percent of failed change management efforts is flawed implementation—flawed management of the change.[20] This means, for example, that even if a firm's innovation committee has a fantastic leader, if they don't manage (and market) the efforts, they will be doomed to failure, left without structure, an end date, goals, roles, or identifiable metrics. Research demonstrates that "[w]hen executives ignore project management, products launch late, strategic initiatives don't deliver, and company transformations fail, putting the organization's future seriously at risk."[21] This is one of the main reasons why leaders need to focus not only on honing their leadership and collaboration skills but also on their management skills. So when leading an innovation or complex problem-solving effort of any kind, leaders need to be managers as well. And I "get" the producer-manager dilemma that exists for all professional service providers. When focused on management, they can't produce, that is, bill, or work on client matters. But increasingly client matters require teams to work together on projects. Although there needs to be a balance, as it stands, it seems there is an imbalance, with too little attention on the manager side of the equation.

You might now be wondering why we need leaders who are also managers as opposed to two different people (one leading and one managing) in collaboration. Here's why.

When we are in charge of both, our tendencies to go to one extreme or the other are checked. For example, managers who are not leaders might tend toward micromanaging, as opposed to being a resource for the team to help guide them. While it is true that not all micromanagement is bad or ineffective,[22] the yin to the yang is that leadership skills nonetheless help prevent the manager in us from certain myopia. With leadership skills intact, a manager checks in on the teams as opposed to checking *up* on the team.[23] Without this check, a manager might focus only on process improvements, which research shows hinders innovation over time.[24] Further, in managing innovation, a manager might create new structures that seem to support co-collaboration across diverse groups but might, in turn, create protocols and checkpoints that create new barriers.[25] As a leader-manager we are able to strike that balance to ensure that we aren't managing creativity to death but instead managing to enable creativity to flow.[26] Also, professionals in the knowledge service industry tend to work autonomously, moving from one task to another with little time spent on reflection and acknowledgment of change and the effort required and resulting frustrations and emotional toil that comes with change. There is a famous saying that leadership is "disturbing" or "disappointing people at a rate they can absorb."[27] A manager, working under the "progress principle"[28] might be great at getting the team to results, and even celebrating those results, but may lose some people along the way by not walking through the changes and implementing them at a bearable pace.

According to experts in adaptive challenges, people don't resist change in and of itself. They resist the loss that change threatens to create.[29] An adaptive leader who is also a manager can identify and *manage* those potential losses by putting them into new contexts to motivate people to embrace the change and move forward individually.[30] An adaptive leader who is also a manager can help teams work through not only what should be given up but also what should be preserved.[31] When leaders also have the skills and mindset of a manager they empower others to change the stories they tell about themselves and to think independently and do their new job. They also set structure and develop strategy, plans, and systems.[32] Although some may call this micromanagement, it isn't. This is because, although leader-managers specify the ends and provide support to get there, they don't specify the details of the means by which the team should pursue those ends and, thereby, waste talent and experience and demotivate people (or cause perverse effects).[33] Instead, they employ a combination of leadership and management skills, which include teaching, interpersonal, strategic, visionary, creative problem-solving, diagnosis, and implementation skills—and it is that combination that others, like me, believe makes the difference.[34]

Being both a leader and manager also gives us the wherewithal to *identify* when we need to be a Big Bird (that's the manager part) and then to truly act as the Big Bird in a way that brings the birdies together (as opposed to falling apart; that's the leader part, which we already discussed). It gives us the wherewithal to structure and organize our teams in a way that ensures that the innovation proceeds toward success (or at worst, competent failure). And it gives us the wherewithal to facilitate a collaboration journey utilizing The 3-4-5 Method™, to create a space for diverse ideation (and prevent jumping to solutions) while at the same time keeping the light on the purpose and highlighting the trajectory forward.[35] As other author experts on design thinking have put it:

> *Leaders can't simply commission design-thinking projects and then step back. They must keep a watchful eye on them and be vigilant in recognizing moments when they need to engage with the team. . . . Leaders who commission design-thinking projects must be coaches who inspire their teams to achieve success, hand-holding when necessary but drawing back when a team hits its stride.[36]*

Additionally, proper management includes having a marketing plan that talks to the key stakeholder and a method or process that identifies key milestones and helps move teams from point A to point Z.

Until now, we have focused on how you can be a better, more inclusive, more self-aware leader and create the right teaming environment for a culture of collaboration and innovation to thrive. That's essential. However, the point of this part of the book is to convince you that even if you master all of that, your efforts to motivate your teams to collaborate on projects, let alone collaborate on an innovation journey, will fail if you fail to manage and market those efforts properly. Earlier, I said that I believed the biggest problem with innovation was that the teams lacked consensus about and a cohesive understanding of the problem. The second biggest problem with collaboration and innovation, why these efforts fail, is the lack of proper management. And proper management includes having a marketing plan and a method or process to get from point A to point Z. It is to this second problem that Part III turns. Chapter 9 addresses how to manage teams and teaming, while Chapter 10 focuses on the importance of marketing to all key stakeholders and using a method that helps put some sanity into the madness that design thinking and innovation efforts create. Chapter 11 provides an overview of the 3-4-5 Method™ and why it can be used by any leader-manager to facilitate collaborative problem solving by multidisciplinary teams.

CHAPTER 9

Progress Needs Procedure: To Lead, You Must Manage

> *"Management is, above all, a practice where art, science, and craft meet."*
>
> —Henry Mintzberg[1]

As you know by now, I don't buy into the segmentation of managers and leaders. I also don't buy into the idea that leadership is an art and management a science. As the opening quote of this chapter suggests, true management has leadership baked into it and therefore is "a practice where art, science, and craft meet": the tangible and intangible. That is what this chapter is all about. It is designed to teach leaders how to manage both the tangible parts of collaboration and culture creation efforts (e.g., the structure and organization of teams) and the intangible things like building trust and accountability. It's one thing to say that accountability is a key ingredient to creating a "safe" culture, it is another thing to "manage" it, to make sure that people actually feel accountable and are held accountable. The reality is that both the tangible and the intangible *can* and *should* be managed.

Teams need to be created, structured, and developed in a way that builds trust and that reaps the benefits of true multidisciplinary teaming and avoids much of the havoc that can ensue if this is not done right.[2] As we dig into this section, a warning. This section attempts to reduce teaming (the management of teaming) and building trust to a regular, customary set of procedures. Of course, the reality is that teaming is an organic process and requires a leader to be alert and creative, as noted in

Part II. However, some parts of teaming and building trust need to be structured, that is, managed, and not left to chance. Also, you may find some recommendations in this part to be what my students would call *cringey*. I believe in cringey. Cringey is often unforgettable, like a catchy song lyric that you wish you could forget but plays on repeat in your head. But I promise you that even if you cringe at these recommendations, even if you feel like they are a waste of valuable time, this section will more than save time because it will help you avoid teaming and collaboration issues on the backend which are a time-suck. That is because these recommendations create more efficient, effective collaboration habits that enhance accountability and results, and, as I tell all my civil procedure students, the process and the *procedure*, matters. Lots of cases are won and lost by strategically using (or not using) the rules of civil procedure to their advantage. The same is true of these recommendations around teaming and building trust. I have *processized* them into rules of teaming procedure that can be used strategically by leader managers to their advantage—if you can get over the cringe factor. And I hope you do because the only way these procedures work is if you are open and up front about them. You should tell your teams what you are doing and why—because these procedures help you manage teams so that teams team "right"—and good teaming is essential to productivity and especially to creativity, collaboration, and innovation.

The best news about following these rules of *teaming* procedure is, even if our projects do not end up getting enough votes to move forward or enough support to fund—we will not only know our colleagues better but *like* them better, and, therefore, even if we are frustrated with the outcome, we won't be frustrated with the process. There's no more lethal killer of innovation than a frustratingly hellish process. People don't forget going through that. These recommended procedures help ensure a better collaboration and/or innovation process.

A. There's Nothing Organic about Team Organization

While it is true that organic interaction at work can help people feel a sense of belonging, there should be *nothing* organic about team organization: it's size, structure, and makeup. It should be organized and orchestrated from the start.

1. Size

First, where team size is concerned, bigger is definitely not better. Most of you have been on committees or task forces made up of 10 to 15 people. (If you're on one at this time, skip the next meeting. You really aren't needed.) A team of more than 10 people is simply too big to get anything done or hold anyone accountable. Worse yet, a large-sized committee isn't really a team and, even if it is, it may encourage bystanders, what economists call *free riding*, which we don't want.[3] In my consulting work with law firms, I have found that innovation committees that are formed based on a combination of politics and good intentions to ensure inclusivity, end up being around 20 to 30 people from the firm—mostly lawyers, with the business professionals sprinkled in for support (as opposed to as real members—trust me, I will say more about that later, critically). And this group of 20 to 30 is generally divided into two groups (or three if I'm lucky) around a topic—often one that is named something like the *legal tech group*, with others possibly named *pricing*, or *new products*, or *process*, or *operations*, or *training*, or *recruitment*, etc. (I will also talk more about naming later.) Even so divided, the groups and topics are still too large, and the committee is generally ineffective. American comedian Fred Allen described it this way: "Committee: A group of people who individually can do nothing but together can decide that nothing can be done."[4]

So, what is the ideal size of a team? In my experience it is between five and eight people, with nine (if absolutely necessary) being the maximum; and research shores this up.[5] But I also go further than that. If a team is made up of six or more people, there absolutely needs to be subgroups within the team (as noted later) because eight people can't collaborate at once. It's just not possible, and it enhances performance problems exponentially.[6] So I always divide people into subgroups of three to four people. You might ask: why not divide them into groups of two? Given the nature of professional services and unpredictable client demand, groups of two are super risky and super tough if one person can't pull their weight for whatever reason, that is, client needs, personal emergency, job transition, etc.—not to mention that it would be hard to follow (and gain the benefits of) the Open Door Rule of Engagement with only two people.

2. Structure

Second, subgrouping is also important because every team needs structure related to tasks and roles. Every team needs some doers, and every team needs some mentors or guides. Every team needs a project manager to keep the team from drift. And every team needs a coach who is arguably the ultimate leader-manager but not involved in the day-to-day; instead, the coach is in charge of driving and motivating the team toward a viable solution. They come in and out as interveners at key moments, sometimes only to provide encouragement, other times to prevent groupthink, and still other times to provide tough love (and serve as a Big Bird) on interpersonal and strategic issues. All these interventions should focus the team on its goal: delivering an outcome that adds value (as opposed to inputs and outputs).[7]

After writing the first draft of this book, I found research to support how in LawWithoutWalls we use coaches substantively at key intervals of time, namely the beginning (the KickOff), the middle, and the end.[8] Note: I like to use the title of coach over leader, especially when there are people of equal seniority on the team. Calling one person "the" leader is a sure-fire way to make the others defensive. Also, in my experience it works best if there is one main leader (lead facilitator) overseeing multiple teams, whereas there is one coach assigned to each team for whom they are responsible and to whom they are loyal. A picture of a typical team is shown in Figure 9.1.

When building and naming subgroups within a team of five to nine people based on roles, it is useful to remember that status can be a trigger.[9] So name the subgroups carefully, for example, labeling one group of people as "juniors" and other people as "seniors" can be threatening. Don't assume that there is a need to segment groups based on level within an organization and, in fact, our Open Mind and Open Door Rules of Engagement beg for the opposite approach. My experience bears this out.

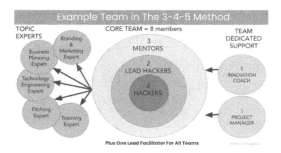

FIG. 9.1. Example Team Makeup and Structure in The 3-4-5 Method™.

I have tested it in LawWithoutWalls many times and I also tested it when I was working with Microsoft. We had six groups one year. We made two groups where the "doers" or "hackers" were the more junior people and the mentor-leaders were more senior. Then, we had two groups where we did just the opposite. Finally, we had two groups where each subgroup was a mix of seniors and juniors. We didn't find any difference in their ability to collaborate or in their work product. Instead, we found what other researchers have found and that is that when expectations and tasks are clear, people play the role they are assigned.

Some of you might remember the book called the *Six Thinking Hats*,[10] which was premised on the power of roles and, more specifically, role-play. In this book, the author, Edward De Bono, argues that we must be deliberate and proactive in our thinking. He recommends people pick one of the six types of thinking and figuratively wear one as a hat. In intentionally putting on one of the six thinking hats, you take on that role, and your ego is protected because you've been assigned and agreed to play that role. In fact, it frees up your ego so it can help you play the role well (even if that role is one that you wouldn't have chosen for yourself or you believe is "beneath" you). And when you "wear" the hat (or the role) it serves as a conditioning signal that triggers our brains and impacts our thinking and behavior.[11] Thus, the roles assigned on a team can provide the same signals and license to our egos to play those roles (as the hats do)—even when the assigned role might not match the internal title "hierarchy" of the organization or firm. Similarly, experts on organizational behavior and leadership maintain that reorganizing people into new roles with new responsibilities and relationships is one the most effective ways to elicit new attitudes and types of behavior.[12]

Roles matter for other reasons too. They help create structure and they also motivate accountability on multiple levels. As long as roles are created in a fair manner, and are really clear as to what each subgroup is going to do, by when, how they will be assessed, and why they matter—and they are delineated in a nontriggering way—role identification can empower people to take charge while enabling each individual to focus on leveraging their expertise to fulfill their assigned role.[13] It can also create a shared leadership approach where the team members feel jointly responsible with the leader, not only about accomplishing the tasks but also working in a way that is truly collaborative—that is, with an Open Mind, Open Heart, and Open Door.[14] In fact, my experience indicates that both subgrouping and role identification actually help prevent the five main triggers that cause the fight or flight reaction as identified by David Rock's SCARF model: S: status, C: certainty, A: autonomy, R: relatedness, and F: Fairness.[15] Everyone who is put into the same subgroup is now (by nature of being in the same subgroup) of the same Status, which helps them feel safe and Related to others in the role. There is Certainty because the subgroup has an identified purpose and goals with Autonomy within to meet those goals and tasks in their own way. Plus, the subgroup is of a size that shirking one's role cannot go unnoticed. This, along with the clarity around roles and expectations assures the participants that the work load is being divvied Fairly.

As will be mentioned below in describing The 3-4-5 Method™, in addition to the members of the team, we identify expert advisors who support the teams but are not "part" of a team. Generally, these are professionals who are experts in substantive areas that teams may not have the expertise on while developing their projects, such as branding/marketing, technology/AI, data analysis, business planning, and teaming. This type of structure can work really well, as long as the experts have the bandwidth and, importantly, as long as they are truly treated as experts. In other words, as long as they are not seen as administrative help and expected to do as much work as the other members of the team or asked to jump in and do the grunt work at the end. I have seen this happen at firms where the business professionals who support the internal professionals are considered second-class citizens within the company because they don't have the same kind of expertise. Unfortunately, it is not uncommon that the head of marketing at a law firm, even if they used to practice law, may be viewed as not having the same level of expertise and understanding of what lawyers do and thus treated as inferior. Yes, this does happen, and it is a shame. I have seen this type of behavior wreak havoc in innovation journeys when the marketing, learning and development, and IT professionals are not positioned as EXPERTS who serve and "advise," and it has not been made clear they are not there to do all the work, crunch all the numbers, conduct all the research, or create the final presentation and script for the team. These professionals either need to be ON the team as an equal team member and fulfilling a role (that others also have been assigned) OR separate from the team and clearly delineated and treated as *expert* advisors. Of course, all of this depends on the culture, the people on the team, and you, the leader-manager. Reasonable people can (and do) disagree on how exactly to structure teams and delineate roles. However, there is consensus that team structure and a shared understanding of roles and goals enhance team effectiveness.[16]

One aspect of role identification where there is likely more debate is related to authority and the process by which the team will make decisions. I believe havoc reigns when authority and decision-making power and process are not transparent (or are left undecided until a decision has to be made). I believe it is crucial to identify the authority of and within the team. Of course, when it comes to level and type of authority, each team's needs are different. For some teams, final decision-making authority will rest on one individual who may be a part of the team, or even outside the team (the latter is okay but it's important that the team has some autonomy to self-manage its work).[17] Other teams will decide differently depending on the issue and who is in the best position to make the decisions that ensure the team accomplishes the result. This hierarchy of authority in the decision-making process doesn't ruffle feathers if there is clarity and the team members believe their ideas are truly being properly considered. This has worked for Disney and its Braintrust sessions in which candor is expected, and input is taken from a diverse group of people, but the ultimate decision is left to the director.[18]

Of course, some teams will still lean toward consensus as the decision tool. It may seem like the latter is the best option, but that hasn't been proven by research and, in fact, experts have argued the opposite.[19] In my experience, if the team prefers the consensus route, it is still good to have one person identified as the final decision maker. Moreover, it is important to understand and agree on the process for how a team will approach consensus. An obvious way, of course, is voting, and there are some great tools out there that make voting more inclusive, take into account the gradients in agreement (as opposed to assuming the vote is yes or no), and enable each person's opinions to be seen and heard.[20] However, instead of voting I prefer trying to build consensus with conversation, understanding that it can be tricky because debate and discussion can increase tension; and silence can sometimes be mistakenly assumed to equate to agreement. This is why experts recommend a combination of time for debate and discussion along with some breaks for processing and reflection, which can lead to increased creativity and help manage the intensity of the discussion and reduce the level of conflict.[21]

Holding these debates and discussions in a way that embraces disagreement but contains conflict does not always come naturally to teams. In LawWithoutWalls we use different exercises to practice building consensus *before* teams actually have to do it for real. One exercise we have borrowed is called *Pancakes or Waffles*. It is a teaming exercise designed to practice making decisions collectively as a team. The name is indicative of the "either/or" choice the team is making. Here's how it works: The premise is that this team is responsible for designing a new world and gets to choose what to keep and what to get rid of. The set-up is that the choices the team makes will have consequences for the world. Whichever choice the team rejects will cease to exist and everything that derives from that will also cease to exist. Each team plays between four and six rounds. After each round a new option is added with higher stakes. Every team member must advocate for a choice, but ultimately the team must reach consensus in whatever way the team can do so. The team's first task is to decide on whether the world is going to keep *Pancakes or Waffles*, a rather easy debate. After making that decision, the prompt changes. The team must then select between the winner and something else like rabbits. So, if waffles had won out, team members then debate whether waffles or rabbits should prevail. After that, then shoes, then cell phones, then soap, etc. The choices they make will have greater and greater consequences for them as they move through the options. The longer they play, the more intense the debate gets, and the more team members will share their values. The game mechanics are helpful for team building because the initial conversation of *Pancakes or Waffles* is low stakes, and it only gradually becomes more challenging as they get to later stages.

We practice building consensus so that we emulate the same type of behavior when the stakes are higher than a game about pancakes or waffles. But even after we believe we have reached consensus it is important to check in to ensure that voices are heard and that everyone is on the same *problem* or *solution* or *decision plane*. I say this because as a team goes around and around in debate towards consensus, it can start to feel like it's never going to end and that they are never going to agree. Sometimes, someone on the team helps stop the never-ending spiral. For example, one team member might stand up and say *"I've got it. I think I've got a compromise that will work."* And it's like a breakthrough. By that time, everyone is ready to agree and move on. We must be careful, though, with these Aha! breakthroughs because sometimes the majority in the room is so powerful that the minority doesn't feel they can once again speak up. They really want to be in agreement, and they really want the euphoria from hard fought and won consensus to occur. So, they go with the flow. They accept the compromise. The problem is, the next day? The euphoria will have waned because the team will be entering the next hard step, whatever that is at the time, and that next step won't go well because that minority won't be in agreement with what follows because they weren't in alignment with what came before.

We had this exact situation occur with one team at the end of our very long second day of a 3-day LawWithoutWalls Sprint. The evening's cocktail party had started more than 30 minutes before, and everyone needed a break. The Aha! moment came, and it was joyous, really joyous. We were all so exhausted and trying so hard and desperately wanted to join the rest of the community at the party to celebrate that we had come to agreement on the essence and key parts of the problem that needed to be solved. But just to be sure, just in case we had one naysayer left, I suggested we do what I call *The Temperature Take Exercise*. Here's how it works. If the meeting is in person, you start by asking everyone to put their heads down. Then you ask people to shout out in unison whether they are feeling like rotten tomatoes, happy bananas, or peaceful palms with what just was agreed upon or where they netted out. The cool thing about this is you can always HEAR the ending of the word tomatoes: "toes" and you can't tell who said it. But "toes" is the team's clue that consensus was not truly reached and so they need to discuss more. (Note: if doing this virtually, an anonymous survey works, or you can have people type it in the chat all at once). Unfortunately, for us, in the scenario I've described, we heard the dreaded "toes . . ." of "tomatoes." So, we had to back up and try again to gain consensus. We ended up missing the entire cocktail party, but after 45 minutes, when we had come back up from our big downer and were starting to feel euphoria again from another hard-fought consensus, I called out *"OK, let's do a Temperature Take!"* We all looked at each other and I'm sure a few people said a prayer, and we put our heads down. This time not only were there no rotten tomatoes—everyone was a happy banana. The funny thing? Where we ended up was only inches away from where we had ended the hour before, but those few inches gained by the painful process of listening with an Open Mind, Open Heart, and Open Door meant a difference in miles for the next day's ideation work because now everyone was on the same *problem plane*.

3. Makeup

Third, after size and structure, the makeup of the team and subgroups is essential. The most important factor, as emphasized in the Open Door Rule of Engagement, is ensuring that teams are diverse in many ways. I like to say that teams should multiply the "multi" beyond only multidisciplinary, that is, multicultural, multigenerational, multi-gender-identified, and the list goes on. However, as to the former (multidisciplinary), there are some roadblocks.

First, as alluded to previously, in knowledge fields like that of professional service firms, sometimes the business support professionals are considered (and treated like) second-class citizens. So they can be overlooked when forming teams.

Second, even when the team values diversity (as opposed to having to be convinced of it), some professionals don't understand what a multidisciplinary team is. For example, a recent study by Bloomberg Law found that lawyers believe that multidisciplinary teams can include *only* lawyers as long as they include lawyers in different practice areas at different levels of seniority.[22]

This problem doesn't occur only in professional service firms but also in professional services departments within companies. Part of the problem can be the historical notion of roles, jobs to be done, and organizational structure. A recent Harvard Law School Executive Education Case Study of the legal department at Google brings this problem to light. When Mary O'Carroll (who was not a lawyer) was hired to take over legal ops in Google's legal department, there was no group assigned to "regulation." This made sense at the time. The legal department was organized around product verticals, for example, lawyers were assigned to Chrome or Android, etc. However, the regulatory issues that were springing up crossed product lines. They also involved issues that went beyond law, that required solutions that could not come from precedent (i.e., adaptive challenges) and that would need to be at the intersection of law, marketing, PR, company governance, etc. The lawyers were excited and wanted to collaborate. They knew that in some ways, this was a beautiful opportunity for the legal department to take the lead because these were new legal and regulatory issues that had ramifications across the company. Hip hip hooray! But the way they decided to collaborate and navigate the ship was not the way I have recommended in this book. Instead, they did what many professional services professionals do when left to their own devices.

They formed committees (big ones without leader-managers). Which meant that everyone—and no one—had any responsibility or the lead role for any one task. As such, there was no thought about project management or innovation management, let alone doing the things recommended in the next section, like taking professional assessment tests, or doing a *Talent & Topic Expertise Exploration Exercise* (as discussed later in the chapter) to discover and harness hidden talents.

They also didn't do an innovation/collaboration check to determine the barriers that existed within their own company, as suggested in the S in S.A.F.E.T.Y. described in Chapter 7. And although they held many cross-disciplinary meetings, the teams themselves were not multidisciplinary. When the people who are diverse are subordinated or extricated and they do not have roles that are equal and respected (as mentioned earlier in the section on Structure), then the team is not multidisciplinary in the true sense of the word. This is problematic on many levels but especially because it prevents transdisciplinarity. The goal of having diverse, multidisciplinary teams is so that they collaborate in a truly *trans*disciplinary way. You might think this is just a theoretical nuance that doesn't make a difference but that is not the case. There is a difference, and it makes a difference.

Multidisciplinary problem-solving incorporates perspectives from two or more disciplines in an additive, sequential manner, with little interaction between the various disciplines. Think of it like having two team participants from two different disciplines who coach the team separately and impart their expertise and knowledge from their discipline to the team without altering their approach. Interdisciplinarity like multidisciplinarity involves incorporating two or more disciplines but there is more integration between the different perspectives, knowledge, and methods. Here, the two team leaders have to collaborate to synthesize their disciplines to provide a more cohesive, integrated coaching approach. With transdisciplinarity, the boundaries between the disciplines dissolve and result in a new, holistic approach and cohesive solution to a shared goal.[23] Importantly, the aim of transdisciplinarity, as distinguished from the other cross-disciplinary approaches, is finding practical solutions to real problems. This is what The 3-4-5 Method™ is designed to get teams to do, that is, to motivate team members from different disciplines to cross discipline boundaries by sharing responsibilities (and sometimes roles) and, importantly, to coach, learn, and collaborate together to accomplish their shared goal. In fact, all of these processes that are laid out herein on how to "team right" are designed to move teams from simply sequentially adding their perspectives to more holistically integrating them to form a new and viable solution to a real business or social problem. You won't be surprised to hear that research supports this tack. Specific actions and interventions to cultivate positive team processes enhance overall effectiveness, conflict management, and transdisciplinary integration.[24]

True, as mentioned, diversity, especially multidimensional diversity, can create conflict and disruption when not managed properly; and there are times when the leader needs to be a Big Bird to help manage the conflict for the team. But just as important to managing that conflict are the procedural rules the team adopts from which the processes follow. Above, we dealt with the organizational procedures needed to help teams collaborate in the right way. Now we turn to the importance of delineating time as an integral part of the procedure.

B. Teaming Takes Trust and Trust Takes Time

"Time is the most valuable thing a man can spend."

—Theophrastus

Creating a positive team culture and developing your team's rules of engagement or core norms of conduct doesn't take a ton of time away from "real work." In fact, spending the time to create rules of procedure so that the processes are culture-appropriate saves time in the long run and builds trust and accountability, and, therefore, results. As I mentioned earlier, of the dysfunctions that exist in teams, the most important is a lack of trust.[25] Patrick Lencioni, in his book, *The Five Dysfunctions of a Team*,[26] explains that when there is a lack of trust, people aren't willing to behave vulnerably. If that is the case, then they won't share what they *really* think let alone *feel* about what others think and say and do. So when they disagree, they won't speak up. This is because when people don't trust, they fear (or want to avoid) conflict because it is not worth it—it might rock the boat, or worse yet, require a difficult, challenging conversation which many would rather avoid.

When team members fear or avoid conflict, they live in what Lencioni calls "artificial harmony."[27] In artificial harmony, we don't debate, not for real, not with skin in the game. Unfortunately, artificial harmony is what often exists between partners at professional service firms, in part due to social embeddedness and strong relationships that are formed by having worked together for years.[28] However, without real debate and difficult conversations, feedback is avoided, and people fail to change behavior. Further, without real debate before decision making, people lack commitment. When we have a lack of commitment, we have low standards and a lack of accountability. Without accountability, there are poor or no results. When you follow the Three Rules of Engagement, your team will trust you and when you insist on teaming exercises among the team, the team will learn to trust each other. And if they learn to trust each other, they will be willing to engage in the type of debate that moves teams forward, and they will avoid artificial harmony. This leaves the door open to accountability and results. Without trust, that door is slammed shut. So insist on teaming exercises that enable team members to practice your team's behavioral norms and build trust. And hold your team leaders accountable for doing them, if not every time they meet with their teams, at least almost every time! Teaming exercises and icebreakers don't have to be super long to be effective.

In the next section of this chapter, I provide different examples of teaming exercises, some of which take less than 30 seconds per person. The key is that they are fun and they help the members of the team get to know each other, build trust, and get in the right mood for the meeting objectives. To loop back to what we were talking about in Chapter 7, vast research on the science of motivation demonstrates that fun, engaging, interactive experiences such as these serve as intrinsic rewards that motivate people to act.[29] So instead of thinking of these teaming exercises as vegetables, think of them as dessert. Better yet, think of them as dessert *before* dinner. This is because if you keep up on the teaming exercises, you might avoid some of the times you need to be the Big Bird.

Importantly, there are different types of trust that need building. It can't all be just lumped into one word: Trust. In fact, experts have identified at least four different types of trust that are critical for successful teaming and that occur along a trajectory: swift-based (conditional trust that develops swiftly due to limited time that is not based on evidence but needs to be verified later), calculus-based (trust based on the calculated risks and benefits for trusting that includes acceptance of a level of vulnerability), knowledge (or competence)-based (trust based on the history of interaction, the person's ability or expertise, and predictability of behavior), and identity-based (trust due to the compatibility among team members with respect to values, goals, emotional connection, or bond).[30] We start with the first, swift trust, with the intention to verify it by building the other three types of trust over time. However, all types of trust (including swift trust) only start when you start and when you strategically manage for it and set the time to do it. It doesn't just happen on its own; you need to create the right organizational structure (as noted above) and the right teaming procedures so that the right processes (actions, steps, exercises) are taken in the right order at the right time for the right amount of time—to make it happen.

Remember when teams are artificially harmonious, they lack commitment. People sit in the meeting with their inner voices saying things like *Who put them in charge?* Or, *they might think we are going to do that, but I never agreed to do that.* These voices justify shirking, that is, lack of responsibility and accountability, which in our world means: There's no creativity, or collaboration, or innovation. So every recommendation in this section proposes a certain procedure related to time or timing that can help build trust so that our teams reach accountability and the results we care about.

1. Take the Time to Build Trust by Teaming The "Right" Way *Right Away* with a Team KickOff

Whether you are leading a strategic planning committee, an innovation committee, a holiday party planning committee, or a team on an innovation journey, the only way to start right, right away, is to spend the first portion of any *first* meeting of an initiative conducting a teaming KickOff. In the last chapter of this book, I briefly describe how we run a KickOff in The 3-4-5 Method™, but there are other ways to do it. However, a Kick-Off should not be skipped entirely if you don't want to encounter teaming and/or other substantive problems later. This is because the main purpose of any team KickOff is to first and foremost build that "swift trust" mentioned above and to set the stage for growing the other three forms of trust. To do that, however, we must meet three objectives:

1. We need to enable people to get to know each other personally and professionally.
2. We need to create a sense of team identity and community for the team (and an *esprit de corps* across the teams, if there is more than one team involved).

3. We need to identify and create accountability around (1) the team's rules of engagement (social norms, which include not only how to behave but also how NOT to behave) and importantly, (2) around the team's goals and team members' respective roles and deliverables (and the timing of it all).

I believe a KickOff should also include some substantive preparation for the work that lies ahead, but this can be done *after* the first three objectives are attempted. I say "attempted" because if your KickOff is the first 30 minutes of a 60-minute meeting, you will have more work to do to actually achieve the three objectives. And that's okay but starting *right* with a KickOff of some sort is essential to collaborative integration, group cohesion, and the creation of a solid team identity.[31] As mentioned earlier, one of the main reasons change efforts fail is the failure on the part of the leader to make sure the right thing is done first. My significant other has a more colloquial way of saying this. He says: "good never follows bad." Thus, taking the time to have a KickOff is essential but even more essential is the timing. It needs to be done first, to set the right *high* expectations.

a. Building Swift Trust and Team Identity

So how do you go about tackling these three goals in a KickOff? For the first goal, getting to know each other personally and professionally, the most important thing is to make sure you do not start with professional titles. Too often, we go around the room and tell our names followed immediately by our title and an explanation of what we do at work. Then *maybe* (if the facilitator forces us) we might tag on something that isn't on our resume. But, in my experience, when we begin with titles, or what we do at work, we either immediately create hierarchies or boredom, or both, and in either and both cases, people tune out. Even if people are asked to add something quirky that's non-resume-based, they are probably busy thinking about what they will say that will be "cool *and* professional" instead of listening to others. Thus, my preference is to start with something personal (that can and should absolutely inform others about the person as a professional as well). One of the reasons LawWithoutWalls is so successful is that at the KickOff we are on a first name basis only and employ casual dress (absolutely no ties allowed); we don't include people's work or school organization on our name cards. This way, you can't tell who is a student from who is the VP of a big bank, nor whether their organization is more or less elite or successful or conservative or liberal, etc.

We also introduce ourselves in Simon Sinek[32] fashion by describing WHY we do what we do and NOT what we do. I call this *The "Start with Why" Networking Exercise* and people love (and hate it). They hate it because it makes them uncomfortable to answer a "what do you do" question with "why they do what they do." They love it because they always find the other person's answer to be richer and more interesting than the response would have been (e.g., their title and company). They also love it because it is super short: 30 seconds per person which avoids the long-winded answers people always have to listen to.

I recommend KickOffs start with a simple teaming exercise that loosens people up because just like yawning, smiling is universal and contagious.[33] The best thing about smiling (vs. yawning) is that the act of smiling changes our mood, even if we are faking it. As I mentioned before, icebreakers work, even if people hate them. You can use one of the many teaming exercises I have mentioned in this book and that are available on my website, or you can make up your own.

My two favorites that I have made up and that help teammates get to know each other both personally and professionally at the same time are *The Pet, Peeve, Motto Exercise* (approximately one minute per person) and *The Restaurant Exercise*. I will describe them only briefly here. But in addition to being a two-for-one (enabling personal and professional sharing), the other great aspect of these exercises is that they cue in other teammates about work style preferences, which helps the team learn to adapt as needed. They can also serve as communication tools for the future to help teammates connect with one another or lighten the mood when needing to have what would otherwise be a heavy conversation when teaming is tough.

The Pet, Peeve, Motto Exercise is lovably short as it only takes about one minute per person. However, it has to be explained a little bit if you have people from different countries on the team (which I hope you do). I have found that the idiom "pet peeve" does not translate from American culture into other cultures and languages easily. Begin this exercise by explaining that in the United States, "pet peeves" are habits by others that drive us a bit crazy but may seem perfectly okay to others. Although this idiom does not translate easily, what I have found does, is the love of animals or pets. There are animal or pet lovers all over the world and in lots of cases you can't spot them from their outward appearances or mannerisms or what they do for a living (unless they work with animals or for animal organizations). Yet cute puppies are a leveler, as are cute names of cute pets.

In this exercise, I ask everyone to share (out loud) the following in less than 60 seconds: (1) their current or past pet (name, kind) or if they don't have a pet, why they don't have one (often these stories are very telling); (2) their "pet peeve" that is, what drives them nuts related to work or teaming; and (3) their life motto. Note: If you are really pressing for the professional stuff then you can request their professional motto but, generally, I have found if you just ask for their motto in life, even if they go personal, it still gives a glimpse into the person's work style preferences and values. To get them started, and to prove that this really can be done in less than a minute, I share mine in colloquial form. It is important that it isn't scripted. And since you aren't giving them time to script, it should be off-the-cuff. You can, of course, give people 2 minutes to think first. Whether you are giving thinking time virtually or in person, I'm a big fan of playing some "thinking music" because silence can be not only awkward but also louder than noise. The introverts in the room will appreciate this! I also always remind people that they don't have to come up with something funny or cute or witty. Instead, I tell them to just be real. Just be themselves. And say it like it is. Sometimes I provide some examples like these:

> Example 1 (female, senior partner at a law firm): (1) I have two dogs, Goldendoodles named Bumper and Lassie; (2) my peeve is people thinking they know what I think instead of asking me; and (3) my motto is "live in the moment and act with love."
>
> Example 2 (female, in-house lawyer): (1) I have two dogs. Oakley, my Jack Russell, and Skunk, my pit bull; but if you met them, you'd think the Jack Russell was the pit bull. (2) My peeve is when people don't take notes (seriously, do they think they can remember all of this?) and (3) My motto: "be the change."

As you can see from these examples, the answers to the questions enable us to get to know the people a little bit both personally and professionally. In example 2, we learned something personal, that is, that they love their dogs and that they have a sense of humor. We also learned a little about their work style and mission in life. Further, we learned that the person is detail oriented and wants not just to embrace change but "be" change. With example 1, we learned that they are a lover not a fighter and want to be heard and believe in inclusivity. These learnings help teaming on a go-forward. In the future, if someone is trying to connect with either of these people, they might share something about their dogs with example 1 or crack a joke with example 2. Or if they sense one of the people in these examples is not participating, they might know from their answers to ask them their point of view. If you were example 2's supervisor, and you want to motivate that person, you might begin by mentioning their motto and then ask them what they'd like to see changed in their current job. This exercise works in the moment to begin to break down barriers between people, to start to build that swift trust, and it works on a go-forward in aiding connection and communication to, hopefully, verify and shore up the trust so that it lasts longer than temporarily.

The second exercise, *The Restaurant*, similarly works on both a professional and personal level. However, it takes a lot more time. It entails people sharing work style preferences based on one of those work personality tests mentioned in Chapter 5. We use DiSC in LawWithoutWalls, which is divided into four colors or types: RED, Dominant doers (D); YELLOW, persuasive Influencers (I); GREEN, Steady cooperators (S); and BLUE, Conscientious planners focused on compliance (C). *Note*: You can have the participants take the actual DiSC personality test prior to the meeting. It takes 10 minutes for about US $25 to $35 per person. If you do that, individuals receive an overview plus about 30 pages of typed explanation. Alternatively, you can shortcut that prior process by explaining the four work styles and analogizing those work styles to how we keep our desks and how we grocery shop and ask people to self-identify. For self-identification related to groceries you might describe the differences as follows: (D) is the impulse shopper. They don't have a list but they know what they want and they are moving fast to put the items in the cart. The (I) tells you where everything is in the store, whether you ask or not. (S) is ready to help; willing to unpack. (C) has a list and wouldn't think of going shopping without coupons and a calculator.

All of this takes about 15 minutes to set up. Then people are asked to pretend they are a team that is about to open and run a new restaurant. Each person shares their work style letter or color, the type of food or dish that most represents them, and then what role they would play at the restaurant that would best use their talents and fit their work style, for example, chef, sous chef, bartender, hostess, financial backer, manager, head of PR/marketing, head of procurement, waiter, etc. In doing so, people learn about each other professionally (their work styles and preferences) but also personally. Warning: when you ask team members to state what food best describes them make sure to clarify that this is not the food they like the best. It is the food that most represents their essence. The example I provide is as follows. I show a picture of my daughter when she was 17 years old. Then I say: *If I were to pick a food that most represents my 17-year-old daughter, it would be a Hass avocado.* (I show a picture of a Hass avocado which is bumpy, rough, dark, and old looking). I then explain: *I chose this food because like the avocado, my daughter looks old and like she's been around the world a bit on the outside.* (*She's looked 21 since she was 12 years old!*). *People trust her beyond her years and tell her things that they might not normally tell someone of her age. But actually, she is quite "green" on the inside meaning not only "young" but also exemplifying renewal and energy. Plus, like an avocado, she has a slight sweetness (but not too sweet) and goes well with almost anything (anyone). She adds a splash of unique color (like that unique green/yellow of this avocado) that is irresistible and brings life and flavor to any situation.* As for her role, I say: *Reading would likely best serve as the maître-d'.*

You will be surprised at the foods people pick to describe themselves and at the roles they choose. Their answers will tell you something personal and often something professional about them or something that will be useful to connect with them at work in the future. For example, someone very senior might say they want to be the waiter and explain that they are great at (and enjoy) memorizing long lists (like today's specials), and they feel a sense of satisfaction in writing things down and serving people what they want. Alternatively, you might learn that someone really likes to cook and dreams of becoming a chef one day. Like the answers from the *Pet, Peeve, Motto Exercise,* the answers here can be used later to warm up a cold room or to bring the heat down in a tense conversation. They can also be used when the group is deciding who should do what and play what role; and they might be the reason you give someone a shot at doing something that you might not otherwise have pictured them doing.

The best thing about both of these teaming exercises is that they lend themselves to the second goal of the KickOff, and that is creating a team identity. There is a reason sports teams have names and mascots. The history of LawWithoutWalls has proven what external research shows: creating a team identity helps individual team members feel a sense of belonging and helps teams not just survive but thrive. It also creates a collective identity that helps teams think of themselves as a "we," and that they are "in this together" which, in turn, helps individual members change focus from their own self-interest to the team's charge, their shared vision, and well-being.[34] In fact, team identity has been shown to be *the* most important factor in overcoming the challenges that diversity can introduce into team dynamics—and it also helps wash away differences in status and integrate demographic, disciplinary, and organizational differences.[35]

Therefore, at every KickOff, with some teaming exercise or another, we have the teams create their own identity/name and even logo. For example, with the *Pet, Peeve, Motto Exercise,* if you are using it as a first teaming exercise, you can easily add in a second step around team identity either right then or during the next meeting. Simply explain that the next step is to create a team name based on the types of pets or the names of the pets. Or you could instead have the teams create a team name and logo that represents a common thread or theme (or pet) that runs between all the members of the team. But be sure to warn the teams that this will be their team name going forward because that will make them take it seriously. Of course, explain *why* you are having them do this. First, you can simply say what I said: There's a reason sport teams have names and mascots. Second, you can explain as I did earlier that Hugh McLeod, a famous cartoonist, claims that we are all born creative, but somewhere along the way, we forgot where we put our crayons.[36] This part of the exercise—the creative naming and the drawing of the logo, is designed to bring them back their crayons.

b. Building Calculus- and Competence-Based Trust

As stated earlier, expectations that aren't set, aren't met. This is true for social norms as well as the substantive goals, purpose of the team, and individual goals. In a similar way, when we move on to the third goal of a KickOff, the norms, purpose, goals, and roles that aren't prescribed aren't imbibed, and the holes that aren't identified aren't filled. It is important for the entire community to know what the social norms are, what the goals are for each subgroup, and for the team at large. It is also important for everyone to know not only what roles each person is supposed to play, but also their goals and their potential, that is, all the roles they *could* play and the *value* they bring related not only to their substantive expertise but also their past and current talents. This is the calculus that helps us begin to build competence-based trust.

As mentioned, there is a right way and a wrong way to team, no matter your age or culture or experience. The right way begins by establishing purpose and goals not only for the entire community or on an individual level, but also for each team or group within the community (organization, department, practice group). We have been doing this for years in LawWithoutWalls and other organizations (outside of LawWithoutWalls) have as well. In Carlos Valdes-Depena's book, *Lessons from Mars*, he discusses the importance of "crystallizing intent" for individuals and subgroups within the team and the team itself.[37] As explained in Chapter 7, having a shared mission, purpose, or vision helps rally teams because this higher purpose helps teams and individuals see how they can contribute and make a difference. And as mentioned in the Empowerment part of the S.A.F.E.T.Y. recipe, including the individuals in the creation of the mission or purpose leads to even better results! Therefore, during our KickOff, we collaborate on identifying each team's purpose.

It is also important for everyone to have individual goals. Therefore, we also focus on individual goals to increase a sense of ownership and understanding of the value each of us provides and put it in the context of the mission or North Star for the team and larger community (the organization, company, or firm). In keeping with that, to successfully meet the challenge of innovation on a multidisciplinary global team of diverse participants, we also need transparency around roles, responsibilities, and time commitments, as mentioned before. We all can't serve as coaches, we all can't serve as mentors, we all can't serve as doers. It's worth repeating: We need to have different roles and, like the goals, they need to be identified and people need to agree and commit to playing those roles. This is not to say that some people will not end up playing multiple roles or giving more time (or less) than originally anticipated. But at the outset we don't know who should play what role because we don't know everyone's talents and expertise. If that is true, we also don't know what talents or expertise our team is lacking, what holes exist in our team. Because there is an "i" in the word "teaming," as discussed, individual performance is key to successful teaming. The opposite, however, is also true—individual performance issues related to teaming can create holes that prevent progress. Therefore, to help participants hone this important (individual) skill of teaming, some focus on the individual is essential. It is only by understanding our own work styles that we can learn to work with others whose work styles are different from our own.

We create a team DiSC map of each team member's work styles to understand our individual and combined work styles, and to identify strengths and weaknesses that exist in work styles. We also do this to build a common language for the team that proves useful when giving and receiving feedback. And we do this to encourage people to stretch and flex, that is, to offer to adopt a new work style to fill in the holes. If we are all RED dominant, domineering, demanding, decisive, and direct doers, who is going to be the GREEN stable, steady, sincere, and supportive doer; who is going to be BLUE cautious, careful conscientious; who is going to be YELLOW and inspire?

Research shores all of this up. These critical team processes encourage knowledge sharing and creation, and they help foster a working environment that enables team members to engage in collaborative learning while understanding (and acknowledging) their differences.[38]

We have two exercises to help teams create and congeal around team and individual goals, set expectations around the Three Rules of Engagement and creative cadence, and identify strengths (roles and tasks) based on talent expertise and also holes in expertise (or willingness) to fill those holes.

The first is the exercise mentioned in Chapter 7 in the section explaining the "A" in S.A.F.E.T.Y.: *The P.A.C.T. Exercise*, which, in addition to involving agreement around purpose and goals and working norms, also involves commitment to social norms/Three Rules of Engagement like Open Heart, Open Mind, Open Door. These P.A.C.T.s are detailed, specifying how the team shall go about achieving the purpose and goals, etc. As such, these P.A.C.T.s have served the teams well in LawWithout-Walls. Evidently researchers have hypothesized that teams that have a more direct communication style, set deadlines for tasks, and establish consistent ways and times to connect receive higher Net Promoter Scores from clients than others.[39] These P.A.C.T.s are strategically designed to build calculus-based trust because they are situation-specific; they are like a contract about a certain project. These P.A.C.T.s establish norms and procedures and expectations and through discussion of roles and procedures they enhance effectiveness, efficiency, and the success of the project and make clear that shirking is not acceptable.

The theory is that people adhere to the established ways of working and live up to expectations because the rewards outweigh the risks if they don't.[40] This is even more true when team members take part in defining the "why,"[41] that is, the North Star for the group, which is why the first part of P.A.C.T. is "P" for "Purpose." For those out there trying desperately to entice (and retain) the millennials and digital natives new to the workforce, an emphasis on purpose resonates (as mentioned in Chapter 7, the millennials have been called "the Purpose Generation").

Further, there is nothing more debilitating to a team than when the members disagree on their mission, their purpose, their "why." This is why in the *Problem Plane Exercise*, we not only ask for team members to agree on the problem statement but also the *reason* solving *this* problem matters. In fact, the *Problem Plane Exercise* is a useful tool for teams that have trouble agreeing on the "P" in P.A.C.T. Exapting this exercise here as a *Purpose Plane Exercise* can do wonders.

Recently, I led a law firm's innovation journey, which consisted of approximately five multidisciplinary teams wherein it was clear at the start that due to the managing partner's communication, some of the members believed their mission was to create a new rocket ship, that is, a big wow innovation. Others believed it was to make the current rocket ship (the firm) run better, that is, TNT as in tiny noticeable things. Knowing this disagreement as to the purpose would be debilitating going forward, I incorporated a *Purpose Plane Exercise* into our KickOff, which greatly helped get everyone charged up and in agreement about their mission (which was NOT to create a new rocket ship!). Importantly, part of the *P.A.C.T. Exercise* is writing it down. It starts with individuals writing their own P.A.C.T.s and ends with the group agreeing to the group P.A.C.T. in writing (much like we do with the *Problem Plane Exercise*). And writing it down has been proven to help not only set the intention but enable future dialogue as teams can revisit the preliminary ideas of the group purpose, processes, and outcomes and refine as needed.[42] In essence, these P.A.C.T.s along with the DiSC assessments create a shared language that is often otherwise absent in collaboration among diverse disciplines and which can lead to misunderstandings and conflict (not to mention inhibit team performance).[43]

The second exercise is the *Talent & Topic Expertise Exploration Exercise* which is designed to build competence-based trust. As described in Chapter 7, this exercise is designed for team members to share their expertise related to the team's goal and their talents (sometimes hidden) that will enhance their contributions. It is also designed so that they connect both talent and expertise to the tasks at hand. The goal is to ensure that everyone's experience, smarts, and talents can be uncovered and put to good use, connected somehow to the topic challenge at hand. This exercise, like the one before, also serves to help develop a shared vocabulary. In addition, it helps participants connect the dots that might not otherwise be connected between a person's expertise, talent, and their ability to add value to the team and its goals. It thereby enhances trust in team members' ability to perform and make good decisions. It also makes teams more effective. Although teams sometimes fail because they lack the right internal resources, other times they fail because they do not realize and utilize the internal resources on the team to perform as well as they could.[44] Because they make assumptions about talent, expertise, and spheres of influence based on current titles and roles,[45] they fail to uncover the full gamut of diverse talents and skills on the team. That may sound obvious but it seems counterintuitive that teams fail in this way.

Think about it. In emergency situations, we do the opposite instinctively. If someone is in physical distress on a plane, we might first ask if anyone aboard is a doctor or nurse but if not, we don't quibble over credentials. We seek anyone with any expertise or knowledge on how to help the hurting person. We are also able, in emergency situations, to connect things that might not otherwise be connected and quickly. If someone knows how to sew and there are no people trained in sewing stitches, this person is quickly trusted to be our new stitches person. But in work teams, people don't speak up for how their skills might be leveraged in new ways. As individuals, we don't realize that our prior careers can add value. For example, if someone's prior career is as a nurse, this experience might provide expertise that is different and valuable to the team related to problem diagnosis, prioritizing, or project management. This is not dissimilar to what happened during the COVID-19 health crisis across industries. According to a recent study of human capital trends by Deloitte, companies were forced to be more creative and adaptive and to unleash the power of worker potential.[46] They had to "make real-time decisions and to redeploy workers to areas where they are needed the most, and where they had the capabilities, interest, and passion to contribute."[47]

The Talent & Topic Expertise Exploration Exercise, therefore, is designed to build "competence-based trust" with knowledge sharing. We have all heard about the importance of knowledge management and knowledge sharing in creating value, innovations, and a competitive edge for organizations of all kinds, including those in the law marketplace. Indeed, many of our LawWithoutWalls teams' topic challenges are related to knowledge management or knowledge sharing or the lack thereof. Knowledge sharing is not only critical for organizations or departments within organizations, but also essential to teams for effective teaming. Research shows that if knowledge is not shared within a team, the cognitive resources of the team will be underutilized. However, knowledge sharing doesn't always happen naturally. Time and time again, we hear of stories about repeated mistakes due to lessons learned not being shared or failure to scale or leverage great ideas or best practices (or best routines, or best processes!) because they weren't shared. True, there may be negative reasons why this might be so (including fear of ridicule, wanting credit, etc.); however, a non-nefarious reason for lack of sharing is simply that we don't have a process or a habit of knowledge sharing in our teams. So, in the field of organizational behavior, this exercise might be described as one designed to help teams uncover their *collective intelligence*, which, by the way, is more predictive of team performance than individual members' intelligence scores.[48]

Leveraging collective intelligence, however, requires team members with relevant knowledge not only to recognize it as such (i.e., connect otherwise unconnected dots) but to speak up when their prior expertise can be helpful[49] so that there is a shared understanding of what expertise each member has and how they can contribute in that moment.[50] This leads to what experts call "critical awareness," which enables group members to "consider and identify the potential contributions of multiple disciplines and areas of practice—including their own and others—to effectively address the target problem. This helps eliminate bias toward a particular disciplinary approach."[51] This opens the door to that transdisciplinarity discussed above. However, that door is only opened if we return to the opening of this section: trust. Without trust and a psychologically safe culture, this type of communication or transference won't occur. Without it, our ability to connect the dots to reach Stephen Johnson's "adjacent possible" in the Open Door Rule of Engagement is stymied. Without trust and knowledge sharing around expertise and talents, there will be more times that the team will need the Big Bird.

c. Take the Right Time to Team Right Almost Every Time

One of the mistakes that teams often make is to fail to account for time. Teams are like pets. They need attention *every* time you see them. They may sleep all the time in between visits and be perfectly happy doing so. But when you meet back up with them, they need love and care like they did the last time, and the time before that and before that. It might not always be the SAME amount of time that is needed. For example, when you first bring your pet home, they need more time. This is true for teams. As discussed earlier, the initial amount of time is critical and more time spent on teaming is essential. Later, however, although the amount of time might be less, time still needs to be taken for teaming the right way. This helps to shore up the swift trust built initially and to build identity trust (over time). So, unfortunately for you, those teaming exercises I mentioned earlier (or if you prefer the word "icebreakers") need to be done almost *every* time you team. Good feelings only last on reserve for so long, not only with pets but with teams, too. If not fed, they don't wag their tails like they used to.

I get pushback all the time about icebreakers. Just last week, I was teaching in Harvard Law School's Leading Law Firms Executive Education course for managing partners. After I presented some of the content of this section of this book (in abbreviated form), a partner came up to me and said, *"I really have to take issue with this idea that we need icebreakers and especially that you think we need them all the time."*

Given my affinity for the 5 Whys, I'm sure you can guess at my first response. I asked her why #1: *"Why do you think we don't need them?" And she said, "Well, it's not that we don't need them; I can see how they help, and likely lawyers need them more than others do. It's just that lawyers hate them."*

Then I asked her why #2: *"Why do lawyers hate them?"* She said, *"Well, they put us out of our comfort zone. I hate when they ask us to share something personal that no one knows about ourselves. I mean I guess sometimes it's cool to hear what others say and some icebreakers work. Like yours today, I learned a lot more about the person with your "Start with Why" Networking Exercise versus them telling me what they do for a living. But that exercise didn't put me on the spot in the same way as sharing a personal secret. It didn't make me feel stupid like when they ask us to share something that's just bizarre or silly. For example, recently before a team gathering, the leader actually gave us icebreaker homework. We were supposed to come to the meeting having thought about who our favorite animated character was. That was sooo annoying."*

Then I asked her why #3: *"Why did that annoy you?"* Her reply: *"I mean really? When I got her long-winded email about the meeting and then saw I had some ridiculous homework (in addition to other prep I had to do), I was taken aback. I don't have time to think of something so stupid before a meeting. There is a lot of other prep I should be doing, not thinking of some silly animated character. I mean what's the point? I didn't even have an answer which made it even worse. And then I was annoyed with myself that I was worried about not having an answer about something that just doesn't matter."*

I asked her why #4: *"Why were you upset about not having to provide an answer to something you just pointed out didn't really matter?"* She said, *"I'm already seen as a little too serious. So not having an answer was going to make it clear I wasn't 'cool' or laid back. I guess it's not that I don't think icebreakers matter and setting the right tone to the meeting is important. I agree that those things matter. But in this instance, it had no relevance to our strategic planning meeting."*

And then I said, *"ahhh, well I agree with you, in part, and in this instance."* I then explained that I didn't think it was the best execution of a teaming exercise. First, teaming exercises shouldn't feel like "work." Second, they don't have to be silly (although, of course, as discussed in the Open Mind Rule of Engagement, silly can really help the mood and creativity). Third, other than during a planned KickOff designed to get the team to know and trust each other, teaming exercises work best when they are super short and have a substantive connection, that is, when they are related to the topic of the meeting, the theme of the project, the goal for the day, etc. For example, if the meeting is about rebranding the department or the firm, everyone could quickly share their favorite brand or favorite commercial and say why they like it or three words that come to mind when they see it. This gets everyone thinking about branding—and it can be done in 30 seconds or less. And yes, I created a *My Favorite Brand Exercise* for this purpose. The key is: having a related reason for the teaming exercise gives people an understanding of the "why"—why they have to do the dreaded exercise that helps justify the "what" even if they hate teaming exercises and icebreakers.

Let's say the meeting is about overhauling some outdated or underused tech in the firm or department or about the rollout of a new matter management system. A great exercise that would be relevant and promote knowledge sharing but not of the "too personal" kind is one I made up called: *The Tools' Tools Exercise.* For this icebreaker, in 45 seconds or less, each person shares one tech tool or app that they use that makes their lives (professional or personal) better or more efficient or effective. Each person explains the tool that they use to be a more effective "tool" of a person. Although this exercise is centered on "Tech Tools" that team members use as best practices, it can be used to apply to other types of "tools" or best practices or lessons learned, etc. The goal is for team members to learn some new tools (practices or policies) that they might want to adopt individually, or maybe as a team. After all, teams work more effectively when they all use the same tech tools!

Oh, and finally, I explained to this female managing partner, teaming exercises should never (ever) stump you. There should always be an example provided (that can be copycatted!), that is, an easy answer or an acceptable out. I don't mean an opt out but, for example, in my *Pet, Peeve, Motto Exercise* mentioned earlier, I always give an example and explain what to do or say if you don't have a pet, that is, make one up, like "a rock," or mention a former pet or someone else's pet or explain why you don't have a pet.

She then said, "*OK, but I still don't see why you recommend this every time we team.*" I replied "*Well, I said almost every time,*" explaining there may be situations where you are meeting every day and people are not of major varying hierarchies and the group is made up of a bunch of extroverts or talkative introverts. In those situations, no, you don't have to do a teaming exercise every time. But at least have a nice opening, as opposed to just getting right down to business. And then consider doing teaming exercises once a month to show you care about the group dynamic so that you, as a leader, remain open to others and ensure you aren't assuming things are going as well as you think they are. These exercises work to show you care about your people *as people*. Also, some people are uncomfortable talking in meetings and so they don't talk much in meetings. A short icebreaker at the beginning might help them learn how easy it is to have a voice and help others notice them in a different way. They, literally, break the ice. They are called icebreakers for that reason. A short teaming exercise can also open different avenues of conversation for follow up among members ('oh . . . will you send me the link to that?'). Importantly, icebreaker exercises can help fill in until the next more personal and in-depth teaming exercise or event can be conducted. And, of course, if you are talking about virtual meetings? I absolutely think they should be done—even if the team meets regularly—because it creates focus, especially if the exercise is related to the theme or substance or goal of the meeting (and again, especially if it is short!).

Then I re-emphasized: *"The icebreaker can and should be quick—less than 30 seconds per person. Remember: we won't take the time to do teaming exercises if they end up taking too much time! Select a teaming exercise or icebreaker that uses the right amount of time and pick a timekeeper that keeps time by either holding up a phone into the video screen or playing a timer on the PowerPoint slide in an in-person meeting so the team can see the countdown and know you are serious about teaming but also cognizant of their time."* Then I went one step further and asked, *"Have I convinced you? I hope so and I hope you will email me in a few weeks to tell me you started implementing teaming exercises with your team."*

She looked at me with a wry smile and said, *"Hmm . . . that might be pushing it. I'll keep an open mind to participating in them, but running them? That's a different story. I'm not like you. I can't do what you do. It doesn't match my personality and people would think I was ridiculous."*

Of course, I asked why again, my why #5: *"Why would you think you need to conduct the teaming exercises like I do?"* And she said, *"I don't know. It just seems like teaming exercises are always done by the more gregarious extroverts who enjoy these kinds of things."* I replied, *"I get that entirely. You can't and shouldn't try to run them like I do. You need to be authentic to YOU. That said, sometimes role-playing can help. I often tell my students to put on their 'judge' robe and speak in their 'judge' voice before they start writing their draft motions or memos. This type of role-play can work at work as well. You could even wear a costume to signify that you are playing a new role. Sometimes surprising our teams by taking risks like that can open them up in a new way to taking more risks themselves."* She cringed at the costume idea (like you, the reader did too I bet). I responded, *"Alternatively, you could pick a song to play that signifies its icebreaker time. Or, as I do, you could start every meeting with a song or a video that relates to the theme of the session. I do that because people learn this about me and, because they want to see the video I play, they show up on time (another reason TIME matters). The song or video can also be related to the icebreaker. I'll ask everyone to give a reason I played that song or that video related to the work we are doing. Sometimes, no one gets the real reason, but the answers I get are pretty creative and they break the ice amongst the group."*

She seemed more amenable to the song/video idea than the costume one but just in case she was still feeling stumped, I said, *"Of course, you can simply call it out, like it is, in your voice, and say 'Hey, I don't like these teaming icebreaker things any more than you do, and I definitely don't like lead-ing them, but we're doing it anyway.' Or you can rotate the responsibility for it. Set parameters (including time!) and have a different person run the teaming exercise each time. That's another way to 'empower' others on the team (going back to our discussion earlier about the E in S.A.F.E.T.Y., the recipe for culture creation."*

My reward for this conversation was the woman's LinkedIn message to me later that day that said, "I promise you will be the first to know of my icebreaker success! Thank you for such an awesome thought-provoking session today."

A second aspect of time that matters related to trust-building is the time at which the most senior person speaks. As mentioned in Chapter 6, research shows that the most senior people often speak first in meetings and that people generally follow the statements and actions of the person who speaks first in a meeting. Even the best efforts to prevent it from happening can be stymied. For example, law school faculty meetings often have a "queue" to help ensure that those that want to be heard can be heard, and the person in charge of the queue is supposed to jot down the names of the professors who raise their hand in the order in which they raise their hand. However, you can already imagine what generally hap-pens. Those with the loudest voices, those who believe they are the most senior and important, have their hands raised (before they even know what they want to say) so that they are first in the queue. Unsurprisingly, over time it is the same people doing that during every meeting. That behavior intimidates the newcomers (who are often the most junior) and creates a hierarchy between the old guard and the new and it just continues like tradition. The same group of professors get on the queue first, and, as a result, they monopolize the conversation.

A third aspect of time that is definitely *not* paid attention to by many professional service providers (and most professors in academia) is the *amount of time* a person speaks in a team meeting. In one faculty meeting that started at 12:30 p.m. but absolutely had to end by 1:50 p.m. for those faculty that taught class at 2:00 p.m., it was apparent that we had 20 faculty in the queue who wanted to make a comment. So, I recommended that, to be inclusive and ensure that everyone's thoughts were heard, we use a timer and limit people's comments to 3 minutes each, which would save 20 minutes at the back end for more collaborative discussion. I can't tell you the uproar that this suggestion received. As a civil procedure professor who prides herself on teaching the importance of the opportunity to be heard, I was shocked at the reaction to my suggestion. Not only did many professors attack me (without raising hands, lol) and accuse me that in making that suggestion, I was also silencing voices, they wasted about 35 minutes doing so. I won't bore you with the details of how the rest of the meeting went, except to say that my recommendation for equally limiting the amount of time each person could speak was not adopted.

Ignoring the realities of time is a death knell for progress on a team, not to mention focus and trust in the process. One way I prevent this from happening is to provide time limits for everyone and stick with them no matter how senior the person is. For our very senior judges in LawWithoutWalls, when they are giving feedback to teams at the final event (the ConPosium), we tell them they must respond in 2 minutes or less. To reinforce this, we have a huge timer up on-screen. In other words, we shame them into stopping. When I am running interactive virtual workshops, I do what I recommended to the female managing partner above: I hold up my phone so people can see the time count down—I do this when managing partners are speaking as well. Another reason why the length of time that someone speaks matters is that in more productive teams, there is equal airtime across all members (which, of course, may be hard to accomplish especially given the research that indicates that people who speak more are more likely to be considered leaders).[52] The good news is that it is not essential that everyone speaks an equal amount of time at every meeting but equal airtime *over time*, over the course of the project—is essential to building trust and teaming right.

It may seem small, but one other point about *time* is critical to teams being able to trust their leader. Make sure individual meetings have a set ending point that is not too long, for example, a virtual meeting that is over 90 minutes without a break is too long. In addition, make sure the meetings end on time, or even early. Giving people the gift of time, even 5 minutes, is welcomed in today's world where we zoom from one meeting to another. People will trust you as a leader if you start and, especially, if you end on time.

▶...Reflection Point Ask yourself: are you really *managing* your teams and committees? Are any of your teams or committees too big? Are they structured in a way that makes roles clear? Are there roles at all (or is everyone just a member?) Has the committee or team been working on the same project for more than 4 months? Take a moment to fill out the following chart for yourself (the committees or teams you are a part of) and for your group (i.e., the people you lead or who report to you). Compare your answers to the second row, which lists the ideal size/amount/structure. Circle any that fall outside the recommended parameters and consider how you might "fix" them. One way to do that is to conduct a *P.A.C.T. Exercise* (as described above and in more detail in Chapter 7). Also, consider whether each committee or team is on the same *Problem or Purpose Plane* and if not, then consider conducting that exercise as described briefly above and in more detail in Chapter 8.

Team or Committee Name	# People	# Subcommittees & # of People on each	Project Length to Date	# Roles	Ideas for change:
Ideal Setup	<10 people	Subgroups for any team of 6 or more people; Subgroups should be 3 to 4 people each.	<4 Months	2 or more roles for groups of 4 or more people	
Example: Innovation Team	15	*None*	*2.5 months*	*none*	• *Divide group into 3 subgroups* • *Create 2 roles per group* • *Hold a mid-KickOff to create P.A.C.T. and set an end date/check in at the 4 month mark*

⬤...Reflection Point Here is a list of the teaming exercises/icebreakers explained in this chapter. Which one do you like the least? Which one do you like the most? And why? What about teaming exercises/icebreakers makes you uncomfortable? What might you gain by trying one of these exercises (especially one that makes you uncomfortable) with your team? (Hint: think about our discussion related to the importance of vulnerability in Chapter 6).

List of Teaming Exercises in this Chapter

Exercise or Resource	Purpose	Timing
The Tools' Tools Teaming Exercise	To enhance knowledge sharing and teaming	Setup: 2 minutes Thinking time: 1 minute Share per person: 45 seconds
Pancakes Or Waffles Exercise[1]	To enhance teaming and practice consensus building	Setup: 5 minutes Exercise Time: 25 minutes
The Pet-Peeve-Motto Exercise	To learn about teammates' work style preferences, practice listening, and enhance teaming (and create a team identity)	Setup: 2 minutes Thinking time: 1 minute Share per person: 30 seconds Create Team Identity: 5 minutes
Quick Mood Check Exercise	To gauge the energy and level of satisfaction of the team	Setup: 30 seconds Thinking time: NONE! Share per person: 15 seconds
The P.A.C.T. Exercise	To prepare and secure buy-in and commitment from participants for the personal and professional work ahead and agree to a joint team purpose, individual and group accountability, creative cadence, and timing	Setup: 10 minutes Exercise Time: 50 minutes
The Restaurant Exercise	To share work style preferences, practice negotiating roles and ideating, and to create a team identity	Setup: 5 minutes Exercise: 30–45 minutes for a Team of 6 or less
The Start with Why[2] *Networking Exercise*	To enhance networking and community building	Setup: 2 minutes Thinking time: 1 minute Share per person: 30 seconds

(Continued)

Exercise or Resource	Purpose	Timing
Getting on the Same Purpose Plane Exercise	To get the team on the same "plane" as it relates to their purpose for this meeting or project or initiative	Setup: 3 minutes Silent Individual Time: 10 minutes Group Time: 20 minutes
My Favorite Brand Exercise[3]	To instigate team thinking about branding and client/ consumer centricity (and to get to know each other)	Setup: 2 minutes Thinking time: 1 minute Share per person: 45 seconds
Talent & Topic Expertise Exploration Exercise	To identify and share team members' respective exper- tise related to the project and other talents that might help the team on their mission (and to get to know each other)	Setup: 5 minutes Thinking time: 1 minute 30–45 minutes for a Team of 6 or less

[1] Renditions of this exercise are widely available on the internet. Anita Ritchie, the Director of LawWithoutWalls, created this version from various sources.

[2] I developed this exercise entirely on my own but it was inspired by the book, *Start with Why*, by Simon Sinek.

[3] This exercise was co-developed with Anita Ritchie, the Director of LawWithoutWalls.

CHAPTER 10

Managing Without a Marketing Plan and a Method Is Madness

> *"Though this be madness, yet there is method in't."*
>
> —William Shakespeare, Polonius in *Hamlet*[1]

Just as there's a recipe for creating the right culture, there is a recipe for managing teams on an innovation journey, and that recipe includes all that was recommended in the previous chapter and also what is recommended here in Chapter 10: creating the right marketing and messaging around the efforts and following a method, like The 3-4-5 Method™. While it is true that creativity, collaboration, and innovation can be messy, managing them without a marketing plan and a method is madness. As Polonius in Hamlet is famous for saying, "Though this be madness, yet there is method in't."[2]

A. "Innovation Isn't an Idea Problem,"[3] It's a Marketing Problem

Even if we do all of the things recommended in the Chapter 9 and more, part of successfully managing collaboration and innovation involves marketing and messaging the right way so that people believe and feel as if they are a part of the purpose behind it, and they do not have unrealistic expectations. Another reason the messaging and marketing is important is so that leaders can "sell" change efforts and groups can sell their new project ideas. Despite the logic in this, marketing and messaging about these efforts (like managing them) has been given short shrift—as have the roles of chief marketing officers (CMOs) within some professional service firms. This is a shame because I believe the professional service firms that learn how to leverage their CMOs will have a competitive edge. Research supports this—including what I see as the five problems related to marketing that create barriers to innovation.[4]

In addition to being a management problem, innovation is a marketing problem in the following five ways.

1. A Bad Rap

First, overall, innovation in professional services has a bad rap. It might be cool (and even necessary) in the tech or start-up world but in professional services, no one is convinced it is really needed or that it is worth the benefit. Even more broadly, no one really knows what is meant by "innovation" and as a result there is little definition of it and little measurement of it. Perhaps this is because a professional service provider's business is about people and relationships and currently, their business model is not broken. In fact, there has been an increase in revenue in the past few years by professional services firms around the world, including law firms, accounting companies, and insurance brokerages.[5] During the pandemic, lots of professional service providers made a lot of money (a lot more money). So much money that heads of innovation couldn't do their jobs. I recently went to lunch with the former head of innovation at a global law firm and she said, "The reason I took the job was to create innovation at the firm, to change the way we provide services and to productize some of the services we already provide. There was a lot of interest in that before the pandemic. But now? No one sees the need."

To make the business case for innovation worse, the benefit of innovation has been marketed as coming later, as in 10 years down the line, whereas investments by partnerships are usually made with a shorter-term view.[6] Furthermore, the value of innovation can be difficult to prove, which makes it difficult to convince professional service providers that it is going to be useful and not just a waste of time. Given this, it's not surprising that many professional service providers do not believe that they need to change[7] and there is a lack of investment in innovation[8] not only financially but also from a time commitment standpoint. This is disappointing. While it is true that the short-term benefits of innovation efforts can be hard to measure, I have interviewed hundreds of clients of professional service providers and the majority tout the more immediate benefit of collaborating, innovating, and honing the innovator's mindset together with the client. Indeed, it is why many want their firms to sponsor them in LawWithoutWalls. Consider these two quotes.

I think it is inevitable. I think if firms are prepared to partner in that way, they will be inside the DNA of our department and they will know how we go about our internal processes. I see this as a building block thing . . . So I think naturally, it will be worth their investment.—Head of legal, large international airline.[9]

How do you measure innovation? You could force a quantitative analysis, e.g., how many new ideas have translated into something. . . . Just change in the service delivered or how delivered and the how will become apparent and become part of the experience and people will accept that the difference is driven by a change in focus and mindset. We will recognize that the change has happened and there is a driver of that change, and the driver is thinking in a new way.—Head of knowledge and development, compliance and secretariat, a Big Four Australian bank and financial service provider[10]

However, these types of benefits don't instill urgency nor are they sufficient to combat a huge obstacle and that is timing. A group's readiness and openness for change is relative based on how urgent the need for change is for that group. Theorists have developed what is called the crisis curve.[11] It identifies three categories of urgency ranging from low urgency (anticipatory change when strategic performance is good and there is time to spare) to mid-level urgency (reactive change when strategic performance is average) to high urgency (crisis change when strategic performance is poor and tanking and there is no time to spare).

Essentially, as strategic capabilities decrease, the readiness for change (the urgency) increases. Further, within one organization, different departments and key stakeholders affected by any collaboration or innovation effort might vary on where they are on this curve. Complicating the matter, key stakeholders and target groups might also vary on their level of commitment based on whether they feel threatened, understand the need, and are in agreement.

What does this have to do with marketing? Well, understanding where key stakeholders are on this curve helps the leader craft the right messages at the right times. Failing to get buy-in from a group whose level of urgency is low but whose budget will be impacted can tank a project. This is another reason why identifying and empathizing with all the stakeholders is essential to any transformation effort, yet it is not sufficient. In addition, it is critical to creating the right amount of urgency at the right time. In fact, failing to do so and under-communicating about the vision and to the right channels in the right way have been identified as key reasons why change efforts fail.[12]

2. Sold as a Pathway to Failure

A second reason why innovation suffers from a "marketing" problem and a poor reputation among professional service providers is the way that design thinking has historically been marketed and sold, which is as a pathway to failure that only the hardiest or audacious should attempt. This touches on two common aversions among professionals: aversion to failure and aversion to taking risks. Studies support the idea that the culture of professional services firms is anything but one of taking risks and failing fast,[13] while the literature on design thinking and innovation often touts failure as something to be celebrated. Too often research highlights entrepreneurs who have failed before succeeding—instead of research that shows that just as many entrepreneurs who succeed had never failed before and entrepreneurs who previously failed were even more likely to fail than new, first-time entrepreneurs.[14]

It's no wonder that professional service providers of all kinds have a lowered appetite for the type of experimentation that innovation requires. Failure for failure's sake is unpalatable to many but especially to lawyers, accountants, engineers, and financial advisors. The only type of failure that is palatable is the kind from which we can learn, that is, competent failure. In fact, this is why past experience is valuable not for itself but only if it enhances ability. Unless the past success or failure "educates" the entrepreneur, it doesn't help.[15] Perhaps unbelievably so, there is research that shows that the reason that serial entrepreneurs are not more successful and are more likely to fail again is because they do not learn from failure.[16] To fill this gap, there is that conference called the FailCon which, as mentioned in Chapter 4, is designed to teach founders of startups how to learn and prepare for failure so they can iterate and grow from it.[17] This is when the difference between competent and incompetent failure must be stressed. As Professor Pisano states, "Failure should be celebrated only if it results in learning."[18] With intentionality, in LawWithoutWalls, we have a low tolerance for mediocrity and sloppy work, both of which can cause team dysfunction and incompetent failures. Instead, we have high expectations and concrete deliverables. As mentioned in Chapter 8, when a team or an individual fails to meet these expectations, we don't celebrate that, we step in as Big Birds and work to correct the action. We try to find a happy medium between complete intolerance of any failure and celebrating incompetent failure.[19] But this medium is hard to find, and many professional service providers who are introduced to design thinking aren't taught about that balance. Moreover, many are not taught how their education helps them avoid failure.

A key variable that researchers have found that predicted success for entrepreneurs was education—not experience.[20] This is good fodder for my mantra (that by now you know so well) which is that all professional services providers should try their hand at innovating. Since they are usually highly educated, research indicates it should give them a leg up.

3. Lack of Marketing Targeted to Key Stakeholders

A third marketing problem with innovation is the lack of effective internal marketing about the organization's innovation or collaboration efforts and their importance. There is mixed messaging by the senior professional service providers about the importance of innovation—which is underscored (negatively) by the fact that "collaboration" is generally not "billable to a client," is often not compensated, or if it is, it is a soft factor that is not counted the same way or with the same weight as other compensation metrics. There is also often a lack of clear *and motivating* messaging about the purpose of a new innovation initiative, committee, or group. What is the North Star? Often the goals are touted as being much bigger than any innovation committee could achieve, which puts professional service providers off because it raises the stakes too high. Remember, think tiny! Other times the messaging is unclear (or absent) because of disagreement about the goals—like the example I mentioned in the prior chapter wherein the managing partner kept pushing the innovation committee to think BIG and HUGE about creating a new rocket ship, whereas many of the members of the committee (and I) thought that was a mistake and that instead, they should be focusing on making the current rocket ship better. I'm a big believer that any first innovation effort can and should be positioned as a "pilot." Everyone can handle a pilot (whether it succeeds or fails). A pilot means that the stakes are lower, which takes some of the pressure off. The word "pilot," therefore, works like grease and it is related to the MVS (minimum viable solution) we talked about earlier. Calling it a pilot reminds everyone to focus on what is minimally necessary for the solution to be viable so that it fits the problem like a glove. Leave the bells and whistles for year 2 or 3.

This lack of internal marketing (or the right kind of messaging) is a big problem for any transformation effort. Harvard Business School professor John P. Kotter, widely regarded as an expert on the topics of leadership and change, explains that one of the eight reasons why transformations fail is "undercommunicating the vision by a factor of 10":[21]

> *In more successful transformation efforts, executives use all existing communication channels to broadcast the vision. They turn boring and unread company newsletters into lively articles about the vision. They take ritualistic and tedious quarterly management meetings and turn them into exciting discussions of the transformation. They throw out much of the company's generic management education and replace it with courses that focus on business problems and the new vision. The guiding principle is simple: use every possible channel, especially those that are being wasted on nonessential information.[22]*

Successful transformation teams understand that they cannot capture the "hearts and minds" of the troops if they under-communicate the vision and the why.[23] Kotter also points out that the executives involved in successful cases of major change "walk the talk" and "consciously attempt to become a living symbol of the new corporate culture."[24] This is exactly what we talked about in Part II (which focused on you as an individual leader). That point is tied to marketing because communication is both what we say and what we do (and of course the latter is often the most influential).

Marketing to external stakeholders is also essential. Remember the scene from the movie, *The Founder*, described in Chapter 3. Because the burger company had not included its external stakeholders in the transformation of how it served burgers 30 seconds faster, it angered its customers (who didn't want to have to get out of their car or eat burgers wrapped in paper). The burger company sidestepped the disaster by creating a huge advertising campaign explaining "why" they made the changes to convince their target audience that the inconvenience was worth it. Evidently this worked! I'm not suggesting you ever take such a risk. The point is more that you should check in and include your key customers or clients when making changes to your products and services, and market the reasons for the changes along the way (not after the fact).

4. Lackluster Marketing of Small Wins and Progress

There is also often a lack of internal marketing and messaging about progress as initiatives move forward even though there are small wins that could be promoted. For example, it is success when a team finally converges around a narrow problem that is fixable, yet professional service firms often don't celebrate or recognize that milestone—though narrowing the problem often is the hardest part of the innovation journey. Measuring and marketing the wins—the small and big wins—are important to keep the teams engaged but also for buy-in by others. Innovation needs different ways of measuring success and different ways of marketing it, for example, through storytelling and award giving and career advancement. This isn't surprising given research on how technological innovation is adopted.

According to experts, to fill in the credibility gap, we need to win over more than just the early adopters (the first 34 percent); we need to convince at least half of the majority (the next 34 percent, the "early majority").[25] Given that the "early majority" tend to deliberate longer (than early adopters) before completely adopting a new idea,[26] convincing them requires a strategic marketing plan that takes into account their values and needs (as all successful marketing plans do).[27] Yet creating and executing such a plan is often not made a priority by many professionals (especially when it involves internal marketing). Perhaps this is because they don't value "marketing." Or they see it as soft and unnecessary thinking perhaps: *if it works, it doesn't need marketing; it will market itself.* But that belief is wrong and misguided. Unfortunately, sometimes there exists the same feeling about branding, which sabotages marketing efforts when they are attempted. Without a true understanding of the department's or practice group's brand (and how it fits in and aligns with the company or firm's brand), how can anyone develop a marketing and messaging plan that resonates?

5. Failure to Create a Brand and Solution in a Sentence That Packages and Sells the Innovation

Finally, there is a lack of internal marketing, messaging, and branding of the innovation itself, the idea or solution. This is a failure of packaging. I insist that my participants give their idea or solution a name and a tagline, and that they determine its brand essence. We have a dedicated exercise to do just that called *A-Brand-and-Solution-in-a-Sentence-or-2 Exercise* that is designed to help teams succinctly describe the branded solution, highlighting its point of difference and benefits and what it does, for whom, and why. Prior to this exercise, teams have to complete *The Brand Matrix Exercise* to help develop a brand for their solution and identify their solution's physical brand attributes, rational and emotional brand benefits, and the brand image/personality.

"Why do we need to do that?" team participants from my Microsoft program asked. *"Our company has a brand already. What's the purpose of that?"*

My reply: *"Because in doing this exercise you tighten up the solution, ensure it talks to the target audience and determine how to sell this internally to the powers that be. If you have 3 minutes in the elevator with Brad Smith (president and chief legal officer of Microsoft), you need to be able to sell him on your idea. These exercises will enable you to do this."*

The pushback is a bit concerning because by this point, the teams have learned about the importance of storytelling, and they have all created consumer stories that bring to life the various audiences that are impacted by their problem or the solution that they created. They've done all this and have come so far, but when it comes to bringing their idea to life with a story and a brand or a message, there is push back. *"That's something marketers do, not us,"* they complain. Perhaps the negative attitude stems from the fact that they don't really understand the influence of branding or marketing or know how to utilize either to their advantage.

Unfortunately, there is anecdotal evidence that many professional service firms (especially law firms), don't understand branding and marketing even though they can help a firm win business over a competitor.[28] That aside, any internal innovation, new idea, or new plan needs a marketing campaign, messaging care, and well-crafted, well-targeted pitches. Research shows that HOW you present your idea and the information (if you personalize the information and make it tangible and based on what the listener values) can change the impact greatly.[29] However, many professional service providers do not know how to create a beautiful PowerPoint deck, stand powerfully (with presence) in front of a crowd, and make a motivating presentation without "umms" and "you knows" and reading from notes. This is why we focus on presentation skills (part of those C.O.S.T. skills in the third level of the Skills Delta) and learning how to give pitches of different kinds to different types of audience. It is also why we rehearse and rehearse and rehearse. The reality is, marketing (and presenting) is a skill we all need because all professional service providers are in sales and marketing of some sort—as the title of Daniel Pink's book makes clear, *To Sell Is Human.*

In essence, creating the right branding, marketing, and messaging is the spoonful of sugar that helps the medicine aka "dreaded change" (and management of that change) go down easier. In other words, for each change effort, we need management techniques and for each change and management effort, we need the right messaging and the right branding—for the initiative *and* for the individual leaders.

Just as important as walking the walk, the personal branding of the leader (you!) is key (and often not paid as much attention as we should). A personal brand is different from a company or firm brand, but they can be intertwined, and a personal brand should not be inconsistent with the company/firm brand. The company/firm's brand is the promise the company/firm makes to its target consumers. It is the story it tells about its product or services, why it exists and what it offers to the target consumer to convince them to buy. But branding is not just for companies and products. As mentioned in Chapter 3, as part of digital transformation efforts, today's large corporate legal departments are determining their unique selling proposition (the unique benefits that the in-house legal department provides that distinguish it from other providers) to clarify what the department stands for, that is, what its "brand" is.[30] Branding can help departments, professionals service firms, practice groups, and teams message with influence, inspire culture change, prioritize initiatives, "resonate" with clients, and innovate.

A personal branding statement is a few sentences that sum up who you are, what you do, and why you do it. A personal brand should get to your essence, describe your inner super power, convey what drives you (why you do what you do and your values), and portray what makes you a YOUnicorn (your uniqueness). And it shouldn't sound like a sales pitch! A good start to developing your personal brand is to go through the exercise of creating a personal branding statement, which is a few sentences that sum up who you are, what you do, and why you do it. It is a dynamic, evolving, messaging strategy that includes multiple types of communication channels and tools (and that is backed up by action, results, and a lot of effort) to convey your point of difference, your unique value in an authentic way.

I have a *Mad-Lib Personal Branding Exercise* that I have used with LawWithoutWalls participants and partners attending executive education programs. The process of creating a personal branding statement forces you to think critically and to be honest about yourself, all so that you better understand your goals, aspirations, strengths, and values, when you only have a few minutes to make a good impression. Understanding your personal brand also helps you determine which requests you should accept (and decline). Of course, developing a personal brand takes strategy, help, effort, and many communication channels. Also, of course, a personal brand grows and evolves over time and must be backed up with actions and results, that is, credibility.

Personal branding is itself a type of storytelling and messaging that helps leaders champion change. When we combine this authentic narrative with the mindset and skill set on the Skills Delta—especially empathy—our ability to convince others to join us in our change efforts is enhanced.[31] But what does personal branding have to do with branding and marketing the product? You are the mouthpiece for the product. Understanding your own brand and owning it helps you present and market any idea or project more authentically.

Overcoming some of these barriers by embracing marketing and branding will get us some of the way there. However, in addition to needing a marketing and messaging plan, we need a method in order to innovate successfully.

B. The 3-4-5 Method™ Is Designed for Change in Professional Services

While it is true that all innovation processes include a little messiness, trying to manage any collaborative problem-solving journey or innovation initiative without a method is madness. Consider McKinsey—famous for always delivering advice in "threes"—or the book, *The 7 Habits of Highly Effective People*,[32] or the 5 Ps of Marketing.[33] They offer a structure, a way to understand what needs to be done and where the end-state of these tasks or steps or strategies lies. However, when it comes to innovation and design thinking, it is often presented as a messy almost nonprocess. Although it is true that the application of design thinking in the corporate world to innovate both products and services has been the subject of several well-known books, I have not found the methods easily understood. Perhaps this is because it is hard for people who have not been formally educated in innovation and design to read about overlapping iterative spaces like IDEO's (inspiration, ideation, and implementation) and thereby understand how to actually lead multidisciplinary teams on an innovation journey from problem to solution.[34] Why would you need to hire IDEO or attend Stanford's design thinking course if you can understand how to do everything simply by reading it?

However, I think there is more to it than that. Perhaps the problem is one of nomenclature. Perhaps these are not *really* methods in that they aren't actually intended to explain a systematic way of doing or accomplishing each of the phases or steps or a process by which the tasks are completed. Instead, perhaps these approaches are more like a list of activities that must be conducted or accomplished (not necessarily in order) to create a new product or service. Yet, I often find they do not describe the method in detail and exactly how to move through the steps or phases, what exercises and which tools can help a team do so, when they should occur, and how long they should take—which is why I did exactly that in my recently published accompaniment to this book: *The Leader Upheaval Handbook*. It might also be the case that I'm entirely wrong. There may be easy-to-understand instructional books out there that I simply haven't found.[35]

If these books or manuals exist, that's great. In fact, I hope they do because the point of this section is twofold. First, it is to convince you that *all* teams on *any* collaborative problem-solving journey need to use a method, but this is especially true for those in professional services. Second, its purpose is to provide an overview of a real method, The 3-4-5 Method™ that has been tested on over 230 teams and explain why it works and what makes it a good method. That way, even if you don't decide to read *The Leader Upheaval Handbook* and use my method, you can pick whatever method you prefer. I, of course, hope you will use The 3-4-5 Method™ because it is a truly methodical process and I've packaged and marketed it that way. True, it includes some back and forth among the steps, but there IS a trajectory forward and it makes sense to people with a less creative artistic backdrop in their lives.

Essentially, The 3-4-5 Method™ educates and provides structure for professional service providers who are attempting to lead collaborative innovation initiatives. As a method, it identifies how and when to move from one stage to another in the problem identification and ideation process and who should be doing what. It delineates time frames and role identification and differentiates competent from incompetent failure. I created The 3-4-5 Method™ with all of the gaps previously identified in mind. It's also why I wrote *The Leader Upheaval Handbook*, which provides detailed instructions on how to use and implement the method and run exercises that make it work. However, before we delve into the method, let's turn to why professional service providers need a method, what The 3-4-5 Method™ is, and why it works.

1. Why Professional Service Providers Need a Method

Professional service providers need a real method for many reasons but the first and foremost reason is because of the gaps in mindset and skill set identified in Part I. As mentioned, these gaps need to be filled before or during any innovation journey to prevent them from hindering progress. Hopefully, I have already convinced you that the art of collaboration and innovation starts with you, but the leader needs to convince each member of each multidisciplinary team on the journey of the same thing. Most design thinking methods seem to assume you already have people who are not only willing but also *able* to collaborate in the ways needed and with the right mindset and skill set. But that's not necessarily true, especially for professional service providers. There are many lawyers, accountants, and consultants alike who graduated with their respective expert degrees having never had to truly collaborate on a team project and have never taken a course on collaboration, innovation, or design thinking. So even if they are willing (which isn't always a given), they may not be able as is.

Further, unless they attended business school, likely the majority (if not all) of their grades and assessments were based on individual contributions (not team work). Furthermore, like the culture and curriculum of the schools, the firms in which they now work may be more individualistic and competitive and discourage risk taking and encourage conformity. Further, many professional service providers are assessed based on their own contributions and, in some industries, based on billable hours or individual commissions. This means there is an inherent lack of extrinsic motivation to collaborate well on an innovation journey. This (combined with the lack of training) means that the expectations aren't understood. Moreover, it's not clear that professional service providers really *get* what we mean by collaboration. I interviewed a managing partner of a law firm who had recently reorganized the firm by industry group, and she said "You know, we have learned that we are not supposed to use the word *cross-sell*. That's a no-no. Instead, we are supposed to use the word *collaborate*. But I don't think we know what *collaborate* means." And wow did this ring true! In fact, whenever I dig into what has been pointed to with pride as an example of collaboration by a law firm, I often find that it isn't really collaboration. For example, I often hear about request for proposal processes wherein the lawyers divide up the work so that they can each work individually and independently on the pieces related to their expertise and then give all the pieces to the business development and marketing people to pull it together and package it. That's not proactive collaboration. That's coordinating and cooperating—reactively. My interviews with hundreds of legal professionals and experience teaching thousands of current and future legal professionals shores this up. Some don't see the difference, but some do, and they still struggle to make it happen at their firms. Consider the following typical response:

> *I don't think we are as proactive as we can be. Most of us (not all of us) are more reactive. We answer a phone call from a client who says they need to talk to a tax partner, and we give them the contact information of our partner in tax. This is not a collaboration. It's cross-selling. We need to collaborate in a different way, to anticipate the needs of clients and to see the client among the firm in a different way. It's not what can I do for the client. Instead, it's what we do for the client. But we are only just beginning to try this.*—Partner, one of the top law firms in Brazil[36]

The emphasis that many design thinking methods place on how iterative and unpredictable and prone to failure innovation journeys can be may be off-putting to professional service providers who are, as described in Part I, often risk-averse, analytical, and methodical. If they can't see the reason for it and they are put off, then they lack not only extrinsic motivation but also intrinsic motivation.

Further, consider that if you haven't been trained to ideate in the way design thinkers do, the process can be uncomfortable, difficult, and, unfortunately, unsuccessful. Group ideation sessions in which people gather around a white board and are required to think on the spot—or, worse yet, put all the thoughts on a bunch of Post-it® notes—are antithetical to how many professional service providers prefer to think and ideate. They prefer to work behind closed doors, often solo, and almost always rationally and objectively—with a concentration on converging on an answer. Being asked to employ methods that require empathy and emotional connection with users and that prevent teams from quickly identifying a solution can seem overly subjective and inefficient.[37] Having to squeeze brilliant thoughts into one or two words on a small bit of paper isn't how many professional service providers prefer to communicate. Not to mention the fact that this is also antithetical to how introverts work and, therefore, is not inclusive. This is unfortunate because this format isn't necessary for collaboration or innovation efforts to succeed; however, it seems part and parcel of many methods.

Also, many methods do not identify how or when to move from one stage to another in the ideation process or who should be doing what. They also do not delineate time frames and role identification, nor do they differentiate competent from incompetent failure, as noted earlier. Professional service providers are paid for their knowledge, expertise, and time, even if they charge a flat rate instead of a billable hour, even if they work internally within a company and not at an external firm. So, any time that they are not working with or for a client is unleveraged, invaluable time. I often hear professional service providers say that their firm is doing so well, they don't have time to collaborate or innovate.[38] So convincing them to go on an innovation journey without a real method (without a process) to get them from A to Z and without transparent time boundaries is super hard. They don't have the time or patience (as mentioned earlier regarding their eagerness to rush to solve). Without a method, professional service providers are likely to be skeptical and untrusting and, frankly, unwilling to "play" and collaborate the way that you might want them to. A quote by W. Edwards Deming, a famous American engineer, sums this idea up: "If you can't describe what you are doing as a process, you don't know what you are doing." Professional service providers do not like *not* knowing what they are doing. They like to be buttoned up and they will not follow a leader who does not seem to know what they are doing. Having a real process overcomes both hurdles.

Thus, a method that *assumes* that professional service providers understand the phases or stages as described—and assumes that they want to actually complete the phases (because generally I find professional service providers questioning why they have to do this or that)—isn't going to work. Instead, they need a method (and a leader) that helps them navigate the journey.[39] They need a leader who educates and convinces them along the way of the importance of collaboration and who forces them to commit to a new type of collaboration, one that fills the gaps regardless of whether the gaps exist due to a lack of training, temperament, extrinsic or intrinsic motivation, or a combination thereof.

This is why I created The 3-4-5 Method™, a team-based innovation process grounded in design thinking principles and constructed especially for professional service providers' temperament, training, and work preferences. It emphasizes the *how* and *who*. Further, it makes the *what* and *when* super, super clear so that collaboration comes easier (and perhaps with more certainty in the process) than it might otherwise. It does this in three phases for a set amount of time and in 5 Steps. Although the steps are iterative, this method details instructions and exercises for each step, along with deliverables, role identification, time commitment, and, importantly, a timeline: the series of meetings and activities that must occur among the team and with external advisers along the innovation journey. This method focuses on purpose, goals, accountability, and transparency. It also focuses on *service* innovation, not just products, which is key for many professional service providers who aren't yet interested or don't quite understand what people mean when they talk about *productizing a service*, that is, when services are sold like products, with defined parameters and pricing. Armed with this level of information and predictability of the innovation journey, I find that professional service providers are willing to put in the time to get the results of new skills, new mindsets, and new behaviors, not to mention an innovation.

Interestingly, even after learning The 3-4-5 Method™, and going through it, some participants are still impatient with the messiness of the process that innovation entails. A piece of feedback that made me smile came from a survey of a law firm innovation committee after their 4-month journey. When asked to complete the following sentence "I hope in the future we can . . .," their answer was "Duplicate the process, but hopefully in a more streamlined way now that we understand the process." The beauty of this response is twofold. First, this respondent realizes that innovation is a process and that it can be "duplicated." It's not just a hot mess. Yes, progress! Second, the respondent realizes that *managing* innovation is critical. Yes, even more progress! What they still don't understand, however, is even with good facilitation and management, the process is guaranteed to be a bit less than "streamlined," and it's always going to be difficult and hard. Therefore, I always stress the importance of a method and in teaching it, I explain that although the 3 Phases go in order and the 5 Steps are generally sequential, they may also be recursive and iterative. That is, insights during Step 3 about the key stakeholders' pain points may mean we have to revert to Step 2 to revise or add more detail to the problem statement. After that, we might need to return to Step 1 to do some more investigative research to support the importance of solving the problem. Being able to explain the method as a process is key to convincing them to take the time because in many ways what M. S. Dhoni, an Indian professional cricketer, is famous for saying is true: "The process is more important than the results. And if you take care of the process, you will get the results."[40] But some processes and methods are better than others. In the next chapter, I provide an overview of The 3-4-5 Method™, its goals and benefits, and an explanation of why it works, that is, why it has been so successful among hundreds of teams from companies and professional service firms of different kinds and industries, headquartered in different countries around the world

Before turning to the method, however, let's explore the theory behind it.

2. The Theory: The Seven Essential Experiences for Creativity, Collaboration, and Innovation

It is not true that professional service providers are not creative or that the practices of law, consulting, or finance are not creative practices. They are. But as many of my interviewees aptly point out, professional service providers don't appreciate the extent to which what they do is creative, and that creativity is a skill they have honed for years. Even if they do, many don't know how to apply that type of creativity to help them innovate. The challenge of applying creativity to the professional services field is that lawyers, consultants, bankers, and so on are taught to use the same thinking in which they have engaged before, the same reasoning, the same processes, and the same methods to solve new problems. However, as Albert Einstein said: "We can't solve problems by using the same kind of thinking we used when we created them." Therefore, what we need is a new kind of thinking, a new theoretical framework. To that end, this section presents seven essential experiences that all professionals must go through (and master) to achieve creativity, collaboration, and innovation when multidisciplinary teaming on an innovation journey.

These seven experiences are those that every highly successful innovation team must not only go through but also own—often repeatedly but not always in the same order. If you were to put the experiences in an ideal chronology, they would be as follows (even though they don't always occur in this order): (1) nurturing (self and the team); (2) falling in love (with the problem and the target audience); (3) celebrating important moments (births, anniversaries, and deaths); (4) moving in (with a narrower problem and target audience); (5) getting engaged, then married (to a problem and solution); (6) reflecting (monitoring and evaluating); and (7) working hard.

a. Nurturing: Self and the Team

At the core of most successful innovation journeys is a multidisciplinary team made up of very different types of individuals. Therefore, an essential element throughout an innovation journey—and actually the very first stage of any journey—should be nurturing, focusing on the strengths and weaknesses of ourselves, the other individuals on the team, and the team as a whole. Every innovation cycle should start here, with nurturing and building trust, which is why, in The 3-4-5 Method, we start with a KickOff (described in the next chapter) that includes individual assessments, team personality mapping, individual and team goals setting, communication training, and teaming exercises. During the KickOff, we are first introduced to and practice the Three Rules of Engagement, including how to give constructive feedback, of course.

To enhance this nurturing in LawWithoutWalls, we provide teams with an anonymous hotline and a teaming coach. Regrettably, I didn't originally replicate this in my consultancy work, as I thought the same types of teaming issues that occurred with and between students would not occur on teams composed solely of professionals already in the workplace. I was wrong. As alluded to earlier, in the programs that I run with law firms and in-house legal departments like DXC Technology and Microsoft, I have found that conflict can still arise when the teams do not spend enough time nurturing the teaming aspect of the team. No matter how old we are, we can "fight" and have conflict with team members, and that dissonance can derail progress regardless of how professional we are and how thick-skinned we are and how *above all that* we think we are. But airing these differences can help. Sometimes nurturing the self and nurturing the team can be in conflict because what is good for you individually and for your growth may not always coincide with what is good for the team and its growth and progress on its journey toward innovation. Effective teaming is a balance between our own goals, our own cultures, and our own preferences and the needs of others and the objectives of the team.

b. Falling in Love (with the Problem and the Target Audience)

A core essential experience of innovation is what IDEO calls "inspiration." I call it "falling in love." When we are falling in love in our personal lives, we are interested in every little detail (past, present, and future) of the other person. We ask all kinds of questions and attempt to connect with the other person on multiple levels—from music, to food, to hobbies, to intellectual interests. We might even be fascinated with how our love interest brushes their teeth—seriously? That's wacky. And it is that crazy experience that we all need in innovation (multiple times). We need to fall in love with the problem. We need to fall in love with the people experiencing the problem.

Like the falling-in-love stage in our personal lives, in an innovation cycle, this is the time when we explore not only everything about the problem but also everything about the target audience: the user experiencing the problem or opportunity. It is at this stage that we create the consumer story from the point of view of the person who is experiencing the problem or has a need. The consumer (customer, target audience) is the focal point. This is why, as mentioned earlier, Amazon's founder Jeff Bezos places one empty chair in each meeting. He does this to represent the customer.[41] When we are falling in love, all we see is the empty chair. We learn to empathize with the target audience (the group with whom we are falling in love) sitting in that chair and experiencing every facet of the problem.

Pretend for a moment that you were charged with solving the problems that a busy working woman has in making a salad as part of dinner for her three children. Your first reaction might be, seriously? How hard is it to make a salad? Then take a moment and think again. Try to put yourself in her shoes. She is 43. She is a divorced, single parent with three teenage children, two of whom are girls aged 14 and 15 who won't eat anything but salad because they are obsessed with their diet. True, she could just buy a salad from the same store she buys a grilled chicken for her son, but then it won't be "healthy," meaning it has more calories than a McDonald's hamburger and vanilla shake combined. Even if she can figure out a way to save time and have both the chicken and the lettuce delivered (bearing in mind that Instacart is not known for its ability to select produce), she must painstakingly wash each piece of lettuce to get rid of the dirt and grit. Then she has to pat the lettuce dry with a paper towel. And she must navigate between washing too little so that when her daughters begin to eat, she doesn't hear that little crunch when they bite down on a piece of grit that didn't get washed away or washing too much so that the lettuce tastes more like overcooked spinach than salad. Can you picture that? Then you understand what this part of the innovation experience is all about. It's about the problem. And it's about the person experiencing the problem and how they are feeling related to two different aspects of the problem (that we know now) were (thank goodness) fixed with prewashed and prebagged lettuce (now I just wish someone would fix the inevitable smell of the bagged lettuce! Even when the date of expiration is five days away, it still has that *awful* smell.)

Ironically, the group of people that empathized with the working woman with teenage children who developed bagged lettuce were not the lettuce growers. According to Professor Ranjay Gulati, this is because they were focusing on an "inside-out perspective"—on metrics related to sales of lettuce and customer satisfaction with the quality—instead of what a pain it was for customers to prepare salad.[42] In a similar vein, in Bruce Turkel's book *All About Them*, he warns us about the danger of seeing the world through our own personal understanding instead of attempting to see the world through our customer's point of view.[43] He calls this "depending on one's own self-referencing criteria."[44] During this stage of design thinking, it is imperative that you consider the consumer's frame of reference, that you look at the problem from the consumer's point of view (not your self-referencing criteria) so that you can see what they see and feel how they feel. It is about storytelling—but not yours. It's about telling the consumer's story in their voice through their lens. We have all of our teams create consumer stories in The 3-4-5 Method™ for this purpose.

This is especially tough for people in power. Daniel H. Pink cites studies showing that there is "an inverse relationship between power and perspective-taking."[45] Those in power are more likely to look at things from their own vantage point and less likely to adjust to that of others.

This means that this may be especially tough for leaders, who often have the most power in the room. And it is for this exact reason that the CEO of Uber started driving an Uber periodically, so that he could really get into the shoes of the drivers.

Of course, the goal is not just to empathize with the consumer/user, but to be inspired by them because when we are inspired, when we have passion for something, we are willing to put more work into it. Warren Buffett, Steve Jobs, and Mark Zuckerberg all have famous quotes about following your passion. As in our personal lives, when we are in the falling-in-love stage, the best part is the passion. And passion is the only thing that helps us last through the arduous and long process of problem finding. In a study of industrial design students, research concluded that creative results were more likely to be achieved by students who were problem-oriented (as opposed to solution-oriented.)[46] In other words, the more time a person spent understanding, defining, and framing the problem, the more creative the results were. This ability to frame and reframe is essential to the innovation process. We need to spend more time questioning to make sure we have identified the right problem in the right way for the right target group. In doing so, we are able to find a more effective solution more efficiently. This harkens back to the quote by Albert Einstein, mentioned in Chapter 2, which essentially stated that if he had an hour to solve a problem, he'd spend 55 minutes analyzing the problem and 5 minutes on the solution.[47]

People may say that our job is to solve our clients' problems, but that's not accurate. Our real job is to help our clients better understand their problems. As mentioned and as both Tina Seelig and Daniel H. Pink make clear, the best problem solvers are the best problem finders.[48] Consider this example by Pink. If someone says that they need a new vacuum, a problem solver might suggest that the person go online and compare the different options and prices and order a vacuum online. A problem finder, on the other hand, might ask questions to determine *why* this person thinks they need a new vacuum. I often ask professionals to role-play this scenario with me, and they struggle. After I tell them my vacuum cleaner is broken, I tell them to ask me "why?", and they laugh. They think: *What a silly question. Why would I ask you "why" you think your vacuum is broken when you have just told me it is and, frankly, it doesn't matter "why"?* Ah, but it does matter. In asking why, we might determine that the problem isn't that the vacuum needs replacing; instead, the problem may be that I just installed a new carpet, and it is too thick for this type of vacuum. Or perhaps the carpet is made of such a material that no vacuum will work on it. If so, then what the person "needs" is a new carpet, not a new vacuum. In asking why, we bypass symptoms and find problems. Indeed, this is why we have all our teams practice the 5 Whys (also discussed in Chapter 2).

A similar example came from a group of my students. I used to teach a course at the University of Miami School of Law called Innovation, Technology, and the Law. For one of the group exercises, I had the students interview another group of students on a problem they had identified related to law school. Then their job was to try to solve that other group's problem. The problem was identified as follows: too many undergraduates were using the law library, making it hard to find a quiet place to study. The team developed a solution that would track undergraduates entering the library by utilizing a key card so that after a certain number had entered, no more could come in. When they presented the solution, the students who had complained about the problem originally were disappointed because the solution didn't solve the problem. The problem was not the amount of space the undergraduates took up; the problem was that they didn't follow the noise rules and thus made it hard to study. What the students needed was not a way to prevent undergraduates from entering the law library and using it; instead, they needed a way to get the undergrads to comply with the rules about making noise. This group of students was eager to create a cool solution, and indeed their solution was pretty cool. But because they didn't spend more time interviewing their target audience (the group of students who had experienced the problem) and asking questions such as "why?", their solution missed the mark.

Furthermore, sometimes there is an opportunity to make something better that we don't see because we don't register the problem. What we have might work okay as it is. Consider bagged lettuce or bagless vacuums. We didn't *really* need either. But no one has likely ever changed a vacuum bag successfully without that gross "poof" of air and dirt that erupts from the bag when it is removed from the tube.[49] Tina Seelig calls this "need finding." She explains, "The key to need finding is identifying and filling gaps, that is, gaps in the way people use products, gaps in the services available, and gaps in the stories they tell when interviewed about their behavior."[50] Need finding is the exact opposite of one of the sayings I have already stated that I hate the most: if it ain't broke, don't fix it. One of the exercises I have created to help teams problem and need find is actually called just the opposite: *If It Ain't Broke, Twist It and Fix It.*

The most important thing to remember at this stage is that what we are falling in love with is the problem or need—not the solution. So many times, teams rush to solve a problem—rush to "move in" (the terminology we are using later in this chapter) before making sure they have fallen in love with the right problem. But once they finally do, it's important to celebrate the finding first because the finding is often the hardest part.

c. Celebrating Important Moments (Births, Anniversaries, and Deaths)

At this point, we have decided to zero in on one problem and one discrete audience. Now it's time to celebrate. That may sound crazy; we just started this journey, and now we are celebrating only that we have identified a problem (or perhaps the problem within a problem)? We are because (as mentioned and worth repeating) problem finding for a discrete consumer or target audience is the most critical element and is often the most frustrating and debilitating to teams, causing conflict and disagreement. Just as you celebrate anniversaries with significant others, it is important to celebrate this transition. It is the thing that everyone forgets to do, and yet it is so easy . . . if only we would stop and take the time to do it.

You will notice that the title in this experience also includes celebrating deaths. Just as people celebrate death with funerals or celebrate love with engagement parties, we need to take moments to celebrate our progress (or lack thereof) in the innovation cycle. This is because all team members likely must do what Stephen King is known for urging (via William Faulkner and he via Sir Arthur Thomas Quiller-Couch), and that is "kill your darlings"[51] at some point—to walk away from their exact interpretation of a problem or their previous framing of it. This "death" is progress: it is competent failure because it is implementing lessons learned. So, this is a time to celebrate the deaths of those ideas and put aside any team conflict that might have arisen along the way. Whether we are moving forward with an idea or moving out to find a new idea we can love, we can celebrate that we took a risk, invested time and energy, and learned. Given how busy we are and that some of us tend to see risk under every rock, we don't always take the time to celebrate moments along the way to winning a case, solving a problem, or prevailing for our clients . . .because we might be wrong. We have likely all heard the lore that the financial analyst's, the lawyer's, and the consultant's job is often to pick things apart and look for what might go wrong. How can we celebrate until we know for sure we have won? Even when we are right about something, there is always the fear (and often the reality) that something even worse is coming next and our job is to prevent it. Yet celebrating short wins early on is important. True, as Kotter warns, we need to be careful about declaring victory too soon (like the teams who latch on to their first idea, which is never the best idea).[52] However, even Kotter lauds planning for, creating, and celebrating short-term wins.[53] Otherwise we risk burnout and team conflict. Unfortunately, celebration may be a talent that many are losing:

> *People of our time are losing the power of celebration. Instead of celebrating we seek to be amused or entertained. Celebration is an active state, an act of expressing reverence or appreciation. To be entertained is a passive state—it is to receive pleasure afforded by an amusing act or a spectacle . . . Celebration is a confrontation, Giving attention to the transcendent meaning of one's actions.—Abraham Joshua Heschel[54]*

d. Moving In (with a Narrower Problem and Target Audience)

The fourth essential experience in an innovation cycle is what IDEO calls "ideation." For me, this part of innovation is like moving in with someone. This is the phase in our personal lives wherein we lock in on one person, perhaps with the hope of getting engaged. One discrete problem for one discrete primary target audience has been chosen, and now we start ideating possible solutions to that problem. Many different types of exercises can be used to generate problem-solving ideas, many of which are described in my companion handbook. Often, though, these exercises involve on-the-spot brainstorming, which can be uncomfortable for introverts. Therefore, I recommend treating these exercises as tools you can use spontaneously during a team meeting not only to spur creative thinking when you are stuck but also as scheduled exercises spaced out over a few days so that you are sure to discover that great thinking of the introverts (who sometimes need a few days to process).

As mentioned above, design thinking is an iterative, overlapping, and integrative process. The experiences are not attacked in order, progress is not incremental, and the enterprise requires a mix of left- and right-brain thinking.[55] This mix of processes can be difficult for professionals who are results-driven, timekeepers, and methodical. The back-and-forth between phases or steps and in types of thinking required can sometimes feel inefficient. Yet generating solutions demands nothing less.

During the moving-in phase, we must focus on both divergent and convergent thinking. First divergent, then convergent, and then divergent and convergent again. Phil Charron provided a short description of both types of thinking in a blog in 2011.[56] He wrote:

> *Divergent thinking is taking a challenge and attempting to identify all of the possible drivers of that challenge, then listing all of the ways those drivers can be addressed. In practice, it's more than just brainstorming. Some analysis is needed so you don't put too many tools in your Swiss Army knife, but you shouldn't hamstring yourself with too many constraints, either.*[57]

Convergent thinking, on the other hand, is what the crew on *Apollo 13* had to do to save the ship. They could only use what they had on board to solve the problem. Convergent thinking "is the practice of trying to solve a discrete challenge quickly and efficiently by selecting the optimal solution from a finite set."[58]

Charron provides the following example to show the difference:

Convergent thinking: I live four miles from work. My car gets 30 MPG. I want to use less fuel in my commute for financial and conservation reasons. Money is no object. Find the three best replacement vehicles for my car.

Divergent thinking: I live four miles from work. My car gets 30 MPG. I want to use less fuel in my commute for financial and conservation reasons. Money is no object. What options do I have to reduce my fuel consumption?

Tim Brown defines the two types of thinking as follows: "During divergence, we are creating choices and during convergence we are making choices."[59]

During this phase, we test whether the solutions we come up with will work. We see what might be improved. Like couples moving in together to do a test run for marriage, we do a test run by creating a prototype and testing it on consumers and refining it and retesting it. Professions new to the world of human-centered design sometimes worry about this step. (Indeed, I see their faces cringe when I describe it). The word *prototype* conjures up three-dimensional images in their minds, and their skeptical side immediately thinks: *What in the world does this have to do with professional services?* But as design thinkers such as Tim Brown emphasize, a prototype can be "[a]nything tangible that lets us explore an idea, evaluate it, and push it forward."[60] It can be a static mock-up of a potential website or app that shows how a user would interface with the potential product.

Let me bring this to life. The winning Project of Worth for a LawWithoutWalls' team a few years ago was Cybird: a game that teaches children how to recognize, report, and prevent cyberbullying. The Cybird team members didn't create the game in its entirety; rather, they mapped out the game flow and illustrated key components of the user experience using short animations to prototype the game and get feedback from our community.

A prototype can also be a skit or video that brings a story to life. For example, one of the teams in LawWithoutWalls was tasked with making the relationship between legal professionals and marketers within the sponsoring healthcare company more effective and efficient. This team (we will hereafter refer to it as the healthcare team) devised Creative License: an artificial intelligence–based solution that gives marketers instant feedback on high-risk words and phrases as they type—like having a lawyer, a compliance officer, and a brand guardian working on the same task at the same time. During its final presentation, the team set the stage for its problem using a video-recorded, humorous skit employing actual marketers and lawyers giving real examples of their concerns. (The skit even involved a LawWithoutWalls team member from the company who played the hero as an anthropomorphized "Creative License.") To show Creative License in action, the team used another video composed of a sequence of screenshots with voice-overs to demonstrate how the product would look, work, and feel in real time.

Prototyping, therefore, is simply a way to bring an idea to life, to give it dimension—but not necessarily three dimensions. We prototype and tweak the prototypes until we are sure (as sure as we can be) that we are ready to implement the solution. However, one part of this phase that seems to be given short shrift in the literature is that during this stage, we must analyze not only the feasibility (workability and profitability) but also the viability of the solution (business growth and sustainability) to which we want to get engaged. This is why we move in with someone we have fallen in love with—to determine whether we can actually "do" this: cohabit, share finances, co-own a dog, etc. After all this analysis, we might still determine that the solution isn't viable for the long term or isn't feasible (e.g., the solution doesn't have a large enough target audience to make it worth creating). So, we break up (i.e., we have to go backward). We must nurture ourselves to heal and then move on to eventually move in with a new, but viable, solution.

e. Getting Engaged, Then Married (to a Problem and Solution)

The fifth essential experience is comparable to getting engaged and then married. We have selected one solution to implement for one target audience. The hope is that this engagement will go smoothly, and we will get married to it (i.e., implement it for years and years to come). The hope is also that the solution is targeted, viable, and feasible and that it achieves its objectives (e.g., makes money, builds brand recognition, etc.). Of course, by now, it should not be just a hope. We should have put some numbers together in the moving-in phase because we cannot select one idea without doing the business analysis. But at this stage, we fully test the business case, including the financials, timing, costs, projected revenue, or savings over the next 5 years.

This is a tough part of the innovation process for professional service providers who don't have to create business plans in their day jobs and weren't taught how to do that in school. After years of leading hundreds of teams wherein at least 50 percent of the teams are lawyers, I can say that lawyers of all kinds from different countries, firms, and legal departments do not like putting time, costs, or task flow into a plan. I constantly get push back: *"Why do we have to build a business case? If so-and-so thinks it is a good idea, they will find the money for it. We already showed you the need for it, and we justified it with some numbers."* I will reply, *"Yes, and we need more— more specifics, more numbers, more time estimates, and an analysis of ROI."* They begrudgingly resist the urge to roll their eyes (because that would not be in keeping with the Open Mind Rule of Engagement).

Another part of this essential experience is positioning and selling the prototype internally. As noted above, this type of branding or marketing can't wait until we bring the product to market. This is why in The 3-4-5 Method™ we require every team to have a brand name, logo, and commercial (in addition to a business case) for its proposal—even if the team's idea is a new organizational structure within its legal department.

When asked: *"Why do we care about marketing or branding the idea when we will hire a team of branding experts to position it to our customers?"* I always answer, *"because how you position and sell an idea internally is as important as the idea itself."* Spoken like a true advertising executive.

Yet another type of branding, marketing, and positioning is involved if the product or service is brought to market. The branding and advertising campaign that is developed "externally" after you sell the idea internally should be thought of as an entirely new project, one that needs to be put through the design thinking process of inspiration, ideation, and implementation. This leads naturally to the discussion of the next essential experience, which continually overlaps with this one (as well as the others).

f.   Reflecting (Monitoring and Evaluating)

Throughout the process, there needs to be constant tweaking, testing, and improving along the way that can only be done by monitoring, evaluating, and getting feedback. Because it can be hard to take time for these activities and because it is hard to be critiqued, we institute feedback into The 3-4-5 Method™ at various intervals along the way and in various forms. For example, at our KickOff, we introduce and provide training on giving and receiving feedback and we hammer home that feedback is a gift (one of our core tenets). Over the course of the 4-month cycle, we have required feedback and coaching sessions and a midterm written reflection progress report.

We also assign every team what we call "shadow teams."[61] Shadow teams are based loosely on the concept of red teams. The term *red team* comes from the practice during the Cold War of having U.S. officers try to "think red" (i.e., like a Soviet trying to figure out how he might defeat U.S. strategies). U.S. red teams utilized Soviet technology and theory to try to destroy its own U.S. Navy submarine forces. The thinking is that by learning how to defeat yourself from the enemy's vantage point, you can protect yourself better. If you are offended by the concept of red teams, it might make you feel better to know that the Soviets did the same thing, calling them blue teams.[62]

In LawWithoutWalls, the purpose of shadow teams is to play the role of devil's advocate, to find weaknesses. This doesn't mean we stop saying "Yes, and . . ." It means we also listen to the people who are saying "No, but" and who are poking holes in our inspiration and ideations. We look to our shadow team to be our naysayers, to assist us in evaluating and reflecting on our projects to develop them further. We call them shadow teams instead of red teams to take the sting out. The shadow teams are there to uncover what the shadow casts. We help teams reflect differently, that is, own the issues they miss by matching shadow teams based on personality gaps within the team (identified through the DiSC maps referred to in Chapter 9). Shadow teams meet with each other periodically to ensure teams are reflecting without blinders and group think.

Reflection is also important later, after implementation. Once a product or service has been created or improved, it must be continually monitored and improved to stay relevant and to compete with other products and services on the market. This is also true of ourselves. We need to continue to reflect on our own behaviors and efforts to ensure that we are living up to our potential—which leads nicely to the last essential experience.

g. *Working Hard*

The last but not least experience essential to any type of human-centered design innovation process is hard work. People often refer to Mozart's music as magic because of a fake letter that was published in a music newspaper in 1815. In this letter, Mozart supposedly claimed that his masterpieces came to him in one swoop, as if in a dream, as if by magic. All he had to do was wake up and write them down. In his book *How to Fly a Horse*, Kevin Ashton explains that the reality as evidenced by letters from Mozart to his family is quite the opposite.[63] Success followed failures. Mozart suffered from bouts of writer's block. He studied other musicians to learn from them. He rewrote and revised his compositions. The reality is that Mozart's music was magical, but it was not magic. Mozart's work was work.

In a similar way, innovation involves taking risks, sharing ideas that are half baked as opposed to perfectly fleshed out, and running with ideas that are good enough as opposed to perfect. As mentioned in Part I, this is what clients want from their professional service providers: partners in co-collaboration that are willing to proceed with something despite risk and incomplete information—even though this is especially tough for those professionals who are consultants or advisors to do.

Thomas Edison's famous quote "Genius is one percent inspiration and 99 percent perspiration" defines design thinking. Indeed, he is in some ways the father of design thinking. Tim Brown has contended that the idea of design thinking was exemplified by Thomas Edison's approach to the creation of a lightbulb because he did so in a customer/user-centric, systems thinking way.[64] If Edison is the father of design thinking, Albert Einstein is the son. That is why I quote him at the beginning of this section. He understood that "We can't solve problems by using the same kind of thinking we used when we created them." Much like design thinkers today, Einstein understood that we need a new kind of thinking—a human-centered perspective—to solve old problems. Einstein used the scientific method, which isn't all that different from the design thinking process. Design thinking also utilizes a scientific approach to discovery. Like the scientific method, it begins with a problem and includes iterative feedback mechanisms to model, test, and revise a solution.[65]

Although it is true that design thinking cannot be distilled entirely cleanly into a step-by-step process, I believe, like Tim Brown does, that we can distill it into a systematic and practicable approach.[66] This in large part is what The 3-4-5 Method™ does for the professional services market: It combines parts of a design thinking framework with other kinds of business, marketing, and creative process methods to form an applicable (if iterative and messy) approach that can be followed to transform the culture of your organization, department, or firm and the ways professionals collaborate to solve problems. It can also help professionals create innovations, new service models, and better service experiences for clients. And the work never stops—neither does the need to keep innovating and changing.

◖ ...Reflection Point Consider the following challenge assigned to a LawWithoutWalls team:

* Cogito Ergo Sum: How can cognitive technologies transform the way financial institutions deal with the impact of regulatory change on their lending documentation?
* Now consider the solution this team created:
* Clear Loan: A training tool for consumer borrowers and an analytics tool for banks to help banks reduce consumer complaints against it. The tool educated the consumer and at the same time gathered standardized evidence of compliance with regulatory rules the bank could use to counter complaints by consumer borrowers that might be later raised during the lending process. Thus, the tool was designed to help protect consumers in the lending process but also help the bank avoid adverse judgments from the ombudsman when disputes arose regarding the terms of the loan and compliance with rules.

- With whom did the team have to empathize to create this solution? How many target audiences are there for the tool the team created? (Hint: There are at least three.)

⬤...Reflection Point As mentioned above, part of design thinking is understanding the consumer's or user's journeys with your product, process, or service. Often innovation teams will create a user journey that maps out the way users currently interact with the service, website, process, or product. They do this to better understand user behavior and identify ways to support and/or enhance the experience. The first step in mapping out a user journey often starts with creating the user/consumer story (i.e., identifying your user's goals, motivations, pain points, and overall character—as discussed in Essential Experience 2: Falling in Love [with the Problem and the Target Audience]). The second step is mapping each interaction the user has with the product or service. If you work at a professional service firm or within a department in a company: How might you map out the "service experience" of your clients? What points of contact does the client have with your firm or department that occurs before you start working on the matter, during the time you are working on the matter, and then after you finish working on the matter? When does the client interact with professionals in your department or firm who are of a different discipline than you are? How else might the client interact with your firm or department (e.g., website, social media, different office, event, product/tool/portal/database)? Each time the client interacts with the firm or department, what is the context for the client, how are they are interacting (through what devices, with how many different people), what type of service, response, functionality are they expecting, and what is their emotional state each step of the way? (Are they happy, annoyed, frustrated, urgent, interested?). Try mapping this out and see what problems or opportunities you discover.

CHAPTER 11

Overview of The 3-4-5 Method™ and Why It Works

> *"Inspiration is for amateurs. The rest of us just show up and get to work. If you wait around for the clouds to part and a bolt of lightning to strike you in the brain, you are not going to make an awful lot of work. All the best ideas come out of the process; they come out of the work itself."*
>
> —Chuck Close[1]

This quote encompasses my attitude toward The 3-4-5 Method™ I have developed over the past 14 years. It's a process, and every piece contributes. Everything matters—every moment and every little detail. This is the execution of innovation as opposed to its vision. It's one thing to describe the seven essential experiences necessary for innovation; it is quite another to map it out into a process with steps, an order (even if repetitive at times and not entirely linear at other times), and exercises so that other people can do it. It is yet still another thing to do this in a way that resonates with professional service providers.

In the following, I provide an overview of the method I created so that professionals working on multidisciplinary, global teams can make sense of the process of innovation and lead their teams in using it. My method draws on my marketing and advertising background, where I was trained not only in business planning but also in professional services and to think not just of the numbers but also the delivery of the service and to take a human-centered approach to the creation of products and services. I was taught how to conduct consumer-focused research on both the end product and the user experience and to utilize that research to empathize with the end user and create solutions and new products that are viable, feasible, and desirable. I worked on the development of new products with people in marketing, advertising, PR, events, legal, merchandising, product development, market research, and sales. I have combined this with my legal training and research, along with my experience leading more than 230 lawyer-managed teams on a 4-month innovation cycle and another 50 on shorter journeys (1 month, 1week, and 3 days long).

Like most innovators or intrapreneurs, I am constantly tweaking my method, adding things that work and revising things that don't. Unlike most design thinkers, my focus is on teaching innovation to professional service providers who are working with other types of professionals on multidisciplinary, multicultural, and often virtual teams. What every participant of my method learns is that following The 3-4-5 Method™ is a process that will help the best ideas unfold because it doesn't let you "wait around for the clouds to part and a bolt of lightning to strike." It's a method that comes alive when we follow it in detail. As Alfred North Whitehead is known for stating, "We think in generalities, but we live in detail."[2] (This is why I published the companion handbook that provides step-by-step instructions that bring the minutia to life and include tools and exercises to lead teams on an innovation and collaboration journey with The 3-4-5 Method™.)

A. The 3-4-5 Method™: An Overview

At its core, The 3-4-5 Method™ is designed for multidisciplinary teaming around a discrete challenge or opportunity. It can be used for one team hacking on one challenge or multiple teams hacking on multiple challenges. The "challenges" can be problems we need to solve, innovations we want to create, opportunities yet to be leveraged, or any other project that is, revamping the current talent retention program. In LawWithout-Walls, we often work with about 12 to 18 teams in each "cohort" which means we have 125 to 180 people involved at some level. Likely, most readers won't be biting off something that big all at once. To determine how to apply The 3-4-5 Method™ to your needs—based on your goals, the opportunity or problem you are tackling, and how many teams you are working with at the same time—definitely check out the *Leader Upheaval Handbook* referenced earlier. This section in this book is simply an over-view so that you understand the basic components and (hopefully) will be convinced that it works.

The 3-4-5 Method™ is a team-based experiential innovation process grounded in design thinking principles constructed especially for pro-fessional service providers based on their temperament, training, work preferences, and innovation needs. It makes clear the "how," "who," and "what" so that creativity, collaboration, and innovation come easier than they otherwise might. As already mentioned, The 3-4-5 Method™ is not only about creating solutions. It is also designed to help train the skills on the Skills Delta in Level 1 (including project management, marketing and branding, communication, etc.) and Level 2 (including self-awareness, empathy, adaptability, cultural competency, creative problem finding and solving, business planning, communication, and collaboration). This thereby leads to the development of inclusive leaders who know how to provide client-centric, full-service client service that is focused on the cli-ent's experience. The transformation of relationships between clients and professional service providers comes from that development but *more so* if clients are on the teams, included in the journey.

At the end of a 3-4-5 journey, in addition to a solution, participants will have developed a new mindset, a new skill set, and new behaviors. Indeed, this was the original vision of LawWithoutWalls and purpose of this method: To develop cross-competent business leaders with excel-lent creative, collaborative problem finding and problem-solving skills who delight clients by approaching service with the mindset, skill set, and behaviors of innovators. This is why we call the solutions Projects of Worth because even if the solution is not brought to fruition, there is so much worth in the progress we have made as individuals along the way. This is also why LawWithoutWalls was given the name LWOW (pro-nounced L-WOW), because there is so much to wow over no matter what the final result. In following The 3-4-5 Method™, if we really embrace it, as individuals, we cannot fail. Of course, the method can't *guarantee* that each team will actually create a viable solution that can be brought to life to solve the problem. It can guarantee, however, a change in mindset, skill set, and behaviors. As long as each person individually commits to the Three Rules of Engagement and attempts the 5 Steps to a Project of Worth (discussed below), they will have grown as leaders and collaborators. In sum, the method is designed to do the following:

1. Foster a climate and culture for innovation and collaboration across a firm's or company's business.
2. Connect people in teams across different offices, departments, and divisions.
3. Develop the skills of participants in all three levels of the Skills Delta.
4. Deepen entities' relationships with clients (internal or external) through team-based collaboration.
5. Find solutions for business problems and identify new opportunities through innovation.

The name of The 3-4-5 Method™ is descriptive as it is divided into 3 Phases over 4 months (or less) with 5 iterative Steps overlaid along the way.

The 3 stands for a process that always (no matter how long) occurs in 3 Phases, which are (1) a KickOff, (2) multidisciplinary teaming to develop a project (usually done virtually), and 3) a ConPosium (pitching presentations to experts to receive feedback and further enhance project development).

The 4 stands for the period of time that the team sets at the outset for the innovation journey, and it stands for the number 4 as in 4 months *or less*. Although the method has been tested and proved successful in various increments of time (4 months, 3 months, 1 intense week, 3 days, and 48 hours), the 4 stands for the maximum number of months any innovation journey should exist before it reaches a ConPosium. Does this mean that a project will be fully baked by then? No, but it does mean that a decision about its viability and a business case and marketing plan justifying further development should be prepared and assessed by this time. Figure 11.1 depicts the phases.

Just as the phases can be done during different time periods, they can be done either in-person or virtually. The very first LawWithoutWalls program (LawWithoutWalls Original) was 4 months long and part-virtual back in 2011. That's crazy. We were in effect zooming before Zoom! We

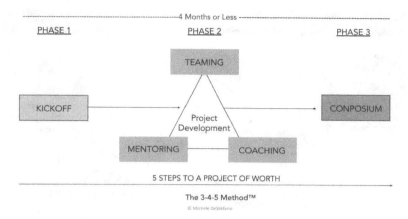

FIG. 11.1. The 3 Phases in The 3-4-5 Method™.

held a 2-day KickOff in person in Phase 1, then worked virtually during the teaming in Phase 2 (using AdobeConnect and other videoconferencing platforms combined with Google Drive). Then, we met again in person for Phase 3, the ConPosium. In 2013, we launched our first all-virtual program (LWOW X) where we did all 3 Phases online, including a 48-hour virtual KickOff. The coolest thing about saying that now is that no one understood how exhausting it was to team virtually. Now everyone does! In 2020, we launched LawWithoutWalls Sprint (3 days in person with a few months of virtual training prior just for the students), but it was delayed in its fruition due to the Pandemic. In 2022 (and again in 2023), the Sprint version was a huge success. So, The 3-4-5 Method™, although it has structure, has baked-in flexibility.

The 5 stands for the 5 Steps to a Project of Worth, that is, the 5 Steps that each team must go through to move from an opportunity or challenge to a solution that has the possibility of viability. Although the steps are iterative, as explained in more detail, they provide a sequential trajectory for the team to measure its progression. For a depiction see Figure 11.2.

1. Phase 1 of The 3-4-5 Method™: The KickOff

> ## *"Existence can be rearranged, a man can be many things."*
>
> —Tom Robbins, *Jitterbug Perfume*[3]

FIG. 11.2. The 5 Steps in The 3-4-5 Method™.

Given how much emphasis I placed on the importance of having a Kick-Off, it will not surprise you to know that the entire Phase 1 in The 3-4-5 Method™ is a KickOff. As mentioned above, the KickOff is the most essential ingredient to team success. It creates the culture and sets the protocols and expectations and, even more importantly, creates commitment and accountability at the individual and group levels. The KickOff is designed to meet three goals.

- First, to train participants on The 3-4-5 Method™ and best practices for multicultural, multidisciplinary teaming and collaboration.
- Second, to knit together engaged and committed teams of individuals to create team cohesion and community culture.
- Third, to prepare and get buy-in and commitment from participants for the personal and professional work ahead.

The members of the teams are intentionally diverse in every way possible: culture, discipline, age, expertise, talents, and backgrounds. The entire team is made up of approximately seven to nine people with varying, yet very clear delineation, of roles, that is, who are the hackers ("doers"), who are the mentors, who are the coaches, and what are their respective expectations.

At the KickOff, we participate in teaming exercises like those mentioned in earlier chapters of this book, including the *Talent & Topic Expertise*

Exploration Exercise, The Restaurant, and *Pet-Peeve-Motto Exercises.* We also conduct the *P.A.C.T. Exercise* mentioned earlier to agree to purpose and garner commitment and accountability. Importantly, we also provide substantive training about leadership and collaboration and also about design thinking and innovation in general, and of course, about The 3-4-5 Method™ itself.

Depending on the length of the KickOff, we do one of two things to teach and prep participants for The 3-4-5 Method™. If it is a shorter KickOff, we show participants how a team progressed through the 5 Steps and a team presents their final Project of Worth like they did at ConPosium, so the bar is set high. If it is a longer KickOff, we do the former PLUS we have each of the teams do a fast run-through of The 3-4-5 Method™. We assign them a "fake" challenge that is accessible to all (e.g., how can we improve higher education) and have them practice the same exercises they will do later "for real" to move through the 5 Steps. We even have them do a mini-presentation like that which will be expected at ConPosium.

The length and content of a KickOff vary based on how long the journey is slated to be and how many teams are starting the journey together. Either way, if there is more than one team involved, it is essential that there is community building across the teams as well as among the members of each team. This can be hard (especially in a virtual setting), but it can be done.

One way we do this in LawWithoutWalls at the KickOff is we introduce each team to their assigned shadow team as described in the Chapter 10 and each team's shadow team will stay with them throughout the entire journey no matter how long or short.

Another way we build community is that prior to the KickOff, we have individuals record themselves lip syncing to a segment of our Kick-Off theme song like *Ain't No Mountain High Enough* or *Start Me Up.* Then we splice it together and play it at the beginning of the KickOff as the first community collaborative endeavor. In watching it together, we transform from individuals to a highly cooperative, socially integrated superorganism like a beehive. Why does this work? Research shows that working (walking, singing, chanting) in unison breaks down psychological walls and creates group cohesion.[4] We do it for the same reasons people sing in church, armies march in unison, dancers dance to the beat. We don't do it just with the lip sync. At least once during every KickOff, we have all our participants sing or dance or do some type of mirroring activity together in unison. I know first-hand that this works, having witnessed it in LawWithoutWalls. Recently, I have also witnessed this working at a law firm retreat. I had the pleasure of working with Allen & Gledhill, a leading law firm and one of the largest in Singapore. And wow, do they do this well! They have their practice groups sing and dance (in unison and in competition) at their annual retreats and they have the teams arrive in a themed costume. The energy and camaraderie developed during the retreat I attended was like no other.

2. Phase 2: The 5 Steps to a Project of Worth

> *"Ring the bells that still can ring.*
> *Forget your perfect offering*
> *There is a crack in everything*
> *That's how the light gets in."*
>
> —Leonard Cohen, "Anthem"[5]

After the KickOff, teams begin project development. Teaming can occur in person or virtually or in a combination of the two. Work is done in team meetings within their subgroups and also as a big group with the project managers, innovation coaches, and external advisors as they progress through the 5 Steps. Through these meetings, teams receive feedback to improve the viability, financial structure, and overall positioning and creativity of the project. This is part of the prototyping, testing, reassessing, and improving process. In LawWithoutWalls, if journeying with more than one team on a 4-month journey, we meet weekly to attend interactive virtual webinars to build community across teams. These webinars serve as community building as well as substantive training as they are focused on topics like consumer storytelling, prototyping, branding, and business planning, and more; or they are designed to provide a deeper understanding of the professional services marketplace around the world and how innovation and technology are impacting the careers and work of professionals. These webinars are a great way to involve many different members of the community (or entice new members to get interested) as guest panelists who can share their stories. They are lively and purposefully engaging to incentivize the community to keep in contact and get to know each other. In other modes, for example, when LawWithoutWalls is conducted in-person over the course of a week or 3 days, we hold these webinars prior to (and after) the event.

We also host LawWithoutWalls PopUps in different places around the world to create glocal (i.e., both local and global) pockets of community. PopUps are short community- and skills-building events designed to help introduce LawWithoutWalls to newcomers and provide refreshers to those who have participated in LawWithoutWalls before. These PopUps vary in content and form but each PopUp includes an interactive exercise related to teaming or creative, collaborative problem-solving that attendees can later utilize in their own teaming efforts at the organizations in which they work. I tell all of this to you because even if you are thinking small and pilot, often innovation initiatives continue and with different cohorts over time. These are ideas to build a community and keep the community alive and previous members involved, even after they have finished their journey.

Phase 2 is when the hard work gets done and lots of battles are not won. It is when the teams must actually apply the Three Rules of Engagement in tough times (as opposed to at a fun KickOff) to get through the 5 Steps to a Project of Worth described below. It is also when teams must live up to the intentions and protocols that they set at KickOff. And, at times, it is when teams face personal and/or professional and/or cultural divides. As such, we recognize that "there is a crack in everything" and working through these issues and tough times is "how the lights get in." It is how team members grow and teams congeal along with "ring[ing] the bells that still can ring" and celebrating the small wins of course!

As mentioned above, The "5" in The 3-4-5 Method™ of Innovation stands for the 5 Steps each team must tackle to meet its objective: a viable, feasible solution to a defined problem for a discrete target audience, along with a prototype, business case, and commercial (some type of 30- to 60-second video that brings the problem and solution, including its brand, to life in a compelling way).

The 5 Steps are as follows:

1. Exploring and investigating the challenge
2. Finding and refining the problem or opportunity
3. Understanding key stakeholders and target audience(s)
4. Solving the problem and prototyping
5. Planning, assessing, and testing the solution

I created the 5 Steps after reading about an entrepreneur named Tim Young who raised $10 million in venture capitalist (VC) money in one year by using just five "magic" slides in his fundraising deck.[6] His reasoning was: "If you can't outline your business in just five slides, you should go back to the drawing board and simplify your messaging."[7] This resonated with me so I decided to break the method into five steps—so that each step could be a slide if someone was pitching to a VC. Let's review the steps in a little more detail.

a. Step 1: Exploring and Investigating the Challenge

Step 1 is about exploring and investigating the background and big picture of the challenge or topic assigned. It starts with asking questions that are open-minded and inspirational. After all, we know well that Einstein's theory of relativity began with an early, beautiful question that was something like, "What if I rode a beam of light across the universe?"

Then the team's job is to dig in and understand everything it possibly can about the challenge assigned. Teams generally start by conducting secondary archival and bibliographical research to explore the context of the challenge, its history and regulatory environment, the demographic trends and global (or glocal) impact affecting it, the current state of the market and the technology, statistical data they can find about the challenge, and more. They do this with the goal of identifying the problems that lie within the challenge. This then helps them identify who to conduct primary research with, that is, through interviews and surveys. Step 1 can be daunting because the topics (even after some narrowing) are broad, thorny, and sometimes outside the scope of knowledge of many participants. An individual will have different interpretations of the challenge given their varied cultures, expertise, and background (which is, as mentioned, a good thing). So, part of Step 1 is to figure out what the challenge means to each individual on the team and also what it means in the context of the team's company, department, or firm and its purpose, values, and goals.

There is a steep learning curve in this step. The good news is that although this step starts out very broad and open-ended, it eventually focuses on seeing the trees and not the forest—studying branches is something lots of professional service providers are good at. Eventually, however, teams need to refocus on the forest; this can prove difficult for individuals who want to cover every aspect of a problem. Perfection in innovation is not possible at the outset of a cycle; once a narrow problem or opportunity is identified, the work lies up ahead and not behind. Also, once progress is made on Steps 2 and 3, there is the need to redo Step 1. The team needs to now use secondary research (studies, data) that prove a real need exists. How many people are impacted by this problem and what are the implications (negative or positive) that have been proven by others? In other words, once a team has narrowed in on a specific problem, Step 1 is a great help in convincing audiences that something needs to be done.

b. Step 2: Finding and Refining the Problem or Opportunity

In Step 2, teams have to whittle down the large challenge they have been assigned to a smaller, narrower problem impacting a discrete audience. There might be a primary audience and a secondary audience or two equally targeted audiences (not to mention other key stakeholders). These audiences will be further defined in Step 3—as such, there may be back and forth movement between Steps 2 and 3. Because in Step 2 the goal is identifying the narrow problem, this also means there is some back and forth with Step 1 to determine the context or history behind the more narrow problem or opportunity, and the stats and data supporting the problem's heft and impact. This is done again with internal or external research and by conducting interviews of the relevant group of people to uncover problems related to the topic. The goal is for teams to literally fall in love with their narrower problem (as mentioned in Chapter 10). If they do not feel passionate about solving it, they won't.

In addition, it is important that the team accurately frames the problem and separates out the true root causes of the problem from the symptoms. This is why Step 2 often turns out to be the hardest of all the steps because problem-framing is really hard, and we are often fooled into thinking that a particular symptom is the problem. Let me give you an example. In 2014, General Motors recalled over 2.5 million cars due to an ignition switch problem that was causing air bags to not deploy (and that killed and injured hundreds of people). This recall might sound responsible; however, GM had known for almost a decade that there was a problem with its ignition switch, that is, that it could easily be turned "off" and that it had been designed with less torque than was originally in the product specification.[8]

They also knew that they had a problem with their airbags not deploying. However, they never connected the two. They didn't realize that the ignition switch problem was the cause of the airbag problem. I know that sounds confusing. Luckily Professor Robert Eli Rosen wrote an article that cleared up the confusion.[9] GM framed the problem as a moving stall, that is, when the ignition switch slipped into the off position (for example, when knocked by someone's knees or a keychain), it caused the car to enter into a moving stall. In a moving stall, the engine stalls but the car is still in motion and can be pulled over to the side of the road and restarted. Therefore, it was not seen as a safety problem. What they failed to see was that the stalled engine was a symptom of a larger problem which was a lack of electricity and that the lack of electricity was causing the airbags to not deploy.[10] Because today's cars are actually computers, a car that is coasting with an engine that is off means it is coasting without any electricity. And like any computer, cell phone, or tablet, when the source of electricity stops, the device doesn't work. The air bags need electricity to deploy. GM might have been able to diagnose the real problem in this case if they had conducted Steps 1 and 2 (and Step 3 in tandem with Step 2). In Step 1, with more digging into the context and history of the current car marketplace, they may have realized the importance of the fact that cars today are electronic computers, whereas they used to be mechanical devices. In Step 2, they may have made headway with the 5 Whys and a root cause analysis. And in Step 3, they may have better understood what happened and how it happened with more interviews of the engineers and of accident survivors. Instead they did the opposite; they blamed drivers for the ignition switch turning off because they were tall or had keychains that were too long.[11] Indeed, Rosen points out that more empathy with the driver and the engineers would have helped to identify the real problem faster.

And this is why Steps 2 and 3 are often done in tandem. It is also why a step back to Step 1 is often needed. Once Steps 2 and 3 are done in tandem, more research needs to be done (via Step 1) to provide the team with the data and stats to hammer home the importance of solving this problem, that is, to create that urgency that is essential to any innovation success. It is only then that the team will likely be successful in getting on the same *problem plane*.

c. Step 3: Understanding Key Stakeholders and Target Audience(s)

The third step is all about understanding everything about the key target audience. However, to do so, often we have to understand other audiences as well. Think Kellogg's Apple Jack, wherein the buyer was the mom and the consumer was the tween, as discussed in Chapter 8. There are often at least two sides to every story and then other stakeholders that might be impacted or have an impact, so multiple key stakeholders (clients or consumers) may need to be investigated. In the GM example, the key stakeholders included the corporate executives in the company, the company itself as its own entity, the actual engineers of the car ignition switch, the drivers of the cars, insurance carriers, regulators, the lawyers, and the list goes on. In fact, in the GM example, some have claimed that people *outside* the company connected the dots between the airbags not deploying and the ignition switch issue.[12] And that these reports were in GM's files for 5 years but ignored because it didn't square with other information and insiders didn't believe the outsiders' information was objective. Unsurprisingly, it was the lawyers and plaintiffs suing GM who connected the dots.

The point of course is to identify and empathize with all key stakeholders (internal and external to the organization) who feel the effects and consequences of the problem. This requires talking to people in each group (via interviews and focus groups) and getting real life examples from them (e.g., times, dates, descriptions of the who, what, where, when, and how it happened) and creating consumer stories for each of them. Also, it is important for the team to understand what other problems their target audiences are experiencing, and other factors influencing key stakeholders, like that described in the crisis curve in Chapter 10. All this investigation is intended to help the teams understand their target audience to a depth that is beyond what they think they need so that the solution they create is tight and relevant in every way: content, design, process, length, size, mood, brand, feel, and message. Like the narrow problem, the team should fall in love with the target audience. The target audience is the focal point. When we are falling in love, we are obsessed with the person. We want to know everything about them, from the small to the big. This requires talking to people in the target audience group and getting real-life examples from them.

Eventually, the team should create an animation or other unique way to bring the target audience or user's problem to life from their perspective and in a way that moves the audience, that is, so that the audience feels as passionately as the team does about solving THIS problem for THIS core key audience(s). However, before doing that, the team likely will need to refine the problem again with some *Problem Trip Mapping* that includes how and when the different audiences are impacted and a *Consumer/Stakeholder Profile and Problem Refining Exercise.*

Finally, during Step 3, the team needs to zero in on one or two target audiences experiencing the problem that are large enough to justify the solution and small enough to test via a pilot or prototype. This is why Step 3 necessarily includes a dash of Step 5—and this goes back to the *Field of Dreams* problem we talked about earlier in Chapter 8. Just because you build it, doesn't mean your target audience will come. If your target audience is not large enough, the bleachers will be almost empty, and you might not be able to cover the costs of running and maintaining the field.

d. Step 4: Solving the Problem

When teams begin Step 4, they may have done Steps 1, 2, and 3 multiple times. However, they also may have started Step 4 too soon, that is, ideating a solution too early, only to realize that they didn't have a real problem. This can occur when a team jumps to a cool idea and then tries to match the solution to some target audience for whom their cool idea solves the problem. Challengingly, sometimes teams come up with solutions that already exist, which is why Step 4 always includes a little bit of Steps 1 and 5. Moreover, often teams become wed to their first idea, although the first idea is rarely the best idea. Experts contend that teams should brainstorm over 100 ideas to get to the ideas that are novel.[13] I like to say to teams: *If it is obvious to you (this early), you are obviously missing something.*

The good news is when teams are finally really ready for Step 4, it is time to ideate. The goals for Step 4 are to determine the forms or manifestation(s) the solution can take. In this step, teams also necessarily must dip their toes into Step 5 just a little bit to ensure that they don't start to create a solution that isn't viable because it costs too much money or it only accounts for one side of the story, or there is no need for it, or because it's already been developed by a competitor. In this way, in addition to a look forward to Step 5 (viability and business planning), this step requires a look back to Steps 2 and 3 (problem refining and understanding the key target audiences).

Of course, The 3-4-5 Method™ includes lots of exercises for Step 4 to help teams creatively "solutionize" that involve many different types of ideation, including *divergent wild idea generation,* that is, outside-the-box thinking, and convergent ideating with constrictions, that is, inside-the-box. Counterintuitively, we use restraints to set us free in ideation. For example, as Tina Seelig has recommended, doing a wild and crazy idea generation exercise and then picking our worst idea and trying to improve it or using the attributes of our favorite app to solve our problem can sometimes help us get more creative—as it did for those doctors described in Part I who exapted the attributes of the puffer fish to create the jelly-like pill to monitor tumors. As mentioned in the Open Door Rule of Engagement in Chapter 6, although they do not call it exaptation, other design thinkers have touted the importance of looking outward to other examples of success within and outside their own companies and industries in order to combine ideas in new ways—or even outright imitate—to fuel successes of their own. If that last word "imitate" gives a bad taste in the mouth, turn back to Chapter 6 and re-read the quote by T.S. Eliot: about how good poets exapt from others and improve upon it. Also, re-read the section about how our most famous musicians of all times (like Mozart, Bach, and Beethoven) imitated others who came before them. Evidently, portions of the Beatles' song "Because" is Beethoven's Moonlight Sonata backwards.[14] If you still aren't convinced, watch the Ignite Presentation called "Great Designers Steal" by True Ventures Design Partner and entrepreneur, Jeff Veen.[15]

People often think finding the solution (Step 4) is the hardest part, but it should be easiest. If the team has done Steps 2 and 3 right (and multiple times, including *Problem Trip Mapping,* an *MVS Steeple People Exercise,* and a *Consumer/Stakeholder Profile and Problem Refining Exercise*), the solution follows almost naturally. The time spent on refining the problem and the consumer stories enables the brains to percolate. Then when the team is truly ready to solutionize (as I like to call it), the solution *pops pops pops* almost like an Aha! moment. But although it might feel that way, the reality is that the ideas have been simmering. One person's thoughts have spurred another person's thoughts. This migration is what Stephen Johnson calls the slow hunch theory that leads to the "pearl of the oyster."[16] As he points out: "There are good ideas, and then there are good ideas that make it easier to have other good ideas."[17] This is another reason why exaptation is a critical concept of Step 4. This is also why we need to beware the team's inclination to go with their first idea (which is rarely the best) and instead make sure the team members build on each other's ideas to get to that pearl.

I find the hardest part for teams is narrowing the solution so that it is an MVS (minimum viable solution). Sometimes in the ideation phase they forget to solutionize for the narrow problem at hand and there is scope creep. Recall the *MVS Steeple People Exercise* mentioned earlier. If the team identified three issues that need to be addressed, the solution should address those three and fit like a glove. Anything more might be a bell or whistle to save for after a pilot test of the MVP. To prevent scope creep and to get the team ready for the prototyping that also occurs in Step 4, I have all teams conduct a *Flushing Out the Solution Exercise* to help ensure all components of the solution are mapped out. After that, teams need to create a prototype and a user-journey map to show the user experience journey with its solution/prototype.

Let's pause here for a moment to do a refresh on what a prototype is, because I find that the word itself causes fear and confusion, or worse yet, push-back. In their minds, people think: "*How are we going to create a prototype if our solution is a new process?*"

Before answering that question, let's start with explaining why we prototype. A prototype helps improve your solution because it forces you to map out each feature and define the user interface. Further, it enables you to test the solution with the target audience and refine the user experience based on feedback. It also helps you bring your solution to life more effectively, which enhances the probability that your pitch will be successful.

Now, let's answer the naysayers who don't think a prototype is needed if the solution isn't a product. Here's what I tell them: *A prototype is a way to bring your solution to life visually no matter what form the solution takes. A prototype can be many things, including a skit, a storyboard, a simple sketch, a scene-by-scene flow chart, a three-dimensional depiction, a visual mock-up, or a video, that is, a videotaped demo of how a user would interact with your website.* And I give the following advice. *First, a first prototype should be simple to the core, that is, it should have fewer than five features (and those features had better match the problem statement). Second, pretty is NOT pretty in prototyping, meaning it's OK to start with a simple sketch and refine and refine before making it fancier (with a three-dimensional depiction or a video). Third, fake it to make it, that is, demonstrating how it will work is more important than making it work for real. Mockups that are merely visuals on a mobile phone (as opposed to actual real software or apps working on an iphone) are fine! You can show and explain a web, app, or software project using template pictures of an iPhone, tablet, or desktop. If you really want to make it for real (vs. faking it), there are a ton of free UI (user interface) kits, tools, and open-source software to do so. But don't make it fancy until you have tested it with your target audience, that is, dip back into Step 3 and forward into Step 5 (assessing).*

Also, before spending too much time perfecting the solution and prototype, teams need to move even further into Step 5 to do some business planning to support the business case, research the competitive landscape, and assess viability. After they do that, they can return to Step 4 to perfect their prototype. Part of perfecting it is developing a brand by first building a brand matrix or pyramid. Eventually, in Step 4, teams will create a logo, tagline, and a "Solution and Brand in a Sentence or 2" (via an elevator-speech exercise I created). Essentially, we spend almost two thirds of the cycle redefining and solving the problem (Steps 1 to 3). Then we spend the last one third ideating and prototyping (Step 4) and then, testing, business-case planning, and refining the solution (Step 5). Step 5 is not only one of the most time-intensive steps, it is also, in some ways, one of the most important steps.

e. *Step 5: Planning, Assessing, and Testing the Solution*

Step 5 is the last step sequentially, but it is the step that has been in the background the entire time and the step that almost never ends. Think iPhone. We are constantly getting updates that actually are mini-Step 5 tests to improve our user experience but also to test new updates to see if it enhances our experience or increases profitability for Apple. In Step 5, teams create a timeline and action plan to create the solution. They also develop the business case. Although the business planning will feel foreign to some types of professional service providers, it is only by creating that business plan that the team can really assess the strengths, weaknesses, opportunities, and threats. The two go hand in hand.

The business plan doesn't have to be long and, depending on your needs, a one- or two-page business plan might be sufficient. However, it is important that teams make a business plan that identifies their business model and ROI (return on investment) and projects the future date by when the solution will be self-sustaining or profitable, what expertise will be needed on the team, potential sources for funding, revenue streams, and the costs for marketing, production, sales, development, operations, etc. Of course, part and parcel to this is creating a roadmap for what will be created and piloted and measured by when before a full roll out is justified. Additionally, a thorough understanding and assessment of the competition along with identifying the solution's point of difference is essential. The good news is, by the time teams fully dive into Step 5, they have already developed many parts of the standard business plan in the previous steps. For example, in Steps 2 and 3 with a backward dip into Step 1, they have identified their target market, market needs, and size of market opportunity. In Step 4, they have identified how they will solve their target audience's problems with a unique value proposition and looked at the competition with a dash of Step 5.

Step 5 is not just about testing the substance (the feasibility) of the solution, but also about testing the viability with the target audience. Assessment is critical to this step. Therefore, there are many opportunities for such assessments in Step 5 and this is how it lurks in the background. Teams, in Step 4, dip their toes in Step 5 to test the prototype they have developed with people internal and external to the organization. Of course, part of the main reason we have so many meetings is that they serve as part of the assessment process that is so important to Step 5. In this way, Step 5 is really occurring throughout the process during the various milestone meetings, the coach sessions, the shadow team meetings, and the optional external expert meetings (with branding, tech, business planning, or pitch coach experts). It is also a big part of the rehearsals before the ConPosium. Then, of course the ConPosium itself is a Step 5 assessment and test within an intense confined time frame.

Also included in Step 5 is a focus on developing scripting, storytelling, presentation, and communication skills. Participants have to learn how to put together a beautiful PowerPoint deck and a compelling, engaging presentation that brings the consumer story and problem to life in a clear and succinct way to outsiders who know nothing about the topic. Participants must ensure they set up the problem so that the solution spreads like butter. Participants also have to learn how to present out loud in front of different types of professionals and different sizes of audiences, sometimes in front of hundreds of people (without notes) with powerful presencing, clear oration, and an absence of umms, "you-knows," and other tics.

Rehearsals (and the art of giving and receiving feedback) are key to this step. For many, this last part (the rehearsal and presentation part) is the hardest. Senior executives at many professional service firms have never had to pitch an idea in this way in front of so many people and in collaboration with others. One reason we love to use the Ignite Presentation format is because it is so very hard: 20 self-moving slides (every 15 seconds), and once the slide is gone, you have to stop talking and turn it over to the next person, and it is short: 5 minutes. As mentioned, it takes a lot of trust and vulnerability (and practice) to do this—core skills that we are focusing on honing in the Skills Delta.

The hardest part about The 3-4-5 Method™ is having to repeat steps. They are iterative. They go back and forth. Sometimes, we take huge steps back and only baby steps forward. Sometimes progress feels chaotic before it feels integrative. There is no certainty that progress is being made by moving from Step 1 to Step 2 or from Step 2 to Step 3 because what we find in Step 3 can send us back to Step 2. Further, we often have to go through some mourning for the ideas we had to let go to move forward. However messy it may appear, the results can often be sublime. The most difficult steps to progress through are Steps 2 and 3. As mentioned in Part I, research shows the best problem solvers are the best problem finders. Problems need to be refined and whittled down, and a consumer story (from each point of view) needs to be uncovered and understood. And the team needs to really empathize with the target audience(s) to ensure that the team understands why this problem or opportunity matters, and to ensure that they are solving a real problem (and not a symptom of the problem) for a real target audience.

But all of these steps and all the back and forth and all the hard work results in a creation, which British technology pioneer, Kevin Ashton, defines as: "the consequence of acts that appear inconsequential by themselves but when accumulated, change the world."[18]

3. Phase 3: The ConPosium

> *"Ends and beginnings—there are no such things.*
> *There are only middles."*
>
> —Robert Frost, *Mountain Interval*[19]

Teams then reconvene in person or online to pitch their Projects of Worth (dynamic pitch, prototype, business case, commercial, and tagline) at what is for some an ending event that has some high stakes. This is why developing your personal brand and a dynamic presentation style is an essential skill on the Skills Delta and something we emphasize in The 3-4-5 Method™. We call this event a ConPosium because it is a quasi-conference-symposium. The presentation pitches are 10 to 15 minutes with a 5-minute question and answer (Q&A) session with expert judges. Alternatively, the ConPosium is done in Ignite style, as mentioned above, with Q&A from expert judges. But the ConPosium is much more than simply a set of presentations.

First and foremost, the ConPosium is a community celebration to reunite the community as one, even though, in some ways, the process may have been a competition. The reality is an entity can't bring all projects to life; and in a journey of 10 teams, it is likely that only two will be baked enough to warrant investing in by this time. It is also a form of reflection (of assessing and testing). It feels like the end; it is not. As part of the 5 Steps to a Project of Worth, the ConPosium is a time for feedback, for testing our prototypes, and for analyzing our business cases. The ConPosium is an opportunity to present the problem, solution, and prototype in front of the community and receive critique from learned experts and from each other. Indeed, we often include a live chat that is featured on a screen in the room so community audience members can provide support to their fellow teams, live feedback on projects, and their own questions or responses to the judges' questions. These chats are saved so they can be reviewed by the presenting team later and used to refine their presentations and Projects of Worth. Perhaps counterintuitively, the ConPosium, although it is an ending point for the team, is not the end. This might be the hardest part for professional service providers to swallow because at the end they want to be done with it. This might be the case, or it can be that other teams take up where the ConPosium teams leave off. However, the only downside to that is the loss of control and influence the original founders of the idea will have. That said, it is likely a good thing for the idea and its implementation. So, the ConPosium, even if it is an end for the specific individuals, it is not an end for the Projects of Worth. It is a continuation of the middle. Thus, despite there being three phases in The 3-4-5 Method™ that feel like a beginning, middle, and end, the reality is that they are all middles. As Robert Frost aptly put: "Ends and beginnings—there are no such things. There are only middles."[20]

B. Why The 3-4-5 Method™ Works

You might still be wondering after this short overview of a mere 5 Steps, why The 3-4-5 Method™ works with professional service providers (given all the critiques that are often made and have been reviewed in this book about them). Therefore, this section, although it may seem like me tooting my own horn about how great my method is, isn't there for that reason. Instead, it's there to *convince you* because you are likely doubting that The 3-4-5 Method™ works—recall the research provided earlier that demonstrated that professional service providers were more skeptical than other types of professionals. Therefore, I provide five reasons why The 3-4-5 Method™ works in the hopes to overcome your skepticism.

1. Reason #1: There Are a "Multiplicity of Reasons for It"

As mentioned in Chapter 4, one of my favorite quotes from one of my favorite books *Children of God* is: "The sign of a good decision is the multiplicity of reasons for it. If more than one goal is served, then a decision is more likely to be wise."[21] This is one of the main benefits of The 3-4-5 Method™: there is a "multiplicity of reasons" for using it (over some other method). This is because it is not only useful for innovation. It works to move any project team or committee forward—even if that committee is focused on creating a forward-looking strategic plan for the department or company at large. Although there is a plethora of analytical tools to help the strategic planning process,[22] without a method, tools, or exercises to spark and manage creative ideation, it is difficult for committees to find new, game-changing strategies that reshape the future and incentivize. This method provides that structure and the crayons for creativity.

Additionally, this method is not only designed to help multidisciplinary teams meet their end goal, whether that is innovate, problem-solve, or strategize. It is also designed to hone the skills on the Skills Delta that are desired by clients (including innovation, cultural competency, creative problem finding and problem-solving, business planning, communication, leadership, and collaboration); and it is designed to transform relationships between professional service providers and clients; that is, transform how participants collaborate with others within their organization (including clients) and outside their organizations. Thus, in addition to innovation, the goal is to develop cross-competent business leaders with excellent creative, collaborative problem finding and problem-solving skills who delight clients by approaching service with the mindset, skill set, and behaviors of innovators.

There is yet another reason. The 3-4-5 Method™ is designed to *train-the-trainers* so that participants (i.e., YOU) can lead a journey (or a movement) at their organizations. As mentioned earlier, for a successful innovation journey, you need a strong leader-manager to lead and manage that process and to ensure that the people who are involved in the initiative are on board with the method. While it is true that research on new technology shows that you only need approximately 34 percent of people to adopt a new initiative for the rest to follow, that number may be a bit more like 40 percent to 45 percent when it comes to professional service providers given their training and mindset, discussed in Part I.

So, how do you get the 34 percent to 45 percent? As mentioned above, you start small (with a pilot). Use The 3-4-5 Method™ on the first group of eager beavers as a *train-the-trainers* opportunity so that they can then be the leader-managers of one to two new teams later on. If you start with two teams of seven to eight eager beavers, that gives you 15-16 leader-managers who can then each lead one or two teams in the future. Now you have 30 to 48 potential leader-managers and can really start to exponentially make a difference with The 3-4-5 Method™. Again, this is why we call our final presentations Projects of Worth. Even if the proposed solution is not implemented or implementable—for whatever reason—the project is still one of worth because of the substantive learnings and skills training of the members of the team.

2. Reason #2: There Is the Ability to Work on Any Type of Problem or Project

Another benefit of The 3-4-5 Method™ is that it works for any type of challenge, opportunity, or problem that any type of multidisciplinary, diverse team (innovation team, taskforce, committee) is hacking on. It even works in strategic planning. This method has been used on topics relating to internal operations, relationships between departments, training, learning and development, recruitment, compensation, cognitive bias, diversity, client retention, social justice, access to justice, compliance, ethics, knowledge management, data mining, etc. Here are a few example topics tested in The 3-4-5 Method™ to exemplify its range:

- Bridging the gaps. How can we use external and internal data to map business needs, risks, and opportunities to enhance efficiency, drive value, and provide outstanding customer experience for the global organization? (Sponsored by Dentons + NextLaw In-House Solutions.)
- Accessing sustainable finance. How can lenders (like Standard Chartered) digitize its customers' supply chain information to achieve

transparency about their sustainability credentials and verify sustainable finance criteria? (Sponsored by McGuireWoods.)

- Twice as nice. How can firms improve knowledge sharing among trainees so that past successes, learnings, and insights further (or enhance) future trainees' performance and training? (Sponsored by White & Case.)
- Heading off hoarding. How do we prevent knowledge hoarding so that data and information can be collected, analyzed, and shared to enhance services and create value? (Sponsored by iManage.)
- Paving the path forward. How can GSK help refugee women and children more easily access health care relief (food, shelter, and consumer products) after they cross international borders? (Sponsored by Morae Global.)
- Eye in the sky. How can we foresee new opportunities to drive revenue for Spotify? (Sponsored by Spotify.)
- Law by design. How might digital channels and design thinking be leveraged to improve access to existing legal advice for the people who need it the most? (Sponsored by iManage.)

Although LawWithoutWalls is geared toward topics related to the business of law, the method works on any business challenge, as exemplified in this list.

3. Reason #3: Extrinsic and Intrinsic Motivation Are Baked in

As discussed before, research demonstrates that we need both extrinsic and intrinsic (inner commitment) motivation to change behavior.[23] This is why The 3-4-5 Method™ includes both. The extrinsic motivators (external rewards) include being selected to do something different, being recognized as able to do something different, and being invested in—because the method invariably costs any organization money, at least in terms of time (and there are costs associated with hiring an external facilitator if they do so). There is also the extrinsic motivation of fear and rising to the challenge. The ConPosium is designed to incentivize participants to perform to their best ability. An ending presentation in front of key stakeholders and peers raises the stakes—not to mention creates an opportunity for a team's innovation to be brought to life so that it may save thousands of dollars or generate revenue. The other extrinsic motivator that I often have to push participants to do is including clients on the teams. When a client is present, there is an added motivator to put the work in that is required, as opposed to using the client as an excuse for being too busy to innovate.

My method also contains the 3 key ingredients that, according to research, cultivate intrinsic motivation among professionals: (1) autonomy (sense of control and having a choice), (2) competence (mastery), and (3) relatedness (connection or sense of purpose).[24] I will discuss each in turn further here.

a. Control/Autonomy

According to organizational psychology research, people feel a sense of control or autonomy when they are a part of the agenda and goal-setting process and planning.[25] This is another reason we have the teams make their own P.A.C.T.s. Another way to fulfill the need for control or autonomy is to give participants a sense of choice.[26] Recall that the challenge that the team is originally assigned is always broader than the problem the team ends up solving. As they proceed through Steps 2 and 3 in the 5 Steps of the method, the participants have choice. They select how they narrow the scope of the problem and which discrete target audience their project will serve. However, as mentioned above, The 3-4-5 Method™ inspires experimentation but at the same time, is rigorously planned out, that is, it has strict discipline to it which ensures that there is not too much choice and that participants know how to navigate key decisions. Given the science of how people make choices this yin and yang in the method is essential.[27]

b. Competence

There's nothing more detrimental to innovation than a feeling of incompetence. In fact, I'm convinced that one reason professional service providers are hesitant to try innovating is a fear (not only of failure) but that they aren't good enough at innovating to try doing it. We know the research about people with fixed mindsets versus growth mindsets. Those with fixed mindsets focus on what they are good at, which means that over time, they get better and better at those things, but also start to become even less confident of their skills in other areas. Perhaps counterintuitively, research demonstrates that people are more motivated to change their behavior when they feel competent to do so.[28] This does not mean that people should not be challenged! Quite the contrary. Studies have shown that regardless of role or level, people who feel their jobs are challenging do experience greater job satisfaction and feelings of success.[29] The 3-4-5 Method™ is centered on meeting the assigned challenge.

However, a secret ingredient is to add a bit of positivism to their challenge. Essentially, people are inspired to change their behavior when the strengths they currently possess are stressed as positioning them well to meet the challenge.[30] This is one of the reasons that the method includes the exercise that requires participants to identify their strengths in the Skills Delta, not only their weaknesses. This is also why the method includes the *Talent & Topic Expertise Exploration Exercise*. We all have talents and expertise that can help the team. Another secret ingredient to motivating people to rise to the challenge is, as discussed earlier, progress[31] and praise for that progress. This is also one of the reasons The 3-4-5 Method™ is segmented into 5 Steps. There is progress (although not always in order) just by moving through the steps. The slated exercises and mapped out milestone meetings help teams progress (and see that progress). It may seem daunting to look at the calendar of events and tasks (displayed below) but once on the road to completing them, there is a sense of pride and progress for how much each team (and individual) has done and contributed.

The last piece of competence that is baked into the method is the substantive training we provide on design thinking and The 3-4-5 Method™ itself, that is, what teams need to do to get from problem to solution. First, at the KickOff, we train on the method. As mentioned, we have a prior team present their Project of Worth, or we do a mini-version of the method in its entirety on a topic that everyone can relate to; such as how to improve higher education. The participants practice hacking through the 5 Steps and present at the end of the KickOff. The stakes are, of course, a lot lower than they are at the ConPosium but it teaches them about the concepts, which are altogether unfamiliar at first. Second, either before or during the journey, we provide (live or recorded) webinars along with suggested articles to read and videos to watch to train the participants on the theories and concepts needed to progress through the steps, that is, on what is consumer storytelling and the power it has, how to develop a prototype, etc. Too often, participants on innovation and collaboration journeys are left to just figure it out, which doesn't enhance competence.

c. Connectedness/Relatedness

The third component of intrinsic motivation is a sense of connectedness.[32] As discussed earlier, all three phases in The 3-4-5 Method™ are designed purposefully to create community and connection, that is, relatedness. The KickOff is a bonding experience above all else that sets teams up to collaborate with empathy and a feeling of connectedness going forward. The virtual teaming phases include webinars in which the entire community regroups to learn and engage. This keeps us connected not only to our teams and subteams, but the community at large. Further, each team is deeply connected to the goals of the project because their charge is to solve a real challenge that a client or their organization is facing. The team is taught to "fall in love" with their problem and target audience—yet another type of relatedness and connection. In the process of going through the 5 Steps, many teams have to start over at some point and this is a bonding experience like no other—as long as the starting over was not due to incompetence or irresponsibility. By the end, there isn't a team still teaming that isn't completely connected to each other, to its project, and to its purpose.

4. Reason #4: It Has a Good Beginning and Lots of Effort-Filled Ends That "Let [Us] See Something Happen Now"[33]

As explained earlier in this chapter and in the previous chapter, the KickOff is critical to successful teaming, and The 3-4-5 Method™ always starts with a KickOff. The saying that first impressions matter most is absolutely true here as well. Beginnings matter in life in so many ways and starting off right is crucial. But endings matter almost as much, ends to meetings (as mentioned above), ends to parts of a project, and an actual end of the project entirely. In addition to the individual meetings needing an end, so too do phases or stages of the project—which is why I recommend having a method, like The 3-4-5 Method™, that is structured timewise, as in when project update meetings occur, but also milestone meetings that mark the end of a step, or stage, or phase of a project. We need multiple (accurately spaced out) stopping points to stop and reflect and assess (before we revise and refine). The 3-4-5 Method™ embeds the Progress Principle and is in spirit with Mahatma Gandhi's famous quote: "Have a bias toward action—let's see something happen now. You can break that big plan into small steps and take the first step right away."

One of my favorite recommendations to people trying to solve a problem is to CHUNK IT. It is why we do *Problem Trip Mapping* and, as others might call it, journey mapping in the design thinking process. In *Problem Trip Mapping*, we (1) map the process during which the problem surfaces (where and when it starts or occurs and who causes it or is impacted by it, and how it is currently resolved or sidestepped); (2) identify other problems within the identified problem that occur along the process or trajectory of the problem; and (3) identify the key audiences impacting, experiencing, OR creating the narrower problems within the problem and the pain points. This type of mapping is critical to the success of the team in any collaboration or innovation initiative so that everyone is on the same *problem plane* (as discussed earlier). The other type of map that is essential is a roadmap that provides directions on how to get from A to Z, from problem or opportunity to solution. This is why we have such a detailed calendar and earmarked milestone meetings. Without that, completing the journey seems not only endless but fruitless.

And, these milestone or *ending* meetings need to be timed and planned out as to what deliverables are due and in what form and how they will be reported (format and length, before or during the meeting) and how they will be assessed. For example, if the milestone meeting is scheduled for 30 minutes, are any pre-reading materials to be provided by the team? How long does the team have to present? What is expected to be presented (history or progress to date) and in what format and by whom? Will there be feedback during the meeting? If so, how long will feedback last and by whom, and will there be time for Q&A? This is how all teaming meetings should be managed but most definitely the milestone meetings that mark endings. This is how teams know what is expected, make progress over time, and can measure progress and success—the Progress Principle comes to mind again! Plus, there's nothing like the absence of a due date (or a due date too far in the future) to justify procrastination! To that end we need an actual stopping point to work toward (wherein we can opt out of continuing on this project or committee or, alternatively opt in). Although Ursula K. Le Guin's quote from *The Left Hand of Darkness* is one of my favorites: "It is good to have an end to journey towards; it is the journey that matters, in the end,"[34] if there is no end to journey towards, or if the end is nowhere practical in sight, the dread of the length of the journey sucks the creativity, collaboration, and innovation out of us—yet another reason to keep the length of the journey to 4 months or less!

It is also important for the ending point to have high stakes. It needs to make people sweat. During my days leading teams at Microsoft on their innovation journey, the nine teams that were coached by Brad Smith's nine direct reports presented at the annual meeting in one of the main rooms and often in front of very senior professionals from Microsoft who served as judges. There were also hundreds of people as attendees and the promise that Brad would drop by for a few of the presentations. In addition to that, the winning team won one of the nine awards he gave for the year, and they presented live on stage to over 2,700 people. That's high stakes. And it is the one way I was able to convince the very senior people on the teams that the marketing, messaging, presenting, and communication of the idea was AS important (if not more important) than the idea itself—and that even though they were senior, their presentation styles could be enhanced with some coaching.

Although the ConPosium feels like "the end," like the other milestone meetings, it is more like a safety stop as a diver ascends to the surface, as opposed to closure, which is good because it means there continues to be a journey forward and another milestone to meet. All of these ends take effort (and sweat), which, according to experts, is essential:

> *The reality is that to be effective, learning needs to be effortful . . . The same way you feel a muscle "burn" when it's being strengthened, the brain needs to feel some discomfort when it's learning. [It] might hurt for a while—but that's a good thing.*[35]

5. Reason #5: It's Targeted, Predictable, and Methodical, Yet Also Flexible

The 3-4-5 Method™ is a collaborative, problem-solving process grounded in design thinking principles that is uniquely constructed for professional service providers' temperament, training, and work preferences to develop the skill sets and attributes on the Skills Delta. This is important for all the reasons laid out in Part I of this book. A quote by renowned experts on professional services, Ashish Nanda and Das Narayandas, about "what professional service firms must do to thrive," hits home:

> *A practice's ability to deliver value to clients rests on the skills of its professionals, and the skill set of those professionals affects the choice of clients. In turn, the clients being served affect the development of the professionals' skills. The strategy of a practice therefore is tightly linked to its clients and the professionals serving them. Whom a practice hires affects the clients it can serve, the clients*

it serves affect how the skills of its professionals evolve, how the skill set evolves affects the clients the practice can acquire in the future, and the cycle keeps repeating.[36]

The 3-4-5 Method™ is designed to ensure the cycle is a valuable and growing one as opposed to a cyclone.

In addition to being targeted, The 3-4-5 Method™ provides predictability. It emphasizes the how and who. Further, it makes the *what* and *when* so very clear. Although the steps are iterative, the method details specific instructions and exercises for each step, along with deliverables, role identification, time commitment, and, importantly, a timeline detailing the series of meetings that should occur among the team and external advisers along the innovation journey. The 3-4-5 Method™ focuses on purpose, goals, accountability, and transparency. It also focuses on service innovation. One of the reasons the method works so well is that, armed with this level of information and predictability, professional service providers are willing to put in the time to get the intended results.

A big contributor to the success of The 3-4-5 Method™ is that, although the method embraces the messiness (and madness) that comes when diverse teams collaborate toward innovation, there is a method, a process to it. The 3-4-5 Method™ does not just map out the 5 Steps. It maps out every single meeting, task, and deliverable across the time period. Figure 11.3 shows only a portion of what is really mapped out. For a fuller, more detailed understanding (and mapping), read *The Leader Upheaval Handbook*.

This chart is, I know, daunting but the alternative is worse. Our very first year, I had the teams try to map it themselves so they would feel a part of the process (as recommended earlier). The problem with doing that, however, is they underestimate how much time it will take. That said, charts like this (and The 3-4-5 Method™ itself) perhaps leave little to the imagination and, at the same time, seem a bit "mad." However, Polonius's famous statement in Hamlet bears repeating: "Though this be madness, yet there is method in't."[37]

But flexibility in the method is key. One of the other most beneficial aspects of The 3-4-5 Method™ is that it is a *flexible* method. It can be done over 4 months, 3 days, 1 week, 4 weeks, or 48 hours—all of which I have tested. As mentioned, LawWithoutWalls' latest rendition is the LWOW Sprint: a 3-day in-person "weekender" focused on innovation, collaboration, and transformation in law that requires 48 hours of hacking. Its

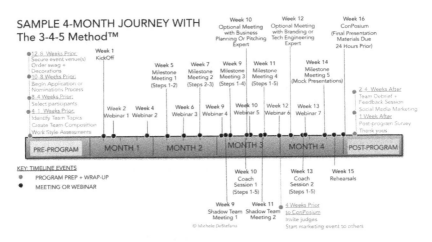

SAMPLE 4-MONTH JOURNEY WITH
The 3-4-5 Method™

FIG. 11.3. Example 4-Month Calendar in The 3-4-5 Method™.

3-day format is designed to match the demanding marketplace today, which often requires extraordinarily talented multidisciplinary teams to be pulled together quickly to work collaboratively on urgent matters. Over the course of three intense, high-energy days, participants hack to solve a real business-of-law problem or social responsibility challenge (or ESG) assigned to them by a sponsoring law firm, legal department, or law company. Teams create the foundation of a practicable solution and, at the end of the Sprint, present it to a panel of expert judges in front of the community of more than 180 people. Given its short length, its focus is less on the innovation and more on the hands-on upskilling for practicing and aspiring professionals who seek to enhance their cross-cultural, creative teaming, problem-solving, communication, and leadership skills while hacking alongside kindred spirits who share a passion for intrapreneurship and community exchange. However, no matter the length, The 3-4-5 Method™ requires hard work and resilience, delivers personal and professional growth and, of course, celebrates small wins along the way.

⬛...Reflection Point Almost any project can be divided into the 3 Phases of The 3-4-5 Method™.

- Take a moment to write down all of the benefits you think might be generated if you divided your next team project (any type of team project) into the 3 Phases of The 3-4-5 Method™:

- A KickOff (a community-wide meeting that was skills-focused)
- Virtual teaming through the 5 Steps of a Project of Worth
- A closure meeting where solutions are shared and reflected upon so that they can be improved and celebrated
- Now make a list of all of the potential downsides.
- Compare the two lists.

⬤...Reflection Point Consider the 4-month program timeline (shown in Figure 11.3) and the 5 Steps to a Project of Worth. How might you map out a similar process and utilize the 5 Steps the next time your team undertakes a project to ensure that the team is taking on the right problem for the right audience, meeting the objectives of the key stakeholders, and doing so in the right amount of time with input from externals to get diverse viewpoints along the way?

Conclusion

> *"You have to have an idea of what you are going to do, but it should be a vague idea."*
>
> —Pablo Picasso

Given the leader upheaval discussed in this book, people often ask me for my predictions of the future as it relates to the professional services market. I usually reply that the direction is up in a way that has never been possible before, up as in *up, up, and away* toward a new level of success.

For the most part in this book, I have defined innovation as lasting incremental change that adds value yet appears small on the surface (i.e., TNT: tiny noticeable things). That definition remains. Clients who fail to demand innovation and professional service providers who refuse to step "up" to innovate, to make those kinds of incremental changes in their practice and in how they service their clients and develop business, will not continue to succeed at the same levels as in the past. True, in the near term, they will continue to be tolerated and make money. But in the long term, over time, they will be ousted. Success will belong to those who embrace and hone the mindset, skill set, and behaviors identified in the lower two levels of the Professional Skills Delta, who are client-centric, and who follow the Three Rules of Engagement: Open Mind, Open Heart, and Open Door as described in Parts I and II of this book. Success will belong to prospective professional service providers who attend those schools that train them differently from the way they always have, that train them in design thinking and leadership. This is the hope; the good news is that even if I am wrong and the traditional way of doing things remains tolerated and schools continue to train as usual, the odds are high that some professional service providers, some firms, some departments, and some schools will still step up in a big, big way. And last, my bet is on you.

A. The Possibility in You: The Quarterbacks of Our Future

You are here. You are reading this book. You are in the small segment of the population that wants to transform how professional service providers collaborate and provide services. And so I see infinite possibility in you: in the people who have asked for earlier drafts of this book and copies of my presentations and in the people who have been inspired by my call to action—my mission—which is to convince all professional service providers (and especially lawyers) to learn *how* to innovate so that they hone the skill set, mindset, and behaviors of innovators even if they do not want to be entrepreneurs and even if they never create or even want to create an innovation in their lifetime. So possibly you will be the intrapreneurs, the potential quarterbacks who harness the right people, the right training, the right networks, the right processes, the right technologies, the right tools, and the right services to create (and bring to life) the vision for professional service firms and departments of the future. Yes, it is as hard to picture as was the "world wide web" was in 1991: What in the world could it be? What will it mean? How will it function? What kind of technology will it use? How will it change and impact us, and how can we harness it? "Yes, and . . ." those same questions are here now for you—only instead of being about the web, the questions are about diversity and inclusion, ESG, and technology (especially generative AI). And the good news is, per the quote at the beginning of this conclusion, although we need an "idea of what [we] are going to do," it doesn't have to be precise; in fact, it is likely "better" that it isn't because the point is to start, and then continue, to explore with an Open Mind, Open Heart, and an Open Door—understanding that "the journey" needs to begin now because now is the only time that matters. So, I conclude with my favorite quote of all:

> *"Remember then: there is only one time that is important—Now! It is the most important time because it is the only time when we have any power."*
>
> —Leo Tolstoy

APPENDIX A

Recommended Further Reading and Watching

Books

1. MICHELE DESTEFANO, LEADER UPHEAVAL: A GUIDE TO CLIENT-CENTRICITY, CULTURE-CREATION, AND COLLABORATION (1st ed. 2024).
2. MICHELE DESTEFANO, THE LEADER UPHEAVAL HANDBOOK: *LEAD TEAMS ON AN INNOVATION & COLLABORATION JOURNEY* (1st ed. 2023).
3. MICHELE DESTEFANO, LEGAL UPHEAVAL: A GUIDE TO CREATIVITY, COLLABORATION, & INNOVATION IN LAW (1st ed. 2018).
4. STEVEN JOHNSON, WHERE GOOD IDEAS COME FROM: THE NATURAL HISTORY OF INNOVATION (2010).
5. SIMON SINEK, START WITH WHY: HOW GREAT LEADERS INSPIRE EVERYONE TO TAKE ACTION (2009).
6. DANIEL H. PINK, TO SELL IS HUMAN: THE SURPRISING TRUTH ABOUT MOVING OTHERS (2012).
7. TINA SEELIG, WHAT I WISH I KNEW WHEN I WAS 20: A CRASH COURSE ON MAKING YOUR PLACE IN THE WORLD (2009).
8. TINA SEELIG, INGENIUS: A CRASH COURSE ON CREATIVITY (2012).
9. CHRISTOPHER CHABRIS AND DANIEL SIMONS, THE INVISIBLE GORILLA: HOW OUR INTUITIONS DECEIVE US (2009).
10. KEVIN ASHTON, HOW TO FLY A HORSE: THE SECRET HISTORY OF CREATION, INVENTION, AND DISCOVERY (2015).
11. CHIP HEATH AND DAN HEATH, SWITCH: HOW TO CHANGE THINGS WHEN CHANGE IS HARD (2010).
12. JASON FRIED AND DAVID HEINEMEIER HANSSON, REWORK (New York, Crown Business Publishing, 2010).
13. ROB CROSS & ANDREW PARKER, THE HIDDEN POWER OF SOCIAL NETWORKS: UNDERSTANDING HOW WORK REALLY GETS DONE IN ORGANIZATIONS (2004).
14. DREW BOYD AND JACOB GOLDENBERG, INSIDE THE BOX: A PROVEN SYSTEM OF CREATIVITY FOR BREAKTHROUGH RESULTS (2013).
15. JON. J. MUTH, ZEN SHORTS (2008).
16. ERNEST CLINE, READY PLAYER ONE (2012).
17. HEATHER FOREST, STONE SOUP (ATLANTA, AUGUST HOUSE LITTLEFOLK, 1998).
18. CARLOS VALDES-DAPENA, LESSONS FROM MARS (2019).
19. DESTEFANO & DOBRAUZ, NEW SUITS: APPETITE FOR DISRUPTION IN THE LEGAL WORLD (2019).
20. CHRIS AVERY, TEAMWORK IS AN INDIVIDUAL SKILL (2001).
21. JACK NEWTON, THE CLIENT CENTERED LAW FIRM: HOW TO SUCCEED IN AN EXPERIENCE-DRIVEN WORLD (2020).

22. J. Richard Hackman, Leading Teams: Setting the Stage For Great Performance (2002).
23. William Duggan, Creative Strategy: A Guide for Innovation (2013).
24. Hal B. Gregersen, Questions Are the Answer: A Breakthrough Approach to Your Most Vexing Problems at Work and in Life (2018).

Articles

1. Jon R. Katzenbach, Ilona Steffen, and Caroline Kronley, *Culture Change That Sticks*, Harv. Bus. Rev. (Jul. 1, 2012).
2. Clayton M. Christensen, Michael E. Raynor, and Rory McDonald, *What Is Disruptive Innovation?*, Harv. Bus. Rev. (Dec. 1, 2015).
3. Alex Moazed, *Why Clayton Christensen Is Wrong About Uber and Disruptive Innovation*, TechCrunch (Feb. 27, 2016).
4. Dr. Larry Richard, *Herding Cats: The Lawyer Personality Revealed*, Altman Weil Report to Management, Vol. 29, No. 11 (2002).
5. Tim Young, *365 Days, $10 Million, 3 Rounds, 2 Companies, All with 5 Magic Slides*, TechCrunch (Nov. 2, 2010).
6. Leslie A. Gordon, *Most Lawyers Are Introverted, and That's Not Necessarily a Bad thing*, ABA Journal (Jan. 1, 2016).
7. Tim Brown, *Design Thinking*, Harv. Bus. Rev. (June 1, 2008).
8. Cass R. Sunstein and Reid Hastie, *Making Dumb Groups Smarter*, Harv. Bus. Rev. (Nov. 1, 2014).
9. Bernadette Dillon and Juliet Bourke, *The Six Signature Traits of Inclusive Leadership*, Human Capital Consulting (Deloitte University Press 2017).
10. *The 5 Whys* by MindTools.
11. Abraham Zaleznik, *Managers and Leaders: Are They Different?*, Harv. Bus. Rev. (Jan 1, 2004).
12. John O' Leary, *Do Managers and Leaders Really Do Different Things?*, Harv. Bus. Rev. (June 1, 2016).
13. Nadya Zhexembayeva, *Stop Calling It Innovation*, Harv. Bus. Rev. (Feb. 1, 2020)
14. Gary P. Pisano, *The Hard Truth About Innovative Cultures*, Harv. Bus. Rev. (Jan 1, 2019).
15. James Clear, *The Three Stages of Failure in Life and Work (and How to Fix Them)* (2020).
16. Adam Brandenburger, *Strategy Needs Creativity*, Harv. Bus. Rev. (Mar. 1, 2019).
17. Christian Bason and Robert D. Austin, *The Right Way to Lead Design Thinking*, Harv. Bus. Rev. (Mar. 1, 2019).
18. Michele DeStefano, Bjarne Tellmann, and Dan Wu, *Don't Let the Digital Tail Wag the Transformation Dog: A Digital Transformation Roadmap for Corporate Counsel*, 17 Journal of Business & Technology Law, 183 (2022).
19. Marcus Buckingham and Ashley Goodall, *The Feedback Fallacy*, Harv. Bus. Rev. (Mar. 1, 2019).

20. Teresa M. Amabile and Steven J. Kramer, *The Power of Small Wins*, Harv. Bus. Rev. (May 1, 2011).

21. Jeffrey H. Dyer, Hal Gregersen, and Clayton M. Christensen, *The Innovator's DNA*, Harv. Bus. Rev. (Dec. 1, 2009).

22. Tina Seelig, *Three Ways to Reframe a Problem to Find an Innovative Solution*, Fast Company (Sept. 8, 2015).

23. Jeremy Utley and Perry Klebahn, *The Brainstorm as We Know It Doesn't Work. Here's What Does*, The Entrepreneur (Nov. 22, 2022).

24. Jill Avery and Rachel Greenwald, *A New Approach to Building Your Personal Brand*, Harv. Bus. Rev. (May 1, 2023).

25. Ed Catmull, *How Pixar Fosters Collective Creativity*, Harv. Bus. Rev. (Sept. 1, 2008).

26. Blair Epstein, Caitlin Hewes, and Scott Keller, Capturing the Value of 'One Firm', McKinsey Quarterly (May 9, 2023), https://www.mckinsey.com/capabilities/strategy-and-corporate-finance/our-insights/capturing-the-value-of-one-firm.

27. Michele DeStefano, *Chicken or Egg: Diversity and Innovation in the Corporate Legal Marketplace*, 91 Fordham L. Rev. 183 (2022).

28. Tojin T. Eapen, Daniel J. Finkenstadt, Josh Folk, and Lokesh Venkataswamy, *How Generative AI Can Augment Human Creativity: Use It to Promote Divergent Thinking*, Harv. Bus. Rev. (Jul. 1, 2023).

Videos

1. Daniel Pink, *Problem Solvers to Problem Finders* (YouTube).

2. *Dr. Brene Brown on Empathy* (YouTube).

3. Derek Sivers, *How to Start a Movement* (Ted.com).

4. Margaret Hefferen, *Forget the Pecking Order at Work* (YouTube).

5. Simon Sinek, *The Art of Listening* (YouTube).

6. John Amaechi, *On Teaming and Collaboration* (start video at 41:38) (Ironclad.com).

7. William Ury, *The Power of Listening* (YouTube).

8. Ross Shafer, *Customer Loyalty* (Rossshafer.com).

APPENDIX B

List of Figures

APPENDIX C

Research Methodology and Interview Characteristics

Research Methodology

To explore the topics in this book, from 2016 through 2023, I conducted 286 interviews of professional service providers of all kinds, including general counsels (GCs) and chief executives from large, international corporations, along with heads of innovation and partners of law firms and consulting firms from around the world. For most of the interviewees, a "snowball sample" approach was used to find potential respondents.[1] To elicit participation, on average, the interviewees were contacted by email one or two times. Interviewees from between 2016 and 2017 were told that the topic was Culture, Collaboration, and Innovation in law. Those from between 2018 and 2023 were told the topic was Culture, Collaboration, and Innovation, Digital Transformation,[2] or Client-Centricity. Interview questions were not provided in advance. All interviewees (except those who were interviewed for podcasts) were assured that they and their companies would remain anonymous. These interviews lasted between 20 and 45 minutes, with an average of about 30 minutes. A large portion of the law firm interviews were conducted as part of my consulting work for the firms. These interviews were shorter in length and had a dual purpose: (1) to understand the culture of the firm and (2) to explore the topics noted above. These law firm interviewees were told of these purposes and were assured that their comments would remain anonymous. For the shorter interviews, I utilized a subset of the same questions I used with my other interviews.

The interviews were conducted via phone or video platform (e.g., Skype, Zoom, or Teams). The questions consisted of both closed- and open-ended questions. The interviews that occurred during 2016 to 2017 (referred to as Part 1 Interviews) were used to inform my first book, *Legal Upheaval*. For these interviews, a codebook was developed consisting of two sections.[3] The first section attempted to measure questions that elicited specific answers to tabulate responses systematically across interviewees. For the most part, the topics were presented in an open-ended fashion; therefore, the second section of the codebook is an analysis of the interview transcripts by certain questions and topics.[4] Various law student research assistants were trained to code the data. The findings from my interviews are not statistically significant, and they are not relied on to show or prove any point empirically. The interviews are merely self-reports by senior executives who have their own agendas and stories to tell. To that end, the interviews conducted during Part 1 (2016-2017) and Part 2 (2018-2023) cannot be used to depict a true picture of how the world is; instead, they depict how "some professionals believe the world is or how it ought to be or how they would like others to believe they see the world."[5] This is sufficient because the research was not designed or used to *prove* anything. Instead, the primary goals of the interviews were to understand how professionals working in the professional services marketplace define, manage, and think about client-centricity, culture, collaboration, and innovation. As such, they provide a lens through which to view my hypothesis and theories and to inform my analysis and conclusions.

Interview Characteristics

The interviews were conducted in two parts. Part 1 interviews were conducted from 2016 to 2017 and used in my first book, *Legal Upheaval*. Part 2 interviews were conducted from 2018 to 2023.

Description of Part 1 Interviews: I interviewed 107 professionals from 30 law firms, 42 large corporations, and 7 professional service firms (that were not law firms) located in 13 different countries. The interviewees consisted of the following:

- 44 clients (referred to as Client Interviewees).
  - These interviewees were generally a mix of GCs and senior business executives within large, international corporations.[6]
- 31 chief innovation officers (referred to as CINO interviewees).[7]
  - These interviewees were individuals in charge of innovation at the professional service firm. Their titles varied. Some were called chief innovation officers; others were called directors of innovation, and heads of innovation; still others had different titles. Some didn't have a title but were recognized as the leader of innovation at the firm, nonetheless.
- 32 senior executives of professional service firms.
  - 23 law firm partners (referred to as PSF Interviewee (law firm partner)).
  - 9 senior executives (referred to as PSF Interviewees).
    - These interviewees were a mix of senior executives from the Big 4 and other professional service and law consulting firms.

Description of Part 2 Interviews: I interviewed 179 professionals from 29 large corporations and 24 professional service firms located in 16 different countries. The interviewees consisted of the following:

- 61 clients referred to as Client Interviewees.
  - These interviewees were generally a mix of senior in-house counsel (mostly GCs) and senior business executives within large, international corporations.
- 2 chief innovation officers (referred to as CINO Interviewees).
  - These interviewees were individuals in charge of innovation at a professional service firm.
- 116 senior executives of professional service firms.
  - 79 partners and 5 senior associates from law firms (referred to as PSF Interviewee [law firm partner[8] or law firm associate]).
  - 32 senior business partners (referred to as PSF Interviewees).
    - These interviewees were a mix of senior executives who are not lawyers who work at professional service firms, including the Big 4 law firms and other consulting firms.

Part	Type & Citation	#	Title	Company Description	Year
Culture, Collaboration, & Innovation Client Interviewee					
1	Client Interviewee	1	Deputy General Counsel	A large international airline	2016
1	Client Interviewee	2	Executive Vice President of Regulatory Strategy	A widely known American brokerage firm	2016
1	Client Interviewee	3	Assistant General Counsel	An educational consulting firm	2016
1	Client Interviewee	4	Assistant General Counsel	An international industrial company	2016
1	Client Interviewee	5	Vice President & Senior Corporate Counsel	A global insurance provider from the United States	2016
1	Client Interviewee	6	Senior Vice President & General Counsel	A global technology solutions company	2016
1	Client Interviewee	7	General Counsel	An energy & electric technologies company	2016
1	Client Interviewee	8	Chief Legal Officer	An office supplies & business solutions retailer	2016
1	Client Interviewee	9	Head of Knowledge & Development, Compliance & Secretariat	A Big 4 Australian bank & financial service provider	2016
1	Client Interviewee	10	Legal Director	A worldwide healthcare group based in the United Kingdom	2016
1	Client Interviewee	11	General Counsel	An Australian division of a worldwide healthcare group based in the United Kingdom	2016
1	Client Interviewee	12	Corporate Legal Director	A cooperative specializing in pension & asset management	2016
1	Client Interviewee	13	Chief Legal Officer	A large Chinese car manufacturer	2016

(Continued)

Part	Type & Citation	#	Title	Company Description	Year
1	Client Interviewee	14	Executive Vice President & Chief Legal Officer	A global insurance provider based in the United States	2016
1	Client Interviewee	15	General Counsel	An international design & consulting firm	2016
1	Client Interviewee	16	Deputy General Counsel	A global insurance company based in the United States	2016
1	Client Interviewee	17	General Counsel	A U.S. iconic software & technology company	2016
1	Client Interviewee	18	Former Chairman	A Swiss-based financial services corporation	2016
1	Client Interviewee	19	General Counsel	An American mortgage investment firm	2017
1	Client Interviewee	20	General Counsel	An American nonprofit that designs public competitions for technological development	2017
1	Client Interviewee	21	General Counsel	A British multinational banking & financial services company	2017
1	Client Interviewee	22	Lead Counsel	A large, global bank headquartered in the United Kingdom	2017
1	Client Interviewee	23	General Counsel	A global music streaming service	2017
1	Client Interviewee	24	Deputy General Counsel	A global network & managed information technology service provider from Germany	2017
1	Client Interviewee	25	General Counsel	A large media & telecommunications company in Australia	2017
1	Client Interviewee	26	General Counsel	A global information technology & consumer electronics company headquartered in the United Kingdom	2017

Part	Type & Citation	#	Title	Company Description	Year
1	Client Interviewee	27	General Counsel	An online legal technology company that helps clients create legal documents	2017
1	Client Interviewee	28	General Counsel	A U.S.-based global cybersecurity company	2017
1	Client Interviewee	29	Vice President & Associate General Counsel	An American multinational enterprise information technology company	2017
1	Client Interviewee	30	Head of Legal	A large international airline	2017
1	Client Interviewee	31	General Counsel	A government department of Australia	2017
1	Client Interviewee	32	Senior Legal Counsel	A global management consulting & professional services company	2017
1	Client Interviewee	33	Senior Corporate Counsel	A multinational insurance company headquartered in Australia	2017
1	Client Interviewee	34	Director	A government department in Australia	2017
1	Client Interviewee	35	General Counsel	A religious organization in Australia	2017
1	Client Interviewee	36	Senior Vice President	A large airline	2017
1	Client Interviewee	37	Senior Vice President & General Counsel	A global chemical distribution company	2017 (and in 2023)
1	Client Interviewee	38	Associate General Counsel	An American bank holding company	2017
1	Client Interviewee	39	CEO	A specialist real estate investment management company in Australia	2017
1	Client Interviewee	40	CEO	One of Australia's largest insurance companies	2017

(Continued)

Part	Type & Citation	#	Title	Company Description	Year
1	Client Interviewee	41	General Counsel	A large financial services group based in Norway	2017
1	Client Interviewee	42	General Counsel	A Chilean division of a French cosmetics company	2017
1	Client Interviewee	43	Vice President of Legal, EMEA Division	An American manufacturer & marketer of cosmetics & hair care products	2017
1	Client Interviewee	44	General Counsel	A Canadian division of a Japanese automobile manufacturer	2017
2	Client Interviewee	45	Assistant General Counsel of Enterprise Operations	An American multinational corporation specializing in worker safety, healthcare, & consumer goods	2020
2	Client Interviewee	46	Associate General Counsel & Managing Counsel	An American multinational corporation specializing in worker safety, healthcare, & consumer goods	2020
2	Client Interviewee	47	Director & Assistant General Counsel	An American multinational corporation specializing in worker safety, healthcare, & consumer goods	2020
2	Client Interviewee	48	Executive Vice President, Regional Head of Logistics Operations	One of the largest international e-commerce operators in Southeast Asia	2020
2	Client Interviewee	49	Head of Venture Risks	One of the largest international e-commerce operators in Southeast Asia	2020
2	Client Interviewee	50	Vice President, Group Procurement	One of the largest international e-commerce operators in Southeast Asia	2020

Part	Type & Citation	#	Title	Company Description	Year
2	Client Interviewee	51	In-House Lawyer	One of the largest international e-commerce operators in Southeast Asia	2020
2	Client Interviewee	52	Senior Digital Transformation Manager	A British multinational telecommunications company	2020
2	Client Interviewee	53	Head of Legal, Partnerships & Alliances	A British multinational telecommunications company	2020
2	Client Interviewee	54	Senior Enterprise Lawyer	A British multinational telecommunications company	2020
2	Client Interviewee	55	Chief Counsel/ General Counsel	A British multinational telecommunications company	2020
2	Client Interviewee	56	Senior Business Executive	A British multinational telecommunications company	2020
2	Client Interviewee	57	General Counsel	An AmLaw 200 law firm	2020
2	Client Interviewee	58	General Counsel	A British multinational pharmaceutical & biotechnology company	2021
2	Client Interviewee	59	Vice President, Legal & Chief Privacy Officer	A British multinational pharmaceutical & biotechnology company	2021
2	Client Interviewee	60	Vice President, Legal N Europe, EMEA & Latam	A British multinational pharmaceutical & biotechnology company	2021
2	Client Interviewee	61	Vice President & Chief Operation Officer Legal, Consumer Healthcare	A British multinational pharmaceutical & biotechnology company	2021
2	Client Interviewee	62	Vice President Legal Americas	A British multinational pharmaceutical & biotechnology company	2021

(Continued)

Part	Type & Citation	#	Title	Company Description	Year
Culture, Collaboration, & Innovation Client Interviewee Chief Innovation Officer					
1	PSF CINO Interviewee	1	Practice & Clients Director	A leading Portuguese law firm	2016
1	PSF CINO Interviewee	2	Quality, Organization, & Innovation Coordinator	A leading Portuguese law firm	2016
1	PSF CINO Interviewee	3	Chairman	An AmLaw 100 firm	2016
1	PSF CINO Interviewee	4	Head of Business Development & Innovation	An international, Spain-based legal & tax services firm	2016
1	PSF CINO Interviewee	5	Head of Innovation	One of the top 50 largest law firms by revenue based in London	2016
1	PSF CINO Interviewee	6	Director of Practice Innovation	An international AmLaw corporate law firm based in the United States	2016
1	PSF CINO Interviewee	7	Chief Practice Management Officer	One of the top 50 largest law firms by revenue headquartered in the northwest United States	2016
1	PSF CINO Interviewee	8	Executive Director of Innovation	A world-renowned law firm based in Asia	2016
1	PSF CINO Interviewee	9	Chief Information Officer	An Australian corporate law firm	2016
1	PSF CINO Interviewee	10	Director of Resources & Technology	A leading law firm based in the United Kingdom	2016
1	PSF CINO Interviewee	11	Chief Strategy Officer	A leading London-based law firm	2016
1	PSF CINO Interviewee	12	Chief Information Officer	A multinational professional services firm from Australia	2016
1	PSF CINO Interviewee	13	Chief Knowledge Officer	A large American law firm	2016

Part	Type & Citation	#	Title	Company Description	Year
1	PSF CINO Interviewee	14	Client Relationship Director	One of Australia's Big 6 law firms	2016
1	PSF CINO Interviewee	15	Innovation Manager	A Dutch law firm with offices in Europe & the United States	2016
1	PSF CINO Interviewee	16	National Innovation Leader	One of Canada's largest law firms	2016
1	PSF CINO Interviewee	17	Senior Director of Professional Services	A business law firm from California	2016
1	PSF CINO Interviewee	18	Director of Knowledge & Innovation	One of the top 50 largest law firms by revenue based in London	2016
1	PSF CINO Interviewee	19	Partner	An AmLaw 100 firm	2016
1	PSF CINO Interviewee	20	Chief Knowledge Officer	An AmLaw 100 firm	2016
1	PSF CINO Interviewee	21	Chief Operating Officer	A multinational, London-based law firm	2016
1	PSF CINO Interviewee	22	Partner	An AmLaw 100 firm	2016
1	PSF CINO Interviewee	23	Global Head of Innovation & Business Change	A magic circle law firm	2016
1	PSF CINO Interviewee	24	Founder & Partner	A leading law firm in India	2017
1	PSF CINO Interviewee	25	Head of Innovation Europe	One of the world's largest law firms from the United Kingdom	2017
1	PSF CINO Interviewee	26	Corporate Services Director	An Australian business law firm	2017
1	PSF CINO Interviewee	27	Director of Innovation	One of Australia's Big 6 law firms	2017
1	PSF CINO Interviewee	28	Partner responsible for innovation	A leading large Australian law firm	2017
1	PSF CINO Interviewee	29	Global Chief Innovation Officer	A London-based law firm with four dozen offices worldwide	2017

(Continued)

Part	Type & Citation	#	Title	Company Description	Year
1	PSF CINO Interviewee	30	Head of Innovation	One of the world's top law firms headquartered in both London & Washington, D.C.	2017
1	PSF CINO Interviewee	31	Innovation & Networks Leader	A multinational professional services firm & one of the Big 6 law firms in Australia	2017
2	PSF CINO Interviewee	32	Chief Innovation & Value Officer	An international AmLaw 100 firm	2018
2	PSF CINO Interviewee	33	Director, Practice Innovation	One of the world's 50 largest law firms by revenue	2021

Culture, Collaboration, & Innovation Client Interviewee PSF Law Firm Partner

Part	Type & Citation	#	Title	Company Description	Year
1	PSF Interviewee (Law Firm Partner)	1	Partner	One of the world's 100 largest law firms by revenue with offices in the United States & Europe	2017
1	PSF Interviewee (Law Firm Partner)	2	Partner	One of the world's 100 largest law firms by revenue with offices in the United States & Europe	2017
1	PSF Interviewee (Law Firm Partner)	3	Partner	One of the world's 100 largest law firms by revenue with offices in the United States & Europe	2017
1	PSF Interviewee (Law Firm Partner)	4	Partner	One of the world's 100 largest law firms by revenue with offices in the United States & Europe	2017
1	PSF Interviewee (Law Firm Partner)	5	Partner	One of the world's 100 largest law firms by revenue with offices in the United States & Europe	2017

Part	Type & Citation	#	Title	Company Description	Year
1	PSF Interviewee (Law Firm Partner)	6	Partner	One of the world's 100 largest law firms by revenue with offices in the United States & Europe	2017
1	PSF Interviewee (Law Firm Partner)	7	Partner	A leading independent Australian law firm	2017
1	PSF Interviewee (Law Firm Partner)	8	Partner	A leading independent Australian law firm	2017
1	PSF Interviewee (Law Firm Partner)	9	Partner	A leading independent Australian law firm	2017
1	PSF Interviewee (Law Firm Partner)	10	Partner	A leading independent Australian law firm	2017
1	PSF Interviewee (Law Firm Partner)	11	Partner	A leading independent Australian law firm	2017
1	PSF Interviewee (Law Firm Partner)	12	Partner	A leading independent Australian law firm	2017
1	PSF Interviewee (Law Firm Partner)	13	Partner	A leading independent Australian law firm	2017
1	PSF Interviewee (Law Firm Partner)	14	Partner	A leading independent Australian law firm	2017
1	PSF Interviewee (Law Firm Partner)	15	Partner	A leading independent Australian law firm	2017
1	PSF Interviewee (Law Firm Partner)	16	Partner	A leading independent Australian law firm	2017
1	PSF Interviewee (Law Firm Partner)	17	Partner	A leading independent Australian law firm	2017
1	PSF Interviewee (Law Firm Partner)	18	Deputy Chief Executive Partner	One of Australia's Big 6 law firms	2017
1	PSF Interviewee (Law Firm Partner)	19	Chief Executive Partner	One of Australia's Big 6 law firms	2017
1	PSF Interviewee (Law Firm Partner)	20	Partner	One of Australia's Big 6 law firms	2017
1	PSF Interviewee (Law Firm Partner)	21	Partner	One of Australia's Big 6 law firms	2017
1	PSF Interviewee (Law Firm Partner)	22	Deputy Chief Executive Partner	One of Australia's Big 6 law firms	2017

(Continued)

Part	Type & Citation	#	Title	Company Description	Year
1	PSF Interviewee (Law Firm Partner)	23	Partner	New York City–based law firm	2017
2	PSF Interviewee (Law Firm Partner)	24	Managing Partner	One of the top 200 largest law firms in the United States	2018
2	PSF Interviewee (Law Firm Partner)	25	Founding Partner	One of the top 200 largest law firms in the United States	2018
2	PSF Interviewee (Law Firm Partner)	26	Partner	One of the oldest & largest law firms in the western United States	2018
2	PSF Interviewee (Law Firm Partner)	27	General Counsel	One of the oldest & largest law firms in the western United States	2018
2	PSF Interviewee (Law Firm Partner)	28	Partner	An AmLaw 100 firm	2018
2	PSF Interviewee (Law Firm Partner)	29	Partner	An AmLaw 100 firm	2018
2	PSF Interviewee (Law Firm Partner)	30	Partner	An AmLaw 100 firm	2018
2	PSF Interviewee (Law Firm Partner)	31	Partner	An AmLaw 100 firm	2019
2	PSF Interviewee (Law Firm Partner)	32	Managing Partner	An AmLaw 100 firm	2019
2	PSF Interviewee (Law Firm Partner)	33	Partner	An AmLaw 100 law firm that is one of the world's 30 largest global law firms by revenue	2019
2	PSF Interviewee (Law Firm Partner)	34	Partner	An AmLaw 100 law firm that is one of the world's 30 largest global law firms by revenue	2019
2	PSF Interviewee (Law Firm Partner)	35	Managing Partner	One of the top 200 largest law firms in the United States	2019
2	PSF Interviewee (Law Firm Partner)	36	Partner	One of the top 200 largest law firms in the United States	2019

Part	Type & Citation	#	Title	Company Description	Year
2	PSF Interviewee (Law Firm Partner)	37	Partner	One of the top 200 largest law firms in the United States	2019
2	PSF Interviewee (Law Firm Partner)	38	Partner	An AmLaw 100 law firm	2019
2	PSF Interviewee (Law Firm Partner)	39	Partner	An AmLaw 100 law firm	2019
2	PSF Interviewee (Law Firm Partner)	40	Partner	An AmLaw 100 law firm	2019
2	PSF Interviewee (Law Firm Partner)	41	Chair/Managing Partner	An AmLaw 100 law firm	2019
2	PSF Interviewee (Law Firm Partner)	42	Partner	An AmLaw 100 law firm	2019
2	PSF Interviewee (Law Firm Partner)	43	Partner	An AmLaw 100 law firm	2019
2	PSF Interviewee (Law Firm Partner)	44	Partner	An AmLaw 100 law firm	2019
2	PSF Interviewee (Law Firm Partner)	45	Partner	An AmLaw 100 law firm	2019
2	PSF Interviewee (Law Firm Partner)	46	Partner	One of the world's 100 largest global law firms by revenue	2020
2	PSF Interviewee (Law Firm Partner)	47	Partner	One of the world's 100 largest global law firms by revenue	2020
2	PSF Interviewee (Law Firm Associate)	48	Associate	One of the world's 100 largest global law firms by revenue	2020
2	PSF Interviewee (Law Firm Partner)	49	Managing Partner	One of the world's 100 largest global law firms by revenue	2020
2	PSF Interviewee (Law Firm Partner)	50	Partner	One of the world's 100 largest global law firms by revenue	2020
2	PSF Interviewee (Law Firm Partner)	51	Partner	One of the world's 100 largest global law firms by revenue	2020

(Continued)

Part	Type & Citation	#	Title	Company Description	Year
2	PSF Interviewee (Law Firm Partner)	52	Partner & Global Head of Finance	One of the world's 100 largest global law firms by revenue	2020
2	PSF Interviewee (Law Firm Partner)	53	Partner Employment Law	One of the world's 100 largest global law firms by revenue	2020
2	PSF Interviewee (Law Firm Partner)	54	Partner	An AmLaw 200 firm	2020
2	PSF Interviewee (Law Firm Partner)	55	Partner	An AmLaw 200 firm	2020
2	PSF Interviewee (Law Firm Partner)	56	Partner	An AmLaw 200 firm	2020
2	PSF Interviewee (Law Firm Partner)	57	Senior Counsel (former partner)	An AmLaw 200 firm	2020
2	PSF Interviewee (Law Firm Partner)	58	Senior Associate	An AmLaw 200 firm	2020
2	PSF Interviewee (Law Firm Partner)	59	Managing Partner	An AmLaw 200 firm	2020
2	PSF Interviewee (Law Firm Partner)	60	Partner	An AmLaw 200 firm	2020
2	PSF Interviewee (Law Firm Partner)	61	Partner	An AmLaw 200 firm	2020
2	PSF Interviewee (Law Firm Partner)	62	Partner	An AmLaw 200 firm	2020
2	PSF Interviewee (Law Firm Partner)	63	Partner	An AmLaw 200 firm	2020
2	PSF Interviewee (Law Firm Partner)	64	Partner	An AmLaw 200 firm	2020
2	PSF Interviewee (Law Firm Partner)	65	Partner	An AmLaw 200 firm	2020
2	PSF Interviewee (Law Firm Partner)	66	Partner	One of the top law firms in Brazil	2021
2	PSF Interviewee (Law Firm Partner)	67	Partner	One of the top law firms in Brazil	2021
2	PSF Interviewee (Law Firm Partner)	68	Partner	One of the top law firms in Brazil	2021
2	PSF Interviewee (Law Firm Partner)	69	Partner	One of the top law firms in Brazil	2021

Part	Type & Citation	#	Title	Company Description	Year
2	PSF Interviewee (Law Firm Partner)	70	Partner	One of the top law firms in Brazil	2021
2	PSF Interviewee (Law Firm Partner)	71	Partner	One of the top law firms in Brazil	2021
2	PSF Interviewee (Law Firm Partner)	72	Partner	One of the world's 10 largest global law firms by revenue	2021
2	PSF Interviewee (Law Firm Partner)	73	Co-Managing Partner	One of the world's 10 largest global law firms by revenue	2021
2	PSF Interviewee (Law Firm Partner)	74	Partner	One of the world's 10 largest global law firms by revenue	2021
2	PSF Interviewee (Law Firm Partner)	75	Partner	One of the world's 10 largest global law firms by revenue	2021
2	PSF Interviewee (Law Firm Assoc.)	76	Associate	One of the world's 10 largest global law firms by revenue	2021
2	PSF Interviewee (Law Firm Assoc.)	77	Associate	One of the world's 10 largest global law firms by revenue	2021
2	PSF Interviewee (Law Firm Partner)	78	Partner	One of the world's 10 largest global law firms by revenue	2021
2	PSF Interviewee (Law Firm Partner)	79	Partner	One of the world's 10 largest global law firms by revenue	2021
2	PSF Interviewee (Law Firm Assoc.)	80	Associate	One of the world's 10 largest global law firms by revenue	2021
2	PSF Interviewee (Law Firm Partner)	81	Partner	One of the Big 5 law firms in South Africa	2022
2	PSF Interviewee (Law Firm Partner)	82	Partner, Head of Finance Group	One of the Big 5 law firms in South Africa	2022
2	PSF Interviewee (Law Firm Partner)	83	Managing Partner	One of the Big 5 law firms in South Africa	2022

(Continued)

Part	Type & Citation	#	Title	Company Description	Year
2	PSF Interviewee (Law Firm Sr. Assoc.)	84	Senior Associate	One of the Big 5 law firms in South Africa	2022
2	PSF Interviewee (Law Firm Partner)	85	Partner	One of the Big 5 law firms in South Africa	2022
2	PSF Interviewee (Law Firm Partner)	86	Shareholder/ Partner	A top 300 American healthcare-focused law firm	2022
2	PSF Interviewee (Law Firm Partner)	87	President/CEO	A top 300 American healthcare-focused law firm	2022
2	PSF Interviewee (Law Firm Partner)	88	Shareholder/ Partner	A top 300 American healthcare-focused law firm	2022
2	PSF Interviewee (Law Firm Partner)	89	Partner	One of the world's 10 largest global law firms by revenue	2023
2	PSF Interviewee (Law Firm Partner)	90	Partner	One of the world's 10 largest global law firms by revenue	2023
2	PSF Interviewee (Law Firm Partner)	91	Partner	One of the world's 10 largest global law firms by revenue	2023
2	PSF Interviewee (Law Firm Partner)	92	Partner	One of the world's 10 largest global law firms by revenue	2023
2	PSF Interviewee (Law Firm Partner)	93	Partner	One of the world's 10 largest global law firms by revenue	2023

Culture, Collaboration, & Innovation Client Interviewee PSF Interviewee

Part	Type & Citation	#	Title	Company Description	Year
1	PSF Interviewee	1	Director	A consultancy firm with expertise in growth & strategy projects	2016
1	PSF Interviewee	2	Director of Legal Transformation	A consulting firm specializing in legal practice management	2016

Part	Type & Citation	#	Title	Company Description	Year
1	PSF Interviewee	3	Partner & Head of Technology	A global consultancy firm that provides advice across a wide range of business ventures	2016
1	PSF Interviewee	4	Independent Consultant	A U.K.-based consulting firm	2016
1	PSF Interviewee	5	Director	A Big 4 global consulting firm	2016
1	PSF Interviewee	6	Chief Financial Officer	One of Australia's Big 6 law firms	2017
1	PSF Interviewee	7	Executive Director	A Big 4 global consulting firm	2017
1	PSF Interviewee	8	Former CEO	An AmLaw 100 law firm based in the Midwest United States	2017
1	PSF Interviewee	9	Partner & Head of Legal	A Big 4 global consulting firm	2017
2	PSF Interviewee	10	Marketing & Attorney Recruiting Coordinator	One of the oldest & largest law firms in the western United States	2018
2	PSF Interviewee	11	Head of Legal Ops	A British multinational insurance company headquartered in London	2019
2	PSF Interviewee	12	Director of Admin	One of the world's 100 largest global law firms by revenue	2020
2	PSF Interviewee	13	Senior Director Pricing & Legal Project Management	One of the world's 100 largest global law firms by revenue	2020
2	PSF Interviewee	14	Senior Manager of Talent	One of the world's 100 largest global law firms by revenue	2020
2	PSF Interviewee	15	Director of Attorney Recruiting	One of the world's 100 largest global law firms by revenue	2020

(Continued)

Part	Type & Citation	#	Title	Company Description	Year
2	PSF Interviewee	16	Chief Human Resources Officer	One of the world's 100 largest global law firms by revenue	2020
2	PSF Interviewee	17	Director Pricing & Legal Project Management	One of the world's 100 largest global law firms by revenue	2020
2	PSF Interviewee	18	Chief Operating Officer	An AmLaw 100 national law firm with more than 1,200 attorneys	2020
2	PSF Interviewee	19	Chief Marketing Officer	An AmLaw 100 national law firm	2020
2	PSF Interviewee	20	Chief Talent Officer	An AmLaw 100 national law firm	2020
2	PSF Interviewee	21	Chief Information Officer	An AmLaw 200 firm	2020
2	PSF Interviewee	22	Chief Marketing Officer	An AmLaw 200 firm	2020
2	PSF Interviewee	23	Global Director of Strategy	One of the world's 10 largest global law firms by revenue	2021
2	PSF Interviewee	24	Chief Marketing Officer	One of the top law firms in Brazil	2021
2	PSF Interviewee	25	Events Coordinator	One of the top law firms in Brazil	2021
2	PSF Interviewee	26	Director of Practice Operations, Corporate	One of the world's 50 largest global law firms by revenue	2021
2	PSF Interviewee	27	Chief Legal Operations Officer	One of the world's 50 largest global law firms by revenue	2021
2	PSF Interviewee	28	Director of Business Transformation Office, Enterprise Applications, Practice Support & Solutions	One of the world's 50 largest global law firms by revenue	2021
2	PSF Interviewee	29	Senior Analyst	One of the world's 10 largest global law firms by revenue	2021

Part	Type & Citation	#	Title	Company Description	Year
2	PSF Interviewee	30	Head of Knowledge Management	One of the Big 5 law firms in South Africa	2022
2	PSF Interviewee	31	Chief Marketing Officer	A top 300 American healthcare-focused law firm	2022
2	PSF Interviewee	32	Senior Manager: Business Development & Data Analytics	One of the Big 5 law firms in South Africa	2022
2	PSF Interviewee	33	Head of Strategy & Market Engagement	One of the Big 4 professional services firms	2023

Digital Transformation Interviewee

Part	Type & Citation	#	Title	Company Description	Year
2	DT Client Interviewee	1	Vice-President, Global Head of Legal, General Corporate	An American multinational Global 500 & Fortune 500 information technology services & consulting company	2019
2	DT Client Interviewee	2	Associate General Counsel, International Operations	An American multinational Global 500 & Fortune 500 corporation operating in many fields including healthcare & consumer goods	2019
2	DT Client Interviewee	3	Associate Chief Counsel	A Global 500 & Fortune 500 health services organization	2019
2	DT Client Interviewee	4	Senior Vice President & General Counsel; Chief Compliance Officer	An international Global 500 chemical producer.	2019
2	DT Client Interviewee	5	Group General Counsel	A Global 500 large multinational pharmaceutical company	2019
2	DT Client Interviewee	6	Senior Vice President, Legal Affairs & General Counsel	An American multinational Global 500 & Fortune 500 corporation operating in many fields including healthcare & consumer goods	2019

(Continued)

Part	Type & Citation	#	Title	Company Description	Year
2	DT Client Interviewee	7	Executive Vice President, Secretary & General Counsel	An international Global 500 & Fortune 500 international distributor of information technology products	2019
2	DT Client Interviewee	8	Executive Vice President & General Counsel	One of the largest global providers of insurance, annuities, & employee benefit programs	2019
2	DT Client Interviewee	9	Senior Vice President & General Counsel	An American multinational personal care corporation that manufactures paper products & surgical & medical instruments	2019
2	DT Client Interviewee	10	General Counsel UKI & Data Protection Officer	A British multinational insurance company that is one of the largest general insurers	2019
2	DT Client Interviewee	11	Deputy General Counsel,	Global 500 & Fortune 500 information technology services/ consulting & computer hardware/software company	2019
2	DT Client Interviewee	12	General Counsel, Senior Vice President	Large Global 500 & Fortune 500 defense contractor	2019
2	DT Client Interviewee	13	General Counsel & Chief Legal Officer	FTSE 100 international education & publishing company	2019
2	DT Client Interviewee	14	Executive Vice President & Sr. Deputy GC	American multinational Fortune 500 financial services company	2019
2	DT Client Interviewee	15	General Counsel Tech	Fortune 500 international e-commerce company	2020

Part	Type & Citation	#	Title	Company Description	Year
2	DT Client Interviewee	16	General Counsel Tech	Global 500 British multinational telecommunications holding company	2020
2	DT Client Interviewee	17	Director of Strategy & Transformation	One of the world's largest bottlers in terms of volume & sales	2021
2	DT Client Interviewee	18	Group General Counsel & Company Secretary	A Global 500 British multinational telecommunications company	2020
2	DT Client Interviewee	19	General Counsel	An American multinational Global 500 & Fortune 500 information technology services & consulting company	2020
2	DT Client Interviewee	20	VP, General Counsel, APAC/ Middle East Global Lead Counsel	An American data communications & telecommunications equipment provider	2021
2	DT Client Interviewee	21	General Counsel	A Fortune 500 global pharmaceutical company.	2021
2	DT Client Interviewee	22	Chief Digital & Information Officer	A commercial, national airline	2020
2	DT Client Interviewee	23	VP of Digital Business	An American multinational Global 500 & Fortune 500 information technology services & consulting company	2020
2	DT Client Interviewee	24	Chief Legal Innovation Officer	A multinational worldwide pharmaceutical, healthcare company corporation	2020
2	DT Client Interviewee	25	Group Legal Chief Operating Officer	A multinational investment bank & financial services company	2021

(Continued)

Part	Type & Citation	#	Title	Company Description	Year
Client-Centricity Interviewee					
2	CC PSF Interviewee	1	Global Chief Communications Officer	One of the world's 10 largest global law firms by revenue	2023
2	CC Client Interviewee	2	Global Digital Ethics Manager	One of the largest drink & brewing companies in the world	2023
2	CC Client Interviewee	3	Head of Core Solutions	A major retail & commercial bank in the United Kingdom	2023
2	CC Client Interviewee	4	Head of Colleague Platforms & Network Services	A major retail & commercial bank in the United Kingdom	2023
2	CC Client Interviewee	5	Head of Cloud Services	A major retail & commercial bank in the United Kingdom	2023
2	CC Client Interviewee	6	Chief Compliance Officer	A global leader in the development & manufacture of plant remedies	2023
2	CC PSF Interviewee	7	Global Inclusion & Diversity Officer	One of the world's six largest global law firms by revenue	2023
2	CC PSF Interviewee	8	Global Chief Clients & Markets Officer	One of the world's six largest global law firms by revenue	2023
2	CC Client Interviewee	9	Associate General Counsel	American multinational technology corporation	2023
2	CC Client Interviewee	10	Former General Counsel	One of the largest mutual insurers in the United Kingdom	2023
2	CC Client Interviewee	11	Chief Financial Officer	A boutique investment advisory firm based in the United States	2023
2	CC Client Interviewee	12	Information Technology & Commercial Lawyer	One of the United Kingdom's largest financial services organizations	2023

Part	Type & Citation	#	Title	Company Description	Year
2	CC PSF Interviewee (Law Firm Partner)	13	Chairman (& Partner)	An AmLaw 100 firm	2023
2	CC PSF Interviewee (Law Firm Partner)	14	Chairman (& Partner)	An AmLaw 200 firm	2023
2	CC PSF Interviewee	15	Director, Pricing & Legal Project Management	An AmLaw 200 firm	2023
2	CC Client Interviewee	16	Head of Outsource, Tech & IP Legal Team	A major retail & commercial bank in the United Kingdom	2023
2	CC PSF Interviewee	17	Co-founder	A U.K.-based Professional Services Firm	2023
2	CC Client Interviewee	18	Global Head of Outside Counsel Management	A multinational investment bank & financial services company	2023
2	CC PSF Interviewee	19	Co-founder	A legal startup	2023
2	CC PSF Interviewee	20	Marketing Strategy Consultant	A U.S.-based strategic marketing consulting firm	2023
2	CC PSF Interviewee (Law Firm Partner)	21	Law Firm Partner	An AmLaw 100 firm	2023
2	CC PSF Interviewee	22	Chief Marketing Officer	An AmLaw 100 firm	2023
2	CC PSF Interviewee (Law Firm Partner)	23	Law Firm Partner	An AmLaw 100 firm	2023
2	CC PSF Interviewee (Law Firm Partner)	24	Law Firm Partner	An AmLaw 100 firm	2023
2	CC PSF Interviewee (Law Firm Partner)	25	Law Firm Partner	An AmLaw 100 firm	2023

(Continued)

Part	Type & Citation	#	Title	Company Description	Year
2	CC PSF Interviewee (Law Firm Partner)	26	Law Firm Partner	An AmLaw 100 firm	2023
2	CC PSF Interviewee	27	Chief Client & Innovation Officer	An AmLaw 100 firm	2023
2	CC PSF Interviewee (Law Firm Partner)	28	Law Firm Partner	One of the largest law firms in Singapore	2023
2	CC PSF Interviewee (Law Firm Partner)	29	Law Firm Partner	One of the largest law firms in Singapore	2023
2	CC PSF Interviewee (Law Firm Partner)	30	Law Firm Partner	One of the largest law firms in Singapore	2023
2	CC Client Interviewee	31	In-House Lawyer	Government Agency in Southeast Asia	2023
2	CC Client Interviewee	32	In-House Lawyer	Government Agency in Southeast Asia	2023
2	CC PSF Interviewee (Law Firm Partner)	33	Law Firm Partner	Government Agency in Southeast Asia	2023
2	CC Client Interviewee	34	In-House Lawyer	Government Agency in Southeast Asia	2023
2	CC Client Interviewee	35	In-House Lawyer	Government Agency in Southeast Asia	2023
2	CC Client Interviewee	36	In-House Lawyer	Government Agency in Southeast Asia	2023
2	CC Client Interviewee	37	In-House Lawyer	Government Agency in Southeast Asia	2023
2	CC PSF Interviewee (Law Firm Partner)	38	Law Firm Partner	One of the largest law firms in Singapore	2023
2	CC Client Interviewee	39	In-House Lawyer	Government Agency in Southeast Asia	2023
2	CC PSF Interviewee (Law Firm Partner)	40	Law Firm Partner	A large corporate law firm in Malaysia	2023

My research was global, as depicted in the following chart. I conducted interviews with professionals from 23 different countries.

	23 Countries	Total	Part 1 2016–2018	Part 2 2018–2023
1	United States	141	36	105
2	Australia	37	36	1
3	England	36	13	23
4	Singapore	19	0	19
5	Brazil	8	0	8
6	Germany	7	3	4
7	South Africa	7	0	7
8	Canada	4	3	1
9	Netherlands	3	3	0
10	Scotland	3	0	3
11	Spain	3	3	0
12	Chile	2	2	0
13	France	2	1	1
14	India	2	2	0
15	Norway	2	2	0
16	Portugal	2	2	0
17	Switzerland	2	0	2
18	Belgium	1	0	1
19	China	1	1	0
20	Greece	1	0	1
21	Israel	1	0	1
22	Italy	1	0	1
23	Qatar	1	0	1
		286	**107**	**179**

NOTES

Introduction

1. "Professional services" is a broad term that includes any firm, business, department, or individual who creates value by providing knowledge, expertise, or services (versus a manufactured product). Professional services "range from technology services to business consulting services, managed services, legal and recruitment services and everything else in between." Catherine Lynch, *How Digitalization Is Transforming The Professional Services Industry*, FORBES: SAP (July 16, 2021) https://www.forbes.com/sites/sap/2021/07/16/how-digitalization-is-transforming-the-professional-services-industry/; *Professional Services Basics: A Guide to Project Management for Professional Services*, Wrike, https://www.wrike.com/professional-services-guide/professional-services-basics/ (last visited Aug. 9, 2022). Professional service providers include lawyers, consultants, accountants, human resources professionals, engineers, financial advisors, public relations professionals, advertising executives, marketing professionals, compliance officers, architects, and insurance brokers, to name a few. *See* David L. Deephouse et al., *Reputation, Diversification, and Organizational Explanations of Performance in Professional Service Firms*, 16 ORG. SCI. 661, 661 (2006); Henry Mintzberg, *Structure in 5's: A Synthesis of the Research on Organization Design*, 26 MGMT. SCI. 322, 322–41 (1980); Andrew H. Van de Ven & André L. Delbecq, *The Effectiveness of Nominal, Delphi, and Interacting Group Decision Making Processes*, 17 ACAD. MGMT. J. 605, 605–71 (1974). Organizing 4 Innovation, *Why's It so Hard? Innovation Management In Professional Service Firms*, https://www.organizing4innovation.com/whys-it-so-hard-innovation-management-in-professional-services-firms/ (last visited Aug. 9, 2022).

2. *See* Victor Lipman, *New Study Explores Why Change Management Fails — And How to (Perhaps) Succeed*, FORBES (Sept. 4, 2013), https://www.forbes.com/sites/victorlipman/2013/09/04/new-study-explores-why-change-management-fails-and-how-to-perhaps-succeed/; *see also* N. Anand & Jean-Louis Barsoux, *What Everyone Gets Wrong About Change Management*, HARV. BUS. REV., Nov.-Dec. 2017, at 79, 80; *cf.* Mark Hughes, *Do 70 Per Cent of All Organizational Change Initiatives Really Fail?*, 11 J. CHANGE MGMT. 451, 451-64 (2011) (citing studies that show a 70 percent to 75 percent failure rate but contending the empirical evidence may be lacking).

Part I

1. SIMON SINEK, START WITH WHY: HOW GREAT LEADERS INSPIRE EVERYONE TO TAKE ACTION (1st ed. 2009).

Chapter 1

1. J.D. SALINGER, THE CATCHER IN THE RYE 122 (17th ed. 1991).

2. For a longer discussion of how socioeconomics, demographics, and globality are continuing to transform global industries and occupations, see generally WORLD ECON. FORUM, THE FUTURE OF JOBS: EMPLOYMENT, SKILLS AND WORKFORCE STRATEGY FOR THE FOURTH INDUSTRIAL REVOLUTION, GLOBAL CHALLENGE INSIGHT REPORT v–vi (2016), https://www3.weforum.org/docs/WEF_Future_of_Jobs.pdf [hereinafter 2016 WEF REPORT]; Michael Leimbach, *Leadership Development in the Age of Disruption: Best Practices to Reinvent Leadership Development Amidst Continued Turbulent Times and Technological Transformatio*n, TRAINING MAG. (May 9, 2023), https://trainingmag.com/leadership-development-in-the-age-of-disruption/.

3. Ziad Haider, Jon Huntsman Jr., & Chris Leech, *Geopolitical resilience: The new board imperative*, McKINSEY & Co. (Aug. 8, 2023) https://www.mckinsey .com/capabilities/risk-and-resilience/our-insights/geopolitical-resilience -the-new-board-imperative.

4. *See generally* WORLD ECON. FORUM, THE FUTURE OF JOBS REPORT 2023, at 4 (2023), https://www3.weforum.org/docs/WEF_Future_of_Jobs_2023.pdf [hereinafter 2023 WEF REPORT].

5. ESG "broadly refers to a company's efforts to address stakeholder interests that involve your company, its workforce, its products, or its impact on society." Michael J. Callahan et al., *The General Counsel View of ESG Risk*, HARVARD LAW SCHOOL FORUM ON CORPORATE GOVERNANCE 4 (Sept. 23, 2021), https://corpgov .law.harvard.edu/2021/09/23/the-general-counsel-view-of-esg-risk/.

6. Stephanie Neal, *The Human Factor: The Top 3 Concerns Keeping CEOs Up at Night*, CEO WORLD MAG. (Mar. 21, 2023), https://ceoworld.biz/2023/03/21/the -human-factor-the-top-3-concerns-keeping-ceos-up-at-night/ (surveying 13,695 leaders worldwide—including 529 CEOs—about the state of leadership).

7. *Cf.* David M. Mayer et al., *To Get Companies to Take Action on Social Issues, Emphasize Morals, Not the Business Case*, HARV. BUS. REV. (Feb. 14, 2019), https://hbr .org/2019/02/to-get-companies-to-take-action-on-social-issues-emphasize -morals-not-the-business-case (suggesting that managers are more likely to act on social issues when they are presented in "moral terms" rather than in "economic language.").

8. *See* Vijay Eswaran, *The Business Case for Diversity Is Now Overwhelming*, WORLD ECON. Forum 22–25 (Apr. 29, 2019), https://www.weforum.org/agenda/2019/04/ business-case-for-diversity-in-the-workplace/; *see also* Dieter Holger, *The Business Case for More Diversity*, WALL ST. J. (Oct. 26, 2019), https://www.wsj.com/articles/ the-business-case-for-more-diversity-11572091200?shareToken=stc911902db 723474d92eb5843b4ea1732; *see also* Paul Gompers & Silpa Kovvali, *The Other Diversity Dividend*, HARV. BUS. REV., July–Aug. 2018, at 72, 72–77; *see also* Matthew Corritore et al., *The New Analytics of Culture*, HARV. BUS. REV. (Jan. 1, 2020), https://hbr.org/2020/01/the-new-analytics-of-culture.

9. World Econ. Forum, Diversity, Equity and Inclusion 4.0, at 6 (2020), https://www3.weforum.org/docs/WEF_NES_DEI4.0_Toolkit_2020.pdf.

10. Richard Kersley et al., Editorial, *The CS Gender 3000 in 2019: The Changing Face of Companies*, Credit Suisse Rsch. Inst., Oct. 10, 2019, at 22–23 (finding that companies in which women held 20 percent or more of management roles created EBITDA margins that were 2 percent higher than companies in which women held 15 percent or less in management roles); Marcus Noland et al., *Is Gender Diversity Profitable?: Evidence from a Global Survey* 3 (Peterson Inst. for Int'l Econ., Working Paper No. 16-3, 2000), https://www.piie.com/publications/working-papers/gender-diversity-profitable-evidence-global-survey (finding a positive correlation between profitability and women in senior leadership positions).

11. Noland, *supra* note 10.

12. World Econ. Forum, *supra* note 9, at 6.

13. *See, e.g.*, Juan M. Madera et al., *Top Management Gender Diversity and Organizational Attraction: When and Why It Matters*, 7 Archives Sci. Psych. 90, 96-97 (2019); Cara C. Maurer & Israr Qureshi, *Not Just Good for Her: A Temporal Analysis of the Dynamic Relationship Between Representation of Women and Collective Employee Turnover*, 42 Org. Stud. 85, 86, 98-100(2021); Christine M. Beckman & Damon J. Phillips, *Interorganizational Determinants of Promotion: Client Leadership and the Attainment of Women Attorneys*, 70 Am. Soc. Rev. 678, 696 (2005) ("[C]orporate clients with women in leadership positions affect the growth of women partners in their law firm.").

14. Neal, *supra* note 6.

15. *See, e.g.*, Deloitte, Unleashing the Power of Inclusion 4 (2017), https://www2.deloitte.com/content/dam/Deloitte/us/Documents/about-deloitte/us-about-deloitte-unleashing-power-of-inclusion.pdf; Lydia Dishman, *The New Rules of Work: Millennials Have a Different Definition of Diversity and Inclusion*, Fast Co. (May 18, 2015) https://www.fastcompany.com/3046358/millennials-have-a-different-definitionof-diversity-and-inclusion (studying more than 3,500 millennials); *What Job Seekers Really Think About Your Diversity and Inclusion Stats*, Glassdoor (Jul. 12, 2021), https://www.glassdoor.com/employers/blog/diversity/; Jennifer Miller, *For Younger Job Seekers, Diversity and Inclusion in the Workplace Aren't a Preference. They're a Requirement*, Wash. Post (Feb. 18, 2021), https://www.washingtonpost.com/business/2021/02/18/millennial-genz-workplace-diversity-equity-inclusion/.

16. Michael Dimock, *Defining Generations: Where Millennials End and Generation Z Begins*, Pew Rsch. Ctr. (Jan. 17, 2019), https://www.pewresearch.org/fact-tank/2019/01/17/where-millennials-end-and-generation-z-begins/.

17. Kim Parker & Ruth Igielnik, *On the Cusp of Adulthood and Facing an Uncertain Future: What We Know About Gen Z so Far*, Pew Rsch. Ctr. (May 14, 2020), https://www.pewresearch.org/social-trends/2020/05/14/on-the-cusp-of-adulthood-and-facing-an-uncertain-future-what-we-know-about-gen-z-so-far-2/.

18. Sara Martinez, *How Gen Z Employees Evaluate Companies Based on Their Morals and Values*, UNTAPPED (June 27, 2022), https://www.untapped.io/blog/how-gen-z-employees-evaluate-companies.

19. Richard Fry & Kim Parker, *Early Benchmarks Show 'Post-Millennials' on Track to Be Most Diverse, Best Educated Generation Yet*, PEW RSCH. CTR. (Nov. 15, 2018), https://www.pewresearch.org/social-trends/2018/11/15/early-benchmarks-show-post-millennials-on-track-to-be-most-diverse-best-educated-generation-yet/.

20. CHRISTIE SMITH, STEPHANIE TURNER, & DELOITTE U. LEADERSHIP CTR. FOR INCLUSION, THE RADICAL TRANSFORMATION OF DIVERSITY AND INCLUSION: THE MILLENNIAL INFLUENCE 3-4 (2015), https://www2.deloitte.com/content/dam/Deloitte/us/Documents/about-deloitte/us-inclus-millennial-influence-120215.pdf; WORLD ECON. FORUM, *supra* note 9.

21. Juliet Bourke & Andrea Espedido, *Why Inclusive Leaders Are Good for Organizations, and How to Become One*, HARV. BUS. REV. (Mar. 29, 2019), https://hbr.org/2019/03/why-inclusive-leaders-are-good-for-organizations-and-how-to-become-one.

22. Emily Heaslip, *5 Benefits of Age Diversity* (Aug. 1, 2022), https://vervoe.com/age-diversity/; Katie Saba & Jacob Diker, *5 Benefits of Age Diversity in the Workplace*, JD SUPRA (July 20, 2021), https://www.jdsupra.com/legalnews/5-benefits-of-age-diversity-in-the-9504111/; Stefanie K. Johnson, *The Diversity Employers Need to Remember: Age Diversity*, FORBES (July 19, 2020), https://www.forbes.com/sites/nextavenue/2020/07/19/the-diversity-employers-need-to-remember-age-diversity/?sh=2c6aedcc4b6b.

23. Luisa Alemany & Freek Vermeulen, *Disability as a Source of Competitive Advantage: Employing People with Disabilities Can Significantly Improve an Organization*, HARV. BUS. REV. (July 1, 2023), https://hbr.org/2023/07/disability-as-a-source-of-competitive-advantage.

24. WORLD ECON. FORUM, *supra* note 10, at 6 (reporting a 20 percent increase in both); Rocío Lorenzo et al., *How Leadership Teams Boost Innovation*, BOS. CONSULTING GRP. (Jan. 23, 2018), https://www.bcg.com/publications/2018/how-diverse-leadership-teams-boost-innovation [hereinafter *How Leadership Teams Boost Innovation*]; Rocío Lorenzo et al., *The Mix That Matters: Innovation Through Diversity*, BOS. CONSULTING GRP. (Apr. 26, 2017), https://www.bcg.com/publications/2017/people-organization-leadership-talent-innovation-through-diversity-mix-that-matters [hereinafter *The Mix That Matters*]; *see also* Mohammed Hossain et al., *Do LGBT Workplace Diversity Policies Create Value for Firms?*, 167 J. BUS. ETHICS 775, 776 (2019).

25. *See* Gunter K. Stahl & Martha L. Maznevski, *Unraveling the Effects of Cultural Diversity in Teams: A Retrospective of Research on Multicultural Work Groups and an Agenda for Future Research*, 52 J. INT. BUS. STUD. 4, 4–22 (2021).

26. Maria Del Carmen Triana et al., *The Relationship Between Deep-Level Diversity and Team Performance: A Meta-Analysis of the Main Effect, Moderators, and Mediating Mechanisms*, 58 J. MGMT. STUD. 2137, 2139–42 (2021); Daan van Knippenberg

et al., *Synergy from Diversity: Managing Team Diversity to Enhance Performance*, 6 Behav. Sci. & Pol'y 75, 75–92 (2020).

27. Kara L. Hal et al., *A Four-Phase Model of Transdisciplinary Team-Based Research: Goals, Team Processes, and Strategies*, Translational Behav. Med. at 1, 14 (2022); Susan E. Jackson et al., *Understanding the Dynamics of Diversity in Decision-Making Teams, in* Richard A. Guzzo, Eduardo Salas, & Assocs., Team Effectiveness And Decision Making in Organizations 223–24 (1995).

28. PSFs of all kinds tout the importance of DEI and are attempting to make progress. *See, e.g., Diversity, Equity, and Inclusion at BCG: Our 2023 US Report*, Bos. Consulting Grp. (2023), https://www.bcg.com/about/commitments/diversity/us-diversity-equity-inclusion-report (detailing how they have "held [themselves] accountable to [their] commitment to embrace diverse perspectives, strive for equitable outcomes, and create an inclusive culture.").

29. *See* Erin Geiger Smith, *Wal-Mart Will Slash Firms That Don't Have Flex-Time Policies*, Bus. Insider (Oct. 27, 2009, 2:35 PM), https://www.businessinsider.com/wal-mart-will-slash-firms-that-dont-have-flex-time-policies-2009-10; Christopher J. Whelan & Neta Ziv, *Privatizing Professionalism: Client Control of Lawyers' Ethics*, 80 Fordham L. Rev. 2577, 2596–99 (2012).

30. *See* Caroline Spiezo, *Microsoft Raises Reward for Outside Law Firms That Promote Black and Latino Lawyers*, Reuters (Sept. 30, 2020, 2:14 PM), https://www.reuters.com/article/lawyer-diversity-microsoft/microsoft-raises-reward-for-outside-law-firms-that-promote-black-and-latino-lawyers-idUSL1N2GR1LH.

31. Ruiqi Chen, *HP Legal Chief Rivera: Demand Diversity, Law Firms Will Listen*, Bloomberg L. (Oct. 13, 2020, 6:01 AM), https://news.bloomberglaw.com/business-and-practice/hp-legal-chief-rivera-demand-diversity-law-firms-will-listen.

32. *Diversity Plan for Shell Legal Services–United States*, Minority Corp. Couns. Ass'n, https://mcca.com/resources/pathways-research/a-study-of-law-department-best-practices/diversity-plan-for-shell-legal-services/ (last visited Dec. 19, 2022).

33. *See Novartis Launches New Preferred Firm Program for Legal Services*, Novartis (Feb. 12, 2020), https://www.novartis.com/news/novartis-launches-new-preferred-firm-program-legal-services.

34. *See, e.g.,* Lisa Kirby & Caren Ulrich Stacy, *Client Call for Greater Diversity at Fever Pitch*, Am. Lawyer (July 17, 2017, 5:03 PM), https://www.law.com/sites/almstaff/2017/07/17/client-call-for-greater-diversity-at-fever-pitch/; Letter from Bradley Gayton, Senior Vice President & General Counsel, Coca-Cola Co., to U.S. Law Firms Supporting Coca-Cola Co. (Jan. 28, 2021) (on file with author); *see also* Ruiqi Chen, *Coke GC Tired of 'Good Intentions,' Wants Firm Diversity Now*, Bloomberg L. (Jan. 28, 2021, 4:15 PM), https://news.bloomberglaw.com/business-and-practice/coke-gc-tired-of-good-intentions-wants-law-firm-diversity-now; Debra Casens Weiss, *Afternoon Briefs: Coca-Cola GC Leaves after 8 Months; Wrongly Jailed Man Challenges 4000 Bill for Confinement*, Am. Bar Ass'n J. (April 22, 2021, 2:50 PM), https://www.abajournal.com/news/article/afternoon-briefs-coca

-cola-gc-leaves-after-8-months-wrongly-jailed-man-challenges-4000-bill
-for-confinement.

35. Virginia G. Essandoh, *Tear Up the Old Diversity Plan; Forget Just Doing Something. You Must Do Something Dramatically Different*, NAT'L L.J. (Nov. 5, 2007) (stating that 99 percent of the Am Law top 200 firms spend tens of thousands of dollars on programs promoting diversity); *see generally* MINORITY CORPORATE COUNSEL ASS'N, DO GOOD, DO WELL LIST (2015), https://mcca .com/wp-content/uploads/2017/05/2016-Do_Good_Do_Well-v01.pdf (showcasing law firms with successful DEI initiatives); *see also* Stacey, Zaretsky, *The First Biglaw Firm to Offer Billable Diversity Hours for All Timekeepers*, ABOVE THE LAW (Jan. 29, 2021) https://abovethelaw.com/2021/01/the-first-biglaw-firm -to-offer-billable-diversity-hours-for-all-timekeepers/.

36. Rebecca L. Sandefur, *Staying Power: The Persistence of Social Inequality in Shaping Lawyer Stratification and Lawyers' Persistence in the Profession*, 36 Sw. U. L. REV. 539, 545–46 (2007); *see 2022 National Lawyer Population Survey*, AM. BAR ASS'N (2022), https://vokalapress.ir/wp-content/uploads/2022/06/2022-national-lawyer -population-survey.pdf; *NALP Report Shows Small Gains of Diversity in Law Firms*, AM. LAWYER (Jan. 12, 2023), https://www.law.com/americanlawyer/2023/01/12/ nalp-report-shows-small-gains-of-diversity-in-law-firms/?kw=NALP%20 Report%20Shows%20Small%20Gains%20of%20Diversity%20in%20Law%20 Firms&utm_source=email&utm_medium=enl&utm_campaign=newsroomupdate& utm_content=202 (stating NALP 2022 results show that progress at the partnership level "continues to lag far behind that of associates and summer associates, with people of color and women comprising just 11.40 percent and 26.65 percent of all partners."); *See 2021 ABA MODEL DIVERSITY SURVEY*, AM. BAR ASS'N 8 (2021) https://www.americanbar.org/content/dam/aba/administrative/diversity -inclusion-center/2021-md-survey-2nd-edition.pdf; *see also* MINORITY CORPORATE COUNSEL ASS'N, THE LAW FIRM DIVERSITY SURVEY 7 (2023), https://mcca.com/wp -content/uploads/2021/12/2021-MCCA-Law-Firm-Diversity-Survey-Report.pdf.

37. For further discussion of the lack of diversity in the law marketplace despite calls to action by clients and efforts on the part of law firms, see Michele DeStefano, *Chicken or Egg, Diversity and Innovation in the Corporate Legal Marketplace*, 91 FORDHAM L. REV. 1209 (2023).

38. Ahva Sadeghi, *Why Insurance Companies Need To Recruit More Strategically*, FORBES (Feb. 24, 2023), https://www.forbes.com/sites/forbeshumanresourcescouncil/ 2023/02/24/why-insurance-companies-need-to-recruit-more-strategically/ ?sh=335bcfb3842b.

39. Alicia McElhaney, *Consulting Firms Are Overwhelmingly White, Data Show*, INSTITUTIONAL INV. (Dec. 10, 2020), https://www.institutionalinvestor.com/article/ b1plyvx3pjzw6d/Consulting-Firms-Are-Overwhelmingly-White-Data-Show (reporting that Diverse Asset Managers' Initiative Survey showed "on average, about 73 percent of consulting firms' employees are white and so are 80 percent of their

owners and partners.""); Fergus Navaratnam-Blair, *Management Consulting's Diversity Problem—and Why You Should Care*, DIVERSITYQ, (Sept. 24, 2020), https://diversityq .com/management-consultings-diversity-problem-and-why-you-should-care/.

40. Loreal Jiles et al., *Diversifying U.S. Accounting Talent: A Critical Imperative to Achieve Transformational Outcomes*, INST. MGMT. ACCTS. 16–19 (Oct. 12, 2021) (Report on file with author) (surveying over 3,000 professionals and demonstrating a diversity gap in the accounting profession).

41. Marty Swant, *New Ad Industry Diversity Data Provides a New Benchmark—And Room for Improvement*, FORBES (Sept. 22, 2020) https://www.forbes.com/sites/ martyswant/2020/09/22/new-ad-industry-diversity-data-provides-a-new -benchmark-and-room-for-improvement/?sh=305d67e535e4 (surveying sixty-five advertising, marketing, and PR agencies representing more than 40,000 employees and reporting a diversity gap); Angela Chitkara, *PR Agencies Need to Be More Diverse and Inclusive. Here's How to Start*, HARV. BUS. REV. (Apr. 12, 2018), https://hbr.org/2018/04/pr-agencies-need-to-be-more-diverse-and-inclusive -heres-how-to-start#:~:text=My%20interviews%20suggest%20five%20things, culture%20by%20conducting%20bias%20training; Patrick Coffee & Sean Czarnecki, *The PR Industry Continues to Struggle with Diversity*, BUS. INSIDER (June 17, 2020), https://www.businessinsider.com/the-pr-industry-continues-to-struggle-with -diversity-2020-6.

42. Tina Sha Paikeday & Jean Lee, *Unleashing the Power of Diversity Through Inclusive Leadership*, HARV. L. SCH. FORUM ON CORP. GOVERNANCE (May 20, 2019), https://corpgov.law.harvard.edu/2019/05/20/unleashing-the-power-of-diversity -through-inclusive-leadership/; *see also* Deborah L. Rhode, *Foreword: Diversity in the Legal Profession: A Comparative Perspective*, 83 FORDHAM L. REV. 2241, 2241–42 (2015) (highlighting firms' "organizational culture that do not support diversity" and "unconscious and concealed biases"); THE WOLTERS KLUWER FUTURE READY LAWYER: LEADING CHANGE SURVEY 23 (2022) (on file with author) (reporting that law firms rank a "diverse and inclusive" culture last); Jiles et al., *supra* note 41, at 18–20.

43. Paikeday & Lee, *supra* note 43; Jiles et al., *supra* note 40, at 18–20.

44. *The Top 10 Reasons Attorneys Go In-House*, LHH (May 23, 2023) https://www .lhh.com/us/en/insights/top-10-reasons-attorneys-go-in-house/; Olga V. Mack, *Understanding and Thriving in the Role of In-House Lawyers*, ABOVE THE LAW (Sept. 26, 2022) https://abovethelaw.com/2022/09/understanding-and-thriving -in-the-role-of-an-in-house-lawyer/; ALM Media, *Are Legal Departments Really Better Than Firms at Diversity?*, LAW.COM (Mar. 9, 2019), https://www.yahoo.com/ now/legal-departments-really-better-firms-030230565.html (explaining that legal departments—like law firms—have subjective assignment or mentorship models that enable similar biases to impact which lawyers get those opportunities).

45. *Unleashing the Human Element at Work: Transforming Workplaces Through Recognition*, WORKHUMAN, (May 11, 2022), https://www.workhuman.com/resources/

reports-guides/unleashing-the-human-element-at-work-transforming
-workplaces-through-recognition.

46. *See, e.g.,* Madison Hoff, *The Great Resignation Is Giving Way to the 'Big Stay' as Job-Hopping Slows Down,* Bus. Insider (May 13, 2023), https://www.business insider.com/quit-job-great-resignation-big-stay-changing-jobs-market-2023-5.

47. Ranjay Gulati, *The Great Resignation or the Great Rethink?,* Harv. Bus. Rev. (Mar. 22, 2022), https://hbr.org/2022/03/the-great-resignation-or-the-great-rethink

48. Joseph Fuller & William Kerr, *The Great Resignation Didn't Start with the Pandemic,* Harv. Bus. Rev. (Mar. 13, 2022), https://hbr.org/2022/03/the-great-resignation -didnt-start-with-the-pandemic (claiming that the Great Resignation may have been provoked by the pandemic but that it is actually a "continuation of a long-term trend").

49. *ESG Assets Rising to $50 Trillion Will Reshape $140.5 Trillion of Global AUM by 2025, Finds Bloomberg Intelligence,* Bloomberg (July 21, 2021), https://www.bloomberg .com/company/press/esg-assets-rising-to-50-trillion-will-reshape-140-5 -trillion-of-global-aum-by-2025-finds-bloomberg-intelligence/.

50. Joel Makower, *Inside the War for ESG Talent,* GreenBiz, July 19, 2021, https:// www.greenbiz.com/article/inside-war-esg-talent.

51. Robert G. Eccles & Alison Taylor, *The Evolving Role of Chief Sustainability Officers,* Harv. Bus. Rev., July 1, 2023, https://hbr.org/2023/07/the-evolving -role-of-chief-sustainability-officers.

52. Vivienne Walt, *A Top CEO Was Ousted After Making His Company More Environmentally Conscious. Now He's Speaking Out,* Time (Nov. 21, 2021), https://time .com/6121684/emmanuel-faber-danone-interview/#.

53. Dambisa Moyo, *10 ESG Questions Companies Need to Answer,* Harv. Bus. Rev. (Jan. 3, 2022), https://hbr.org/2022/01/10-esg-questions-companies-need-to -answer.

54. Walt, *supra* note 52.

55. Mark R. Kramer & Marc W. Pfitzer, *The Essential Link Between ESG Targets & Financial Performance,* Harv. Bus. Rev., Sept. –Oct. 2022, at 128, 132.

56. Pippa Stevens, *1 in 4 Investing Dollars Are Now Going into ESG Strategies. How to Play it, According to Cowen,* CNBC (Mar. 18, 2021), https://www.cnbc .com/2021/03/18/sustainable-strategies-attract-1-in-4-investing-dollars .html?ref=ardentprivacy.ai. Research has shown that in 2020, one in every four dollars invested in the United States was allocated into sustainable companies using an ESG evaluation and that sustainable funds attracted a record $51.1 billion in investments. *Id.*

57. Stephanie Ebbs, *What Are ESG and 'Woke Capitalism'? State Treasurers Weigh in on Fight Over Where Tax Money Goes: The Divide Is Over Whether ESG Investing Is Socially Conscious or Partisan,* ABC News (Oct. 12, 2022), https://abcnews.go.com/ Politics/esg-woke-capitalism-state-treasurers-weigh-fight-tax/story?id=91114475.

58. Eccles & Taylor, *supra* note 51.

59. Sanjai Bhagat, *An Inconvenient Truth About ESG Investing*, Harv. Bus. Rev. (Mar. 31, 2022), https://hbr.org/2022/03/an-inconvenient-truth-about-esg-investing.

60. Alex Castro, *Basecamp CEO Apologizes to Staff in New Post: 'We Have a Lot to Learn,'* The Verge (Apr. 27, 2021), https://www.theverge.com/2021/5/4/22419799/basecamp-ceo-apologizes-staff-new-post; Luke Rosiak, *Software Firm Rejects Woke Workplace, Saying 'We Are Not A Social Impact Company,'* Daily Wire (Apr. 27, 2021), https://www.dailywire.com/news/basecamp-rejects-woke-workplace-we-are-not-a-social-impact-company.

61. *What Is the "G" in ESG?*, S&P Global (Feb. 24, 2020), https://www.spglobal.com/en/research-insights/articles/what-is-the-g-in-esg.

62. Eccles & Taylor, *supra* note 51.

63. *Id.* at 801.

64. *SEC Proposes Rules to Enhance and Standardize Climate-Related Disclosures for Investors*, SEC (Mar. 21, 2022), https://www.sec.gov/news/press-release/2022-46.

65. *Corporate Sustainability Reporting*, Eur. Comm'n: Finance, https://finance.ec.europa.eu/capital-markets-union-and-financial-markets/company-reporting-and-auditing/company-reporting/corporate-sustainability-reporting_en.

66. *New Climate-Related Financial Disclosure Regulations for UK Companies*, Lexology (Apr. 25, 2022), https://www.lexology.com/library/detail.aspx?g=b72fa6bf-ad2d-4dc1-aff8-4504898efd9e.

67. Audrey Jenna & Rona F. Davis, *An Evolving ESG Landscape for Professional Service Firms*, AON (July 2022), https://www.aon.com/risk-services/professional-services/an-evolving-esg-landscape-for-professional-service-firms.

68. CC Client Interviewee 12.

69. *See* Moyo, *supra* note 53.

70. Michele DeStefano, Bjarne Tellman, & Daniel Wu, *Don't Let the Digital Tail Wag the Transformation Dog: A Digital Transformation Roadmap for Corporate Counsel*, 17 J. Bus. Tech. L. Rev. 183, 255 (2022). *See, e.g.,* Thibaut Millet, *How to Weave ESG Factors Into Your Digital Strategy*, EY (Jan. 2020), https://www.ey.com/en_ca/mining-metals/how-to-weave-esg-factors-into-your-digital-strategy; Peter Gassmann & Colm Kelly, *How ESG Will Drive the Next Wave of Transformation*, PWC (Jan. 2021), https://www.pwc.com/gx/en/issues/reinventing-the-future/take-on-tomorrow/esg-transformation.html; *see also* World Econ. Forum, Digital Culture: The Driving Force of Digital Transformation 7 (2021), https://www3.weforum.org/docs/WEF_Digital_Culture_Guidebook_2021.pdf [hereinafter WEF 2021 Report, Digital Culture]; Liz Davis, *5 Key Takeaways for a Successful ESG Digital Transformation*, Benchmark Gensuite (Feb. 2, 2021), https://benchmarkgensuite.com/ehs-blog/5-key-takeaways-for-a-successful-esg-digital-transformation/; Kerry Clarke-Potter, *ESG Should Be at the Core of Every Business' Digital Strategy*, Blockchain Blog (Nov. 19, 2020), https://blockheadtechnologies.com/esg-should-be-at-the-core-of-every-business-digital-strategy. (last visited July 25, 2021).

71. DT Interview #5.

72. For an easy to understand description of how generative AI is different than what is called analytical AI or Predictive Analytics, see Arslan H, *Predictive Analytics vs Generative AI: Explanation with 10 Differences*, AI Munch (Apr. 25, 2023) https://www.aimunch.com/what-is-predictive-analytics-vs-generative-ai/ ("Predictive analytics primarily supports decision-making processes by providing forecasts and insights that enable risk mitigation, customer insight, and operational optimization. Generative AI, on the other hand, is used for creative generation and innovation, producing novel outputs for applications like content creation, design, and data augmentation.").

73. For an easy to understand overview of the relationship between AI, generative AI, LLM, GPT, and Chat GPT see Nicola Shaver, LinkedIn, https://www.linkedin.com/posts/nicola-shaver_ai-llms-generativeai-activity-7062045828814663681-RPXa/?trk=public_profile_post_view (last visited Aug. 22, 2023, 2:21 p.m.) (defining LLM as a language model consisting of a neural network with many parameters that has been pretrained on large quantities of text using self-supervised or semisupervised learning—forms of machine learning—LLMs are a type of generative AI since they generate new combinations of text).

74. Mark Wilson, *ChatGPT Explained: Everything You Need to Know About the AI Chatbot* (Mar. 15, 2023), https://www.techradar.com/news/chatgpt-explained.

75. Irving John Good, *Speculations Concerning the First Ultraintelligent Machine*, in Advances in Computers 31, 31–88 (Franz L. Alt and Morris Rubinoff eds., 1965).

76. Danielle Chemtob, *Forbes Daily: Artificial Intelligence: What You Need to Know*, Forbes (July 20, 2023), https://www.forbes.com/sites/daniellechemtob/2023/07/20/forbes-daily-artificial-intelligence-and-what-you-need-to-know/?sh=5510cfa3ba31.

77. Adam Fletcher, The Freedom Figure: How to Work Less, Live More, and Thrive in the Digital Age (2016).

78. Nikolai Vassev, *Artificial Intelligence and the Future of Humans*, Forbes (May 6, 2021), https://www.forbes.com/sites/forbestechcouncil/2021/05/06/artificial-intelligence-and-the-future-of-humans/?sh=1d443a1b6e3b.

79. Richard Susskind, *AI in the Law: Six Thoughts*, LinkedIn (July 5, 2023), https://www.linkedin.com/pulse/ai-law-six-thoughts-richard-susskind/.

80. For an easy to understand explanation of the difference between predictive analytics and AI (which includes machine learning), see Michael Rutty, *Predictive Analytics vs. AI: Why the Difference Matters*, TechBeacon, https://techbeacon.com/enterprise-it/predictive-analytics-vs-ai-why-difference-matters (last visited Aug. 22, 2023, 2:52 p.m.).

81. Aebra Coe, *Will a Robot Lawyer Take Your Job? What AI Means for You*, Law360 (May 31 2017), https://www.law360.com/technology/articles/930096/will-a-robot-lawyer-take-your-job-what-ai-means-for-you?nl_pk=0b4f7f93-5efc-420e-94f0-98e085b43c37&utm_source=newsletter&utm_medium=email&utm_campaign=technology&read_more=1; Eleanor Weaver, *Big Four vs Big Law: How AI Is*

Raising the Stakes in the Legal Market, Lawyer Monthly, LawyerMonthly (Mar. 18 2021), https://www.lawyer-monthly.com/2021/03/big-four-vs-big-law-how-ai-is -raising-the-stakes-in-the-legal-market/.

82. Mike Thomas, *25 AI Insurance Examples to Know*, BuiltIn (Mar. 14, 2023), https:// builtin.com/artificial-intelligence/ai-insurance.

83. Vishal Chawla, *Why the Big Four Audit Firms PwC, EY, Deloitte & KPMG Are Investing Heavily in AI*, Endless Origins, (Jan. 7, 2020), https://analyticsindia mag.com/why-the-big-four-audit-firms-pwc-ey-deloitte-kpmg-are-investing -heavily-in-artificial-intelligenc/; Ben Kepess, ComputerWorld (Mar. 16, 2016), https://www.computerworld.com/article/3042536/big-four-accounting-firms -delve-into-artificial-intelligence.html.

84. Alyssa Schroer, *AI in Marketing and Advertising: 19 Examples to Know* (Apr. 13, 2023), https://builtin.com/artificial-intelligence/ai-in-marketing-advertising.

85. Tojin T. Eapen et al., *How Generative AI Can Augment Human Creativity: Use It to Promote Divergent Thinking*, Harv. Bus. Rev. (July 1, 2023), https://hbr .org/2023/07/how-generative-ai-can-augment-human-creativity.

86. *Id.*

87. *Id.*

88. For a great summary of the benefits of AI for professional service firms, see Arpan Patra, *How AI Overcomes the Professional Services Industry's Challenges*, ReadWrite (Mar. 31 2023), https://readwrite.com/how-ai-overcomes-the-professional -services-industrys-challenges/#:~:text=Professional%20services%20firms%20 can%20utilize%20AI-based%20technologies%20to,skills%20and%20can%20 help%20create%20a%20value-based%20system.

89. Susskind, *supra* note 79.

90. *See, e.g.*, Vishes Raisinghani, *Do Not Go to Law School: This Fund Manager Warns that the Legal Field Is in Big Trouble—Says Folks Are Using ChatGPT for Complex Contracts. Time to Get into Trades?*, Yahoo (June 21, 2023), https://moneywise.com/ employment/will-ai-make-law-school-pointless; Eleanor Lightbody & Forbes Tech. Council, *Here's Why Generative AI isn't Coming for Lawyers*, Forbes (May 25, 2023), https://www.forbes.com/sites/forbestechcouncil/2023/05/25/heres -why-generative-ai-isnt-coming-for-lawyers/; Ramnath Balasubramanian et al., *Insurance 2030—The Impact of AI on the Future of Insurance*, McKinsey (Mar. 12, 2021), https://www.mckinsey.com/industries/financial-services/our-insights/ insurance-2030-the-impact-of-ai-on-the-future-of-insurance.

91. Thomas, *supra* note 83; Sian Townson, *AI Can Make Bank Loans More Fair*, Harv. Bus. Rev., (Nov. 6, 2020), https://hbr.org/2020/11/ai-can-make-bank-loans-more-fair.

92. *See, e.g.*, Don Fancher et al., *AI Model Bias Can Damage Trust More Than You Know. But It Doesn't Have To*, Deloitte (Dec. 8, 2021), https://www2.deloitte.com/us/ en/insights/focus/cognitive-technologies/ai-model-bias.html; Kristin Johnson, Frank Pasquale & Jennifer Chapman, *Artificial Intelligence, Machine Learning, and Bias in Finance: Toward Responsible Innovation*, 88 Fordham. L. Rev. 499, 505, 512

(2019); James Manika, Jake Silberg & Brittany Presten, *What Do We Do About the Biases in AI*, Harv. Bus. Rev. (Oct. 25, 2019), https://hbr.org/2019/10/what-do -we-do-about-the-biases-in-ai. *Cf.* Drew Simshaw, *Access to AI Justice: Avoiding an Inequitable Two-Tiered System of Legal Services*, 24 Yale. J.L. & Tech. 150, 199–202 (2022) (exploring the harmful effects that can result from bias used in AI-driven legal processes but contending that "[e]ffectively-calibrated AI, on the other hand, can actually help combat bias."). *But see* Frida Polli & Will Uppington, *Resetting the Conventional Wisdom: Using AI to Reduce Bias*, Informs (Aug. 24, 2022), https:// pubsonline.informs.org/do/10.1287/LYTX.2022.05.02/full/; Kate Crawford, *The Hidden Biases in Big Data*, Harv. Bus. Rev. (Apr. 1, 2013), https://hbr.org/2013/04/ the-hidden-biases-in-big-data.

93. Robert Bartlett et al., *Consumer-Lending Discrimination in the FinTech Era*, Haas Sch. Bus. U.C. Berkeley (Nov. 2019), http://faculty.haas.berkeley.edu/morse/ research/papers/discrim.pdf

94. Richard Susskind & Daniel Susskind, *Generative AI Will Upend the Professions*, Fin. Times (June 18, 2023), https://www.ft.com/content/96a1877f-0bbb -48c7-be8f-4fed437810e8.

95. Peter Hayes & Justin Wise, *Attorneys Must Certify AI Policy Compliance, Judge Orders*, Bloomberg L. (May 31, 2023), https://news.bloomberglaw.com/ business-and-practice/attorneys-must-certify-ai-policy-compliance-judge-orders.

96. Jack Queen, *Comedian Sarah Silverman Sues Meta, Open AI for Copyright Infringement*, Ins. J. (July 10, 2023), https://www.insurancejournal.com/news/ national/2023/07/10/729351.htm.

97. TY Roush, *FTC Investigating ChatGPT Maker OpenAI for Providing False Information in Chaat Results, Report Says*, Forbes (July 13, 2022), https://www.forbes .com/sites/tylerroush/2023/07/13/ftc-investigating-chatgpt-maker-openai-for -providing-false-information-report-says/?utm_source=newsletter&utm _medium=email&utm_campaign=dailydozen&cdlcid=63a21af8f9c34d 131050644c&section=tech&sh=77cb23b44

98. Rhys Dipshan, *A Legal and Regulatory Reckoning for Generative AI*, Law.com: Barometer (June 8 2023), https://www.law.com/2023/06/08/a-legal-and -regulatory-reckoning-for-generative-ai/.

99. Jacques Bughin et al., *The Case for Digital Reinvention*, McKinsey Dig. (Feb. 9, 2017), https://www.mckinsey.com/capabilities/mckinsey-digital/our-insights/the -case-for-digital-reinvention (reporting that professional services and financial services are among the four lowest for digital penetration).

100. For a definition of AI, see B.J. Copeland, *Artificial Intelligence*, Britannica (Mar. 18, 2022), https://www.britannica.com/technology/artificial-intelligence (defining AI as "the ability of a digital computer or computer-controlled robot to perform tasks commonly associated with intelligent beings"). For a discussion of how to define AI, see IBM Cloud Education, *Artificial Intelligence*, IBM (June 3, 2020), https://www.ibm.com/cloud/learn/what-is-artificial-intelligence.

101. For a comprehensive discussion of how AI is transforming the corporation and the implications thereof, *see* MARCO IANSITI & KARIM R. LAKHANI, COMPETING IN THE AGE OF AI: STRATEGY AND LEADERSHIP WHEN ALGORITHMS AND NETWORKS RUN THE WORLD (2020).
102. DeStefano, Tellman & Wu, *supra* note 70, *at* 197–99.
103. ERIC LAMARRE ET AL., REWIRED: THE McKINSEY GUIDE TO OUTCOMPETING IN THE AGE OF DIGITAL AND AI 1–2, 6 (2023).
104. Silvio Palumbo and David Edelman, *What Smart Companies Know About integrating AI: Talent and Data Are Just as Important as Technology*, HARV. BUS. REV. (July 1, 2023), https://hbr.org/2023/07/what-smart-companies-know-about-integrating-ai.
105. DeStefano, Tellman & Wu, *supra* note 71, at 194, 235–23; KPMG INT'L COOP., DESTINATION (UN)KNOWN: KEY STEPS TO GUIDE YOUR DIGITAL TRANSFORMATION JOURNEY, at 8 (2017), https://assets.kpmg/content/dam/kpmg/uk/pdf/2017/09/digital_transformation_guide_2017.pdf (describing what KPMG identifies as the four steps to digital transformation; the third step is articulating an enterprise-wide operational strategy). For more discussion, *see infra* Part I.
106. ERNST & YOUNG, HOW HAS ADVERSITY BECOME THE SPRINGBOARD FOR GROWTH FOR AUSTRALIAN AND NEW ZEALAND CEOS?: CEO IMPERATIVE STUDY 2021, PART 1, at 18 (2021), ey-the-ceo-imperative-study-2021.pdf; WEF 2021 REPORT, DIGITAL CULTURE, *supra* note 71, at 7–11 (explaining that "[e]xisting organizational culture is often at odds with digital culture (collaboration, innovation, data-driven insights and customer-centricity). That's why it is important to recognize the behaviors, mindsets, values and organizational practices that inhibit or promote its adoption.").
107. Experts in the field agree that DT and DT strategy are multifaceted. Rogers, for instance, identifies five domains of DT: customers, competition, data, innovation, and value. DAVID L. ROGERS, THE DIGITAL TRANSFORMATION PLAYBOOK: RETHINK YOUR BUSINESS FOR THE DIGITAL AGE 1–19 (2016).
108. LAMARRE ET AL., *supra* note 103, at 6.
109. GOLDMAN SACHS, GLOBAL ECONOMICS ANALYST. THE POTENTIALLY LARGE EFFECTS OF ARTIFICIAL INTELLIGENCE ON ECONOMIC GROWTH, 1, 10 (Mar. 26, 2023), https://www.gspublishing.com/content/research/en/reports/2023/03/27/d64e052b-0f6e-45d7-967b-d7be35fabd16.html.
110. Chemtob, *supra* note 76.
111. For a longer discussion of these three forces continuing to transform global industries and occupations *see generally* WORLD ECON. FORUM, THE FUTURE OF JOBS REPORT: EMPLOYMENT, SKILLS AND WORKFORCE STRATEGY FOR THE FOURTH INDUSTRIAL REVOLUTION, at v (2016) [hereinafter 2016 WEF REPORT].
112. ERNST & YOUNG, HOW CAN TODAY'S CEO BRIDGE THE GAPS TO REALIZE TOMORROW'S OPPORTUNITIES?: CEO IMPERATIVE STUDY 2021, PART 2, at 10 (2021), https://assets.ey.com/content/dam/ey-sites/ey-com/en_gl/topics/ceo-imperative-study/ey-ceo-imperative-study-part-2.pdf (explaining that there are gaps).

113. DeStefano, *supra* note 37, at 1233–38.

114. Nathan Furr & Jeffrey H. Dyer, *Leading Your Team into the Unknown*, Harv. Bus. Rev. (Dec. 1, 2014), https://hbr.org/2014/12/leading-your-team-into-the -unknown; Donald J. Polden, *Lawyers Leadership and Innovation*, 58 Santa Clara L. Rev. 427, 443-446 (2018) (explaining the necessary environment, change management, and monitoring required by leaders and describing the large barriers).

115. *Id.*; David Horth & Dan Buchner, Innovative Leadership: How to Use Innovation to Lead Effectively, Work Collaboratively, and Drive Results 6–10 (2014) (ebook).

116. *See generally* Bernadette Dillon & Juliet Bourke, *The Six Signature Traits of Inclusive Leadership: Thriving in a Diverse New World*, Deloitte Univ. Press 8 (2016), https://www2.deloitte.com/content/dam/Deloitte/au/Documents/human -capital/deloitte-au-hc-six-signature-traits-inclusive-leadership-020516 .pdf; Katherine Graham-Leviss, *The 5 Skills That Innovative Leaders Have in Common*, Harv. Bus. Rev. (Dec. 20, 2016), https://hbr.org/2016/12/the-5 -skills-that-innovative-leaders-have-in-common.

117. The adaptive leadership model was first developed by Harvard Professor Ronald Heifetz. *See generally* Ronald Heifetz, Leadership Without Easy Answers (Harv. Univ. Press, 2009) (1994). It was further developed in a second book coauthored by Professor Heifetz and Professor Marty Linsky. *See generally* Ronald Heifetz & Marty Linksy, Leadership On the Line: Staying Alive Through the Dangers of Leading (2002); *see also* Ben Ramalingham et al., *5 Principles to Guide Adaptive Leadership*, Harv. Bus. Rev. (Sept. 11, 2020), https://hbr. org/2020/09/5-principles-to-guide-adaptive-leadership.

118. Susskind & Susskind, *supra* note 94.

119. J. D. Salinger, *supra* note 1, at 122.

120. Susskind & Susskind, *supra* note 94.

121. Nicky Wakefiled & Karen Pastakia, *Leadership Awakened*, Deloitte (Feb. 29, 2016), https://www2.deloitte.com/us/en/insights/focus/human-capital-trends/2016/ identifying-future-business-leaders-leadership.html.

122. Milhnea Moldoveanu & Das Narayandas, *The Future of Leadership Development*, Harv. Bus. Rev., Mar.–Apr. 2019, at 46 ("The need for leadership development has never been more urgent."); Laci Loew, Improving Leadership Development: The Time to Act Is Now, Brandon Hall Grp. (Jul. 30, 2015) (finding that 84 percent of organizations anticipate a shortfall of leaders in the next 5 years), https://trainingmag.com/ improving-leadership-development-the-time-to-act-is-now/. For a summary of Brandon Hall's leadership study see Robert Velasquez, *13 Shocking Leadership Development Statistics*, Infopro Learning (Jul. 13, 2020), https://www.infoprolearning .com/infographic/13-shocking-leadership-development-statistics-infopro-learning.

123. Dev. Dimensions Inc., Global Leadership Forecast 2023, at 11 (2023), https:// media.ddiworld.com/research/glf2023.pdf (surveying nearly 14,000 global leaders); Stephanie Neal, *CEO Priorities in 2023: 3 Critical Talent Trends*, DDIWorld .com, (Feb. 9, 2023), https://www.ddiworld.com/blog/ceo-priorities-in-2023

(explaining that only 12 percent of organizations report that they have quality professionals to fill critical leadership positions).

124. Dev. Dimensions Inc., *supra* note 124, at 9 (surveying nearly 14,000 global leaders); *New DDI Study Reveals Largest Drop in Leadership Confidence in a Decade*, Dev. Dimensions Inc., (Feb. 8, 2023), https://www.ddiworld.com/about/media/global-leadership-forecast-2023.

125. Jean Brittain Leslie, The Leadership Gap: What You Need, And Still Don't Have, When it Comes to Leadership Talent, Ctr. for Creative Leadership, 2, 8–11 (2015) https://cclinnovation.org/wp-content/uploads/2020/03/leadership-gap-what-you-need.pdf.

126. *See Psychological Safety and the Critical Role of Leadership Development*, McKinsey & Co. (Feb. 11, 2021), https://www.mckinsey.com/capabilities/people-and-organizational-performance/our-insights/psychological-safety-and-the-critical-role-of-leadership-development (reporting that "[f]ew leaders display the behaviors that can instill psychological safety, and employee experiences vary greatly depending on how leaders act."); Northeastern Graduate Programs Staff, *Top 5 Leadership Skills for the Workplace of Tomorrow*, Ne. Univ. Graduate Programs (Sept. 4, 2019), https://www.northeastern.edu/graduate/blog/essential-leadership-skills-for-tomorrow; Ernst & Young, How Has Adversity Become the Springboard to Growth for CEOs?: CEO Imperative Study 2021, EYQ third edition, at 18 (2021), ey-ceo-imperative-study-2021.pdf. (reporting that only "44% affirm having an innovation mindset across the organization; only 32% say mid-level leadership personally models shared purpose and visions, and a meager 28% say they create diverse and inclusive teams at all levels.").

127. Neal, *supra* note 6.

128. Loew, *supra* note 125; Dev. Dimensions Inc., *supra* note 124, at 5; Neal, *supra* note 7 (noting that the top concerns are retaining talent, and keeping talent engaged and developing the next generation of leaders who need to be at the helm on these challenges).

Chapter 2

1. Dov Seidman, *How: Why How We Do Anything Means Everything* (expanded ed. 2011).

2. *See* John Cawley & Jim Korkis, *Encyclopedia of Cartoon Superstars: Mr. Magoo*, Cataroo, http://www.cataroo.com/cst_MAGOO.html (last visited Jan. 27, 2022). Mr. Magoo is known for his good-hearted nature that drives him on adventures. *See id.* What makes Mr. Magoo unique in his character is that Magoo "stumbles" through life with little awareness of what is going on. *See id.* Most notably he confused a bear for his nephew in a racoon coat. Despite his silliness and lack of awareness, he is incredibly popular by both the other characters in his cartoon and the viewers. *See id.*

3. LawWithoutWalls (LWOW) is a part-virtual, experiential learning initiative designed for practicing and aspiring legal and business professionals who seek to enhance their cross-cultural, creative teaming, problem finding and solving,

and leadership skills while hacking alongside kindred spirits who share a passion for intrapreneurship and community exchange. LWOW unites law and business professionals with students from 30 law and business schools around the world to co-create innovative solutions to problems at the intersection of law+business+technology using The 3-4-5 Method™ developed by its founder, Professor Michele DeStefano. Leveraging intergenerational, cross-cultural, multidisciplinary exchange and design thinking principles, LWOW changes mindsets, skillsets, and behaviors. Specifically, LWOW focuses on: upskilling and re-skilling, transforming culture and relationships, creating innovative solutions to real business of law and social justice problems, and building a change-agency community. For more information, see https://lawwithoutwalls.org/.

4. *See generally*, RICHARD SUSSKIND AND DANIEL SUSSKIND, THE FUTURE OF THE PROFESSIONS: HOW TECHNOLOGY WILL TRANSFORM THE WORK OF HUMAN EXPERTS (updated ed. 2022).

5. The adaptive leadership model was first developed by Harvard Professor Ronald Heifetz. *See generally*, RONALD HEIFETZ, LEADERSHIP WITHOUT EASY ANSWERS (Harv. Univ. Press, 2009) (1994) [hereinafter WITHOUT EASY ANSWERS]. It was further developed in a second book coauthored by Professor Heifetz and Professor Marty Linsky. *See generally*, RONALD HEIFETZ & MARTY LINKSY, LEADERSHIP ON THE LINE: STAYING ALIVE THROUGH THE DANGERS OF LEADING (2002) [hereinafter ON THE LINE]. To learn more about how to apply adaptive leadership, read RONALD HEIFETZ ET AL., THE PRACTICE OF ADAPTIVE LEADERSHIP: TOOLS AND TACTICS FOR CHANGING YOUR ORGANIZATION AND THE WORLD (2009) [hereinafter TOOLS AND TACTICS] and consider attending Harvard Law School's Executive Education Program on Adaptive Leadership in which Ron Heifetz is a faculty member. *See* Harv. Law School Exec. Educ., *Adaptive Leadership: Lawyers Driving Change*, https://execed.law.harvard.edu/masterclass/adaptiveleadership/ (last visited Jul. 7, 2022).

6. *See, e.g.*, Tim Brown, *Design Thinking*, HARV. BUS. REV., June 2008, at 84, 92 (explaining that "[a]s more of our basic needs are met, we increasingly expect sophisticated experiences that are emotionally satisfying and meaningful. These experiences will not be simple products. They will be complex combinations of products, services, spaces, and information.").

7. MICHELE DESTEFANO, LEGAL UPHEAVAL: A GUIDE TO CREATIVITY, COLLABORATION, AND INNOVATION 241-65 (John Palmer et al. eds., 2018).

8. "Thumbs-up smiley face" and "Thumbs-down smiley face" icons are generated by *Icons Mind*. Image# 68448, https://thenounproject.com/icon/like-68448/; Image# 68446, https://thenounproject.com/icon/dislike-68446/.

9. Henrik Kniberg, *Making Sense of MVP (Minimum Viable Product)—and Why I Prefer Earliest Testable/Usable/Lovable*, CRISP. (Jan. 25, 2016, 12:14 PM), https://blog.crisp.se/2016/01/25/henrikkniberg/making-sense-of-mvp. Note: I was first introduced to this chart by a presentation delivered by Professor David

Wilkins at Harvard Law School in one of the Executive Education programs we both teach.

10. Client Interviewee 30 ("It sounds trite, but I am amazed how many times it is missed in practice.").

11. Client Interviewee 39.

12. CC Client Interviewee 12.

13. *Amplifying the Voice of the Client in Law Firms*, LEXISNEXIS 5-7 (2017).

14. *See generally* JENNIFER CURRENCE, DEVELOPING BUSINESS ACUMEN: MAKING AN IMPACT IN SMALL BUSINESS HR (2017) (discussing the need for HR professionals to have business acumen and providing recommendations for how to develop it); *see also* Lin Grensing-Pophal, *HR Skills Aren't Enough: Why CHROs Need Business Acumen*, FORBES (Feb. 23, 2018), https://www.forbes.com/sites/adp/2018/02/23/hr-skills-arent-enough-why-chros-need-business-acumen/.

15. CC Client Interviewee 11.

16. Client Interviewee 25.

17. Client Interviewee 33.

18. CC Client Interviewee 12.

19. Max Hübner, *The Case of PGGM: The Transformational Legal Department*, PGGM NV 123, 128_ https://files.m17.mailplus.nl/user317000253/2437/Hubner%20inhouse%20counsel.pdf (last visited July 6, 2023).

20. Client Interviewee 9.

21. Hübner, *supra* note 18.

22. Reena SenGupta, *Legal Success Comes from Turning Orthodoxies on Their Heads*, FINANCIAL TIMES (June 2, 2016), https://www.ft.com/content/48a7b0a2-2069-11e6-aa98-db1e01fabc0c; *see also* Herbert Smith Freehills Wins Financial Times Top Asia Pacific Innovation Award (June 14, 2016), https://www.herbertsmithfreehills.com/news/herbert-smith-freehills-wins-financial-times-top-asia-pacific-innovation-award.

23. Jamie Smyth, *Australian Law Firms—Up from Down Under: Fierce Competition Has Made Them Inventive at Home and Ambitious Overseas*, FINANCIAL TIMES (June 1, 2017), https://www.ft.com/content/734c3c98-2922-11e7-bc4b-5528796fe35c.

24. Law Firm Partner Interviewees confirm this over and over again. *See, e.g.*, PSF Interviewee (Law Firm Partner) 23 ("At the end of the day, what they want you to do is run their business and tell them, confidently what to do . . . with instantaneous responsiveness.").

25. Client Interviewee 29.

26. Steven Walker, *6 Things Modern GCs Really Want: From Their Law Firms*, LINKEDIN (November 27, 2017), https://www.linkedin.com/pulse/6-things-modern-gcs-really-want-from-law-firms-steven-walker/ (making a similar point, "Once again, this is an opportunity for law firms. Many GCs would welcome guidance from their trusted partner law firms on technology they might look at. Firms are in a unique position to provide expertise and communicate a point of view; they are vendor-agnostic and have a history of service delivery for established

clients, putting them in an excellent position to support their clients on technology strategies and requirements. Such services may not be core to today's law firms and may even seem incongruous or beyond their current capabilities, but they are most certainly going to be core to the Big 4 and the new generation of alternative legal service providers.").

27. Client Interviewee 29.

28. Leo Staub, *8 Steps to Management Excellence in Law Firms, The Comprehensive St. Gallen Approach* 38 (2014) (unpublished manuscript, on file with author) (pointing out that the "strategic challenge" for the lawyer is to "stabilize this sporadic contact with the client" and "develop a significantly more intensive, and above all more permanent, relationship with the client").

29. Client Interviewee 31.

30. Justin Connor, *Leading General Counsel Speak About the GC Summit*, LINKEDIN (May 5, 2017), https://www.linkedin.com/pulse/leading-general-counsel-speak -gc-summit-justin-connor/.

31. Client Interviewee 33.

32. Bernadette Dillon & Juliet Bourke, *The Six Signature Traits of Inclusive Leadership: Thriving in a Diverse New World*, DELOITTE (April 4, 2016), https://www2 .deloitte.com/za/en/insights/topics/talent/six-signature-traits-of-inclusive -leadership.html (identifying the six essential traits of inclusive leaders as courage, cognizance, commitment, curiosity, cultural intelligence, and collaboration); Daniel Goleman, *What Makes a Leader?*, HARV. BUS. REV. (Jan. 2004), https://hbr .org/2004/01/what-makes-a-leader; Sunnie Giles, *The Most Important Leadership Competencies, According to Leaders Around the World*, HARV. BUS. REV. (Mar. 15, 2016), https://hbr.org/2016/03/the-most-important-leadership-competencies- according-to-leaders-around-the-world; Katherine Graham-Leviss, *The 5 Skills That Innovative Leaders Have in Common*, HARV. BUS. REV. (Dec. 20, 2016), https:// hbr.org/2016/12/the-5-skills-that-innovative-leaders-have-in-common; Bill McBean, *The 5 Characteristics of Great Leaders*, FAST COMPANY (Jan. 24, 2013), https://www.fastcompany.com/3004914/5-characteristics-great-leaders; Olivia Fox Cabane & Judah Pollack, *Your Brain Has A 'Delete' Button—Here's How to Use It*, FAST COMPANY (May 11, 2016), https://www.fastcompany.com/3059634/ your-brain-has-a-delete-button-heres-how-to-use-it; Ben Ramalingham et al, *5 Principles to Guide Adaptive Leadership*, HARV. BUS. REV. (Sept. 11, 2020), https:// hbr.org/2020/09/5-principles-to-guide-adaptive-leadership. *See also supra* note 4 (citing to the Harvard professor who developed the adaptive leadership model).

33. TINA SEELIG, WHAT I WISH I KNEW WHEN I WAS 20: A CRASH COURSE ON MAKING YOUR PLACE IN THE WORLD 8-14 (HarperOne 2009); DANIEL H. PINK, TO SELL IS HUMAN: THE SURPRISING TRUTH ABOUT MOVING OTHERS 88-89 (Riverhead Books, 2012).

34. TINA SEELIG, INGENIUS: A CRASH COURSE ON CREATIVITY 19–30 (HarperCollins Publishers 2012).

35. Client Interviewee 33.
36. Client-Centricity Interviewee #4.
37. Client Interviewee 23.
38. Client Interviewee 11.
39. Client Interviewee 9.
40. Christoph Senn, *Stop Selling. Start Collaborating. The Secret to Fostering Lasting Client Relationships*, Harv. Bus. Rev. (May-June 2022), https://hbr.org/2022/05/stop-selling-start-collaborating.
41. Client Interviewee 23.
42. *Sakichi Toyoda*, Wikipedia, https://en.wikipedia.org/wiki/Sakichi_Toyoda (last visited Jan. 27, 2022); Shubhangi Choudhary, *5 Whys—Getting to the Root of a Problem Quickly*, Medium (Feb. 16, 2019), https://medium.com/@i.shubhangich/5-whys-getting-to-the-root-of-a-problem-quickly-a779f8ae7e3c.
43. *See, e.g.*, Paul Brest and Linda Hamilton Krieger, *Lawyers as Problem Solvers*, 72 Temple Law Review 811, 811-812 (1999); Arthur N. Turner, *Consulting Is More Than Giving Advice*, Harv. Bus. Rev. (Sept. 1, 1982), https://hbr.org/1982/09/consulting-is-more-than-giving-advice; *cf.* Larry Richard, *The Lawyer Personality: Why Lawyers Are Skeptical, What Makes Lawyers Tick?*, LawyerBrain, (Feb. 11, 2013), https://www.lawyerbrainblog.com/2013/02/the-lawyer-personality-why-lawyers-are-skeptical (explaining that lawyers' skepticism enables critical thinking).
44. Jeff Dyer et al, The Innovator's DNA: Mastering the Five Skills of Disruptive Innovators (Harv. Bus. Rev. Press 2011) 23-27.
45. Heidi K. Gardner, *When Senior Managers Won't Collaborate*, Harv. Bus. Rev., Mar. 2015, at 74, 74-78; Heidi K. Gardner, Smart Collaboration: How Professionals and Their Firms Succeed by Breaking Down Silos 2-3 (Harvard Business Review Press, 2016).
46. *Philips*, Wikipedia, https://en.wikipedia.org/wiki/Philips (last visited Aug. 31, 2023); *Philips Healthcare History*, Zippia, https://www.zippia.com/philips-healthcare-careers-34824/history/ (last visited Aug. 31, 2023).
47. *Our strategic focus*, Philips, https://www.philips.com/a-w/about/our-strategy.html (last visited Aug. 31, 2023).
48. Mark R. Kramer and Marc W. Pfitzer, *The Essential Link Between ESG Targets & Financial Performance*, Harv. Bus. Rev. (Sept. 1, 2022) https://hbr.org/2022/09/the-essential-link-between-esg-targets-financial-performance.
49. *Id.*
50. Client Interviewee 29.
51. Client Interviewee 30.
52. Tsedal Neeley and Paul Leonardi, *Developing a Digital Mindset: How to Lead Your Organization into the Age of Data, Algorithms, and AI*, Harv. Bus. Rev. (May 1, 2022), https://hbr.org/2022/05/developing-a-digital-mindset.
53. Client Interviewee 29.

54. Client Interviewee 32.

55. STEVEN JOHNSON, WHERE GOOD IDEAS COME FROM: THE NATURAL HISTORY OF INNOVATION 159-61 (Riverhead Books, 2011).

56. Michael Mankins et al., *Strategy in the Age of Superabundant Capital*, HARV. BUS. REV. (March 1, 2017), https://hbr.org/2017/03/strategy-in-the-age-of-superabundant -capital.

57. W. Chan Kim, & Renee Mauborgne, *Innovation Doesn't Have to Be Disruptive: Create New Markets for Growth Without Destroying Existing Companies or Jobs*, HARV. BUS. REV., May-June 2023, at 74-76.

58. *Id.*

59. *Id.* at 79-81 (explaining that Blue Ocean innovation, like Cirque du Soleil, created a new market space across the existing theater and circus industries).

60. Client Interviewee 25.

61. *Id.*

62. *Id.*

63. *Id.*

64. Client Interviewee 30.

65. CARLOS VALDES-DAPENA, LESSONS FROM MARS: HOW ONE GLOBAL COMPANY CRACKED THE CODE ON HIGH PERFORMANCE COLLABORATION AND TEAMWORK 102-105 (2018).

Chapter 3

1. MARSHALL GOLDSMITH, WHAT GOT YOU HERE WON'T GET YOU THERE (Generic 2013) (2007).

2. We created two campaigns to gain popularity among trend-setting young males and increase our market share of course: The "make room" campaign that featured male teens in urban settings looking rough and tough. Then we created the "It's Wide Open" campaign to expand beyond teens to males in their 30s. Some of you might remember a fairly racy/romantic commercial called the "elevator fantasy," which was a ton of fun to work on! For more detail about the advertising campaigns, see *Levi Strauss & Co.*, ENCYCLOPEDIA.COM: MARKETING, https://www .encyclopedia.com/marketing/encyclopedias-almanacs-transcripts-and-maps/ levi-strauss-co (last visited Aug. 31, 2023); *see also* Julia Angwin, *Levi's Hopes Wide-Leg Jeans Will Grab Urban Youth Market*, SFGATE (July 26, 1996), https://www .sfgate.com/business/article/Levi-s-Hopes-Wide-Leg-Jeans-Will-Grab-Urban -Youth-2972401.php. To watch the commercial, see Kevin V., Levi's Elevator Fantasy (FULL VERSION!!), YouTube (Feb. 1, 2007), https://www.youtube .com/watch?v=t_5o4b9aC4w.

3. ERNST & YOUNG, HOW CAN TODAY'S CEO BRIDGE THE GAPS TO REALIZE TOMORROW'S OPPORTUNITIES?: CEO IMPERATIVE STUDY 2021, PART 2, at 13 (2021), https://assets.ey.com/content/dam/ey-sites/ey-com/en_gl/topics/ceo-imperative -study/ey-ceo-imperative-study-part-2.pdf (explaining that there are gaps).

4. CC PSF Interviewee (Law Firm Partner) 40.

5. Client Interviewee 37 (whom I interviewed in 2017 and also in 2023 related to client-centricity).

6. *Id.*

7. *John Keats: Quotes*, GOODREADS, https://www.goodreads.com/quotes/622634-nothing -ever-becomes-real-till-experienced-even-a-proverb (visited July 10, 2023).

8. CC PSF Interviewee 17.

9. Client Interviewee 20.

10. PSF Interviewee (Law Firm Partner) 19.

11. PSF Interviewee (Law Firm Partner) 10.

12. PSF Interviewee 6.

13. SUBIR CHOWDHURY, THE DIFFERENCE: WHEN GOOD ENOUGH ISN'T ENOUGH 11-13 (2017).

14. Henry N. Nassau, *Collaboration as Superpower: Optimizing Value to Lead in the Future*, N.Y.L.J., (Apr. 24, 2017), https://www.law.com/newyorklawjournal/almID/ 1202784074939/.

15. CHOWDHURY, *supra* note 11, at 11-13. *Id.* at 36–37 (describing the difference as "a caring mindset" made up of four "STAR principles": "Being Straightforward," "Being Thoughtful," "Being Accountable," and "Having Resolve.").

16. DT Client Interviewee 17.

17. *Id.*

18. A recent 2021 study by EY in collaboration with Harvard Law School consisting of over 2,000 interviews reported that digitization is the number one priority among CEOs. EY LAW & HARVARD L. SCH. CTR. ON LEGAL PROFESSION, THE GENERAL COUNSEL IMPERATIVE SERIES: HOW DO YOU TURN BARRIERS INTO BUILDING BLOCKS? 8 (2021), https://assets.ey.com/content/dam/ey-sites/ey-com/en_gl/topics/law/ law-pdf/ey-general-counsel-imperative-series-how-do-you-turn-barriers-into -building-blocks.pdf?download; *see* John De Young, *The CEO Imperative: How Has Adversity Become the Springboard to Growth for CEOs?*, EY (July 19, 2021), https://www.ey.com/en_us/ceo/the-ceo-imperative-how-has-adversity-become -a-springboard-to-growth; *see also* KPMG, *U.S. CEO Outlook 2017*, KPMG: INSIGHTS (2017), https://home.kpmg/us/en/home/insights/2017/06/us-ceo-outlook -2017.html.

19. THE FOUNDER (Netflix 2016).

20. *Id.*

21. *Id.*

22. *Id.*

23. *Id.*

24. *Id.*

25. *See, e.g., 10% of Clients Like Sitting Through Your Pitch - Why This Spells Trouble*, BTI CONSULTING GRP. (Aug. 19, 2020), https://bticonsulting.com/themadclientist/ 10-of-clients-like-sitting-through-your-pitch-why-this-spells-trouble.

26. For more on perfectionism and fear-preventing progress, see generally BRENÉ BROWN, DARE TO LEAD: BRAVE WORK, TOUGH CONVERSATIONS, WHOLE HEARTS (2018) [hereinafter DARE TO LEAD].
27. CC PSF Interviewee 17.
28. Rob Shafer, *Customer Loyalty, Cracking the Experience Code in a Revolutionary Way*, https://rossshafer.com/topics/customer-loyalty/ (last visited July 9, 2022).
29. CC Client Interviewee 35.
30. CC Client Interviewee 4.
31. Client Interviewee 28.
32. CC Client Interviewee 10.
33. CC PSF Interviewee 17.
34. CC Client Interviewee 16.
35. CC Client Interviewee 10.
36. CC Client Interviewee 9.
37. *Id.*
38. I am a cofounder of The Digital Legal Exchange, a global nonprofit institute of leading thinkers and practitioners in academia, business, government, technology, and law, committed to accelerating digital transformation. For more information, see www.dlex.org.
39. DIG. LEGAL EXCHANGE, THE DIGITAL DISCONNECT 5 (2021) (on file with author).
40. Andreas Bong & Stuart Fuller, *Global Legal Department Benchmarking Survey*, KPMG INT'L 26 (2021) (finding that most GCs do not view adding business value as valuable—only 25 percent found it significant) https://assets.kpmg/content/dam/kpmg/xx/pdf/2021/03/global-legal-department-benchmarking-survey.pdf.
41. Gene Cornfield, *The Most Important Metrics You're Not Tracking (Yet)*, HARV. BUS. REV. (Apr. 30, 2020) (providing the example of "nothing broke" as a CPI of a grocery store delivery service), https://hbr.org/2020/04/the-most-important-metrics-youre-not-tracking-yet.
42. *Id.*
43. PETER F. DRUCKER, MEN, IDEAS, AND POLITICS ix (2nd ed., Harvard Business Press, 2010) (1971).
44. John Amaechi, *The State of Digital Contracting: Deep Collaboration and the Uncertain Future of MS Word*, IRONCLAD.COM https://ironcladapp.com/lp/thankyou-webinarod-the-state-of-digital-contracting-deep-collaboration-the-uncertain-future-of-ms-word/?utm_campaign=2020Q3VirtualEventIroncladKeynote&utm_medium=email&utm_source=sales&utm_term=prospect&utm_content=Q3Keynot (last visited on Aug. 14, 2023).
45. CC Client Interviewee 18.
46. Client Interviewee 22.
47. CC Client Interviewee 9.
48. CC Client Interviewee 16.
49. CC Client Interviewee 9.
50. CC Client Interviewee 12.

51. CC Client Interviewee 15.

52. CC Client Interviewee 18.

53. CC Client Interviewee 4.

54. CC Client Interviewee 10.

55. CC Client Interviewee 39.

56. Client Interviewee 37 (whom I interviewed in 2017 and also in 2023 related to client-centricity).

57. DT Client Interviewee 6.

58. CC Client Interviewee 40.

59. Ian Craib, *Narratives as Bad Faith*, in THE USES OF NARRATIVE: EXPLORATIONS IN SOCIOLOGY, PSYCHOLOGY, AND CULTURAL STUDIES 64, 65 (3d prtg. 2009) (citing Jerome Bruner, *Life as Narrative*, 54 SOC. RES. 11, 15 (1987)).

60. STEVEN JOHNSON, WHERE GOOD IDEAS COME FROM: THE NATURAL HISTORY OF INNOVATION 174 (2010).

61. TINA SEELIG, WHAT I WISH I KNEW WHEN I WAS 20: A CRASH COURSE ON MAKING YOUR PLACE IN THE WORLD 10 (HarperOne 2009)

62. Tsedal Neeley & Paul Leonardi, *Developing a Digital Mindset: How to Lead Your Organization into the Age of Data, Algorithms, and AI*, HARV. BUS. REV. (May 1, 2022), https://hbr.org/2022/05/developing-a-digital-mindset.

63. JOHNSON, *supra* note 57, at 174.

64. *Id.*

65. RON HEIFETZ, LEADERSHIP WITHOUT EASY ANSWERS 6–7 (2009) (ebook). For a description of how the model of adaptive leadership was conceived and developed, see Chapter 1, footnote 118.

66. *Id.* at 8.

67. *Id.* at 71–72.

68. *Id.* at 73–76

69. *Id.* at 72–73.

70. This term was first used by the U.S. Army War College to describe the impact that the Cold War had on the world. *See* U.S. Army Heritage and Education Center, *Who First Originated the Term VUCA (Volatility, Uncertainty, Complexity, and Ambiguity)?*, U.S. ARMY WAR COLLEGE (December 6, 2022), https://usawc.libanswers .com/faq/84869. In the past few years, this term has been used to frame the issues facing large corporations and especially compliance and legal departments within the increasingly global world we live in wherein regulations in places all over the world impact how corporations operate. *See generally*, S. Tamar Cavusgil et al., *International Business in an Accelerated VUCA World: Trends, Disruptions, and Coping Strategies*, 6 RUTGERS BUS. REV. 220 (2021); *see also* Bill Carter, *Top Trends Driving the Business of Law in a VUCA World*, ALM (September 28, 2023), https://www .alm.com/blog/top-trends-driving-the-business-of-law-in-a-vuca-world-2/.

71. HEIFETZ, *supra* note 62, at 268 ("Even if the weight of carrying people's hopes and pains may fall mainly, for a time, on one person's shoulders, leadership cannot be exercised alone. The lone-warrior model of leadership is heroic suicide. Each of us has blind spots that require the vision of others.").

72. Michael Leimbach, *Leadership Development in the Age of Disruption*, Training Mag. (May 9, 2023), https://trainingmag.com/leadership-development-in-the-age-of -disruption/.

73. Heifetz, *supra* note 62, at 268.

74. *Id.* at 49.

75. *Id.* at 60.

76. Chat GPT 3, *Adaptive vs. Traditional Leaders* https://chat.openai.com/share/ c3522ae2-f9dc-4d5f-88e4-6f831b893e8c (conversation generated July 12, 2023) (asking how are the traits of adaptive leaders different than the traits of traditional leaders).

77. *Id.*

78. *Id.*

Chapter 4

1. Client Interviewee 25.

2. Client Interviewee 9.

3. Client Interviewee 30.

4. Cranla Warren, Financial Investment Advisor Professional Arrogance and Performance 38-39 (March 2019) (Ph.D. dissertation, Walden University), https://scholarworks .waldenu.edu/cgi/viewcontent.cgi?article=7980&context=dissertations.

5. Heidi K. Gardner, *When Senior Managers Won't Collaborate*, Harv. Bus. Rev., Mar. 2015, at 74, 74–78; Heidi K. Gardner, Smart Collaboration: How Professionals and Their Firms Succeed by Breaking Down Silos 72–78 (Harvard Business Review Press, 2016).

6. *Id.*

7. Client Interviewee 9.

8. Tina Seelig, What I Wish I Knew When I Was 20: A Crash Course on Making Your Place in the World 10 (HarperOne 2009)

9. Failcon, www.thefailcon.com/ (last visited Dec. 7, 2017).

10. Walter Frick, *Research: Serial Entrepreneurs Aren't Any More Likely to Succeed*, Harvard Bus. Rev. (Feb. 20, 2014), https://hbr.org/2014/02/research-serial -entrepreneurs-arent-any-more-likely-to-succeed (concluding that founders who had previously failed were more likely to fail than first-time entrepreneurs after accounting for education and industry experience).

11. Kenneth A. Grady, *Why Your Law Firm Can't Innovate: The Rise of the Innovation Killers*, Medium (June 1, 2017), https://medium.com/the-algorithmic-society/ why-your-law-firm-cant-innovate-58524ca2ec9.

12. Client Interviewee 17.

13. Client Interviewee 9. Note: A tick is a positive thing such as a check mark.

14. Client Interviewee 11.

15. Client Interviewee 41.

16. Client Interviewee 9.

17. Client Interviewee 16.

18. TIM BROWN, CHANGE BY DESIGN: HOW DESIGN THINKING TRANSFORMS ORGANIZA-
TIONS AND INSPIRES INNOVATION 138-39 (New York: HarperCollins Publishers, 2009).

19. Portia Crowe, *IT'S OFFICIAL: Intel Is Buying the Autonomous-Driving Company
Mobileye for $15.3 Billion*, BUSINESS INSIDER, March 13, 2017, www.business
insider.com/intel-mobileye-acquisition-report-2017-3.

20. Robert Musil, *The Man Without Qualities, Vol. I: A Sort of Introduction and Pseudor-
eality Prevails into the Millennium* (New York: Vintage Books, 1996) 62.

21. There is debate about who this quotation should be attributed to, but it is often
attributed to Winston Churchill. *See, e.g., Attitude Is a Little Thing That Makes a Big
Difference*, THE QUOTE INVESTIGATOR, https://quoteinvestigator.com/2013/03/13/
attitude-little-big/ (last visited April 18, 2018).

22. MADELEINE L'ENGLE, A WRINKLE IN TIME 95 (New York: Square Fish, 2007) 95.

23. Bernadette Dillon & Juliet Bourke, *The Six Signature Traits of Inclusive Leadership: Thriving in a Diverse New World*, DELOITTE (April 4, 2016), https://www2
.deloitte.com/za/en/insights/topics/talent/six-signature-traits-of-inclusive
-leadership.html (identifying the six essential traits of inclusive leaders as courage, cognizance, commitment, curiosity, cultural intelligence, and collaboration);
Daniel Goleman, *What Makes a Leader?*, HARV. BUS. REV. (Jan. 2004), https://hbr
.org/2004/01/what-makes-a-leader; Sunnie Giles, *The Most Important Leadership Competencies, According to Leaders Around the World*, HARV. BUS. REV. (Mar. 15,
2016), https://hbr.org/2016/03/the-most-important-leadership-competencies
-according-to-leaders-around-the-world; Katherine Graham-Leviss, *The 5
Skills That Innovative Leaders Have in Common*, HARV. BUS. REV. (Dec. 20, 2016),
https://hbr.org/2016/12/the-5-skills-that-innovative-leaders-have-in-common;
Bill McBean, *The 5 Characteristics of Great Leaders*, FAST COMPANY (Jan. 24, 2013),
https://www.fastcompany.com/3004914/5-characteristics-great-leaders; Olivia
Fox Cabane & Judah Pollack, *Your Brain Has A 'Delete' Button—Here's How to
Use It*, FAST COMPANY (May 11, 2016), https://www.fastcompany.com/3059634/
your-brain-has-a-delete-button-heres-how-to-use-it.

24. PSF Interviewee (Law Firm Partner) 10.

25. Michele DeStefano, *The Chief Compliance Officer: Should There Be a New "C" in the
C-Suite?*, THE PRACTICE, July 2016, https://clp.law.harvard.edu/knowledge-hub/
magazine/issues/the-compliance-movement/the-chief-compliance-officer/;
Michele DeStefano, *Creating a Culture of Compliance: Why Departmentalization
May Not Be the Answer*, 10 HASTINGS BUS. L.J. 71 (2013).

26. PSF Interviewee (Law Firm Partner) 18.

27. DeStefano, *supra* note 25.

28. Jon R. Katzenbach et al., *Cultural Change That Sticks*, HARV. BUS. REV., July–August
2012, https://hbr.org/2012/07/cultural-change-that-sticks.

29. JASON FRIED AND DAVID HEINEMEIER HANSSON, REWORK 249 (New York: Crown
Business Publishing, 2010).

30. *See FT Innovative Lawyers Awards 2013*, FINANCIAL TIMES (Oct. 3, 2013), https://
im.ft-static.com/content/images/4aa3b5c6-2b12-11e3-8fb8-00144feab7de.pdf.

31. Nathan Cisneros et al., *Vieira de Almeida (VdA): Legal Innovation Pioneers in Portugal*, Product number: HLS 15-15 (November 24, 2015); *see also Innovating to Grow: Building an Integrated Firm in Portugal*, THE PRACTICE (Nov. 2016), https://clp.law.harvard.edu/knowledge-hub/magazine/issues/marketing-and-business-development-in-law/innovating-to-grow/.

32. MARY DORIA RUSSELL, CHILDREN OF GOD 225 (New York: Villard Books, 1998).

33. They were all discoveries or inventions that were made independently but almost simultaneously by multiple inventors or scientists. It's the theory of multiples.

34. Lian Chenyu, *Renren, Once China's Answer to Facebook, Is a Digital Ghost Town*, SIXTH TONE (Sept. 3, 2018), https://www.sixthtone.com/news/1002846.

35. Brown, *supra* note 18, at 138–139 and 161–165.

36. Shirley Gregor and Alan Hevner, *The Knowledge Innovation Matrix (KIM): A Clarifying Lens for Innovation*, INFORMING SCIENCE: THE INTERNATIONAL JOURNAL OF AN EMERGING TRANSDISCIPLINE, *17, 217–39* (2014).

37. Greg Satell, *How to Manage Innovation*, FORBES *(March 7, 2013)*, https://www.forbes.com/sites/gregsatell/2013/03/07/how-to-manage-innovation-2/?sh=2c1f1e4b4785.

38. Hutch Carpenter, *The Four Quadrants of Innovation: Disruptive vs Incremental*, WORDPRESS (Dec. 1, 2009), https://bhc3.com/2009/12/01/the-four-quadrants-of-innovation-disruptive-vs-incremental/.

Part II

1. STEPHEN R. COVEY, *FIRST THINGS FIRST* (2015) (ebook).

2. *See* Victor Lipman, *New Study Explores Why Change Management Fails – And How to (Perhaps) Succeed*, FORBES (Sept. 4, 2013), https://www.forbes.com/sites/victorlipman/2013/09/04/new-study-explores-why-change-management-fails-and-how-to-perhaps-succeed/?sh=6f5281ed7137.

3. N. Anand & Jean-Louis Barsoux, *What Everyone Gets Wrong About Change Management*, HARV. BUS. REV., Nov.–Dec. 2017, at 79, 80.

4. CHRISTOPHER M. AVERY ET AL., TEAMWORK IS AN INDIVIDUAL SKILL: GETTING YOUR WORK DONE WHEN SHARING RESPONSIBILITY (2001) (identifying five themes for team wisdom: personal responsibility, partnership, shared purpose, trust, and the collaborative mindset).

5. In addition to my experience in LawWithoutWalls, there is research to support this ordering. *See, e.g.,* WORLD ECON. FORUM, DIGITAL CULTURE: THE DRIVING FORCE OF DIGITAL TRANSFORMATION 34–40 (2021) (suggesting starting with personal actions before moving to organizational initiatives).

Chapter 5

1. "Man in the Mirror" by Glen Ballard and Siedhah Garrett, Sung by Michael Jackson, Fourth Single from Album *Bad* (1987).

2. There is a lot of research and scholarship supporting the idea that humility and self-awareness contribute to effective leadership and management of interdisciplinary

teams. *See, e.g.*, L. Michelle Bennett & Howard Gadlin, *Collaboration and Team Science: From Theory to Practice*, 60 J. INVESTIGATIVE MED. 768, 768–75 (2012); Jack Zenger & Joseph Folkman, *We Like Leaders Who Underrate Themselves*, HARV. BUS. REV. (Nov. 10, 2015), https://hbr.org/2015/11/we-like-leaders-who-underrate -themselves (writing about data describing 69,000 managers as seen through the eyes of 750,000 respondents); *see also* Jack Zenger, *Humble Versus Egocentric Leaders: When Lacking Self-Awareness Helps*, FORBES (Nov. 19, 2015), https://www .forbes.com/sites/jackzenger/2015/11/19/humble-versus-egocentric-leaders -when-lacking-self-awareness-helps; *see, e.g.*, PETER F. DRUCKER, MANAGING ONE-SELF 17–22 (2008); Paul J. Brouwer, *The Power to See Ourselves*, HARV. BUS. REV. (Nov. 1, 1964), https://hbr.org/1964/11/the-power-to-see-ourselves.

3. Jenna (Britton) Arak, *Real Talk: Are Leaders Born or Made?*, THE MUSE (June 19, 2020), https://www.themuse.com/advice/real-talk-are-leaders-born-or-made.

4. Milhnea Moldoveanu & Das Narayandas, *The Future of Leadership Development*, HARV. BUS. REV., Mar.–Apr. 2019, at 40, 42.

5. For more detail on why The 3-4-5 Method™ of Innovation works to hone inclusive leadership traits and the traits of an innovator, see Michele DeStefano & Guenther Dobrauz, *The Secret Sauce to Teaching Collaboration and Leadership to Lawyers*, in NEW SUITS APPETITE FOR DISRUPTION IN THE LEGAL WORLD 635–56 (2019).

6. *Taught Leaders – Executive Training for the Ambitious GC*, THE LEGAL 500 (June 21, 2021), https://www.legal500.com/special-reports/taught-leaders-executive-training -for-the-ambitious-gc.

7. *See, e.g.*, NANCY J. COOKE ET AL., ENHANCING THE EFFECTIVENESS OF TEAM SCI-ENCE 141-44 (2015); Israel Sánchez-Cardona, *Leadership Intellectual Stimulation and Team Learning: The Mediating Role of Team Positive Affect*, 17 UNIVERSITAS PSY-CHOLOGICA 9–10 (2018). *But cf.* J. RICHARD HACKMAN, LEADING TEAMS: SETTING THE STAGE FOR GREAT PERFORMANCE 88–90 (2002) (disagreeing with the value of leadership training).

8. *See, e.g.*, Bennett & Gadlin, *supra* note 2, at 768–75 ("Self-awareness and strong communication skills contribute greatly to effective leadership and management strategies of scientific teams."); DRUCKER, *supra* note 2, at 17–22; Brouwer, *supra* note 2.

9. DRUCKER, *supra* note 2, at 17–22; Brouwer, *supra* note 2.

10. Bennett & Gadlin, *supra* note 2, at 3-4; J. P. Flaum, *When It Comes to Business Leadership, Nice Guys Finish First*, GREENPEAK PARTNERS 5, https://greenpeakpart ners.com/wp-content/uploads/2018/09/Green-Peak_Cornell-University-Study _What-predicts-success.pdf (last visited Jan. 21, 2018) (studying 72 senior exec-utives at public and private companies ranging from $50 million to $5 billion in revenue in a variety of industries and finding that self-awareness was the strongest predictor of a leader's overall success).

11. Flaum, *supra* note 10, at 5; Rob Nielsen et al., *A New Look at Humility: Exploring the Humility Concept and Its Role in Socialized Charismatic Leadership*, J. LEADERSHIP & ORGANIZATIONAL STUD. 17, 35 (2010) (defining self-awareness as "the degree to which

individuals understand their own strengths and weaknesses" and one's ability to "focus attention on oneself").

12. There is much research and many articles and books on the value of knowing and focusing on one's strengths. *See generally,* Yonghong Zhang & Mengyan Chen, *Character Strengths, Strengths Use, Future Self-Continuity and Subjective Well-Being Among Chinese University Students,* Frontiers in Psychol. (June 29, 2018), https://www.ncbi.nlm.nih.gov/pmc/articles/PMC6034163/pdf/fpsyg-09-01040.pdf; Ryan Niemiec & Robert E. McGrath, The Power of Character Strengths: Appreciate and Ignite Your Positive Personality (2019); Brian J. Brim, *The Powerful Duo of Strengths and Engagement,* Gallup (May 9, 2023), https://www.gallup.com/workplace/505523/powerful-duo-strengths-engagement.aspx#:~:text=Gallup's%20strengths%20meta%2Danalysis%20highlights,fewer%20safety%20incidents%2C%20for%20example; Wayne Hammond, *Principles of Strength-Based Practice,* Resiliency Initiatives (2010) http://17963711.s21d-17.faiusrd.com/61/ABUIABA9GAAg5Kyi7AUoo6-vnQM.pdf; P. Alex Linley et al., *Using Signature Strengths in Pursuit of Goals: Effects on Goal Progress, Need Satisfaction, and Well-Being, and Implications for Coaching Psychologists,* 5 Int'l Coaching Psychol. Rev. 6, 6–15 (2010).

13. Zachary A. Rosner et al., *The Generation Effect: Activating Broad Neural Circuits During Memory Encoding,* 49 Nat'l Libr. Med. 1901, 1901-1903 (2013).

14. Gail Matthews, *Goals Research Summary,* Dominican U. Cal. 3 (2015), https://www.dominican.edu/sites/default/files/2020-02/gailmatthews-harvard-goals-researchsummary.pdf (last visited Sept. 4, 2023); Mark Murphy, *Neuroscience Explains Why You Need To Write Down Your Goals If You Actually Want To Achieve Them,* Forbes (Apr. 15, 2018), https://www.forbes.com/sites/markmurphy/2018/04/15/neuroscience-explains-why-you-need-to-write-down-your-goals-if-you-actually-want-to-achieve-them/?sh=4c5310ec7905; *see also* Kumar Mehta, *This One Action Will Help You Achieve Your New Year's Resolutions,* Forbes (Jan. 3, 2022) https://www.forbes.com/sites/kmehta/2022/01/03/this-one-action-will-help-you-achieve-your-new-years-resolutions/?sh=e05555153ace.

15. *Are Smart Goals Dumb?,* Leadership IQ, https://www.leadershipiq.com/blogs/leadershipiq/35353793-are-smart-goals-dumb (last visited Aug. 24, 2023) (surveying almost 17,000 people).

16. *Id.* (finding that visuals help people avoid setting too vague a goal).

17. *See* Matthews, *supra* note 14, at 3.

18. Amy Edmondson, *How to Turn a Group of Strangers Into a Team,* TED (Oct. 2017), https://www.ted.com/talks/amy_edmondson_how_to_turn_a_group_of_strangers_into_a_team/transcript?user_email_address=94d09e65b40912676ebcc090ad0a89c6&lctg=62d19a721c794c328c7843af.

19. Jack Zenger & Joseph Folkman, *We Like Leaders Who Underrate Themselves,* Harv. Bus. Rev. (Nov. 10, 2015), https://hbr.org/2015/11/we-like-leaders-who-underrate-themselves (writing about data describing 69,000 managers as seen

through the eyes of 750,000 respondents); *see also* Jack Zenger, *Humble Versus Ego-centric Leaders: When Lacking Self-Awareness Helps*, FORBES (Nov. 19, 2015), https://www.forbes.com/sites/jackzenger/2015/11/19/humble-versus-egocentric-leaders-when-lacking-self-awareness-helps/?sh=75cbe6555bf4.

20. Zenger & Folkman, *supra* note 19; David Dunning et al., *Why People Fail to Recognize Their Own Incompetence*, 12 CURRENT DIRECTIONS IN PSYCH. SCI. 83–87 (2003).

21. Oliver Sheldon et al., *Emotionally Unskilled, Unaware, and Uninterested in Learning More: Reactions to Feedback about Deficits in Emotional Intelligence*, 99 J. APPL. PSYCHOL. 125, 125–37 (2014).

22. *Id.*

23. BENJAMIN FRANKLIN, POOR RICHARD'S ALMANAC (1750) ("There are three things extremely hard: steel, a diamond, and to know one's self.").

24. Deborah L. Rhode, *Developing Leadership*, 52 SANTA CLARA L. REV. 689, 718 (2012).

25. JAMES M. KOUZES & BARRY L. POSNER, A LEADER'S LEGACY 28 (2006).

26. Keith Ferrazzi, *A New Social Contract for Teams*, HARV. BUS. REV. (Sept. 1, 2022), https://hbr.org/2022/09/a-new-social-contract-for-teams.

27. Zenger & Folkman, *supra* note 19; *see also* Amy Y. Ou et al., *Do Humble CEOs Matter? An examination of CEO Humility and Firm Outcomes*, 44 J. MGMT. 1147, 1147–77 (2018) (finding that humble leaders had stronger company performance, greater staff satisfaction, and lower employee turnover).

28. Dunning, *supra* note 20, at 83–87.

29. Nielsen et al., *supra* note 11, at 34; Stanley B. Silverman et al., *Arrogance: A Formula for Leadership Failure*, 50 INDUS.-ORGANIZATIONAL PSYCHOLOGIST 22, 25 (2012).

30. Nielsen et al., *supra* note 11, at 35.

31. Brouwer, *supra* note 2.

32. *Id.*

33. *Id.*

34. Brouwer, *supra* note 2; *see also* Danielle D. King et al., *Personality Homogeneity in Organization and Occupations: Considering Similarity Sources*, 32 J. BUS. AND PSYCHOL. 641, 641–53 (2016).

35. *See, e.g.*, Paul Brest and Linda Hamilton Krieger, *Lawyers as Problem Solvers*, 72 TEMPLE LAW REVIEW 811, 811-812 (1999); Arthur N. Turner, *Consulting Is More Than Giving Advice*, HARV. BUS. REV. (Sept. 1, 1982), https://hbr.org/1982/09/consulting-is-more-than-giving-advice; *cf.* Larry Richard, *The Lawyer Personality: Why Lawyers Are Skeptical, What Makes Lawyers Tick?*, LAWYERBRAIN, (Feb. 11, 2013), https://www.lawyerbrainblog.com/2013/02/the-lawyer-personality-why-lawyers-are-skeptical (explaining that lawyers' skepticism enables critical thinking).

36. *See* Larry Richard, *Herding Cats: The Lawyer Personality Revealed*, 29 ALTMAN WEIL REP. TO MGMT. 9 (2002) (utilizing the Caliper Profile on more than

1,000 lawyers); David Maister, *10 Unique Dynamics of Professional Services Firms that Hinder Change Efforts, And What Partners Can Do About It*, Openside, https://www.openside.group/10-unique-dynamics-of-professional-services-firms-that-hinder-change-efforts (last visited Aug. 9, 2022).

37. Ashish Nanda & Das Narayandas, *What Professional Service Firms Must Do to Thrive*, Harv. Bus. Rev. (Mar. 1, 2021), https://hbr.org/2021/03/what-professional-service-firms-must-do-to-thrive.

38. Bryant G. Garth & Austin Sarat, Justice and Power in Sociolegal Studies 62–63 (1998) (noting a plethora of sources asserting that lawyers are arrogant, paternalistic, unempathetic, rude, and evasive).

39. Danetha Doe, *About Last Night: Why The US Accounting Industry Will Die A Slow Death*, LinkedIn (Jan. 7, 2016), https://www.linkedin.com/pulse/last-night-why-us-accounting-industry-die-slow-death-danetha-doe ("There is an undercurrent of arrogance that the accounting industry is untouchable."); Karen Klein, *The Case Of the Arrogant Accountant*, Bloomberg (Dec. 2, 2002, 12:00 AM EST), https://www.bloomberg.com/news/articles/2002-12-01/the-case-of-the-arrogant-accountant; David M. Boje et al., *Enron Spectacles: A Critical Dramaturgical Analysis*, 25 Org. Stud. 751, 751–74 (2004) (contending that corporate arrogance and greed resulted in the downfall of Enron); C. William Thomas, *The Rise and Fall of Enron*, J. Accountancy 41, 41–48 (2002); Z. De Silva, *Secret Formula For Profit Growth*, 92 Chartered Acct. J. 42, 42–43 (2013) (citing Bain & Company's 2005 survey of 362 chartered accounting firms that revealed that only 8 percent of clients believed they received great customer experience while 80 percent of these firms believed they delivered a great client experience).

40. *See, e.g,* Jack Kelly, *Deutsche Bank: An Ugly Story of the Unbridled Arrogance and Downfall of an Investment Bank*, Forbes (July 12, 2019), https://www.forbes.com/sites/jackkelly/2019/07/12/deutsche-bank-an-ugly-story-of-the-unbridled-arrogance-and-downfall-of-an-investment-bank; *see also* Ronald F. Duska, *Unethical Behavioral Finance: Why Good People Do Bad Things*, 71 J. Fin. Serv. Profs. 25, 27 (2017) (contending that arrogance was a possible culprit of Bernie Madoff's unethical behavior).

41. *See, e.g.,* Kelly, *supra* note 45; Thomas, *supra* note 44, at 41–48; David Streitfeld & Lee Romney, *Enron's Run Tripped by Arrogance, Greed*, L.A. Times (Jan. 27, 2002), https://www.latimes.com/archives/la-xpm-2002-jan-27-mn-25002-story.html.

42. PSF Interviewee 33.

43. Sumit Ghosh, *Humbleness as a Practical Vehicle for Engineering Ethics Education*, 32nd ASEE/IEEE Frontiers Educ. Conf., at S4F-S4F (Nov. 6–9, 2002), https://ieeexplore.ieee.org/stamp/stamp.jsp?arnumber=1158738.

44. Robert Pater, *Overcoming the Top 10 Leadership Mistakes: Change Your Game to Achieve Game-Changing Results*, 55 Prof. Safety 30, 30 (2014).

45. *See* Silverman et al., *supra* note 29, at 24–25.

46. Ho Ma & Ranjan Karri, *Leaders Beware: Some Sure Ways to Lose Your Competitive Advantage*, 34 Organizational Dynamics 63, 68 (2005).

47. Silverman et al., *supra* note 29, at 25–26; Ghosh, *supra* note 47, at SF13 (calling arrogance the "antithesis" to humility); Duska, *supra* note 40, at 24 (explaining that the antidote to arrogance is "knowing and accepting one's limits."); Russell E. Johnson et al., *Acting Superior but Actually Inferior? Correlates and Consequences of Workplace Arrogance* 23 Human Performance 403–27 (2010) (finding a negative correlation between arrogance and humility).

48. Kristin L. Cullen et al., *Biased Self-Perception Tendencies: Self-Enhancement/Self-Diminishment and Leader Derailment in Individualistic and Collectivistic Cultures* 64 Applied Psychol.: An Int'l Rev., 161, 162–171 (2015).

49. Ron Heifetz, Leadership Without Easy Answers 11 (2009) (ebook).

50. Nielsen et al., *supra* note 16, at 35.

51. Edmondson, *supra* note 18.

52. *Id.*

53. Nielsen et al., *supra* note 11 at 37.

54. Derek Sivers, *How to Start a Movement*, TED (Feb. 2010), https://www.ted.com/talks/derek_sivers_how_to_start_a_movement.

55. *Id.*

56. Derek Sivers, *First Follower: Leadership Lessons from Dancing Guy*, YouTube (Feb. 11, 2010), https://www.youtube.com/watch?v=fW8amMCVAJQ.

57. Jon R. Katzenbach et al., *Cultural Change That Sticks*, Harv. Bus. Rev. (July 1, 2012) https://hbr.org/2012/07/cultural-change-that-sticks.

58. Nielsen et al., *supra* note 11, at 37; Silverman et al., *supra* note 34, at 25 ("When employees attribute humility to their leaders, they also perceive the leader as more honest, trustworthy, competent, and confident.").

59. Arménio Rego et al., *The Perceived Impact of Leaders' Humility on Team Effectiveness: An Empirical Study*, 148 J. Bus. Ethics 205, 205–218 (2018).

60. Margaret Heffernan, *Forget the Pecking Order at Work*, TEDWoman (May 2015) https://www.ted.com/talks/margaret_heffernan_forget_the_pecking_order_at_work.

61. William M. Muir and Heng Wei Cheng, Genetics and the Behaviour of Domestic Animals, Chapter 9: Genetics and the Behaviour of Chickens: Welfare and Productivity, 2 (2nd ed., Academic Press) (2013).

62. *Happy and Passive Means More Productive Animals*, Purdue University News, (August 2, 2005), https://www.purdue.edu/uns/html4ever/2005/050802.Muir.behavior.html.

63. Boris Groysberg et al., *The Risky Business of Hiring Stars*, Harv. Bus. Rev. (May 2004), https://hbr.org/2004/05/the-risky-business-of-hiring-stars.

64. *Id.*

65. *Id.*

66. *Id.*

67. *Id.*

68. *Id.*

69. *Id.*

70. *Id.*

71. Coates et al., *Hiring Teams, Firms, and Lawyers: Evidence of the Evolving Relationships in the Corporate Legal Market*, 36 LAW & SOC. INQUIRY 999 (Fall 2011) (analyzing interview and survey data from 166 chief legal officers of S&P 500 companies from 2006–2007).

72. Rachel Moloney, *Freshfields Loses Entire Paris Real Estate Team to Jones Day*, THE LAWYER (February 22, 2017), https://www.thelawyer.com/issues/online-february -2017/freshfields-loses-paris-real-estate-jones-day/.

73. Mark A. Bellis et al., *Dying to Be Famous: Retrospective Cohort Study of Rock and Pop Star Mortality and Its Association with Adverse Childhood Experiences*, BRITISH MEDICAL JOURNAL (December 19, 2012), https://bmjopen.bmj.com/content/2/6/ e002089; Emily Leaman, *Study: Musicians in Bands Live Longer Than Solo Acts*, PHILADELPHIA MAGAZINE (December 20, 2012), https://www.phillymag.com/ be-well-philly/2012/12/20/study-musicians-bands-live-longer-solo-acts/.

74. Bellis et al., *supra* note 72.

75. *Id.*

76. Nielsen et al., *supra* note 11, at 37–38.

77. *Id.*

78. *See* Kim Peters & S. Alexander Haslam, *I Follow, Therefore I Lead: A Longitudinal Study of Leader and Follower Identity and Leadership in the Marines*, BRITISH J. PSYCHOLOGY. 708, 708–23 (2018).

79. Edmondson, *supra* note 23 ("When teaming works, you can be sure that some leaders, leaders at all levels, have been crystal clear that they don't have the answers."); Francesca Gino, *Cracking the Code of Sustained Collaboration: Six New Tools for Training People to Work Together Better*, HARV. BUS. REV., Nov. –Dec. 2019, at 73, 80.

80. HACKMAN, *supra* note 7, at 88–90.

81. HEIFETZ, *supra* note 48, at 187.

82. *Id.* at 188.

83. Ronald Heifetz & Marty Linsky: *A Survival Guide for Leaders*, HARV. BUS. REV. (June 1, 2002), https://hbr.org/2002/06/a-survival-guide-for-leaders.

84. Ghosh, *supra* note 42, at SF4.

85. Ronald Heifetz & Donald L. Laurie, *The Work of Leadership*, HARV. BUS. REV. (Dec. 1, 2001), https://hbr.org/2001/12/the-work-of-leadership ("[A]daptive change is distressing for the people going through it. They need to take on new roles, new relationships, new values, new behaviors, and new approaches to work."); *see also* Eric B. Dent & Susan Galloway Goldberg, *Challenging "Resistance to Change*," 35 J. APPLIED BEHAV. SCI. 25, 26-27 (1999) (explaining that people do not necessarily resist change but instead that they "resist loss of status, loss of pay or loss of comfort"); Sally Maitlis & Scott Sonenshein, *Sensemaking in Crisis and Change: Inspiration and Insights from Weick (1988)*, 7 J. MGMT. STUDIES 47, 558 (2010).

86. HEIFETZ, *supra* note 53, at 236–41; RONALD HEIFETZ & MARTY LINKSY, LEADERSHIP ON THE LINE: STAYING ALIVE THROUGH THE DANGERS OF LEADING 128 (2002) (ebook); Ahmad Hafizh Damawan & Siti Azizah, *Resistance to Change: Causes and*

Strategies as an Organizational Challenge, 395 Advances Soc. Sci., Educ. & Human. Rsch. 49, 51 (2020).

87. Aristotle, Nichomachean Ethics bk. II (W. D. Ross, trans, Internet Classics Archive M.I.T.) (c. 350 B.C.E.).

88. Gloria Steinem, *A New Egalitarian Life Style*, New York Times (August. 26, 1971), https://www.nytimes.com/1971/08/26/archives/a-new-egalitarian-life-style.html.

Chapter 6

1. Quoteresearch, *What You Do Speaks So Loudly that I Cannot Hear What You Say*, QuoteInvestigator (Jan. 27, 2011), https://quoteinvestigator.com/2011/01/27/what-you-do-speaks/.

2. Larry Richard, *The Lawyer Personality: Why Lawyers Are Skeptical, What Makes Lawyers Tick?*, LawyerBrain, (Feb. 11, 2013), https://www.lawyerbrainblog.com/2013/02/the-lawyer-personality-why-lawyers-are-skeptical; *see also* Larry Richard, *Herding Cats: The Lawyer Personality Revealed*, 29 Altman Weil Rep. to Mgmt. 8 (2002) (utilizing the Caliper Profile on over 1,000 lawyers).

3. Keith Ferrazzi, *A New Social Contract for Teams*, Harv. Bus. Rev. (September 1, 2022), https://hbr.org/2022/09/a-new-social-contract-for-teams.

4. So-Ang Park & Lisa Birkenbach, *Quick Overview: The General Counsel's Role in Shaping and Advancing Corporate Culture in the Legal Department*, ACC (May 3, 2021), https://www.acc.com/resource-library/quick-overview-general-counsels-role-shaping-and-advancing-corporate-culture-legal.

5. *Id.*

6. Maureen Broderick, Leading Gently, The American Lawyer, Dec. 2010, at 63, 64.

7. Heidi Grant Halvorson, *Explained: Why We Don't Like Change*, HuffPost (Jan 5. 2012), https://www.huffpost.com/entry/why-we-dont-like-change_b_1072702; Ernst & Young, How Can Today's CEO Bridge the Gaps to Realize Tomorrow's Opportunities?, CEO Imperative Study 2021, part 2, at 10 (2021), https://assets.ey.com/content/dam/ey-sites/ey-com/en_gl/topics/ceo-imperative-study/ey-ceo-imperative-study-part-2.pdf (explaining that there are gaps).

8. Ahmad Hafizh Damawan & Siti Azizah, *Resistance to Change: Causes and Strategies as an Organizational Challenge*, 395 Advances Soc. Sci., Educ. & Human. Rsch. 49, 50 (2020).

9. Carlos Valdes-Dapena, Lessons From Mars: How One Global Company Cracked the Code on High Performance Collaboration and Teamwork 193 (2018); Damawan et al, *supra* note 8, at 50 (explaining people resist change due to logical analysis and/or "selfish hopes and emotions that do not care about the benefits of change widely or for others").

10. Valdes-Dapena, *supra* note 9, at 102–05.

11. John Amaechi, Video: Strategies for Modern Leadership & Collaboration, Meeting of the Digital Minds (Ironclad, 2020) https://ironcladapp.com/lp/thankyou-webinarod-the-state-of-digital-contracting-deep-collaboration-the-uncertain-future-of-ms-word/?utm_campaign=2020Q3VirtualEventIronclad

Keynote&utm_medium=email&utm_source=sales&utm_term=prospect&utm
_content=Q3Keynot, (transcript of Amaechi's presentation on file with author).

12. Eric B. Dent & Susan Galloway Goldberg, *Challenging "Resistance to Change,"* 35 J. Applied Behav. Sci. 25, 27 (1999).

13. *Id.* at 38.

14. *Id.* at 37–39.

15. Valdes-Dapena, *supra* note 9, at 106.

16. I developed this mnemonic in LawWithoutWalls in 2014. As I was writing my first book, Legal Upheaval, I went online to see whether anyone else has used it (as lawyers, we are trained to footnote everything). Unsurprisingly, it has been used before but not in this context. For example, it is the motto for the United Methodist Church faith. *See,* Joe Iovino, *A Welcome and a Call: Open hearts. Open minds. Open doors,* United Methodist Church (Oct. 26, 2018), https://www.umc.org/en/content/a-welcome-and-a-call-open-hearts-open-minds-open-doors.

17. PSF CINO Interviewee 18.

18. Jane M. Howell & Christopher A. Higgins, *Champions of Change: Identifying, Understanding, and Supporting Champions of Technological Innovations,* 19 Organizational Dynamics 40, 42–44 (1990); Antonio Sadarića & Miha Škerlavaj, *Leader Idea Championing for Follower Readiness to Change or Not? A Moderated Mediation Perspective of Prosocial Sensegiving,* 23 J. Change Mgmt 200, 219 (2023).

19. Jennifer Cross, *Three Myths of Behavior Change: What You Think You Know that You Don't,* TEDxCSU (Mar. 20, 2013), https://www.youtube.com/watch?v=l5d8GW6GdR0; *see also* John P. Kotter, *Leading Change: Why Transformation Efforts Fail,* Harv. Bus. Rev. (May 1, 1995), https://hbr.org/1995/05/leading-change-why-transformation-efforts-fail-2 ("Most of the executives I have known in successful cases of major change learn to 'walk the talk.' . . . Nothing undermines change more than behavior by important individuals that is inconsistent with their words."); *cf.* Beer et al., *Why Change Programs Don't Produce Change,* Harv. Bus. Rev. (Nov. 1, 1990), https://hbr.org/1990/11/why-change-programs-dont-produce-change (explaining that although they don't necessarily have to at the start, eventually, "senior managers must make an effort to adopt the team behavior, attitude, and skills that they have demanded of others in earlier phases of change.").

20. Richard Wiseman, The As If Principle, The Radically New Approach to Changing Your Life 177 (2014) [hereinafter The As If Principle].

21. *See* Valdes-Dapena, *supra* note 9, at 86 ("The collaboration-versus-individual-achievement problem is a bit like broccoli versus ice cream. We know collaboration is a good thing but will nonetheless, if given a choice, go for the tasty treat of individual achievement.").

22. Damawan et al, *supra* note 8, at 51; Dan Pontefract, *New Research Suggests an Alarming Decline in High-Quality Leaders,* Forbes (Feb. 8, 2023), https://www.forbes.com/sites/danpontefract/2023/02/08/new-research-suggests-an-alarming-decline-in-high-quality-leaders/?sh=54d50e751493; *cf.* Ernst & Young,

supra note 7 ("80% agree establishing stakeholder trust will become an increasingly important part of the CEO's job."); *see also infra* Chapter 8 for further explanation of the necessity for trust.

23. *See* Valdes-Dapena, *supra* note 9, at 214–22; Amaechi, *supra* note 11 (stating that collaboration is about "exposing weakness . . . [and] sharing before you're ready. It's about jumping in and supporting before things hit critical . . . also it's about being vulnerable."); *see generally* Brené Brown, *The Power of Vulnerability*, TED (June 2010), https://www.ted.com/talks/brene_brown_the_power_of_vulnerability/transcript?language=en.

24. Bruce Tulgan, *Learn When to Say No*, Harv. Bus. Rev. (Sept. 1, 2020), https://hbr .org/2020/09/learn-when-to-say-no; Mike Novotny, *Don't Bow to Pressure. This Is How to Say "No" Effectively*, Forbes (Sept. 27, 2019), https://www.fastcompany .com/90410345/dont-bow-to-pressure-this-is-how-to-say-no-effectively.

25. Ingrid Wickelgren, *Speaking Science: Why People Don't Hear What You Say*, Sci. Am. (Nov. 8, 2012), https://www.scientificamerican.com/article/bring-science -home-speaking-memory; Rebecca Lake, *Listening Statistics: 23 Facts You Need to Hear*, CreditDonkey (Sept. 17, 2015), https://www.creditdonkey.com/listening-statistics.html. *But see* Will Thalheimer, *Debunk This: People Remember 10 Percent of What They Read*, Ass'n for Talent Dev. (Mar. 12, 2015), https://www.td.org/insights/debunk-this-people-remember-10-percent-of-what-they-read (arguing that Edgar Dale's "the Cone of Experience," which depicted that people remember 10 percent of what they read, 20 percent of what they hear, 30 percent of what they see, 50 percent of what they see and hear, 70 percent of what they say and write, 90 percent of what they do, is completely false.); *see also* Will Thalheimer, *People Remember 10%, 20% . . . Oh Really?*, Work-Learning Res. (2002), https:// www.worklearning.com/2006/05/01/people_remember (arguing that the Cone of Experience is inaccurate).

26. Ingrid Wickelgren, *supra* note 25; Rebecca Lake, *supra* note 25. *But see* Will Thalheimer, *People Remember 10%*, *supra* note 25.

27. Simon Sinek, *How to Listen: Simon Sinek*, askmen (June 29, 2010), https://www .askmen.com/money/career_300/364_how-to-listen-simon-sinek.html.

28. Daniel H. Pink, To Sell Is Human: The Surprising Truth About Moving Others 88–89 (2012).

29. Otto Scharmer, *4 Levels of Listening: Be a Better Listener*, World Work Project, https://worldofwork.io/2020/10/otto-scharmers-4-levels-of-listening-be-a -better-listener/ (last visited June 16, 2021).

30. *See* Robert Wright, The Moral Animal 681 (1994) (ebook) ("The human brain is, in large part, a machine for winning arguments, a machine for convincing others that its owner is right – and thus a machine for convincing its owner of the same thing. . . . Like a lawyer, the human brain wants victory, not truth, and like a lawyer it is sometimes more admirable for skill than virtue."); *See* Charles Darwin, His Life Told in an Autobiographical Chapter, and in a Selected Series of His Published Letters 42 (Francis Darwin ed., 1908) (1887).

31. Flow is a concept first introduced by Mihaly Csikszentmihalyi. *See* Mihaly Csikszentmihalyi, Flow: The Psychology of Optimal Experience vii (Harper Perennial Modern Classics, 2008) (1990).
32. Kane Pepi, *Sound Stupid? Dumb Business Ideas That Turned Out to Be Pretty Smart*, business.com (Dec. 11, 2014), on file with author; Devon Scott-Leslie, *18 Random Invention Ideas That Made Millions*, cad crowd: Blog (May 3, 2019), on file with author; Mike Michalowicz, *The Dumbest Business Ideas of All Time (That Made Millions)*, MikeMichalowicz.com (Apr. 1, 2013), https://mike michalowicz.com/the-dumbest-business-ideas-of-all-time-that-made-millions/; Patrick Thorne, *Ski Slope to Open on New Copenhagen Power Plant*, The Guardian (Nov. 16, 2016), https://www.theguardian.com/travel/2016/nov/16/copenhagen -ski-slope-green-power-plant/.
33. *See* Jonah Lehrer, *How to Be Creative*, Wall St. J. (Mar. 12, 2012), https://online .wsj.com/article/SB10001424052970203370604577265632205015846.html (reporting that "[w]hen people are exposed to a short video of stand-up comedy, they solve about 20% more of insight puzzles.").
34. Casper, *Who's Speaking First*, Medium (Jul. 15, 2021), https://casper6.medium.com/ whos-speaking-first-50f57c74e378#:~:text=In%20many%20organizational%20 settings%2C%20the,comes%20time%20to%20discuss%20ideas.
35. Cass R. Sunstein & Reid Hastie, *Making Dumb Groups Smarter*, Harv. Bus. Rev. (Dec. 1, 2014), https://hbr.org/2014/12/making-dumb-groups-smarter.
36. *See* Anita Williams Woolley et al., *Evidence for a Collective Intelligence Factor in the Performance of Human Groups*, 330 Sci. 686, 686–88 (2010) [hereinafter *Evidence for a Collective Intelligence Factor*].
37. Anita Woolley et al., *Why Some Teams Are Smarter Than Others*, N.Y. Times (Jan. 16, 2015), https://www.nytimes.com/2015/01/18/opinion/sunday/why-some -teams-are-smarter-than-others.html [hereinafter *Why Some Teams Are Smarter*]; *see also* Charles Duhigg, *What Google Learned From Its Quest to Build the Perfect Team*, N.Y. Times (Feb. 25, 2016), https://www.nytimes.com/2016/02/28/ magazine/what-google-learned-from-its-quest-to-build-the-perfect-team.html; Cameron Herold, *Why Leaders Should Speak Last in Meetings*, The Globe & Mail (Sept. 19, 2016), https://www.theglobeandmail.com/report-on-business/careers/ leadership-lab/why-leaders-should-speak-last-in-meetings/article31934105/; Mike Myatt, *Why Most Leaders Need to Shut Up and Listen*, Forbes (Feb. 9, 2012), https://www.forbes.com/sites/mikemyatt/2012/02/09/why-most-leaders-need -to-shut-up-listen/?sh=5234d8ed6ef9; Mark Williams, *Why Leaders Should Have the Last Word in ALL Meetings*, mtd (Feb. 24, 2016), https://www.mtdtraining .com/blog/the-3-main-benefits-of-the-leader-closing-every-meeting.htm.
38. *Why Some Teams Are Smarter*, *supra* note 37.
39. Steven Spear, *Learning to Lead at Toyota*, Harv. Bus. Rev. (May 1, 2004), https:// hbr.org/2004/05/learning-to-lead-at-toyota.

40. PSF Interviewee (Law Firm Partner) 2.
41. Kristin Holter, *When Leaders Should Speak First*, LinkedIn (Mar. 1, 2018), https://www.linkedin.com/pulse/when-should-leaders-speak-first-kristin-m-holter-fcipd/.
42. Christopher Chabris & Daniel Simons, The Invisible Gorilla: How Our Intuitions Deceive Us (Broadway Books, 2011) (2010).
43. Daniel Simons, *Failures of Awareness: The Case of Inattentional Blindness*, NOBA, https://nobaproject.com/~/modules/failures-of-awareness-the-case-of-inattentional-blindness#:~:text=We%20think%20important%20objects%20and,now%20known%20as%20inattentional%20blindness (last visited Sept. 8, 2023); *see also* Craig E. Geiss, *Inattentional or Change Blindness*, http://www.cti-home.com/wp-content/uploads/2014/01/Inattentional-Blindness.pdf (last visited Sept. 11, 2023).
44. Chabris & Simons, *supra* note 42, at 38–39 ("Focused attention allows us to avoid distraction and use our limited resources more effectively; we don't want to be distracted by everything around us.").
45. *See generally* Guillaume Hervet et al., *Is Banner Blindness Genuine? Eye Tracking Internet Text Advertising*, 25 Applied Cognitive Psychol. 708–16 (2010); Xavier Drèze & François-Xavier Hussherr, *Internet Advertising: Is Anybody Watching?*, 17 J. Interactive Mktg., 8, 8–23 (2003).
46. Chabris & Simons, *supra* note 42, at 241.
47. *Id.* at 37.
48. The As If Principle, *supra* note 20.
49. Richard Wiseman, The Luck Factor: Four Simple Principles That Will Change Your Luck—and Your Life 38–134 (Arrow Books, 2004) (2003) [hereinafter The Luck Factor]; Richard Wiseman, *Be Lucky—It's an Easy Skill to Learn*, The Telegraph (Jan. 9, 2003), https://www.telegraph.co.uk/technology/3304496/Be-lucky-its-an-easy-skill-to-learn.html/.
50. Carol S. Dweck, Mindset: The New Psychology of Success 12 (2006); Marina Krakovsky, *The Effort Effect*, Stanford Alumni Mag. (March–April 2007), https://stanfordmag.org/contents/the-effort-effect/. For a better understanding of fixed versus growth mindsets, see LawVision, *Fixed Mindset or Growth Mindset? How Learning Mindsets May Be Stifling Law Firm Change*, LawVision INSIGHTS Blog (Sept. 1, 2014), https://lawvision.com/fixed-mindset-or-growth-mindset-how-learning-mindsets-may-be-stifling-law-firm-change/.
51. Carol Dweck, *Teaching a Growth Mindset*, YouTube (Nov. 3, 2015), https://www.youtube.com/watch?v=isHM1rEd3GE.
52. Carol Dweck, *Teaching a Growth Mindset*, *supra* note 51; *see also*, Carol Dweck, *What Having a "Growth Mindset" Actually Means*, Harv. Bus. Rev. (Jan. 13, 2016), https://hbr.org/2016/01/what-having-a-growth-mindset-actually-means.
53. Carol Dweck, *Teaching a Growth Mindset*, *supra* note 51.

54. Darren Orf, *10 Awesome Accidental Discoveries*, Popular Mechs. (June 27, 2013), https://www.popularmechanics.com/science/health/g1216/10-awesome-accidental-discoveries/; Katie Kalvaitis, *Penicillin: An Accidental Discovery Changed the Course of Medicine*, Healio: Endocrinology (Aug. 10, 2008), https://www.healio.com/news/endocrinology/20120325/penicillin-an-accidental-discovery-changed-the-course-of-medicine.

55. Steven Johnson, Where Good Ideas Come From: The Natural History of Innovation 174 (2010).

56. Johnson, *supra* note 55, at 174.

57. Bec Oakley, *Ten Things for Parents to Love About Minecraft*, CodeRev's Blog (Oct. 26, 2016), https://www.coderevkids.com/blog/10-things-for-parents-to-love-about-minecraft/.

58. Jeff Dyer et al., The Innovator's DNA: Mastering the Five Skills of Disruptive Innovators 23–27 (1st ed. 2011).

59. *Blue Light Special: Colored Streetlamps Precede Decline in Crime*, Urbanist (Apr. 19, 2016), https://weburbanist.com/2016/04/19/blue-light-special-colored-streetlamps-precede-decline-in-crime/#:~:text=Blue%20Light%20Special%3A%20Colored%20Streetlamps%20Precede%20Decline%20in%20Crime,-Article%20by%20Urbanist&text=In%20the%20early%202000s%2C%20the,and%20disproportionate%20decrease%20in%20crime; Cameron Allan McKean, *How Blue Lights on Train Platforms Combat Tokyo's Suicide Epidemic*, Next City (Mar. 20, 2014), https://nextcity.org/urbanist-news/how-blue-lights-on-train-platforms-combat-tokyos-suicide-epidemic (explaining that track-jumping suicides actually form "a bigger threat to Tokyo's citizens than natural disasters and traffic fatalities combined.").

60. Dyer et al., *supra* note 58, at 31–32.

61. Antoine de Saint-Exupéry, The Little Prince 70 (Harcourt Brace Jovanovich, 1971) (1943).

62. Duhigg, *supra* note 37; *Evidence for a Collective Intelligence Factor, supra* note 36, *at* 686-88.

63. *See, e.g.*, Adrienne Tanner, *Can Accountants Learn Emotional Intelligence*, Chartered Pro. Acct. Can. (Jul. 2, 2019), https://www.cpacanada.ca/en/news/pivot-magazine/2019-07-02-soft-skills-cpas/ (last visited Jan. 16, 2022) (on file with author).

64. Harry Mills, *Accountants Must Learn to Communicate Warmth*, Ass'n Chartered Certified Acct. (Jan. 1, 2019), https://www.accaglobal.com/my/en/member/member/accounting-business/2019/01/insights/communicate-warmth.html/; Chris Matyszczyk, *Eureka! Engineers Aren't Empathetic Because They Can't Be*, CNET (Oct. 30, 2012), https://www.cnet.com/culture/eureka-engineers-arent-empathetic-because-they-cant-be/.

65. Case Western Reserve University, *Empathy Represses Analytic Thought, and Vice Versa: Brain Physiology Limits Simultaneous Use of Both Networks*, Sci. Daily (Oct. 30, 2012), https://www.sciencedaily.com/releases/2012/10/121030161416.htm.

66. Duhigg, *supra* note 37; *Evidence for a Collective Intelligence Factor*, *supra* note 36, at 686–87.

67. David Engel et al., *Reading the Minds in the Eyes or Reading Between the Lines? Theory of Mind Predicts Collective Intelligence Equally Well Online and Face-To-Face*, Plos One 11–12 (Dec. 16, 2014) https://journals.plos.org/plosone/article/file?id=10.1371/journal.pone.0115212&type=printable (providing strong empirical support for the conclusion that the ability to read others' mental states whether via text-based online interactions or other cues is as important to group effectiveness in online environments).

68. Sunstein & Hastie, *supra* note 35.

69. Karina Schumann, *Addressing the Empathy Deficit: Beliefs About the Malleability of Empathy Predict Effortful Responses When Empathy Is Challenging*, 107 J. Personality & Soc. Psychol. 475, 487, 492 (2013).

70. Stephen M. R. Covey, The Speed of Trust: The One Thing That Changes Everything 12–16 (Free Press, 2008) (2006) (ebook).

71. *See, e.g.*, Susan Fiske, *Stereotype Content: Warmth and Competence Endure*, 27 Ass'n for Psych. Sci. 67–73 (2018); Frederica Durante et al., *Nations' Income Inequality Predicts Ambivalence in Stereotype Content: How Societies Mind the Gap*, 52 Brit. J. Soc. Psychol. 726, 740 (2013).

72. Amy Cuddy, Presence: Bringing Your Boldest Self to Your Biggest Challenges 71–74 (2015) (ebook).

73. Simon Sinek, *The Art of Listening*, YouTube (Oct. 27, 2021), https://www.youtube.com/watch?v=qpnNsSyDw-g.

74. RSA, *Brené Brown on Empathy*, YouTube (Dec. 10, 2013), https://www.youtube.com/watch?v=1Evwgu369Jw.

75. *Id.*

76. *Id.*

77. William Ury, *The Power of Listening | William Ury | TedxSanDiego*, YouTube (Jan. 7, 2015) https://www.youtube.com/watch?v=saXfavo1OQo.

78. RSA, *supra note* 74.

79. Teresa Amabile et al., *IDEO's Culture of Helping*, Harv. Bus. Rev. (Jan. 1, 2014), https://hbr.org/2014/01/ideos-culture-of-helping/ ("Research across many kinds of companies finds that those with higher rates of helping have lower employee turnover, enjoy greater customer satisfaction, and are more profitable."); *see also* Amy C. Edmondson et al., *Speeding Up Team Learning*, Harv. Bus. Rev., Oct. 2001, at 125, 125–26, 130; *see also* Margaret Heffernan, *The Secret Ingredient That Makes Some Teams Better Than Others*, Ideas.Ted.com (May 5, 2015) https://ideas.ted.com/the-secret-ingredient-that-makes-some-teams-better-than-others.

80. Shel Silverstein, *Helping*, Poem Hunter, https://www.poemhunter.com/poem/helping-2/ (last visited Sept. 8, 2023).

81. Steven Spear, *Learning to Lead at Toyota*, Harv. Bus. Rev., May 2004, at 78, 84.

82. Brené Brown, Dare to Lead: Brave Work, Tough Conversations, Whole Hearts at 20, 23–24 (2018) [hereinafter Dare to Lead]; *About Brené*, https://

brenebrown.com/about (last visited July 9, 2022); *see* David Sluss, *Stepping Into a Leadership Role? Be Ready to Tell Your Story*, Harv. Bus. Rev. (Apr. 16, 2020), https://hbr.org/2020/04/stepping-into-a-leadership-role-be-ready-to-tell-your-story.

83. Tracy Brower, *Recruiters Are Passing Over College Degrees for this Essential Soft Skill: A Curious Mindset May Carry More Weight in the Current Hiring Market*, Fast Company (Apr. 25, 2022), https://www.fastcompany.com/90755136/recruiters-are-passing-over-college-degrees-for-this-essential-soft-skill.

84. Hal B. Gregersen, Questions Are the Answers: A Breakthrough Approach to Your Most Vexing Problems at Work and in Life 9 (2018) (ebook).

85. Nancy J. Adler, *Communicating Across Cultural Barriers, in* International Dimensions Organizational Behavior 63–91 (2nd ed. 1991) (1986).

86. *Id.* at 69.

87. *Id.; see generally* Philip C. Burger & Bernard M. Bass, Assessment of Managers: An International Comparison (1979) (conducting a study of managers from 14 different countries and finding that managers assumed that their peers were more like them than they actually were).

88. Annabel Fenwick Elliott, *The Science Behind Why People Who Prefer the Window Seat Are More Selfish* (Mar. 18 2019), https://www.telegraph.co.uk/travel/comment/window-versus-aisle-debate/ (reporting that airline statistics and studies by Expedia and Quartz show that "it's almost an even split" between window and aisle seat preferences).

89. *Id.*

90. *Id.*

91. *Id.*

92. *Id.*

93. Danny Heitman, *The Talented Mr. Huxley*, Humanities Mag. (Nov.–Dec. 2015), https://www.neh.gov/humanities/2015/novemberdecember/feature/the-talented-mr-huxley.

94. Heather Forest, Stone Soup 20 (1998).

95. Johnson, *supra* note 55, at 60.

96. *Id.* at 159–61.

97. Lehrer, *supra* note 33.

98. *See* Carsten K. W. De Dreu & Laurie R. Weingart, *Task Versus Relationship Conflict, Team Performance, and Team Member Satisfaction: A Meta-Analysis*, 88 J. Applied Psychol. 741, 741–49 (2003); Gunter K. Stahl & Martha L. Maznevski, *Unraveling the Effects of Cultural Diversity in Teams: A Retrospective of Research on Multicultural Work Groups and an Agenda for Future Research*, 52 J. Int'l Bus. Stud. 4, 4–22 (2021) (reviewing the literature on diversity and stating that "diversity can be a source of friction and conflict – and, hence, an obstacle to effective team functioning. But it can also be a source of synergy and learning – a powerful seed for something new.").

99. Susan Mohammed & Linda C. Angell, *Surface- and Deep-Level Diversity in Workgroups: Examining the Moderating Effects of Team Orientation and Team Process on*

Relationship Conflict, 25 J. ORG. BEHAV. 1015, 1015–39 (2004) (finding that conflicts related to diversity can be moderated by team orientation and team processes); Daan van Knippenberg et al., *Synergy from Diversity: Managing Team Diversity to Enhance Performance*, 6 BEHAV. SCI. & POL'Y 75, 75–92 (2020); Maria Del Carmen Triana et al., *The Relationship Between Deep-Level Diversity and Team Performance: A Meta-Analysis of the Main Effect, Moderators, and Mediating Mechanisms*, 58 J. MGMT. STUD. 2137–79 (2021); NANCY J. COOKE ET AL., ENHANCING THE EFFECTIVENESS OF TEAM SCIENCE 5–6 (2015).

100. Felix Maringe et al., *Leadership, Diversity and Decision Making*, CTR. FOR EXCELLENCE IN LEADERSHIP 32 (Mar. 2007), https://www.researchgate.net/publication/267817649_Leadership_Diversity_and_Decision_Making (explaining that the advantages of diverse groups "include an increase in the quality of group performance through creativity of ideas, cooperation, and the number of perspectives and alternatives considered."); *Id.* at 13 ("Since then, numerous writers have suggested that diverse teams may be advantageous to organisations, especially in performing decision making tasks."); Samuel R. Sommers, O*n Racial Diversity and Group Decision Making: Identifying Multiple Effects of Racial Composition on Jury Deliberations*, 90 J. PERSONALITY & SOC. PSYCHOL. 597, 598 (2006); Susan E. Jackson et al., *Understanding the Dynamics of Diversity in Decision-Making Teams, in* TEAM EFFECTIVENESS AND DECISION MAKING IN ORGANIZATIONS 204–61 (Richard A. Guzzo et al. ed., 1995); Kara L. Hal et al., *A Four-Phase Model of Transdisciplinary Team-Based Research: Goals, Team Processes, and Strategies*, TRANSLATIONAL BEHAV. MED., Dec. 2012, at 415, 425 ("[M]ore diverse teams are more likely to engage in debate. Because these conflicts and related debate can lead to new perspectives and new knowledge, they ultimately may be helpful for making strategic decisions [3, 40] and enhancing team performance.").

101. *See* De Dreu & Weingart, *supra* note 98, at 741–49; Stahl & Maznevski, *supra* note 98, at 4–22 (reviewing the literature on diversity and stating that "diversity can be a source of friction and conflict – and, hence, an obstacle to effective team functioning. But it can also be a source of synergy and learning – a powerful seed for something new.").

102. *See generally* Clint A. Bowers et al., *When Member Homogeneity Is Needed in Work Teams: A Meta-Analysis*, 31 SMALL GRP. RES. 305, 305–27 (2000).

103. WORLD ECON. FORUM, DIVERSITY, EQUITY AND INCLUSION 4.0, at 6 (2020), https://www3.weforum.org/docs/WEF_NES_DEI4.0_Toolkit_2020.pdf.

104. Sundiatu Dixon-Fyle et al., *Diversity Wins: How Inclusion Matters*, MCKINSEY & Co. (May 19, 2020), https://www.mckinsey.com/featured-insights/diversity-and-inclusion/diversity-wins-how-inclusion-matters; *The Bottom Line: Corporate Performance and Women's Representation on Boards*, CATALYST (2007), https://www.catalyst.org/wp-content/uploads/2019/01/The_Bottom_Line_Corporate_Performance_and_Womens_Representation_on_Boards.pdf.

105. Warren E. Watson et al., *Cultural Diversity's Impact on Interaction Process and Performance: Comparing Homogeneous and Diverse Task Groups*, 36 ACAD. MGMT. J. 590,

596–98 (1993); Lu Hong & Scott E. Page, *Groups of Diverse Problem Solvers Can Outperform Groups of High-Ability Problem Solvers*, 101 PNAS 16385, 16385–89 (2004); Scott E. Page, The Difference: How the Power of Diversity Creates Better Groups, Firms, Schools, and Societies xxvi, xxix (2007); Ralph A. Rodriguez, *Challenging Demographic Reductionism: A Pilot Study Investigating Diversity in Group Composition*, 29 Small Grp. Res. 744, 744–59 (1998) (studying 11 groups over 12 weeks and finding that demographic and value diversity also enhanced group creativity and effectiveness); *see* Anthony L. Antonio et al., *Effects of Racial Diversity on Complex Thinking in College Students*, 15 Psychol. Sci. 507–10 (2004).

106. *Evidence for a Collective Intelligence Factor*, *supra* note 36, at 686–88; *Why Some Teams Are Smarter*, *supra* note 37.

107. Tim Lemke, *Do Companies with Female Executives Perform Better*, The Balance (Aug. 26, 2021), https://www.thebalancemoney.com/do-companies-with-female-executives-perform-better-4586443; *The XX Heartbeat Factor: The Strategic Benefits of Women in Leadership*, Heartbeat by Workday (2019), https://forms.workday.com/en-us/reports/employee-voice-strategic-benefits-of-women-in-leadership/form.html?step=step1_default.

108. Luisa Alemany & Freek Vermeulen, *Disability as a Source of Competitive Advantage*, Harv. Bus. Rev. (July 1, 2023), https://hbr.org/2023/07/disability-as-a-source-of-competitive-advantage#:~:text=So%20the%20general%20attitude%20of,pay%20more%20for%20its%20offering.

109. Based on interviews of people who work creatively in different fields, Frans Johansson, author of *The Medici Effect*, found that the likelihood of innovation is higher when people of different disciplines, backgrounds, and areas of expertise collaboratively work together to problem solve. Frans Johansson, The Medici Effect: What Elephants and Epidemics Can Teach Us About Innovation (2017); *see also The Medici Effect: A Simple Introduction*, World Work Project, https://worldofwork.io/2019/07/the-medici-effect (last visited Jan. 28, 2022).

110. Rob Cross & Andrew Parker, The Hidden Power of Social Networks: Understanding How Work Really Gets Done in Organizations 81–83 (2004) ("Research has shown that people with more diverse, entrepreneurial networks tend to be more successful.").

111. Hanne K. Collins et al., *Relational Diversity in Social Portfolios Predicts Well-Being*, PNAS (Oct. 17, 2022), https://www.pnas.org/doi/full/10.1073/pnas.2120668119 (describing social portfolio diversity as "the number and distribution of the various types of relationships engaged in during specific periods of time" and claiming it is a higher and more reliable predictor of subjective well-being than being married).

112. R. Matthew Montoya et al., *Is Actual Similarity Necessary for Attraction? A Meta-Analysis of Actual and Perceived Similarity*, 25 J. Soc. & Pers. Relationships 879, 880-883 (2008) (discussing the research in support of this); Gwendolyn Seidman, *Why Do We Like People Who Are Similar to Us?*, Psychol. Today (Dec. 18, 2018), https://www.psychologytoday.com/us/blog/close-encounters/201812/why-do-we-people-who-are-similar-us.

113. Adam J. Hampton et al., *You're Like Me and I Like You: Mediators of the Similarity–Liking Link Assessed Before and After a Getting-Acquainted Social Interaction*, 36 J. Soc. & Pers. Relationships 2221, 2224 (2019).

114. A. Aron & E. N. Aron, Love and the Expansion of Self: Understanding Attraction and Satisfaction 6, 66–67, 85–88 (1986).

115. Martin Ruef, *Strong Ties, Weak Ties and Islands: Structural and Cultural Predictors of Organizational Innovation*, 11 Indus. & Corp. Change 427, 429–30, 432, 443 (2002) ("[T]he propensity of individual entrepreneurs to break with convention is both encouraged by social relations—which may bring disparate ideas, routine or technologies to an entrepreneur's attention—and discouraged by social relations—which may introduce pressures for conformity or concerns about trust."); Mark S. Granovetter, *The Strength of Weak Ties*, 78 Am. J. Soc. 1360, 1361–66 (1973); Richard Ogle, Smart World: Breakthrough Creativity and the New Science of Ideas 87–88 (2007).

116. Ray Oldenburg, The Great Good Place: Cafés, Coffee Shops, Community Centers, Beauty Parlors, General Stores, Bars, Hangouts and How They Get You Through the Day 42 (1989).

117. Johnson, *supra* note 55, at 162–63.

118. Tina Seelig, *inGenius: A Crash Course on Creativity* (New York: HarperCollins Publishers, 2012) 95–102.

119. Dr. Seuss, *Oh, The Places You'll Go* (New York: Random House, 1990).

120. However, studies have shown that value diversity among a team (when conflict is managed) can result in greater personal satisfaction and greater perceived creativity by teams. *See, e.g.*, Rodriguez, *supra* note 106, at 744–59; Luis M. Arciniega et al., *Exploring the Effects of Value Diversity on Team Effectiveness*, 28 J. Bus. Psychol. 107, 107–21 (2013) (Finding that team value diversity has a negative correlation with team processes and recommending better leadership and facilitation to counteract that); Stahl & Maznevski, *supra* note 98, at 690–709 ("finding that cultural diversity leads to process losses by increasing potential for conflict. However, these losses are partially offset by process gains from creativity").

121. Johnson, *supra* note 55, at 159–61.

122. Ringo Pebam, *How Steve Jobs Got the Ideas of GUI From Xerox*, YouTube (Jan. 4, 2014), https://www.youtube.com/watch?v=J33pVRdxWbw.

123. Jobs evidently saw the Xerox Alto, which is accredited as the first computer designed from its inception to support an operating system based on a GUI, icons, pop-up menus, and a pointing device to control the computer. However, its focus was not at the time on personal computing. *See History of the Graphical User Interface*, Wikipedia, https://en.wikipedia.org/wiki/History_of_the_graphical _user_interface (last visited Jan. 28, 2022).

124. *Id.*

125. Tendayi Viki, *As Xerox PARC Turns 47: The Lessons Learned Is that Business Models Matter*, Forbes (July 1, 2017, 12:30 AM), https://www.forbes.com/sites/ tendayiviki/2017/07/01/as-xerox-parc-turns-forty-seven-the-lesson-learned-is -that-business-models-matter/?sh=f01338775482.

126. *The Xerox PARC Visit*, STAN. UNIV., https://web.stanford.edu/dept/SUL/sites/mac/parc.html (last visited Jan. 18, 2022) (claiming that Jobs did not steal, copy, or borrow these innovations but that he simultaneously was developing the same ones).

127. Stephen M. Klugewicz, *Copying Mozart: Did Beethoven Steal Melodies for His Own Music?*, THE IMAGINATIVE CONSERVATIVE (Feb. 21, 2018), https://theimaginative conservative.org/2018/02/copying-mozart-beethoven-steal-melodies-music -stephen-klugewicz.html.

128. *Id.*

129. T. S. Eliot, *Excerpts from 'Philip Massinger' p. 206*, TSELIOT.COM, https://tseliot .com/prose/phillip-massinger (last visited Sept. 12, 2023).

130. Mark Twain, *Mark Twain's Own Autobiography: The Chapters from the North American Review*, GOODREADS, https://www.goodreads.com/work/quotes/23640909 -chapters-from-my-autobiography (last visited Jan. 18, 2022).

131. This term has been used in this way by other writers in the innovation context. *See, e.g,* JOHNSON, *supra* note 55, at 159–61; Michele DeStefano, *Nonlawyers Influencing Lawyers: Too Many Cooks in the Kitchen or Stone Soup?*, 80 FORDHAM L. REV. 2791, 2808–14 (2012).

132. *Infra* Part III, Chapter 11.A.2.d (Step 4).

133. Although they do not call it exaptation, other design thinkers have touted the importance of looking outward at other industries and other examples of success to imitate or combine with new ideas to fuel successes of their own. *See, e.g*, *An Activity to Help You Find Inspiration Outside Your Context*, IDEOU https://www .ideou.com/blogs/inspiration/an-activity-to-help-you-find-inspiration-outside -your-context (last visited July 9, 2022); WILLIAM DUGGAN, CREATIVE STRATEGY: A GUIDE FOR INNOVATION 32–29 (2012); Ken Favaro, *The Right Ideas in All the Wrong Places*, STRATEGY & BUS. (Mar. 11, 2013), https://www.strategy-business .com/article/cs00007; BOB EBERLE, SCAMPER: CREATIVE GAMES AND ACTIVITIES FOR IMAGINATION DEVELOPMENT 2–4 (2nd ed. 2008) (1997) (ebook).

134. *Inflatable Puffer Fish Pill 'Could Track Patient's Health,'* BBC (Jan. 30, 2019), https:// www.bbc.com/news/health-47059079; *Printing Press*, History.Com (June 29, 2023), https://www.history.com/topics/inventions/printing-press.

135. As you can likely tell, exaptation is a great source of innovation and in keeping with that I have created an exaptation exercise that I use with teams to help them in the ideation stage.

136. Theresa Lant & Maritza Salazar, *Facilitating Innovation in Interdisciplinary Teams: The Role of Leaders and Integrative Communication*, 21 INFORMING SCI. 157, 166–70 (2018).

137. *See generally* VIORICA MARIAN, THE POWER OF LANGUAGE: HOW THE CODES WE USE TO THINK, SPEAK, AND LIVE TRANSFORM OUR MINDS (2023). *But see* Luca Turin, *The Power of Language by Viorica Marian Review–The Virtues of Multilingualism*, THE GUARDIAN: BOOKS (Apr. 7, 2023), https://www.theguardian.com/ books/2023/apr/07/the-power-of-language-by-viorica-marian-review-the -virtues-of-multilingualism (describing Marian's book as "[a]n eloquent but relentless attempt to prove the superiority of polyglots [that] fails to convince.").

138. *See the Legal Design Lab*, Stan. L. Sch., https://law.stanford.edu/organizations/pages/legal-design-lab/#slsnav-our-mission (last visited Aug. 8, 2022).

139. Dyer et al., *supra* note 58, at 23–27.

140. *Id.* at 31–32.

141. World Econ. Forum, The Future of Jobs Report v–vi (2018) [hereinafter WEF Report 2018]; World Econ. Forum, The Future of Jobs Report 3–4 (2020) [hereinafter WEF Report 2020]; *see* Deloitte Insights, 2021 Deloitte Global Human Capital Trends 20–23 (2021) ("'[P]assion projects' give workers new development experiences and opportunities to learn in the flow of work, further enhancing the skills they bring to the organization.").

142. *Here's Why Creativity Matters More than IQ*, World. Econ. Forum (July 2, 2021) https://www.weforum.org/videos/23081-here-s-why-creativity-matters-more-than-iq; *see* Deloitte Insights, *supra* note 138, at 20–23.

143. Adam Brandenburger, *Strategy Needs Creativity*, Harv. Bus. Rev. (Mar. 1, 2019), https://hbr.org/2019/03/strategy-needs-creativity/.

144. Anthony Rivas, *How Drinking Alcohol Makes You More Creative: Drink Up for More "Aha!" Moments*, Med. Daily (Mar. 11, 2014), https://www.medicaldaily.com/how-drinking-alcohol-makes-you-more-creative-drink-more-aha-moments-271026; Cassie Shortsleeve, *Why Drinking Boosts Creativity*, Men's Health (Mar. 9, 2015), https://www.menshealth.com/health/a19536124/drinking-creativity/#.

145. Csikszentmihalyi, *supra* note 31, at vii.

146. *The World According to Mister Rogers*, The Dorky Daddy (January 6, 2014) (quoting poet Kenneth Koch), https://thedorkydaddy.com/2014/01/06/the-world-according-to-mister-rogers/.

147. Dixon-Fyle et al., *supra* note 104 (showing that the likelihood of team members' psychological safety increases by demonstrating the behaviors associated with consultative and supportive leadership styles).

148. *See generally* Jon. J. Muth, Zen Shorts (2005). To watch a video of Jon Muth reading the story aloud from his book, see Jonah Salsich, *Zen Shorts – "The Farmer's Luck,"* Vimeo, https://vimeo.com/17468634 (last visited Sept. 8, 2023).

149. Adler, *supra* note 85, at 63–91.

150. There are six Fs in the sentence.

151. Adler, *supra* note 85, at 63-91.

152. *Id.*

Chapter 7

1. Gokhan Guley & Tracy Reznik, *Culture Eats Strategy for Breakfast and Transformation for Lunch*, The Jabian Journal (Fall 2019), https://journal.jabian.com/wp-content/uploads/2019/10/701_JJ_Fall_19_Culture_Eats_Strategy.pdf.

2. *Id.*

3. *See* McKinsey & Co., *Psychological Safety and the Critical Role of Leadership Development* (Feb. 11, 2021), https://www.mckinsey.com/capabilities/people-and-organizational-performance/our-insights/psychological-safety-and-the

-critical-role-of-leadership-development; Charles Duhigg, *What Google Learned From Its Quest to Build the Perfect Team*, N.Y. Times (February 28, 2016), https://www.nytimes.com/2016/02/28/magazine/what-google-learned-from-its-quest -to-build-the-perfect-team.html (discussing Google's Project Aristotle and how it demonstrated the importance of psychological safety to a team's accomplishments).

4. *See* Gartner, Measure and Influence Innovation Climate at Your Organi- zation, at 6 (2021), https://emtemp.gcom.cloud/ngw/globalassets/en/innovation -strategy/documents/trends/r-d_innovation_climate_whitepaper.pdf (testing 80 drivers and finding that when done well, senior leader posture is the most impact- ful and can have the biggest improvement to innovation climate strength); *see also* Jennifer Cross, *Three Myths of Behavior Change: What You Think You Know That You Don't*, TedXCSU (Mar. 20, 2013), https://www.youtube.com/watch?v=l5d8GW6 GdR0 (stressing the importance of behavior because "attitudes follow behavior, they do not predict it.").

5. *Id.*

6. *See* Gartner, *supra* note 4, at 3 ("The signals leaders convey, the permissions managers grant, and the processes and practices of an organization shape employ- ees' shared perceptions (innovation climate) on innovation.").

7. *See id.* at 2 ("Employees' shared values and beliefs shape their behavior.").

8. Eric B. Dent & Susan Galloway Goldberg, *Challenging "Resistance to Change,"* 35 (1) J. Applied Behav. Sci. 25, 39 (1999).

9. Russell Eisenstat, Bert Spector, & Michael Beer, *Why Change Programs Don't Pro- duce Change*, Harv. Bus. Rev. (Nov. 1, 1990), https://hbr.org/1990/11/why-change -programs-dont-produce-change ("[T]he most effective senior managers in our study recognized their limited power to mandate corporate renewal from the top. Instead, they defined their roles as creating a climate for change then spreading the lessons of both successes and failures."); *id.* (finding that change management efforts that focus on "programmatic change" actually make the situation worse because they are so general and standardized that they don't speak to the day-to-day realities of particular units and "end up covering nobody and nothing particularly well").

10. Keith Ferrazzi, *A New Social Contract for Teams*, Harv. Bus. Rev. (September 1, 2022), https://hbr.org/2022/09/a-new-social-contract-for-teams ("Companies have traditionally emphasized leadership competencies not team competencies. In focusing so heavily on what it means to be a great leader, they've often lost sight of what it means to be a great team.").

11. David Aycan, *Q+A with IDEO: Six Critical Innovation Qualities the Creative Difference Tool Helps Identify and Measure Qualities Crucial for Innovation* (July 6, 2021), https:// www.steelcase.com/research/articles/topics/innovation/qa-with-ideo-six-critical -innovation-qualities/?pdf (explaining that teams repeatedly struggle with figuring out where to focus to develop innovation practices and identifying six elements that create conditions for creativity) (last visited May 25, 2021) (on file with author).

12. Marcie B. Shunk & Silvia L. Coulter, *The Expanding Role of Professional Development: Preparing Lawyers for Business: Survey of Law Firm Professional Development*, Tilt

INST. & LAWVISION (June 2020), https://static1.squarespace.com/static/582cadac3
e00bed23e1f9b25/t/5ee3cc6482fac1522d5dfdb5/1591987300986/LVG_Tilt
_ExpandingRole_of_ProfessionalDevelopment_June2020.pdf (reporting that the
average ranking for leadership training is a 4 out of 10 based on results from a
study of 40 percent of AM Law 100 conducted by the Tilt Institution in collaboration with LawVision); Milhnea Moldoveanu & Das Narayandas, *The Future of
Leadership Development*, HARV. BUS. REV., Mar.-Apr. 2019, at 40, 42–43 (reporting
that "50% of senior leaders believe that their talent development efforts don't
adequately build critical skills and organizational capabilities" and stating that
"[t]raditional executive education is simply too episodic, exclusive and expensive"
and that executive education programs "have seen demand increase significantly
for customized, cohort-based programs that address companies' idiosyncratic
talent-development needs.").

13. Guley et al, *supra* note 1, at 63–64.

14. Ferrazzi, *supra* note 10 (using similar attributes to diagnose whether a team exhib-
its the essential team behaviors that make a team great). Note: I came across the
Ferrazzi article almost a year after I created my S.A.F.E.T.Y. acronym and was
delighted to see the support for my concept, which was created based on my
13 years leading 230 teams on a 4-month innovation journey.

15. RONALD HEIFETZ ET AL., THE PRACTICE OF ADAPTIVE LEADERSHIP: TOOLS AND
TACTICS FOR CHANGING YOUR ORGANIZATION AND THE WORLD 28–31 (2009)
[hereinafter TOOLS AND TACTICS]; *see also* AMY C. EDMONDSON, TEAMING: HOW
ORGANIZATIONS LEARN, INNOVATE, AND COMPETE IN THE KNOWLEDGE ECONOMY
149–150 (2012) (ebook).

16. HEIFETZ ET AL., *supra* note 15, at 533–34.

17. HEIFETZ ET AL., *supra* note 15, at 562–63; *see also* Ferrazzi, *supra* note 10 ("Before
you can change the ways in which your team members interact and operate, you
need a clear view of how they are functioning right now.").

18. Forbes Expert Panel, *15 Methods to Spot a Company's Leadership Gaps*, FORBES (May 18,
2021), https://www.forbes.com/sites/forbescoachescouncil/2021/05/18/15
-methods-to-spot-a-companys-leadership-gaps/?sh=2b0a7a0d69d1.

19. Many tools to gauge collaboration and innovation readiness exist. Some were
created by academic scholars, researchers, and research organizations. *See, e.g.,*
João Rosas & Luis M. Camarinha-Matos, *An Approach to Assess Collaboration Readiness*, 47(17) INT'L J. PROD. RSCH. 4711, 4711–35 (2009) (proposing an approach
to perform assessment of collaboration readiness and making a distinction
between collaboration readiness and collaboration preparedness); L. Michelle
Bennett & Howard Gadlin, *Collaboration and Team Science Field Guide*, NIH
NAT'L CANCER INST. (2010), https://www.cancer.gov/about-nci/organization/crs/
research-initiatives/team-science-field-guide/collaboration-team-science-guide
.pdf. Other tools, like those listed in the body of this handbook, were created by
consulting companies. *See, e.g., Collaboration Readiness Tool: Does My Organization
Have a Collaborative Mindset?*, THE GIVING PRACTICE, https://philanthropynw.org/

sites/default/files/resources/PGT_Collaboration_Readiness_2020.pdf (last visited Jan. 29, 2022); Rachel Novotny & Jean Butel, *Collaboration Readiness Survey*, Reg'l Nutrition Educ. And Obesity Prevention Ctr. of Excellence, https:// snapedpse.org/wp-content/uploads/2017/08/CollaborationReadinessSurvey -v01-BW.pdf (last visited Jan. 29, 2022); *Collaboration Maturity and Readiness Tool*, Infotech, https://www.infotech.com/research/it-social-collaboration-maturity -and-readiness-assessment (last visited Jan. 29, 2022); *Smart Collaboration Diagnostic*, Gardner & Co.., https://www.gardnerandco.co/services/tools/ (last visited July 9, 2022).

20. Sophie Chow et al., *The Case for Creative Problem Solving: Creativity Should Be in Every Leader's Toolbox*, Medium: IDEO Creative Difference (Nov. 23, 2020), https://medium.com/@ideoCD/the-case-for-creative-problem-solving -f6f1a7a26a0f; Aycan, *supra* note 11.

21. To take Ferrazzi Greenlight's team assessment, *see* https://ferrazzigreenlight.com/ high-impact-team-assessment-questionnaire/ (last visited Sept. 17, 2023).

22. For a study identifying the weaknesses with current collaboration readiness frameworks and claiming that collaboration readiness levels should be measured within the innovation process as opposed to retrospectively, see Eva Kalmar et al., *Address at SciT's 2019 Conference: Building the Collaboration Readiness Framework for Ad-Interim Evaluation of Transdisciplinary Collaboration*, TUDelft (May 2019), https://www.inscits.org/assets/2019/Kalmar%20-%20building%20 the%20collaboration%20readiness%20framework%20for%20ad-interim%20 evaluation%20of%20transdisciplinary%20collaborations.pdf.

23. Michael Mankins & Mark Gottfredson, *Strategy-Making in Turbulent Times*, Harv. Bus. Rev. (Sept. 1, 2023), https://hbr.org/2022/09/strategy-making-in-turbulent-times.

24. *Id.*

25. *See, e.g.*, Jackie Wiles, *Is It Time to Toss Out Your Old Employee Engagement Survey?*, Gartner (Nov. 26, 2018), https://www.gartner.com/smarterwithgartner/ is-it-time-to-toss-out-your-old-employee-engagement-survey.

26. *See, e.g.*, Gartner, *supra* note 4, at 4 ("The signals leaders convey, the permissions managers grant, and the processes and practices of an organization shape employees' shared perceptions (innovation climate) on innovation."); *see* Wiles, *supra* note 25.

27. *A Novel Way to Boost Client Satisfaction: Analyze Email Behaviors and Share Best Practices*, Harv. Bus. Rev. (March 1, 2019), https://hbr.org/2019/03/a-novel-way -to-boost-client-satisfaction (explaining that "email [i]s a resource that leaves behind digital breadcrumbs that can be systematically analyzed).

28. *See, e.g.*, Rob Cross & Andrew Parker, The Hidden Power of Social Networks: Understanding How Work Really Gets Done in Organizations (2004); *see* Wiles, *supra* note 25.

29. Many companies offer tools to create short pulse surveys, including CultureMonkey, SurveyMonkey, Qualtrics, Applauz, and Gallop. For an overview of pulse surveys and their benefits *see* John Biotnott, *What Are Pulse Surveys, and How They Can Help*

Your Company, Entrepreneur (October 12, 2021), https://www.entrepreneur.com/leadership/what-are-pulse-surveys-and-how-they-can-help-your-company/389010.

30. Kara L. Hal et al., *A Four-Phase Model of Transdisciplinary Team-Based Research: Goals, Team Processes, and Strategies*, 2(4) Translational Behav. Med. 415, 415–30 (Dec. 2012) (demonstrating that teams should use self-assessment tools to identify areas for improvement and enhance team processes and suggesting the Teamwork Framework by the National Cancer Institute Division of Cancer Control & Population Sciences, as part of their Team Science Toolkit). For more information about the NCI's teamwork framework and toolkit, *see Team Science Toolkit*, Nat'l Cancer Inst., https://cancercontrol.cancer.gov/brp/research/team-science-toolkit (last visited Jan. 29, 2022). *See also* Joann Keyton & Stephenson J. Beck, *Team Attributes, Processes, and Values: A Pedagogical Framework*, 71 Bus. Commc'n Quarterly 488-504 (2008) (presenting a pedagogical framework that intersects "five fundamental group attributes (group size, group goal, group member interdependence, group structure, and group identity) with three overarching group processes (leadership, decision making, and conflict management) and that weds team member behaviors with the values members espouse and enact" and can be used as a tool to analyze team interaction); *SciTS Evaluation*, Divergent Science LLC., https://teamdivergentscience.com/scits-evaluation (last visited Jan. 29); Jennifer Cross, *I'm Ready, Are You Ready?*, Colorado State University, https://www.inscits.org/assets/2019/Cross%20-%20Im%20ready%20are%20you%20ready.pdf (last visited Jan. 29) (studying the readiness of teams to launch and co-create and surveying teams based on whether team members agree or disagree with the following six statements: I feel like my contributions are valued on the team, I am confident about the team, my team gets thing done, I am confident about the goals of the team, team meetings are fun, I feel like I have something unique to contribute to the team).

31. Chow, *supra* note 20.

32. For further support of this, *see* Teresa Amabile & Muktil Khaire, *Creativity and the Role of the Leader*, Harv. Bus. Rev. (Oct. 1, 2008), https://hbr.org/2008/10/creativity-and-the-role-of-the-leader (noting that Kim Scott, a director at Google, "added that the manager must act as a shepherd—an analogy also used by Christy Jones, founder of Extend Fertility. Both believe that executives must protect those doing creative work from a hostile environment and clear paths for them around obstacles.").

33. For a review of DiSC, see https://discprofile.com/what-is-disc/overview/. For a description of the last test listed, see Suzanne M. Johnson Vickberg and Kim Chrisfort, *Pioneers, Drivers, Integrators, and Guardians*, Harv. Bus. Rev. (March. 1, 2017), https://hbr.org/2017/03/pioneers-drivers-integrators-and-guardians (explaining the assessment as dividing people into pioneers, guardians, drivers, and integrators).

34. Nancy J. Cooke et al., Enhancing the Effectiveness of Team Science 5-8 (2015).

35. Aycan, *supra* note 11.

36. Mark Murphy, *The State of Leadership Development*, LEADERSHIP IQ, https://www
    .leadershipiq.com/blogs/leadershipiq/leadership-development-state (last visited
    Aug. 24, 2023).

37. *Id.*

38. John P. Kotter, *Leading Change: Why Transformation Efforts Fail*, HARV. BUS. REV.
    (May 1, 1995), https://hbr.org/1995/05/leading-change-why-transformation
    -efforts-fail-2; Aycan, *supra* note 11; Heidi K. Gardner, *When Senior Managers
    Won't Collaborate*, Harv. Bus. Rev., Mar. 2015, at 74, 74–78; BRENÉ BROWN, DARE
    TO LEAD: BRAVE WORK, TOUGH CONVERSATIONS, WHOLE HEARTS 183–217 (2018)
    [hereinafter DARE TO LEAD].

39. SIMON SINKE, START WITH WHY: HOW GREAT LEADERS INSPIRE EVERYONE TO
    TAKE ACTION (2009); HEIFETZ ET AL., *supra* note 15, at 28–31.

40. Jennifer Cross, *Three Myths of Behavior Change: What You Think You Know
    That You Don't*, TEDXCSU (Mar. 20, 2013), https://www.youtube.com/
    watch?v=l5d8GW6GdR0.

41. Barbara L. Fredrickson & Marcial F. Losada, *Positive Affect and the Complex
    Dynamics of Human Flourishing*, 60 AM. PSYCH. 678-86 (2005).

42. Alice M. Isen et al., *Positive Affect Facilitates Creative Problem Solving*, 52 J. Pers Soc
    Psych. 1122-1131 (1987); Fredrickson & Losada, *supra* note 40, at 678–86; Jonah
    Lehrer, *How to Be Creative*, THE WALL STREET JOURNAL (Mar. 12, 2012, 6:25 PM),
    https://online.wsj.com/article/SB10001424052970203370604577265632205015
    846.html; Annette Bolte et al., *Emotion and Intuition: Effects of Positive and Negative
    Mood on Implicit Judgments of Semantic Coherence*, 14 PSYCH. SCI. 416-21 (demon-
    strating that positive mood improved intuition).

43. See, e.g., Russell Eisenstat, Bert Spector, and Michael Beer, *Why Change Pro-
    grams Don't Produce Change*, HARV. BUS. REV. (November 1, 1990), https://hbr
    .org/1990/11/why-change-programs-dont-produce-change.

44. As will be discussed further, roles really matter and not just for accountabil-
    ity but also to make clear who makes decisions. *See, e.g.*, Linda A. Hill, Emily
    Tedards, & Taran Swan, *Drive Innovation with Better Decision-Making*, HARV. BUS.
    REV. (November 1, 2021), https://hbr.org/2021/11/drive-innovation-with-better
    -decision-making; Russell Eisenstat et al., *supra* note 43 ("[T]he most effective
    way to change behavior, therefore, is to put people into a new organizational
    context, which imposes new roles, responsibilities, and relationships on them.
    This creates a situation that, in a sense, "forces" new attitudes and behaviors on
    people.")

45. *See, e.g.*, Ferrazzi, *supra note* 10 ("To achieve breakthrough performance, teams
    should commit to a new social contract that emphasizes candor, collaboration
    accountability, and continual improvements.").

46. Howard Gadlin & Kevin Jessar, *"Prenuptials" for Collaborators*, THE NIH CATA-
    LYST, May-June 2002, at 12; *see also*, Joan P. Schwartz, *Silence Is Not Golden, Making*

Collaborations Work, The NIH Catalyst, July-Aug. 1997, at 3. *See also* Dare to Lead, *supra* note 37, at 55 (recommending teams do mini versions of this after each meeting, that is, review meeting notes, agree on content, identify roles and responsibilities, and timing).

47. The American Society of Training and Development (ASTD) did a study on accountability and found that you have a 65 percent chance of completing a goal if you commit to someone. And if you have a specific accountability appointment with a person to whom you've committed, you will increase your chance of success by up to 95 percent. *See* Stephen Newland, *The Power of Accountability*, Ass'n For Fin, Counseling & Plan. Educ. (2018), https://www.afcpe.org/news-and -publications/the-standard/2018-3/the-power-of-accountability; John S. Brown et al., *Commit to a Shared Outcome: Focus on the Outcome that Matters Most to Foster Passion and Amplify Your Actions*, Deloitte (Jan. 31, 2018), https://www2.deloitte .com/xe/en/insights/topics/talent/business-performance-improvement/commit -to-shared-outcomes.html; Bad Decisions Podcast, *#32 Commitment Bias: Why You Should Shout It Out Loud*, PodBean (Dec. 23, 2020), https://baddecisions -podcast.com/archive/2020/12/23/32-commitment-bias [hereinafter Bad Decisions Episode 32].

48. Robert E. Quinn & Anjan V. Thakor, *Creating a Purpose-Driven Organization*, Harv. Bus. Rev. (July 1, 2018), https://hbr.org/2018/07/creating-a-purpose-driven -organization; Mark Bonchek, *Purpose Is Good. Shared Purpose Is Better*, Harv. Bus. Rev. (Mar. 13, 2013), https://hbr.org/2013/03/purpose-is-good-shared-purpose; Hal et al., *supra* note 30, at 415–30; Bennett & Gadlin, *supra* note 19, at 768–75 ("Other critical factors of which both leaders and participants need to be aware include developing a shared vision, strategically identifying team members and purposefully building the team, promoting disagreement while containing conflict, and setting clear expectations for sharing credit and authorship.").

49. *See, e.g.*, DeStefano et al., *Don't Let the Digital Tail Wag the Transformation Dog: A Digital Transformation Roadmap for Corporate Counsel*, 17 J. Bus. and Tech. L. (recommending that legal departments should create mission statements of their own and that they should align with the larger corporation's mission statement).

50. Hal et al., *supra* note 30, at 415–30.

51. Helen Rosner & Greg Morabito, *How Naomi Pomeroy Runs an Empowering Kitchen*, Eater: Eater's Digest (Apr.10, 2017), https://www.eater.com/ 2017/4/10/15182402/eater-upsell-naomi-pomeroy.

52. Frances Frei & Anne Morriss, Unleashed: The Unapologetic Leader's Guide to Empowering Everyone Around You 4 (2020).

53. Craig Eaton et al., *Introduction: The Social Enterprise in a World Disrupted*, Deloitte (Dec 9. 2020), https://www2.deloitte.com/us/en/insights/focus/human-capital -trends/2021/social-enterprise-survive-to-thrive.html.

54. See video on Alphabet Work at https://www.scienceofpeople.com/team-building -activities/.

55. Tricia McKinnon, *Trader Joe's: 10 Ways It Attracts & Retains Great Employees*, INDIGO DIGITAL (March 17, 2022), https://www.indigo9digital.com/blog/traderjoesemployeeretention.

56. Gary P. Pisano, *The Hard Truth About Innovative Cultures: Creativity Can Be Messy. It Needs Discipline and Management*, HARV. BUS. REV., Jan-Feb 2019, at 10.

57. Raychel Lean, *This Law Firm Is Ditching Partner and Associate Titles. Will It Improve Team Culture?*, LAW.COM (July 11, 2022), https://www.law.com/dailybusinessreview/2022/07/11/this-law-firm-is-ditching-partner-and-associate-titles-will-it-improve-team-culture.

58. Amy C. Edmondson & Ranjay Gulati, *Agility Hacks: How to Create Temporary Teams That Can Bypass Bureaucracy and Get Crucial Work Done Quickly*, HARV. BUS. REV. (November 1, 2021), https://hbr.org/2021/11/agility-hacks.

59. Ferrazzi, *supra* note 10.

60. Stephanie Neal, *The Human Factor: The Top 3 Concerns Keeping CEOs Up at Night* (March 21, 2023), https://ceoworld.biz/2023/03/21/the-human-factor-the-top-3-concerns-keeping-ceos-up-at-night/ (surveying 13,695 leaders worldwide, including 529 CEOs, about the state of leadership and reporting that keeping talent engaged was a critical concern of leaders and one way to do that was to include them in a "strong sense of purpose").

61. Quinn & Thakor, *supra* note 47.

62. *The State of Leadership Development*, LEADERSHIP IQ, https://www.leadershipiq.com/blogs/leadershipiq/leadership-development-state (last visited July 9, 2022); Mark Murphy, *Great Leaders Show Vulnerability, But Here's How to Do It Without Seeming Weak*, FORBES (Oct. 29, 2020), https://www.forbes.com/sites/markmurphy/2020/10/29/great-leaders-show-vulnerability-but-heres-how-to-do-it-without-seeming-weak.

63. DARE TO LEAD, *supra* note 37, at dust jacket flap; *id.* at 208 (explaining that leaders build trust when they share their values); *see* David Sluss, *Stepping into a Leadership Role? Be Ready to Tell Your Story*, HARV. BUS. REV. (Apr. 16, 2020), https://hbr.org/2020/04/stepping-into-a-leadership-role-be-ready-to-tell-your-story/.

64. Khrysgiana Pineda, *Generation Create? Gen Z Might Be the Most Creative Generation Yet, Poll Says*, USA TODAY, (Aug. 18, 2020), https://www.usatoday.com/story/news/nation/2020/08/18/generation-z-may-most-creative-yet-study-says/5589601002.

65. ROBERT MUSIL, THE MAN WITHOUT QUALITIES, VOL. I: A SORT OF INTRODUCTION AND PSEUDO REALITY PREVAILS 62 (Vintage Books, 1996) (1930).

66. Conversation with James Batham, Partner, Dentons (2016).

67. Teresa Amabile & Steven J. Kramer, *The Power of Small Wins*, HARV. BUS. REV. (May 1, 2011), https://hbr.org/2011/05/the-power-of-small-wins.

68. Khrysgiana Pineda, *supra* note 64.

69. John P. Kottter, *Leading Change: Why Transformation Efforts Fail*, HARV. BUS. REV. (May 1, 1995), https://hbr.org/1995/05/leading-change-why-transformation-efforts-fail-2 (describing a good short-term win as one that is visible and tangible, unambiguous, clearly related to the change effort's long-term goals).

70. Duhigg, *supra* note 3; Anita Williams Woolley et al., *Evidence for a Collective Intelligence Factor in the Performance of Human Groups*, 330 Sci., 686-88 (2010); Anita Woolley et al., *Why Some Teams Are Smarter Than Others*, The N.Y. Times (Jan. 16, 2015), https://www.nytimes.com/2015/01/18/opinion/sunday/why-some-teams-are-smarter-than-others.html. *See also,* John Gottman, *On Trust and Betrayal*, Greater Good Magazine (Oct 29, 2011), https://greatergood.berkeley.edu/article/item/john_gottman_on_trust_and_betrayal (explaining that "trust is related to the secretion of oxytocin, which is the 'cuddle hormone,' the hormone of bonding" and that "trust is built in very small moments, which [he] call[s] 'sliding door' moments, after the movie *Sliding Doors*. In any interaction, there is a possibility of connecting with your partner or turning away from your partner.").

71. *See e.g.,* Marcus Buckingham & Ashley Goodall, *The Feedback Fallacy*, Harv. Bus. Rev., March-April 2019, at 96–97 (explaining that "learning happens when we see how we might do something better by adding some new nuance or expansion to our own understanding. Learning rests on our grasp of what we're doing well, not on what we're doing poorly, and certainly not on someone else's sense of what we're doing poorly.").

72. Walter Bradford Cannon is credited with having first described the fight-or-flight response (now sometimes referred to as the fight-flight-faint-or-freeze response). *See generally,* Walter Bradford Cannon, Bodily Changes in Pain, Hunger, Fear, and Rage: An Account of Recent Research Into the Function of Emotional Excitement 211 (Martino Fine Books, 2016) (1925).

73. *See Infra* Part 3 for a feedback exercise that helps prevent the feedback from failing. *See also* Dare to Lead, *supra* note 37, at 36 (recommending creating a "safe container" by eliciting from team members what they need to feel open and safe in the feedback conversation).

74. Michele DeStefano, *The Chief Compliance Officer: Should There Be a New "C" in the C-Suite?*, The Practice, July 2016, https://clp.law.harvard.edu/knowledge-hub/magazine/issues/the-compliance-movement/the-chief-compliance-officer/; Michele DeStefano, *Creating a Culture of Compliance: Why Departmentalization May Not Be the Answer*, 10 Hastings Bus. L.J. 71 (2013).

75. Katie R. Bach et al., *Culture Change That Sticks*, Harv. Bus. Rev. (July 1, 2012), https://hbr.org/2012/07/cultural-change-that-sticks/. While writing this handbook, I found a *Harvard Business Review* article on Agile work that I hadn't read before that supports this same approach. Darrell K. Rigby et al., *Embracing Agile: How to Master the Process That's Transforming Management*, Harv. Bus. Rev., May 2016, at 7 ("Start Small and Let the Word Spread."); David Heinemeier Hansson & Jason Fried, Rework (2010) (pointing out that culture cannot be installed in an instant big bang push; it takes time—like the aging of scotch, the good kind).

76. Pisano, *supra* note 56, at 11 (explaining that "innovative cultures" are not "for everyone, so you will need to select very carefully who from the parent organization joins" the autonomous teams you create to experiment with a new culture).

77. *Id.*

78. *Id.*
79. To learn more about Agile innovation and Scrum Sprints, *see* Rigby et al., *supra* note 75, at 7; *see also What Is a Sprint in Scrum?* SCRUM.ORG, https://www.scrum .org/resources/what-is-a-sprint-in-scrum (last visited Jan. 29, 2022).
80. Calleam Consulting Ltd., *Case Study – Denver International Airport Baggage Handling System—An Illustration of Ineffectual Decision Making* (2008), https://www5 .in.tum.de/persons/huckle/DIABaggage.pdf.
81. Cyril Northcote, *Parkinson's Law*, THE ECONOMIST (Nov. 19, 1955), https://www .economist.com/news/1955/11/19/parkinsons-law.
82. Nadim Matta & Ron Ashkenas, *Why Good Projects Fail*, HARV. BUS. REV. (Sept. 1, 2003), https://hbr.org/2003/09/why-good-projects-fail-anyway (recommending a series of mini projects or "rapid-results initiatives" over long-term projects).
83. Robert B. Sherman and Richard M. Sherman, SPOONFUL OF SUGAR (1964).
84. Pisano, *supra* note 56, at 11; *see* Rigby et al., *supra* note 75 at 7.
85. For a video that brings to life what is a Debbie Downer, *see Debbie Downer: Disney World - SNL*, YOUTUBE.com (May 1, 2004), https://www.youtube.com/ watch?v=TfE93xON8jk.
86. *See generally*, JON. J. MUTH, ZEN SHORTS (2nd ed. 2008).
87. *Id.*
88. *See, e.g., Pastoral Message*, SAINTS SIMON & JUDE (Aug. 29, 2021), https://www.ssj. org/pastoral-message/pastoral-message-august-29-2021/; *see also* Archangel16, *Two Monks and a Prostitute*, LIVE JOURNAL (Mar. 1, 2007), https://archangel16.live journal.com/131466.html.
89. Alhalau, *Two Monks and a Woman – Zen Story*, KINDSPRING: STORIES OF KINDNESS FROM AROUND THE WORLD (June 20, 2014) https://www.kindspring .org/story/view.php?sid=63753; *see* Farmer Sean, *Two Monks and a Woman – Zen Story*, MEDIUM (Jun. 30, 2018), https://medium.com/@soninilucas/two -monks-and-a-woman-zen-story-c15294c394c1.
90. Jie Li et al., *Not All Transformational Leadership Behaviors Are Equal: The Impact of Followers' Identification with Leader and Modernity on Taking Charge*, 24 J. LEADERSHIP AND ORG. STUD. 318, 318–34 (2017) ("In an era in which innovation, creativity, and pace of change fuel organizational success, leaders rely increasingly on followers to initiate change-oriented behaviors beyond their role descriptions to improve the workplace."); Jin N. Choi, *Change-Oriented Organizational Citizenship Behavior: Effects of Work Environment Characteristics and Intervening Psychological Processes.* 28 J. ORG. BEHAV. 467–84 (2007).
91. Edward L. Deci et al., *Self-Determination Theory in Work Organizations: The State of a Science*, 4 ANN. REV. ORG. PSYCH. AND ORG. BEHAV. 19-23 (2017) [hereinafter *The State of a Science*].
92. *See generally*, DANIEL H. PINK, DRIVE: THE SURPRISING TRUTH ABOUT WHAT MOTIVATES US (Riverhead Books, 2011); NIK KINLEY & SHLOMO BEN-HUR, CHANGING EMPLOYEE BEHAVIOR: A PRACTICAL GUIDE FOR MANAGERS 810-28 (2015) (ebook);

Edwarm L. Deci & Richard M. Ryan, *Intrinsic and Extrinsic Motivation From a Self-Determination Theory Perspective: Definitions, Theory, Practices and Future Directions*, 61 CONT. EDUC. PSYCH. (2020) [hereinafter *Intrinsic and Extrinsic Motivation*].

93. Amabile & Khaire, *supra* note 32 (citing to research conducted by Georgia Tech Professor Henry Sauermann, with Duke Professor Wesley Cohen, who studied more than 11,000 R&D employees).

94. TEDx Talks, *"Cultivating Intrinsic Motivation and Creativity in the Classroom" Beth Hennessey TEdxSausalito*, YOUTUBE (Nov. 23, 2016), https://www.youtube.com/watch?v=v2eRnhBvI_I.

95. *Id.*

96. *Intrinsic and Extrinsic Motivation, supra* note 92; *The State of a Science., supra* note 90, at 19–23; Richard M. Ryan & Edward L. Deci, *Self-Determination Theory and the Facilitation of Intrinsic Motivation, Social Development, and Well-Being*, 551 AM. PSYCH. 68–78 (2000) [hereinafter *Self-Determination Theory*]; Edward L. Deci et al., *Facilitating Internalization: The Self-Determination Theory Perspective*, 62 J. PERSONALITY 119-42 (1994) [hereinafter *Facilitating Internalization*]; Edward L. Deci & Richard M. Ryan, *Facilitating Optimal Motivation And Psychological Well-Being Across Life's Domains*, 49 CAN. PSYCH. 14-31 (2008) [hereinafter *Facilitating Optimal Motivation*]; Kinley & Ben-Hur, *supra* note 92, at 817–33; *see generally* David Rock, *SCARF: A Brain-Based Model for Collaborating With and Influencing Others*, J. NEUROLEADERSHIP (2015) (explaining the five domains of human social experience that can activate our brain and trigger people into threat mode as an acronym SCARF: S for status, C for certainty, A for autonomy, R for relatedness, and F for Fairness). Research on lawyers also shows that these three ingredients are critical for lawyers to experience high well-being. *See, e.g.*, Lawrence S. Krieger & Kennon M Sheldon, *What Makes Lawyers Happy? A Data-Driven Prescription to ReDefine Professional Services?*, 83 GEO. WASH. LAW REV. 579-88 (2015).

97. TEDx Talks, *supra* note 94 (warning that extrinsic motivators can kill creativity); Edward L. Deci, *A Meta-Analytic Review of Experiments Examining the Effects of Extrinsic Reward on Intrinsic Motivation*, 125 PSYCH. BULLETIN 627–28 (1999).

98. *Facilitating Internalization, supra* note 96, at 119–42; Deci, *supra* note 96, at 627–68; Margit Osterloh et al., *Pay for Performance in the Public Sector – Benefits and (Hidden) Costs*, 20 J. PUB. ADMIN. RSCH. AND THEORY 387-412 (2010).

99. Steven Kerr, *An Academy Classic on the Folly of Rewarding A, While Hoping for B*, 9 THE ACAD. OF MNGMT. EXEC. (1995); *see also* J. Richard Hackman, *Leading Teams: Setting the Stage for Great Performances – The Five Keys to Successful Teams*, HARV. BUS. REV. (Jul. 15, 2022), https://hbswk.hbs.edu/archive/leading-teams-setting-the-stage-for-great-performances-the-five-keys-to-successful-teams (explaining that one pitfall for teams can be when the reward system does not recognize and reinforce "team, as opposed to individual, excellence.").

100. Tracey J. Coates et al., *Law Firm Origination Policies: Climbing the Mountain to Equity*, LAW PRACTICE TODAY (June 15, 2020), https://www.lawpracticetoday.org/

article/law-firm-origination-policies-climbing-mountain-equity/ ("Origination credit is determined based on the dollar value of revenue from clients or matters a partner has brought to a firm, and is awarded to that partner in the compensation process for those clients or matters, regardless of who is currently working on the matter. The most significant component of this compensation factor for our purposes is that . . . it can continue indefinitely as long as the client continues to send work to the firm."); *Id.*(explaining that "[O]rigination has historically come easily for white male attorneys, while it has often come at a price for women, racial minorities, and LGBTQ+ attorneys, who may have actually completed the majority of work on those client matters.").

101. Scott D. Anthony et al., *Breaking Down the Barriers to Innovation*, HARV. BUS. REV. (Nov. 1, 2019), https://hbr.org/2019/11/breaking-down-the-barriers-to-innovation.

102. Bill Murphy Jr., *Google Says It Still Uses the "20-Percent Rule," and You Should Totally Copy It*, INC (Nov. 1, 2020), https://www.inc.com/bill-murphy-jr/google-says -it-still-uses-20-percent-rule-you-should-totally-copy-it.html (noting that there is debate if the program still exists and that some employees were reported as calling it "120-percent time"). To learn more about the benefits of the 20 percent policy, watch this three-minute video of former CEO Eric Schmidt on Masters of Scale. *See* Eric Schmidt, *The Genius of Google's 20% Time*, MASTER OF SCALE MASHABLE (May 11, 2018) https://mashable.com/video/google-20-percent-rule (explaining that in addition to enabling time for innovation it also served as a "check and balance" and empowers the employee when confronted by supervisors who demanded too much).

103. Heidi K. Gardner & Ivan Matviak, *Performance Management Shouldn't Kill Collaboration: How to Align Goals Across Functions*, HARV. BUS. REV. (September 1, 2022), https://hbr.org/2022/09/performance-management-shouldnt-kill-collaboration.

104. Lars de Bruin, *Crossing the Chasm in the Technology Adoption Life Cycle*, BUSINESS2YOU (Mar. 15, 2020), https://www.business-to-you.com/crossing-the-chasm -technology-adoption-life-cycle.

Chapter 8

1. Pixar, *For the Birds*, YOUTUBE (Oct. 13, 2012), https://www.youtube.com/ watch?v=Q6X80IWdS6s.

2. Gary P. Pisano, *The Hard Truth About Innovative Cultures: Creativity Can Be Messy. It Needs Discipline and Management.*, HARV. BUS. REV., Jan.–Feb. 2019, at 4.

3. Jie Li et al., *Not All Transformational Leadership Behaviors Are Equal: The Impact of Followers' Identification With Leader and Modernity on Taking Charge*, 24 J. LEADERSHIP & ORG. STUD. 318, 318–34 (2017) ("[Transformative leadership] is considered the major change-oriented leadership that can move followers beyond their self-interests to transform the status quo into a better future."); Israel Sánchez-Cardona, Susana Llorenes Gumbau, & Marisa Slanova, *Leadership Intellectual Stimulation and Team Learning: The Mediating Role of Team Positive Affect*, 17 UNIVERSITAS PSYCHOLOGICA 1, 2-4 (2018); MCKINSEY & CO., PSYCHOLOGICAL

Safety and the Critical Role of Leadership Development (2021) (describing "challenging leadership" style).

4. Li, *supra* note 3, at 329–30; Sánchez-Cardona et al, *supra* note 3, at 9–10 ("Through intellectual stimulation leaders continuously encourage team members to think and perform in new ways by challenging their own beliefs and supporting new and innovative ways of actions.").

5. Giles Hirst et al., *Context Matters: Combined Influence of Participation and Intellectual Stimulation on the Promotion Focus–Employee Creative Relationship*, 33 J. Org. Behav. 894, 894–909 (2012) ("[t]hus, we theorize that individual participation provides flexibility and opportunities for individuals to voice their opinions but does not necessarily inspire creative actions. In contrast, intellectual stimulation involves the leader posing questions and challenging customary practices. Doing so helps followers develop more detailed strategies on how they will succeed promoting flexible and global processing [], in turn fostering creativity"); Le Cong Thuan, *Motivating Follower Creativity by Offering Intellectual Stimulation*, 28 Int'l J. Org. Analysis, 817, 817–29 (2019) (finding "a positive direct relationship between leader intellectual stimulation and follower creative performance"); Li et al., *supra* note 3, at 318–34; Sánchez-Cardona et al, *supra* note 3, at 1 ("Results provide evidence of the strong relationship that intellectual stimulation has on team learning and team positive affect, as well as the potential of positive affect for stimulating team learning. Team positive affect serves as a partial mediator between intellectual stimulation and team learning, contributing to explain significant additional variance. Leadership intellectual stimulation is a relevant team social resource that provides support for team learning.").

6. Li et al., *supra* note 3, at 318 ("Several contextual factors also affect taking charge, including group-focused transformational leadership, team-directed empowering leadership, organizational support climate, procedural justice, and role definitions."); *see id.* at 320 ("Additionally, intellectual stimulation directly encourages followers to question and change the status quo. It encourages problem solving and creativity to strive toward the vision, which implies the need for proactive and challenging behaviors. Thus, followers will see such leader behaviors as calling for change-oriented efforts, prompting them to develop wider role breadth perceptions that foster taking charge behaviors.").

7. McKinsey & Co., *supra* note 3, at 4 ("Another set of leadership behaviors can sometimes strengthen psychological safety—but only when a positive team climate is in place. This set of behaviors, known as challenging leadership, encourages employees to do more than they initially think they can. A challenging leader asks team members to reexamine assumptions about their work and how it can be performed in order to exceed expectations and fulfill their potential.").

8. *See* Gartner, Measure and Influence Innovation Climate at Your Organization 3 (2021) ("Employees' shared perceptions shape values and beliefs (innovation culture)."); *see id.* at 2 ("Employees' shared values and beliefs shape their behavior.").

9. J. Richard Hackman, Leading Teams: Setting the Stage for Great Performance 127–28 (2002).

10. *See* Carlos Valdes-Dapena, Lessons from Mars: How One Global Company Cracked the Code on High Performance Collaboration and Teamwork 105 (2018) (ebook).

11. *See, e.g.*, Will Felps et al., *How, When and Why Bad Apples Spoil the Barrel: Negative Group Members and Dysfunctional Groups*, 27 Research in Org. Behav.: An Ann. Series Analytical Essays & Critical Rev. 175, 175–222 (2006) (arguing that "[a] single, toxic team member may be the catalyst for group-level dysfunction" due to their "behavioral expressions of negativity" and there may be times where constructive responses are unable to counteract the negative behavior when, for example, the "bad apple" "has seniority, political connections, task expertise, or when teammates choose ineffective response strategies"); J. Keyton, *Analyzing Interaction Patterns in Dysfunctional Teams*, 30 Small Grp. Rsch. 491, 493 (1999) (reviewing dysfunctional teams and finding that "[s]ometimes the source of the dysfunction is one individual"). For academic theory proselytizing that when there is a difficult teammate, the team will either compensate for them or the person will be rehabilitated or ousted, see Jeffrey A. Lepine, & Linn Van Dyne, *Peer Responses to Low Performers: An Attributional Model of Helping in the Context of Groups*, 26 Acad. Mgmt. Rev. 67, 67–84 (2001). For research indicating that negative individuals have an asymmetric negative effect on teams, see M. R. Barrick et al., *Relating Member Ability and Personality to Work-Team Processes and Team Effectiveness*, 83 J. Applied Psych. 377, 377–91 (1998) (finding that scores for the worst member i.e., the least conscientiousness, the least agreeableness, and who had the lowest emotional stability were "substantially stronger predictors" of team performance and more so than "the team's mean personality scores or the highest (e.g. "best") person's score"); *see also* M. L. Camacho & P. B. Paulus, *The Role of Social Anxiousness in Group Brainstorming*, 68 J. Personality & Soc. Psych. 1071, 1071–80 (1995).

12. *See* Felps et al., *supra* note 11, at 207 (explaining that "the three most salient and important behaviors of a negative member are the withholding of effort, the demonstration of negative affect, and the violation of important interpersonal norms").

13. Michael A. West, *Sparkling Fountains or Stagnant Ponds: An Integrative Model of Creativity and Innovation Implementation in Work Groups*, 51 Applied Psych.: An Int'l Rev. 355, 355–87 (2002).

14. *See* Felps et al., *supra* note 11, at 203–06.

15. *See id.* at 212 (recommending intervention by the leader as a solution when teams are not empowered to do so on their own).

16. *See id.* ("[A] quick response minimizes the individual and group level effects of a negative member. . . . Nipping this harmful behavior in the bud . . . avoid[s] the[] downward spiral.").

17. *See* VALDES-DAPENA, *supra* note 10, at 77 (2018) (explaining that it is "almost always an individual performance problem" and that "in the end it's always a problem with the manager . . . it's the manager's failure to take effective action that needs to be addressed first and foremost").

18. RONALD A. HEIFETZ, LEADERSHIP WITHOUT EASY ANSWERS 240 (1998) ("[F]rom a strategic standpoint, some parties often must be excluded from the problem-solving process. They generate more disruption than can be contained effectively by the holding environment—the network of cohesive bonds and authority relationships among members of the community.").

19. *See* Felps et al., *supra* note 11, at 185 ("Across disparate literatures, the same reactions to negative behavior crop up again and again: that can be classified as motivational intervention, rejection, and defensiveness. . . . If either the motivation intervention or rejection is successful, the negative member never becomes a bad apple or spoils the barrel."); *id.* (defining team rejection as changing the "psychological composition" of the group by ostracizing negative members, reducing social interaction, talking at rather than with, exclusion from decisions, or removing responsibilities that require them to interact with others); *see also* J. R. Hackman, *Group Influences on Individuals*, HANDBOOK INDUS. AND ORG. PSYCH. 1455, 1455–1552 (1976).

20. Russell Eisenstat, Bert Spector, & Michael Beer, *Why Change Programs Don't Produce Change*, HARV. BUS. REV. (Nov. 1, 1990), https://hbr.org/1990/11/why -change-programs-dont-produce-change ("Some people, of course, just cannot or will not change, despite all the direction and support in the world. Step three is the appropriate time to replace those managers who cannot function in the new organization—after they have had a chance to prove themselves. Such decisions are rarely easy, and sometimes those people who have difficulty working in a participatory organization have extremely valuable skills. Replacing them early in the change process, before they have worked in the new org, is not only unfair to individuals; it can be demoralizing to the entire org and can disrupt the change process . . . Sometimes people are transferred to other parts of the company where technical expertise rather than the new competencies is the main requirement. When no alternatives exist, sometimes they leave the company through early retirement programs for example. The act of replacing people can actually reinforce the org's commitment to change by visibly demonstrating the general manager's commitment to the new way.").

21. John P. Kotter, *Leading Change: Why Transformation Efforts Fail: Compelling Lessons from the Mistakes Companies Have Made Trying to Implement Change*, HARV. BUS. REV. (May 1, 1995), https://hbr.org/1995/05/leading-change-why-transformation- efforts-fail-2 ("If the blocker is a person, it is important that he or she be treated fairly and in a way that is consistent with the new vision. But action is essential, both to empower others and to maintain the credibility of the change effort as a whole."); Ronald Heifetz & Marty Linsky, *A Survival Guide for Leaders*, HARV.

Bus. Rev. (June 1, 2002), https://hbr.org/2002/06/a-survival-guide-for-leaders (explaining that the "uncommitted" people "will need to see that your intentions are serious—for example, that you are willing to let go of those who can't make the changes your initiative requires").

22. Hackman, *supra* note 9, at 125–27.

23. Suzy Wetlaufer, *The Team That Wasn't*, Harv. Bus. Rev. (Nov. 1, 1994), https://hbr.org/1994/11/the-team-that-wasnt (providing this advice related to a case hypo and explaining that "[e]very organization has some members who make their best contributions as solo performers").

24. Kenwyn K. Smith & David N. Berg, Paradoxes of Group Life: Understanding Conflict, Paralysis, and Movement in Group Dynamics 90–93 (1st ed. 1987).

25. *Id.*

26. Wetlaufer, *supra* note 23 ("Midcourse corrections in team composition can be accomplished, but they are risky and difficult. It is better to get team composition right when the team is formed than to undertake repair work later."); Hackman, *supra* note 9, at 127–28; Nancy J. Cooke et al., Enhancing the Effectiveness of Team Science 7 (2015) ("A strong body of research conducted over several decades has demonstrated that team processes (e.g., shared understanding of team goals and member roles . . .are related to team effectiveness.").

27. Hackman, *supra* note 9, at 222 (emphasizing the importance of expert diagnosis and recommending aiming interventions at the structure and context of the team's interaction).

28. Pisano, *supra* note 2, at 11.

29. *Id.* (noting that "because innovative cultures can be unstable, and tension between the counterbalancing forces can easily be thrown out of whack, leaders need to be vigilant for signs of excess in any area and intervene to restore balance when necessary"); *id.* at 5.

30. Blair Epstein, Caitlin Hewes, & Scott Keller, *Capturing the Value of 'One Firm,'* McKinsey Q. (May 9, 2023), https://www.mckinsey.com/capabilities/strategy-and-corporate-finance/our-insights/capturing-the-value-of-one-firm.

31. David Burkus, *Innovation Isn't an Idea Problem*, Harv. Bus. Rev. (July 23, 2013), https://hbr.org/2013/07/innovation-isnt-an-idea-proble.

32. This exercise also works to help a team align around "purpose," that is, the second question can be used as its own Purpose Plane exercise for a team that is collaborating on anything—a new strategy, a new business model, not just an innovation.

33. There are other strategies to help ensure that the team gets on the same *problem plane*. For example, you can ask the team to develop a common list of facts that they all agree on or co-create what is called a "cognitive artifact, a visual representation for the group to more clearly identify the scope of the problem space as well as the relevance of each member's expertise to the problem space, while working toward consensus about the overarching boundaries of the potential collaborative endeavor." Kara L. Hall et al., *A Four-Phase Model of Transdisciplinary*

Team-Based Research: Goals, Team Processes, and Strategies, TRANSLATIONAL BEHAV. MED., Dec. 2012, at 415–30.

34. Pisano, *supra* note 2, at 6.

35. James Clear, *The 3 Stages of Failure in Life and Work (and How to Fix Them)*, https://jamesclear.com/3-stages-of-failure (last visited June 27, 2021).

36. This may seem chauvinistic, but our research showed that the main purchasing decision makers were moms, not dads, at the time, so that was our focus.

37. To see some of the commercials we created, see 90s Commercials, *Apple Jacks Commercial 1997*, YouTube (Mar. 25, 2017), https://www.youtube.com/watch?v=X7aotPqlmd0; My Commercials *Apple Jacks Commercial 1996*, YouTube (Sept. 27, 2011), https://www.youtube.com/watch?v=ggHae3QNvCc; Chad M, *Apple Jacks Commercial 1995*, YouTube (Jul. 10, 2013), https://www.youtube.com/watch?v=FTtdHjtHOXI; Radio Free Galaxy, *1994 Apple Jacks Baseball Team Commercial*, YouTube (Oct. 27, 2021), https://www.youtube.com/watch?v=m5Aw2gvewto.

38. Erin Griffith, *Why Startups Fail, According to the Founders*, FORTUNE (Sept. 25, 2014), https://fortune.com/2014/09/25/why-startups-fail-according-to-their-founders.

39. For a podcast about commitment bias, see *#32 Commitment Bias: Why You Should Shout It Out Loud*, BAD DECISIONS PODCAST (Dec. 23, 2020), https://baddecisions-podcast.com/archive/2020/12/23/32-commitment-bias. For a series of podcasts identifying 33 reasons why teams make bad decisions ranging from authority bias to availability bias, see generally BAD DECISIONS PODCAST, https://baddecisions-podcast.com/episodes (last visited Jan. 30, 2022).

40. BAD DECISIONS PODCAST Episode 32, *supra* note 39.

41. According to a recent *Harvard Business Review* article, Atlassian has been doing these before starting a project to discuss how it could fail and "doing a seven-step exercise that includes a structured cross-examination (in which a group arguing the 'success' case questions a group arguing the 'failure' case and vice versa), voting to gauge risk severity, assigning risk 'owners' and planning how to minimize threats." Scott D. Anthony et al., *Breaking Down the Barriers to Innovation: Build the Habits and Routines That Lead to Growth*, HARV. BUS. REV. (Nov. 1, 2019), https://hbr.org/2019/11/breaking-down-the-barriers-to-innovation.

42. To read about other reasons why people do not kill their projects and how to kill projects effectively, see Henrico Dolfing, *Why Killing Projects Is So Hard* (Jan. 22, 2019), https://www.henricodolfing.com/2019/01/why-killing-projects-is-so-hard-and-how.html; *see also* Jay Leonard, *Evaluating When to Kill a Project: What Criteria Do You Use?*, BUSINESS2COMMUNITY (Apr. 15, 2014), https://www.business2community.com/strategy/evaluating-kill-project-criteria-use-0848647.

43. Pisano, *supra* note 2, at 1 (noting that "because innovative cultures can be unstable, and tension between the counterbalancing forces can easily be thrown out of whack, leaders need to be vigilant for signs of excess in any area and intervene to restore balance when necessary").

44. Burkus, *supra* note 31 (calling it "idea killing").

45. Brené Brown, *The Power of Vulnerability*, TED Conferences (June 2010), https://www.ted.com/talks/brene_brown_the_power_of_vulnerability? language=en; *see* David Sluss, *Stepping into a Leadership Role? Be Ready to Tell Your Story*, Harv. Bus. Rev. (Apr. 16, 2020), https://hbr.org/2020/04/ stepping-into-a-leadership-role-be-ready-to-tell-your-story.

46. Brené Brown, Dare to Lead: Brave Work, Tough Conversations, Whole Hearts 183–217 (2018); BrenéBrown.com, https://www.brenebrown.com (last visited July 9, 2022).

Part III

1. Jennifer Dublino, *What Your Business Can Learn From Peter Drucker*, Business (August 15, 2023), https://www.business.com/articles/management-theory-of-peter -drucker/.

2. *See, e.g.*, Michael D. Watkins, *How Managers Become Leaders*, Harv. Bus. Rev. (June 1, 2012), https://hbr.org/2012/06/how-managers-become-leaders; Abraham Zaleznik, *Managers and Leaders: Are They Different?*, Harv. Bus. Rev. (January, 1 2004), https://hbr.org/2004/01/managers-and-leaders-are-they-different; John O'Leary, *Do Managers and Leaders Really Do Different Things?*, Harv. Bus. Rev. (June 20, 2016), https://hbr.org/2016/06/do-managers-and-leaders-really-do-different-things.

3. Zaleznik, *supra* note 2.

4. O'Leary, *supra* note 2.

5. *Id.* at 4.

6. Rosabeth Moss Kanter, *What Inexperienced Leaders Get Wrong (Hint: Management)*, Harv. Bus. Rev. (November 21, 2013), https://hbr.org/2013/11/ what-inexperienced-leaders-get-wrong-hint-management.

7. CC Client Interviewee 9.

8. Accelo, The Missing Links of Project Management 5 (n.d.) (reporting that over 57 percent of projects were 3 months or less and that shorter projects can equate to a large percentage of total revenue); Geoff Mcqueen, *3 Management Mistakes That Could Destroy Professional Services Businesses*, entrepreneur.com (July 16, 2015), https://www.entrepreneur.com/article/247186.

9. Bent Flyvbjerg & Alexander Budzier, *Why Your IT Project May Be Riskier Than You Think*, Harv. Bus. Rev. (Sept. 1, 2011), https://hbr.org/2011/09/why-your -it-project-may-be-riskier-than-you-think (conducting a global study of 1,471 IT change projects and finding that "the average overrun was 27%" and that "an unusually large proportion of them incur massive overages."); *id.* ("Tech Projects Aren't the Only Problem. Executives in all areas may fall prey to "projectification"—having their work be the sum of many temporary projects.").

10. Mark Gordon & Andrew Lewis, *Slippery Scope: Common Errors Made by Professional Service Firms in Managing Scope*, Vantage Partners (2016), https://cdn2.hubspot .net/hubfs/594420/Q3_Slippery%20Scope.pdf.

11. Accelo, *supra* note 8, at 3.

12. Simon Drane & Ben Kent, The State of Innovation in Professional Services Firms 8 (Spiranti et al eds., 2020) (studying over 80 professional services firms and finding that 47 percent of firms had no structured process to drive innovation); Sebastian Hartmann & Hans Winterhoff, *The Silent Killers of Future Readiness in Professional Service Firms*, LinkedIn (July 9, 2019), https://www.linkedin.com/pulse/silent-killers-future-readiness-professional-service-firms-hartmann/; *see also* Org. 4 Innovation, *Why's It so Hard? Innovation Management In Professional Service Firms*, Org. 4 Innovation, https://www.organizing4innovation.com/whys-it-so-hard-innovation-management-in-professional-services-firms/ (last visited Aug. 9, 2022).

13. Drane & Kent, *supra* note 12, at 8; Hartmann & Winterhoff, *supra* note 12; *see also* Org. 4 Innovation, *supra* note 12.

14. For example, a 2020 Legal Operations Maturity Benchmarking Report comprising responses from over 300 legal departments across 29 industries and 24 countries with corporations ranging from the millions to the tens of billions of US dollars in company revenue, found that most identified 15 functions of legal operations, including change management and innovation management. Ass'n of Corp. Couns. et al., 2020 ACC Legal Operations Maturity Benchmarking Report 7 (2020). Of the 15, the bottom four, ranked as the lowest in terms of maturity, were metrics & analysis, change management, e-discovery and litigation management, and innovation management (which was ranked as last). *Id.* at 10.

15. Antonio Nieto-Rodriguez, *The Project Economy Has Arrived*, Harv. Bus. Rev. (Nov. 1, 2021) , https://hbr.org/2021/11/the-project-economy-has-arrived.

16. Project Management Job Growth and Talent Gap 2017-2027 Report, Project Management Institute 4-5 (2017).

17. Nieto-Rodriguez, *supra* note 15.

18. Catherine Bailey & Adrian Madden, *What Makes Work Meaningful—Or Meaningless*, MIT Sloan Management Review (June 1, 2016), https://sloanreview.mit.edu/article/what-makes-work-meaningful-or-meaningless/ (describing the five qualities of meaningful work).

19. Teresa Amabile & Steven J. Kramer, *The Power of Small Wins*, Harv. Bus. Rev. (May 1, 2011), https://hbr.org/2011/05/the-power-of-small-wins.

20. N. Anand & Jean-Louis Barsoux, *What Everyone Gets Wrong About Change Management*, Harv. Bus. Rev. (Nov. 1, 2017), https://hbr.org/2017/11/what-everyone-gets-wrong-about-change-management.

21. Nieto-Rodriguez, *supra* note 15.

22. David Goldsmith & Lorrie Goldsmith, *Why "Micromanagement" Is Not a Dirty Word—If You Do It Right"*, Fast Co. (Dec. 6, 2012), https://www.fastcompany.com/3003721/why-micromanagement-not-dirty-word-if-you-do-it-right.

23. Teresa Amabile & Steven J. Kramer, *supra* note 19 (describing the ideal manager as one who "stayed attuned to his team's everyday activities and progress" but "was sure to check in while never seeming to check up on them.").

24. Teresa Amabile & Muktil Khaire, *Creativity and the Role of the Leader*, Harv. Bus. Rev. (Oct. 1, 2008), https://hbr.org/2008/10/creativity-and-the-role-of-the-leader (quoting Mark Fishman, MD, president of the Novartis Institutes for Bio-Medical Research, "if there is one device that has destroyed more innovation than any other, it is Six Sigma," and quoting Bob Sutton as "citing research showing that when organizations focus on process improvements too much, it hampers innovation over the long term.").

25. For further support of this, *see id.* (noting that Kim Scott, a director at Google, added that the manager must act as a shepherd—an analogy also used by Christy Jones, founder of Extend Fertility. Both believe that executives must protect those doing creative work from a hostile environment and clear paths for them around obstacles).

26. *Id.* (explaining that "one doesn't manage creativity, one manages for creativity").

27. Ronald A. Heifetz & Marty Linksy, Leadership on the Line, With a New Preface: Staying Alive Through the Dangers of Change 32, 128 (1st ed. 2002 Kindle Ed.).

28. Amabile & Kramer, *supra* note 19.

29. Heifetz & Linksy, *supra* note 27, at 25 ("People do not resist change, *per se*. People resist loss.").

30. *Id.* at 13, 67–70.

31. *Id.* at 11.

32. Goldsmith & Goldsmith, *supra* note 22.

33. J. Richard Hackman, Leading Teams: Setting the Stage for Great Performance 75–78 (2002).

34. *Id.* at 223–25 (identifying an "enabling team structure" as one of the five conditions that can increase the chances of success for teams).

35. For an article highlighting the dichotomous (and managerial) qualities needed of leaders of design thinking journeys, *see* Christian Bason & Robert D. Austin, *The Right Way to Lead Design Thinking*, Harv. Bus. Rev. (March 1, 2019), https://hbr.org/2019/03/the-right-way-to-lead-design-thinking?autocomplete=true.

36. *Id.* at 91.

Chapter 9

1. *See* AzQuotes, https://www.azquotes.com/quote/531738.

2. *See Chapter 6* C footnotes 96 and 97 (highlighting some of the negative consequences of diversity if not managed appropriately and discussing the benefits).

3. J. Richard Hackman, Leading Teams: Setting the Stage for Great Performance 99–100 (2002).

4. *Fred Allen Quotes*, BrainyQuote, https://www.brainyquote.com/quotes/fred_allen_201549 (last visited Sept. 22, 2023).

5. Ivan Dale Steiner, Group Process and Productivity 76 (1972) (finding that although productivity increases as size increases, such gains level off and begin to decrease when the groups begin to reach eight members or more).

6. Carlos Valdes-Dapena, Lessons from Mars: How One Global Company Cracked the Code on High Performance Collaboration and Teamwork 20, 183–89 (2018); Hackman, *supra* note 3, at 115–22.

7. Antonio Nieto-Rodriguez, *The Project Economy Has Arrived*, Harv. Bus. Rev. (Nov. 1, 2021), https://hbr.org/2021/11/the-project-economy-has-arrived (making a similar point about project managers).

8. *See, e.g.*, Anita Williams Woolley, *The Effects of Intervention Content and Timing on Group Task Performance*, 34 J. of Applied Behav. Sci. 30, 34–49 (1998); Connie J. G. Gersick, *Time and Transition in Work Teams: Toward a New Model of Group Development*, 31 Acad. of Mgmt. J. 9, 31 (1988); Karen A. Jehn & Elizabeth A. Mannix, *The Dynamic Nature of Conflict: A Longitudinal Study of Intragroup Conflict and Group Performance*, 44 Acad. of Mgmt. J. 238, 238-251 (2001).

9. David Rock, *SCARF: A Brain-Based Model for Collaborating With and Influencing Others*, Neuroleadership J., https://schoolguide.casel.org/uploads/sites/2/2018/12/SCARF-NeuroleadershipArticle.pdf.

10. Edward De Bono, Six Thinking Hats (1999).

11. *Id.* at 21–24.

12. *See, e.g.*, Russel Eisenstate, Bert Spector, & Micheal Beer, *Why Change Programs Don't Produce Change*, Harv. Bus. Rev. (Nov. 1, 1990), https://hbr.org/1990/11/why-change-programs-dont-produce-change.

13. Jie Li et al., *Not All Transformational Leadership Behaviors Are Equal: The Impact of Followers' Identification With Leader and Modernity on Taking Charge*, 24 J. Leadership & Org. Stud. 318, 318-334 (2017) ("Several contextual factors also affect taking charge, including group-focused transformational leadership, team-directed empowering leadership, organizational support, climate procedural justice, and role definitions."); Daniel J. McAllister et al., *Disentangling Role Perceptions: How Perceived Role Breadth, Discretion, Instrumentality, and Efficacy Relate to Helping and Taking Charge*, 92 J. Applied Psych. 1200, 1200-1211 (2007).

14. Julia Felton, *Empower, Rather Than Delegate*, Leadchange (Jan. 21, 2020), https://leadchangegroup.com/empower-rather-than-delegate/.

15. Rock, *supra* note 9.

16. Hackman, *supra* note 3, at 93–132; Nancy J. Cooke & Margaret L. Hilton, Enhancing the Effectiveness of Team Science 7 (Comm. on Sci. of Team Sci. et al. eds., 2015) (listing "shared understanding of team goals and member roles," "team composition (assembling the right individuals)," "team professional development," and "team leadership" as critical to team effectiveness); *see also*, Nieto-Rodriguez, *supra* note 7.

17. Hackman, *supra* note 3, at 50–52 (describing clarity around the extent of authority as essential to being a real team); *id.* at 100–101.

18. Ed Catmull, *Inside the Pixar Braintrust*, Fast Company (March 12, 2014), https://www.fastcompany.com/3027135/inside-the-pixar-braintrust.

19. Suzy Wetlaufer, *The Team That Wasn't*, Harv. Bus. Rev. (November 1, 1994), https://hbr.org/1994/11/the-team-that-wasnt.

20. SAM KANER, FACILITATOR'S GUIDE TO PARTICIPATORY DECISION-MAKING (3rd ed. 2014). The Gradients of Agreement Tool was developed in 1987 by Sam Kaner, Duane Berger, and the staff of Community at Work. *See, e.g.,* Hannah Love, *Gradients of Agreement for Democratic Decision-Making,* INTEGRATION AND IMPLEMENTATION INSIGHTS (May 25, 2021), https://i2insights.org/tag/gradients-of-agreement-tool/.

21. Kara L. Hall et al., *A Four-Phase Model of Transdisciplinary Team-Based Research: Goals, Team Processes, and Strategies,* 2 TRANSLATIONAL BEHAV. MED. 415, 423 (2012); *see also,* L. Michelle Bennett & Howard Gadlin, *Collaboration and Team Science: From Theory to Practice,* 60 J. INVESTIGATIVE MED. 768, 768-775 (2012) (identifying "promoting disagreement while containing conflict" as a critical factor in developing a shared vision).

22. Francis Boustany, *Analysis: Lawyers–Consider Expanding Your Multidisciplinary Team,* BLOOMBERG Law (Apr. 22, 2021), https://news.bloomberglaw.com/bloomberg-law-analysis/analysis-lawyers-consider-expanding-your-multidisciplinary-team.

23. Hall et al., *supra* note 21, at 415–30.

24. *See, e.g.,* Ruth Wageman, *How Leaders Foster Self-Managing Team Effectiveness: Design Choices vs. Hands-On Coaching,* 12 ORG. SCI. 559, 559-577 (2001) (finding that design features of a team made a bigger difference in the level of team management and team performance outcomes than leader coaching); HACKMAN, *supra* note 3, at 115 (identifying an "enabling team structure" as one of the five conditions that can increase the chances of success for teams, highlighting the importance of the composition of the team).

25. PATRICK LENCIONI, THE FIVE DYSFUNCTIONS OF A TEAM: A LEADERSHIP FABLE (Jossey-Bass, 2002); *see also,* Bennett & Gadlin, *supra* note 21, at 768–75 (citing trust as "among the most important" supporting features of a team and explaining that "without trust the team dynamic runs the risk of deteriorating over time").

26. *See generally* PATRICK LENCIONI, THE FIVE DYSFUNCTIONS OF A TEAM: A LEADERSHIP FABLE (Jossey-Bass, 2002).

27. *Id.* at 202–204 (describing that absence of trust leads to fear of conflict, which leads to artificial harmony instead of healthy conflict and constructive debate).

28. David Maister, *10 Unique Dynamics of Professional Services Firms That Hinder Change Efforts, and What Partners Can Do About It,* OPENSIDE, https://www.openside.group/10-unique-dynamics-of-professional-services-firms-that-hinder-change-efforts (last visited Aug. 9, 2022).

29. Chapter 7, *supra* notes 41–42 and accompanying text.

30. L. Michelle Bennett et al., *Collaboration and Team Science Field Guide,* NIH NAT'L CANCER INST. 5–6 (2010), https://www.cancer.gov/about-nci/organization/crs/research-initiatives/team-science-field-guide/collaboration-team-science-guide.pdf (identifying three different types of trust: calculus-based, competence based, and identity based); *see also* ROY J. LEWICKI & BARBARA BENEDICT BUNKER, TRUST IN ORGANIZATIONS: FRONTIERS OF THEORY AND RESEARCH 114–39 (Roderick M. Kramer et al. eds., 1996) (explaining that trust emerges along a trajectory in

different phases of group development, from calculus-based trust, to knowledge-based trust, to identification-based trust); *see also* DEBRA MEYERSON ET AL., TRUST IN ORGANIZATIONS: FRONTIERS OF THEORY AND RESEARCH 166–95 (Roderick M. Kramer et al. eds., 1996) (proposing that the kind of trust that occurs early on, for example, in temporary systems, is a unique form that they call "swift trust.").

31. Hall et al., *supra* note 21, at 417.

32. Simon Sinek has a book called *Start with Why*. I made up this exercise after reading that book. If Google, Apple, Microsoft, Amazon, and Facebook, some of the most successful companies on our planet, start with *why* they do what they do, not *what* they do, so should we as individuals.

33. *See, e.g.,* RICHARD WISEMAN, THE AS IF PRINCIPLE, THE RADICALLY NEW APPROACH TO CHANGING YOUR LIFE 177 (2012) (explaining that, if we smile, we eventually feel as we would feel if we had smiled naturally); Deborah Blum, *Face It!*, PSYCHOLOGY TODAY (Sept. 1. 1998), https://www.psychologytoday.com/us/articles/199809/face-it.

34. Marilynn B. Brewer & Wendi L. Gardner, *Who Is This "We"? Levels of Collective Identity and Self Representations*, 71 J. OF PERSONALITY AND SOC. PSYCH. 83, 83-93 (explaining that membership in larger more impersonal collectives like work teams or organizations creates a collective social identity and at this level individuals use the group to assess value); Ronit Kark & Boas Shamir, *The Influence of Transformational Leadership on Followers' Relational Versus Collective Self-Concept*, 2002 ACAD. OF MGMT. 1, 6 (2017) ("[L]eaders can affect followers by highlighting different aspects of followers' social self-concept and possibly change their focus from one level of their self-concept to another."); *id.* (citing other sources for the proposition that "[b]ehaviors of the leader that are focused on the group entity, linking the self-concept of individual followers to the shared values and key role identities of the group, can prime the collective aspect of followers' self-concept and foster individuals' perception of belonging to an organizational unit"); *see also* Jie Li et al., *supra* note 13, at 318–33.

35. Bennett et al., *supra* note 30, at 97.

36. HUGH MACLEOD, IGNORE EVERYBODY AND 39 OTHER KEYS TO CREATIVITY (2009).

37. VALDES-DAPENA, *supra* note 6, at 179–206.

38. Hall et al., *supra* note 21, at 417.

39. Gianni Giacomelli, *A Novel Way to Boost Client Satisfaction*, HARV. BUS. REV., Mar.-Apr. 2019, at 17–21.

40. Hall et al., *supra* note 21, at 415-430.

41. Zachary A. Rosner, Jeremy A. Elman, & Arthur P. Shimamura, *The Generation Effect: Activating Broad Neural Circuits During Memory Encoding*, NIH: NATIONAL LIBRARY OF MEDICINE (Sept. 21, 2012), https://www.ncbi.nlm.nih.gov/pmc/articles/PMC3556209/; *See* Stephen Newland, *The Power of Accountability*, Ass'N FOR FIN, COUNSELING & PLAN. EDUC. (2018), https://www.afcpe.org/news-and-publications/the-standard/2018-3/the-power-of-accountability; John S. Brown et al., *Commit to a Shared Outcome: Focus on the Outcome That Matters Most to Foster*

Passion and Amplify Your Actions, Deloitte, (Jan. 31, 2018), https://www2.deloitte
.com/xe/en/insights/topics/talent/business-performance-improvement/commit
-to-shared-outcomes.html; Bad Decisions Podcast, *#32 Commitment Bias: Why
You Should Shout It Out Loud*, PodBean (Dec. 23, 2020), https://baddecisions
-podcast.com/archive/2020/12/23/32-commitment-bias [hereinafter Bad Decisions Episode 32].

42. Zachary A. Rosner et al., *supra* note 41 (recommending the group write down the
shared mission and goals and broad intentions of the group process and outcomes
so that they can revisit and discuss).

43. *Id.*; Cooke & Hilton, *supra* note 16, at 7 (shared goals and roles help manage the
conflicts from diversity).

44. *Id.*; James R. Larson Jr., In Search of Synergy in Small Group Performance
(2009); Steiner, *supra* note 5; *see also* J. Richard Hackman, *Leading Teams: Setting
the Stage for Great Performances – The Five Keys to Successful Teams*, Harv. Bus. Rev.
(July 15, 2022), https://hbswk.hbs.edu/archive/leading-teams-setting-the-stage
-for-great-performances-the-five-keys-to-successful-teams (explaining "how
incredibly under-utilized members' talents were in most of the teams we studied"
and that "most teams, including senior executive teams, generally leave untapped
enormous pools of member talent.").

45. Anna T. Mayo & Anita William Woolley, *Teamwork in Health Care: Maximizing
Collective Intelligence via Inclusive Collaboration and Open Communication*, 18 AMA
J. Ethics 933, 937 (2016) ("Team members' social or professional categories can
also affect their influence. For example, research on group diversity suggests that
looking different from others in a group might increase a member's influence.
When a person is different from other teammates, he or she is expected to have
different knowledge or perspectives to add to the group, and, if that person speaks
up, others are more receptive than they would be to a similar group member. This
biased attention to status and categorical cues that are unrelated to expertise and
should be irrelevant can lead to undue influence for some members while leaving
relevant knowledge of members with low status or from certain subgroups less
likely to be considered and, therefore, less likely to influence the group's work.").

46. Deloitte, 2021 Deloitte Global Human Capital Trends: The Social Enterprise in a World Disrupted 19–20 (Junko Kaji et al. eds., 2020).

47. *Id.* at 19.

48. Christopher Chabris et al., *Evidence for Collective Intelligence Factor in the Performance of Human Groups*, 330 Sci. 686, 686-688 (2010).

49. *See generally* Mayo & Woolley, *supra* note 45, at 935 ("The process of expertise
used in teams is multifaceted. Team members must first share relevant knowledge (i.e., knowledge about the task at hand) with others, and, second, that voiced
knowledge must impact the team's work. The communication processes of speaking up and influencing others both come with challenges.").

50. Hall et al., *supra* note 21, at 416.

51. *Id.* at 416 (explaining that "developing a shared vocabulary as well as establishing a shared understanding of what expertise a team member has and how each member contributes to the collaborative research endeavor" are key social processes that teams must engage in for transdisciplinarity to occur).

52. Anita Woolley *et al.*, *Why Some Teams Are Smarter Than Others*, NEW YORK TIMES (Jan. 16, 2015), https://www.nytimes.com/2015/01/18/opinion/sunday/why-some-teams-are-smarter-than-others.html; *see also* Charles Duhigg, *What Google Learned From Its Quest to Build the Perfect Team*, NEW YORK TIMES (Feb. 25, 2016), https://www.nytimes.com/2016/02/28/magazine/what-google-learned-from-its-quest-to-build-the-perfect-team.html; *see, e.g.*, Natalie Marchant, *People Who Speak More are More Likely to Be Considered Leaders*, WORLD ECONOMIC FORUM (Aug. 9, 2021), https://www.weforum.org/agenda/2021/08/leaders-talk-more-babble-hypothesis/.

Chapter 10

1. WILLIAM SHAKESPEARE, HAMLET act 2, sc. 2, l. 205–06.
2. *Id.*
3. David Burkus, *Innovation Isn't an Idea Problem*, HARV. BUS. REV. (July 23, 2013), https://hbr.org/2013/07/innovation-isnt-an-idea-proble.
4. Rose Wong, *How to Help Your CMO Boost Global Growth*, HARV. BUS. REV. (Nov. 1, 2021), https://hbr.org/2021/11/how-to-help-your-cmo-boost-global-growth.
5. Gretta Rusanow et al., *Even as Expenses Surged, Law Firms in All Segments Saw Profits Spike in 2021*, AM. LAW. (Feb. 16, 2022, 5:00 AM), https://www.law.com/americanlawyer/2022/02/16/even-as-expenses-surged-law-firms-in-all-segments-saw-profits-spike-in-2021/; Mark Maurer, *Big Four Firms EY, Deloitte Report Higher Revenue*, THE WALL ST. J. (Sept. 9, 2021, 5:26 AM), https://www.wsj.com/articles/big-four-firms-ey-deloitte-report-higher-revenue-11631222772; Mika Pangilinan, *How Did the Global Market for Insurance Broking Fare in 2021?*, INS. BUS. MAG. (June 8, 2022), https://www.insurancebusinessmag.com/uk/news/breaking-news/how-did-the-global-market-for-insurance-broking-fare-in-2021--new-report-408807.aspx.
6. *Id.* at 9.
7. SIMON DRANE & BEN KENT, THE STATE OF INNOVATION IN PROFESSIONAL SERVICES FIRMS 9 (Spiranti et al. eds., 2020).
8. *Id.*
9. Client Interviewee 30.
10. Client Interviewee 9.
11. MARY M. CROSSMAN ET AL., STRATEGIC ANALYSIS AND ACTION 208–23 (Pearson, 8th ed. 2013).
12. John P. Kotter, *Leading Change: Why Transformation Efforts Fail*, HARV. BUS. REV. (May–June 1995), https://hbr.org/1995/05/leading-change-why-transformation-efforts-fail-2.

13. Drane & Kent, *supra* note 7, at 9.

14. Sandra Gottschalk et al., *If You Don't Succeed Should You Try Again? The Role of Entrepreneurial Experience in Venture Survival* (ZEW–Leibniz Centre for Eur. Econ. Rsch. Working Paper No. 14-009, 2014).

15. For a great overview of the research discussed above, see Walter Frick, *Research: Serial Entrepreneurs Aren't Any More Likely to Succeed*, Harv. Bus. Rev. (Feb. 20, 2014), https://hbr.org/2014/02/research-serial-entrepreneurs-arent -any-more-likely-to-succeed.

16. Deniz Ucbasaran et al., *Why Serial Entrepreneurs Don't Learn from Failure*, Harv. Bus. Rev. (Apr. 2011), https://hbr.org/2011/04/why-serial-entrepreneurs-dont -learn-from-failure (explaining that entrepreneurs are more prone to overoptimism" than the general population).

17. Failcon, http://thefailcon.com (last visited July 9, 2022).

18. Gary P. Pisano, *The Hard Truth About Innovation Cultures*, Harv. Bus. Rev. (Jan.–Feb. 2019), https://hbr.org/2019/01/the-hard-truth-about-innovative-cultures.

19. Carlos Valdes-Dapena, Lessons from Mars: How One Global Company Cracked the Code on High Performance Collaboration and Teamwork 20, 77 (2018).

20. Anabela Carneiro et al., *Serial Entrepreneurship, Learning by Doing, and Self-Selection* (Centro de Economia y Financias de Uporto Working Paper No. 2013-12, 2013) ("The positive association found between prior experience and serial entrepreneurs, survival is mainly due to selection on ability, rather than the result of learning by doing."); Simon C. Parker, The Economics of Entrepreneurship 117 (2009) (ebook) (estimating that approximately 60 percent of research studies have found a significant positive relationship between educational attainment and entrepreneurship); Michael Frese et al., *Human Capital and Entrepreneurial Success: A Meta-Analytical Review*, 26 J. Bus. Venturing 341, 341–48 (2011) (finding a significant but small relationship between human capital (experience, education, knowledge, and skills) and a higher relationship for knowledge and skills (than education and experience) because knowledge and skills are the outcomes of human capital investments); Sari Pekkala Kerr et al., *Personality Traits of Entrepreneurs: A Review of Recent Literature* 50 (Harv. Bus. School Working Paper 18-047, 2017) ("Prior studies also suggest that educated business owners run more successful businesses, generate more innovation, and grow their firms faster over time."); Richard Freeman et al., Education and Tech Entrepreneurship 2 (Kauffman Foundation 2008) (finding that over 90 percent of American tech founders hold a bachelor's degree and those with MBAs are able to establish their companies more quickly); William Arruda, *Why Aspiring Entrepreneurs Should Put Their Education First*, Forbes (Feb. 11, 2018, 10:22 AM), https://www.forbes.com/ sites/williamarruda/2018/02/11/why-aspiring-entrepreneurs-should-put-their -education-first/?sh=4a80d2fc467c (recommending entrepreneurs get undergraduate degrees and/or MBAs because education hones networking, collaboration and leadership skills); Ewing Marion Kauffman Foundation, Educational

ATTAINMENT OF BUSINESS OWNERS IN THE UNITED STATES 1 (Kauffman Foundation, 2020) (finding that 51.4 percent of all entrepreneurs held at least a bachelor's degree).

21. Kotter, *supra* note 12.

22. *Id.*

23. *Id.*

24. *Id.*

25. EVERETT M. ROGERS, DIFFUSION OF INNOVATIONS 280–81 (2003) (ebook); GEOFFREY A. MOORE, CROSSING THE CHASM: MARKETING AND SELLING HIGH-TECH PRODUCTS TO MAINSTREAM CUSTOMERS 189 (2006) (ebook).

26. ROGERS, DIFFUSION OF INNOVATIONS, *supra* note 25, at 283.

27. MOORE, *supra* note 25, at 54–55 (describing pragmatists as "hard to win over" but "loyal once won").

28. *See, e.g.,* Charles A. Maddock, *Law Firm Branding: Is It Working?*, ALTMAN WEIL (Feb. 2000), https://altmanweil.com/wp-content/uploads/2022/04/Law-Firm-Branding-Is-It-Working_.pdf; *10% of Clients Like Sitting Through Your Pitch – Why This Spells Trouble*, BTI CONSULTING GRP. (Aug. 19, 2020), https://bticonsulting.com/themadclientist/10-of-clients-like-sitting-through-your-pitch-why-this-spells-trouble; Blake Oliver, *Why Accountants Suck at Marketing*, GOINGCONCERN (Mar. 7, 2016), https://www.goingconcern.com/why-accountants-suck-marketing/.

29. *See* Jennifer Cross, *Three Myths of Behavior Change: What You Think You Know That You Don't*, YOUTUBE (Mar. 20, 2013), https://www.youtube.com/watch?v=l5d8GW6GdR0 (stressing the importance of behavior because "attitudes follow behavior, they do not predict it").

30. *See* DeStefano et al., *Don't Let the Digital Tail Wag the Transformation Dog: A Digital Transformation Roadmap for Corporate Counsel*, 17 J. BUS. & TECH. L. 183, 240 (2022).

31. *See* Antonio Sadarića & Miha Škerlavaj, *Leader Idea Championing for Follower Readiness to Change or Not? A Moderated Mediation Perspective of Prosocial Sensegiving*, 23 J. CHANGE MGMT.: REFRAMING LEADERSHIP & ORGANIZATIONAL PRAC. 200, 220 (2023).

32. *See generally* STEPHEN R. COVEY, THE 7 HABITS OF HIGHLY EFFECTIVE PEOPLE (Simon & Schuster Anniversary ed., 2020).

33. *5 P's of Marketing*, CORP. FIN. INST., https://corporatefinanceinstitute.com/resources/management/5-ps-marketing/ (updated Mar. 23, 2023).

34. TIM BROWN, CHANGE BY DESIGN: HOW DESIGN THINKING TRANSFORMS ORGANIZATIONS AND INSPIRES INNOVATION 14–18 (HarperCollins 2009); *see* Tim Brown, *Design Thinking*, HARV. BUS. REV. (June 2008), https://hbr.org/2008/06/design-thinking. IDEO's *Field Guide to Human Centered Design* is the closest I have seen to providing and describing a method (along with tools and exercises) like I do in my recently published book that serves as a handbook for this book: THE LEADER UPHEAVAL HANDBOOK: LEAD TEAMS ON AN INNOVATION & COLLABORATION JOURNEY

WITH THE 3-4-5 METHOD™ (2023). IDEO.ORG, THE FIELD GUIDE TO HUMAN -CENTERED DESIGN 27–157 (2015), https://d1r3w4d5z5a88i.cloudfront.net/ assets/guide/Field%20Guide%20to%20Human-Centered%20Design _IDEOorg_English-0f60d33bce6b870e7d80f9cc1642c8e7.pdf.

35. In fact, while putting the final touches on this book, I came across a book which was published after my first book, *Legal Upheaval*, that appears to be attempting to provide instructions in an easy-to-understand way. MICHAEL LEWRICK ET AL., THE DESIGN THINKING PLAYBOOK: MINDFUL DIGITAL TRANSFORMATION OF TEAMS, PRODUCTS, SERVICES, BUSINESSES, AND ECOSYSTEMS (John Wiley & Sons, Inc. 2018). And I'm sure there are others. My purpose in writing this book is to share my learnings about leadership, culture-creation, and teaming from leading over 235 teams on a 4-month innovation journey. My purpose for this chapter is to share my method and also to convince readers to find a method that works for them.

36. PSF interviewee (Law Firm Partner) 67.

37. Christian Bason & Robert D. Austin, *The Right Way to Lead Design Thinking*, HARV. BUS. REV. (Mar.-Apr. 2019), https://hbr.org/2019/03/the-right-way-to-lead -design-thinking.

38. DRANE & KENT, *supra* note 7, at 9.

39. For an article relaying research supporting this contention, see Bason & Austin, *supra* note 37 (studying how 24 senior executives lead major design-thinking projects within large private- and public-sector organizations in five countries and finding that key to the success is effective leadership).

40. Lifestyle Desk, *The Process Is More Important Than the Result: M S Dhoni*, INDIAN EXPRESS (Aug. 7, 2019, 11:06 IST), https://indianexpress.com/article/lifestyle/ life-positive/ms-dhoni-process-is-more-important-than-the-result-m-s-dhoni -inspiring-video-good-morning-5882798/.

41. DANIEL H. PINK, TO SELL IS HUMAN: THE SURPRISING TRUTH ABOUT MOVING OTHERS 89 (Riverhead Books 2012).

42. RANJAY GULATI, REORGANIZE FOR RESILIENCE: PUTTING CUSTOMERS AT THE CENTER OF YOUR BUSINESS 2–4 (Harv. Bus. Rev. Press 2009).

43. *See generally* BRUCE TURKEL, ALL ABOUT THEM: GROW YOUR BUSINESS BY FOCUSING ON OTHERS (Da Capo Press, 2016).

44. Bruce Turkel, *Self-Referencing Criteria*, LINKEDIN (May 1, 2017), https://www .linkedin.com/pulse/danger-self-referencing-criteria-bruce-turkel/.

45. PINK, *supra* note 41, at 72.

46. Henri Christiaans, Creativity in Design: The Role of Domain Knowledge in Designing (1992) (Ph.D. thesis, Delft University of Technology, The Netherlands).

47. TINA SEELIG, INGENIUS: A CRASH COURSE ON CREATIVITY 19–30 (HarperCollins Publishers 2012).

48. PINK, *supra* note 41, at 5; TINA SEELIG, WHAT I WISH I KNEW WHEN I WAS 20: A CRASH COURSE ON MAKING YOUR PLACE IN THE WORLD 8–14 (HarperOne 2009); SEELIG, A CRASH COURSE, *supra* note 47, at 19–30.

49. Sir James Dyson created the bagless vacuum cleaner because he was frustrated with the smell from the dust, the lack of power, and the loud noise of traditional vacuum cleaners. *See, e.g.*, Shoshana Davis, *Vacuum Inventor James Dyson on Desire to "Change the World,"* CBS News (Jan. 14, 2014, 12:48 PM), https://www.cbsnews .com/news/why-vacuums-sir-james-dyson-on-the-story-behind-his-invention/.

50. Seelig, What I Wish I knew, *supra* note 48, at 23.

51. Many writers have been credited with saying this, including Stephen King. *See, e.g.*, Forrest Wickman, *Who Really Said You Should "Kill Your Darlings"?*, Slate (Oct. 18, 2013, 1:09 PM), https://slate.com/culture/2013/10/kill-your-darlings -writing-advice-what-writer-really-said-to-murder-your-babies.html.

52. Kotter, *supra* note 12.

53. *Id.*

54. *Abraham Joshua Heschel Quotes*, GoodReads, https://www.goodreads.com/ quotes/268379-people-of-our-time-are-losing-the-power-of-celebration (last visited Sept. 29, 2023).

55. Thomas Lockwood, Design Thinking: Integrating Innovation, Customer Experience, and Brand Value vii–xvii (Allworth Press 2009). Thomas Lockwood is a former president of the Design Management Institute (DMI), a nonprofit institute aimed at advancing design in management and business.

56. Phil Charron, *Divergent vs. Convergent Thinking in Creative Environments*, ThinkCompany (Oct. 26, 2011), https://www.thinkcompany.com/blog/divergent -thinking-vs-convergent-thinking/.

57. *Id.*

58. *Id.*

59. Tim Brown, *What Does Design Thinking Feel Like?*, DesignThinking (Sept. 7, 2008), https://designthinking.ideo.com/?p=51.

60. Brown, *supra* note 34, at 92.

61. I first learned about red teaming from an article by Cass R. Sunstein & Reid Hastie, *Making Dumb Groups Smarter*, Harv. Bus. Rev. (Dec. 2014), https://hbr .org/2014/12/making-dumb-groups-smarter.

62. *See* Stefan Ferron, *Red Teaming – A Cold War Lesson*, LinkedIn (Feb. 8, 2016), https://www.linkedin.com/pulse/red-teaming-cold-war-lesson-stefan-de -carufel-ferron/?trk=related_artice_Red%20Teaming%20-%20A%20Cold%20 War%20Lesson_article-card_title.

63. Kevin Ashton, How to Fly a Horse: The Secret History of Creation, Invention, and Discovery xiii–xiv (Anchor Books 2015).

64. Tim Brown, *Design Thinking*, Harv. Bus. Rev. (June 2008), https://hbr.org/ 2008/06/design-thinking.

65. Alina Bradford & Ashley Hamer, *Science and the Scientific Method: Definitions and Examples*, Live Sci. (Jan. 16, 2022), https://www.livescience.com/20896-science -scientific-method.html.

66. Brown, *supra* note 34, at 176.

Chapter 11

1. *Chuck Close*, GoodReads, https://www.goodreads.com/quotes/682112-inspiration -is-for-amateurs-the-rest-of-us-just-show (last visited Oct. 9, 2023).

2. Alfred North Whitehead, Modes of Thought (1938), http://gpmcf.org/ modes_of_thought.html.

3. Tom Robbins, Jitterbug Perfume (New York: Bantam Books, 1984).

4. Scott Wiltermuth & Chip Heath, *Synchrony and Cooperation*, 20 Psych. Sci. 1, 5 (2009); Selin Kesebir, *The Superorganism Account of Human Sociality: How and When Human Groups Are Like Beehives*, 16 Personality and Soc. Psych. Rev. 233, 233–61 (2011); *See, e.g.,* Piercarlo Valdesolo et al., *The Rhythm of Joint Action: Synchrony Promotes Cooperative Ability*, 46 J. Experimental Soc. Psych. 693, 693–95 (2010) (finding that synchronous rocking enhances connectedness); Sebastian Kirschner & Michael Tomasello, *Joint Music Making Promotes Prosocial Behavior in 4-Year-Old Children*, 31 Evolution & Hum. Behav. 354, 354–64 (2010).

5. Leonard Cohen, Anthem (Omnibus Press 2011).

6. Tim Young, *365 Days, $10 Million, 3 Rounds, 2 Companies, All with 5 Magic Slides*, TechCrunch (Nov. 2, 2010), https://techcrunch.com/2010/11/02/365-days-10 -million-3-rounds-2-companies-all-with-5-magic-slides/.

7. *Id.*

8. Anton Valukas, Report to Board of Directors of General Motors Company Regarding Switch Recalls 40 (Jenner and Block, 2014). Some claim that GM had purposefully created the switch to turn easily so that it would feel more European and appeal to more people. *See GM Redesigned Ignition Switch to Give Small Cars European Feel: Automaker Lands into Legal Hot Water, Myriad of Inquiries*, The Blade (July 8, 2014), https://www.toledoblade.com/business/ automotive/2014/07/08/GM-redesigned-ignition-switch-to-give-small-cars -European-feel/stories/20140707248 (last visited Aug. 15, 2022).

9. Robert Rosen, *The Sociological Imagination and Legal Ethics*, 19 Legal Ethics 97, 97-111 (2016).

10. *Id.* at 100 (explaining that there was a bulletin sent to dealers that indicated someone knew that the ignition switch problem caused loss of electrical system, "it cannot be proven that anyone at GM or its dealers understood that loss of electrical system meant loss of airbags.").

11. Rosen, *supra* note 8, at 100.

12. Howard Darmstadter, *The Times and General Motors: What Went Wrong?*, 3 Cogent Arts and Human. 1, 4 (2016).

13. *See, e.g.,* Tina Seelig, *Innovation Demands Focus and Reframing*, YouTube (Oct. 17, 2014), https://www.youtube.com/watch?v=HHbS1YDhsBg.

14. Riley Fitzgerald, *Rock's Deepest Roots: 7 Tracks You Didn't Know Were Based on Classical Music*, happymag.tv (July 11, 2016), https://happymag.tv/rocks-deepest -roots-7-tracks-you-didnt-know-were-based-on-classical-music/.

15. Jeff Veen, *Great Designers Steal*, YouTube (Aug. 25, 2009), https://www.youtube .com/watch?v=8CtC_qbQ51U.

16. Steven Johnson, Where Good Ideas Come From: The Natural History of Innovation 159–61 (Riverhead Books, 2010).
17. *Id.* at 243.
18. Kevin Ashton, How to Fly a Horse: The Secret History of Creation, Invention, and Discovery 23 (New York: Anchor Books, 2015).
19. Robert Frost, *In the Home Stretch, in* Mountain Interval lines 190–91 (Alexandria, United Kingdom, Chadwyck-Healey, 1924).
20. Robert Frost, The Road Not Taken and Other Poems 11 (David Orr eds., 2015).
21. Mary Doria Russell, Children of God 225 (Villard Books, 1998).
22. Adam Brandenburger, *Strategy Needs Creativity*, Harv. Bus. Rev. (March-April 2019), https://hbr.org/2019/03/strategy-needs-creativity.
23. *See* Daniel H. Pink, Drive: The Surprising Truth About What Motivates Us (Canongate, 2009); *see also* Nik Kinley & Schlomo Ben-Hur, Changing Employee Behavior: A Practical Guide for Managers (Palgrave MacMillan, 2015).
24. Nik Kinley & Schlomo Ben-Hur, Changing Employee Behavior: A Practical Guide For Managers 817–33 (Palgrave MacMillan, 2015); *cf.* David Rock, *SCARF: A Brain-Based Model for Collaborating with and Influencing Others*, Neuroleadership J., https://schoolguide.casel.org/uploads/sites/2/2018/12/SCARF-NeuroleadershipArticle.pdf (explaining the five domains of human social experience that can activate our brain and trigger people into threat mode as an acronym SCARF: S for status, C for certainty, A for autonomy, R for relatedness, and F for fairness). Research on lawyers also shows that these three ingredients are critical for lawyers to experience high levels of well-being. *See, e.g.,* Lawrence S. Krieger & Kennon M. Sheldon, *What Makes Lawyers Happy? A Data-Driven Prescription to Redefine Professional Services*, 83 George Washington L. Rev. 579, 579–88 (2015).
25. Kinley & Ben-Hur, *supra* note 26, at 853.
26. *Id.* at 883.
27. *Id.* at 895; *see also* Gary P. Pisano, *The Hard Truth About Innovation Cultures*, Harv. Bus. Rev. (Jan.-Feb. 2019), https://hbr.org/2019/01/the-hard-truth-about-innovative-cultures.
28. Kinley & Ben-Hur, *supra* note 26, at 817–33.
29. Andrew J. Elliot & Judith M. Harackiewicz, *Goal setting, Achievement Orientation, and Intrinsic Motivation: A Mediational Analysis*, 66 J. of Personality and Soc. Psych. 968 (1994); Gary P. Latham & Edwin A. Locke, *Enhancing the Benefits and Overcoming the Pitfalls of Goal Setting*, 35 Org. Dynamics 332, 332–40 (206).
30. Kinley & Ben-Hur, *supra* note 26, at 970–73.
31. Teresa Amabile & Steven J. Kramer, *The Power of Small Wins*, Harv. Bus. Rev. (May 1, 2011), https://hbr.org/2011/05/the-power-of-small-wins.
32. Kinley & Ben-Hur, *supra* note 26, at 991.
33. *Indira Gandhi Quotes*, BrainyQuote, https://www.brainyquote.com/quotes/indira_gandhi_119762 (last visited August 23, 2022).

34. Ursula K. Le Guin, The Left Hand of Darkness 220 (New York: Ace Books, 2000).
35. Brené Brown, Dare to Lead: Brave Work, Tough Conversations, Whole Hearts 170 (2018) [hereinafter Dare to Lead].
36. Ashish Nanda & Das Narayandas, *What Professional Service Firms Must Do to Thrive*, Harv. Bus. Rev. (Mar.-Apr. 2021), https://hbr.org/2021/03/what -professional-service-firms-must-do-to-thrive.
37. William Shakespeare, Hamlet act 2, sc. 2, l. 205.

Appendix C

1. In snowball sampling, initial participants provide connections to other potential interviewees who might be willing to be interviewed by the researcher. For a more detailed description, see Leo A. Goodman, *Snowball Sampling*, Annals Mathematical Stat., 32, no. 148, 148–49 (1961) (defining snowball sampling); Charles Kadushin, *Power, Influence, and Social Circles: A New Methodology for Studying Opinion Makers*, 33 Am. Soc. Rev., 33, 694–96 (1968) (discussing the strengths and weaknesses of snowball sampling); *see also* Jean Faugier & Mary Sargeant, *Sampling Hard to Reach Populations*, J. Advanced Nursing, 26, 790 (1997); Sarah H. Ramsey & Robert F. Kelly, *Using Social Science Research in Family Law Analysis and Formation: Problems and Prospects*, 3 S. Cal. INTERDISC. L. J., 631, 642 (1994). Legal scholars often base research on snowball samples. *See, e.g.,* Kimberly Kirkland, *Ethics in Large Law Firms: The Principle of Pragmatism*, 35 U. Mem. L. Rev., 631, 631 (2004) (utilizing a snowball sample of 22 lawyers practicing in 10 large law firms to investigate "how bureaucratic legal workplaces shape lawyers' ethical consciousness").
2. For a more specific description of these interviews and their scope, see Michele DeStefano, Bjarne P. Tellmann, & Daniel Wu, *Don't Let the Digital Tail Wag the Transformation Dog: A Digital Transformation Roadmap for Corporate Counsel*, 17 Journal of Business and Technology Law 183 (2022).
3. This could be called quasi-content analysis, which is a type of analysis often used for analyzing transcripts, political speeches, advertisements, and judicial opinions. *See, e.g.,* Klaus Krippendorff, *Content Analysis: An Introduction to Its Methodology* (2004).
4. This approach is similar in some ways to that taken by Robert L. Nelson and Laura Beth Nielsen. *See* Robert L. Nelson & Laura Beth Nielsen, *Cops, Counsel, and Entrepreneurs: Constructing the Role of Inside Counsel in Large Corporations*, 34 Law & Soc'y Rev. 457, 470 (2000).
5. *See* Christine Parker, *The Ethics of Advising on Regulatory Compliance: Autonomy or Interdependence?*, J. Bus. Ethics, 28, no. 4: 339, 341. In other areas of study, examination of narratives is a method used successfully (e.g., critical legal studies literature). Furthermore, the number of interviews in this study generally exceeds the number of interviews utilized to research other topics in professional services, especially in law.

6. For the most part, I interviewed the highest-ranking legal officer at the company, usually having the title GC. However, in some situations, I interviewed the deputy GC. Also, in two situations, I interviewed the top two legal officers.
7. The titles of these interviewees varied. Often, they held the title chief innovation officer or head of innovation. However, sometimes, they were identified as the leader of innovation in their firm but held a different title (e.g., chief information officer).
8. For ease of reference in the body of the document, I refer to all as partners as I did not quote any of the associates. However, their titles are included in the table.

Acknowledgments

1. The Beatles, "With a Little Help from My Friends," title of song from *Sgt. Pepper's Lonely Hearts Club Band* (Parlophone, June 1, 1967) (vinyl, LP, album, mono), written by Lennon-McCartney (June 1, 1967); *see also, The Beatles Lyrics: The Songs of Lennon, McCartney, Harrison and Starr*, 2nd edition (Hal Leonard, May 1, 1992).

ABOUT THE AUTHOR

"The world is full of magic things, patiently waiting for our senses to grow sharper."

—*W. B. Yeats*[1]

My first paying job was as a mini magician when I was 12 years old. One of the tricks I learned was how to pull a pigeon out of a hat. The first time I pulled off this magic trick at a children's birthday party, I saw the eyes of those skeptical children and . . . aah, I felt it: my calling.

And no, my calling wasn't to be the next David Copperfield. It was to change the way people see, think, and behave. After attending Dartmouth College, I went into advertising and marketing for 7 years. My job as an account executive at Leo Burnett in Chicago was to help write creative strategies so that commercials would motivate consumers to buy products (such as Frosted Flakes)—to change their behavior, in other words. After four years, I took a position at Levi Strauss & Co. as a marketing manager, researching urban youth to help create new products that would restimulate the brand and change the way people viewed Levi's and ultimately entice them to buy the product.

I then decided to move from the world of cereal and jeans to a world of principles and ethics—to things that mattered more (i.e., the law). And even though the intellectual and moral stakes were higher, being a lawyer is not that different from being an advertising executive or a marketing manager. In the law, we impact how people see the world and behave and how they think.

After getting my degree at Harvard Law School (HLS), I practiced as a special master on a patent law case, then returned to HLS where Professor David Wilkins hired me to work with him as the associate research director of the Center on the Legal Profession. In addition to being involved in launching the HLS Executive Education Program with Professor Ashish Nanda, we worked on a project studying purchasing decisions by general counsels, specifically the make-buy decision. It was then that I realized I was "home." I had found a way to merge my background in marketing, advertising, and market research with law, the legal profession, and legal education. After working as a Climenko Fellow and Lecturer on Law at HLS for a couple more years, I decided to go back to my childhood home, Miami, to follow my calling.

For the past 14 years through MOVELΔW (my consultancy) and LawWithoutWalls (aka LWOW), an experiential learning initiative grounded in design thinking and designed to transform how law and business professionals collaborate, I have led more than 230 multidisciplinary teams of professional service providers on a 4-month journey of collaborative, creative problem solving. Based on others' human-centered approaches to innovation and some of my own, I lead each team through an innovation cycle. Each of these teams starts with a business of law problem, and at the end, team members have a practicable solution: a business case with a branded prototype and commercial. But the point is not the solution; the point is changing mindsets, skill sets, and behaviors by teaching team members to open their minds, their hearts, and their doors. This unleashes our true collaborative and creative potential.

Professional service providers have been given a bad rap when it comes to creativity, collaboration, and innovation; it is simply not true that they are not creative. The challenge of applying creativity to professional services is that many professional service providers are taught to use the same type of strategy thinking they have engaged in before, the same reasoning, the same processes to solve new problems. What we need is a new kind of thinking, a new theoretical framework, a new method designed not only to create innovation in law but also to hone new skills, mindsets, and behaviors. For any method or framework to resonate, however, it needs to be catered to how professional service providers think and are trained. I wrote this guide to do just that, and I hope you enjoy it.

AUTHOR'S BIO

Michele DeStefano is a highly innovative legal professional with a passion for creative problem solving, collaboration, culture change, and innovation in professional services. As a professor at the University of Miami who teaches design thinking at the law and engineering schools and a Faculty Chair in Harvard Law School's Executive Education Program, Michele is an internationally recognized thought leader who has been named a Legal Rebel by the ABA and one of the top 20 most innovative lawyers in North America by the Financial Times Innovative Lawyers.

Michele is the founder of LawWithoutWalls, a community of over 2,000 lawyers, business professionals, entrepreneurs, and students who collaborate to create innovations in the business of law and develop new mindsets and skill sets. She is also the co-creator of the Digital Legal Exchange, a nonprofit that aims to inspire general counsel and their teams to become digital leaders in their businesses to drive commercial value.

With her extensive research and writing on topics such as client-centricity, collaboration, and innovation in law, Michele has authored multiple books, including *Legal Upheaval: A Guide to Creativity, Collaboration, and Innovation in Law* and *New Suits: Appetite for Disruption.* In addition to this book, *Leader Upheaval,* she has published a companion book, *The Leader Upheaval Handbook: Lead Teams on an Innovation & Collaboration Journey with The 3-4-5 Method(™).* Her latest articles include *Chicken or Egg: Diversity and Innovation in the Corporate Legal Marketplace,* 91 Fordham Law Review 1209 (2023) and *Don't Let the Digital Tail Wag the Transformation Dog: A Digital Transformation Roadmap for Corporate Counsel,* 17 J. Bus. & Tech. L. 183 (2022).

Michele earned a B.A. magna cum laude from Dartmouth College and a J.D. degree magna cum laude from Harvard Law School. Michele is a visionary who is dedicated to leading the way in transforming the professional services industry. Through her consultancy, MOVELAW, she frequently speaks and runs workshops on creative problem solving, collaboration, client-centricity, culture change, strategic influence, personal branding, and innovation for professional service providers. For more information visit movelaw.com or micheledestefano.com.

ACKNOWLEDGMENTS

"With a little help from my friends."

—The Beatles[1]

The truth is, I don't get by "with a little help from my friends." I get by because I have so much help from friends of all kinds, old and new. Without their help, I would not have been able to do the research for this book, let alone write it. Nor would I have been able to bring LawWithoutWalls to life and grow it over the past 14 years. So, this section is about giving thanks to those who have helped me "get by."

To My Family

I start by thanking my three incredible, supportive children: Thank you Jasper, Reading, and Trip for always understanding when I had to write and for being interested in my professional life by reading my other book and volunteering in LawWithoutWalls. Next, I thank Ian, my significant other and partner for working alongside me in the office every Sunday (and many other weeknights well into the early morning), for providing breaks with snacks and wine (lots of wine) and laughs (lots of laughs), and for giving me that harsh-and-from-love advice when things were tough and complicated and hard. Thank you to my two stepchildren, Hayden and Connor, who feel like my own after all these years, who supported me and also read my writing and volunteered in LawWithoutWalls. Likely, the only way I really survived was because of my mom. This is not an exaggeration. Thank you, Mom, for knowing how to say "Yes, and . . ." and for saying "Yes, and . . ." to me over and over (and over) again whether it was to grocery shop, pick up my kids from wherever, water my plants, feed my cat, drop off my dry cleaning or hit the post office with my many return packages when I could not.

I thank my sister, Des, who, in addition to treating my children like her own and inviting them to her house, always supported my determination to finish this book no matter how long it took. And of course, I thank my other sister Pam, for being an inspiration for inclusivity, letting go, and having an open mind.

To My Friends, Mentors, and Supporters

I thank the friends from my past who joined me on my quest to create LawWithoutWalls and who continue to play pivotal roles in keeping LWOW alive and making sure it thrives. Thank you, James Batham, Phyllis Dealy, Chad Fischer, and Moray McLaren, Marcia Narine Weldon for serving as my partners in LWOW every year and for saving me and many teams time and time again. I thank all my colleagues who are now friends (or friends that are now colleagues) who continue to believe in me and LWOW and support me and LWOW with their time (as board members, innovation coaches, and project managers): Kwame Adzatia, Leon Atkins, Diego Baranda, Jana Blount, Caroline Brown, Jeff Carr, Sushruta Chandraker, Mark Cohen, Bill Deckelman, James "Jim" Deoitte, Amir Dhillon, Firoza Dodhi, Wende Fischer, Koren Grinshpoon,

403

David Halliwell, Clifton Harrison, Michael Hertz, Peggy Hollander, Helga Kristín Auðunsdóttir, Peter Lee, Steve Makin (who we are all still painfullly mourning), Brian Micic, Katsiaryna Pozniak, Mari-Cruz Taboada, Horacio Gutierrez, Imogen Lee, Alessandro Philip Maiano, Suzanne McFee, Steve Mehr, Alastair Morrison, Justin North, James Peters, Christian Rioult, Kenny Robertson, Dustin Shay, Stacey Quaye, Hendrik Schneider, Maurus Schreyvogel, Felix Schulte-Strathaus, Reena SenGupta, Fergus Speight, Peter Sudbury, Bjarne Tellmann, Damien Taylor, Juuso Turtiainon, Scott Westfahl, and Drew Winlaw, to name a few–and there are too many to name.

I thank my mentors who were early adopters of LWOW, without whom LWOW would not exist at all or be nearly as robust. Thank you, David Wilkins, for believing in me and jumping into LWOW for that reason only. Thank you, as well, for guiding me in my work and life decisions, for supporting my candidacy for every role I've ever attempted to play, and mostly for being there for me at odd times from whatever time zone you were in to listen and give me advice and send love. Thank you as well to: Ida Abbot, Soledad Atienza, Ray Campbell, Elizabeth Chambliss, Anna Donovan, Jim Ferraro (and his funding support), John Flood, Jordan Furlong, Dame Hazel Genn, Bruce Green, Bill Henderson, Peter Lederer (who we all wish was still here with us), Bruno Mascello, Martha Minow, Deborah Rhode (who I miss dearly), Scott Rogers, Rob Rosen, Susan Sneider, Leo Staub, Laurel Terry, and Trish White for joining LWOW before it was clear what it was and for providing advice to me (both personal and professional) along the way as I attempted to help drive its growth and mine. Thank you, Richard Susskind, for presenting at the very first LWOW KickOff in 2011, for supporting me, and for continuing to give me the gift of feedback. I also owe special thanks to Erika Pagano, former LWOW student and former Director of LWOW who was in the weeds with me for years and years and collaborated with me to grow LWOW in many ways.

Some big thanks also go to the people who mentored me pre-LWOW, without whom I would never have become a professor, including John Coates, Anne-Marie Slaughter, and Judge William Young.

To My Book Advisers and Contributors

Thank you to the people who have been advisers and readers of this book. Thank you to Lynn Gohn, Marisa L'Heureux, and Lorraine Murray and the many dedicated copy editors, who together have proven false everything I have ever heard about how tough the book editing process is.

My deepest thanks and gratitude also go to all of the colleagues who provided insights that I have woven throughout the book and the 286 interviewees who gave me not only their time but also their voices to help me say everything better than I could have myself. I also owe a great deal of gratitude to my research assistants who thanklessly checked every source cited in the book: Annemarie Machado, Annick Runyon, and Allison Rose Simon. I also thank another research assistant, Tiffany Perez, who helped take other tasks off my plate so I could focus on this book.

Perhaps ironically, words cannot express my gratitude to my editor, my Aries friend, Stuart Horwitz of Book Architecture, who helped me pick the right words and find the right balance between my voice and the cacophony of voices I was representing. Stuart was a tireless partner, helping me rewrite and restructure, fearless in his edits, and cuts, and pushbacks. This book is so much better because of him.

My final thanks go to Anita Ritchie, the Director of LWOW, who does the job because she believes in LWOW and in me and who does the job better than I ever did. Thank you as well to Anita for tirelessly reading and providing editing suggestions on every page of this book. She has been one of my best friends since I was 22 years old, and she is STILL one of my best friends after working with me for the past few years. (To say that it is a difficult job is an understatement!) Thank you, Anita: without you and all of your help, I would not (even a little bit) get by.

INDEX